# The HOME BOOK of
# *Musical Knowledge*

# Books by David Ewen

# The HOME BOOK of

# *Musical*

# *Knowledge*

*by*

## DAVID EWEN

*Chicago*
SPENCER PRESS, *Inc.*

# Contents

# PART FOUR

## *Music for Solo Instruments and for Chamber-Music Groups*

# PART FIVE

## *Orchestral Music*

# PART SIX

## *Music for Children*

# PART SEVEN

## *A Glossary of Basic Terms in Music*

# Introduction

## Music — The Heavenly Maid

Many people have tried to say what music is, and what it means to them. The lexicographer provides a definition: "The science and art of the rhythmic combination of tones, vocal or instrumental, embracing melody and harmony for the expression of anything possible by this means, but chiefly emotional." But throughout the ages, poets, philosophers, writers, musicians have found a dictionary definition unsatisfactory to characterize this art. Some have preferred to describe music as "the language of the gods"; others, to say that "music begins where speech ends." To Romain Rolland music is a "promise of eternity"; to Sydney Smith it is "the only cheap and unpunished rapture upon earth." Goethe found that music "raises and ennobles whatever it expresses," while to Edna St. Vincent Millay it represents a "rampart, and my only one." Mendelssohn believed that music reached "regions where words cannot follow it," and Tchaikovsky said that music was a "revelation, revealing to us beauties we find in no other sphere."

From the English author and wit, Horace Walpole, has come the following statement: "Had I children, my utmost endeavors would be to make them musicians. . . . As my aim would be to make them happy, I think it is the most probable method." An American philosopher, Irwin Edman, wrote: "In a world where everything seems to come out desperately wrong, good music comes out exquisitely right. It is the logic of sound. But the logic is not that of a textbook or an

vii

argument. It is an order of vitality, a rich dream of sound become organized and crystallized." The English philosopher Herbert Spencer regarded music "as the highest of the fine arts, as the one which more than any other ministers to human welfare."

Music, then, is a rare, perhaps even incomparable, esthetic experience—as so many people have tried to say in many different ways. Of all the arts, its appreciation is an experience for which we come least prepared. The use of words and the science of reading has equipped us to enjoy literature. The sights of the physical world—not only people, objects and scenes, but also color and design—is an important step towards the enjoyment of painting. Our everyday contact with buildings is an apprenticeship for the understanding of architecture. The everyday movements of the body, hands, feet are idealized in the ballet.

It is true that we get a sense of rhythm in the way we walk and breathe, a feeling for melody from the songs we sing and hear, even a sense of tone color from the inflections of the human voice and the sounds all around us. But all this is of very little use in helping us feel at home in the strange, immense, new world of music—a world that makes its own laws, dictates its own forms, creates its own language, and which bear little relation to our everyday experiences.

We must, then, learn music almost from the very elements, even as a child learns about the physical world around him by acquainting himself with the simplest experiences, sights, and contacts. We must make a conscious and studied attempt to learn and enjoy music before the full blessings of the art are showered upon us.

This book is an attempt to collate within a single volume, and in terms easily comprehended by the unschooled music lover, all the information he requires for an intelligent, mature, and even comprehensive understanding of music: its structure, backgrounds, evolution, creators, basic vocabulary and terminology, its schools and movements, and its literature.

# PART ONE

## The A. B. C. of Music, Its History and Composers

# The A.B.C. of Music

Music, like a human being, has a soul, a heart, a mind, and a skeleton.

The soul of music is—melody. A melody is a succession of tones that make up a pleasing tune. The distance between a tone and the next, or between any two tones, is known as an interval. An interval is measured by counting the number of tones, including the first and the last: Thus, the interval between C and E is a third (C,D,E); and the interval between C and G is a fifth (C,D,E,F,G).

The melodies within the aural experience of the everyday music lover are constructed from the eight tones of a scale. For centuries, composers have been arranging and rearranging the order of these eight notes without exhausting the possible permutations and combinations; for, even today, a composer born with the divine gift of melody can shape new and fresh tunes out of these few notes. The succession of eight notes in the scale follows a set pattern, or to be more accurate two set patterns. One of these is the pattern of the major scale or key: a half step, instead of a whole one, between the third and fourth tones, and the seventh and eight tones, of the scale. The other pattern is that of the minor key: a half step between the second and third tones, and the fifth and sixth tones of the scale. Actually there are two variations of the minor scale, created for functional harmonic and melodic purposes, but these need not concern us here. There are forty-eight scales in the major and minor keys, each scale being made up of eight notes.

There are other scales, too, less frequently used and less familiar: the old church modes; the whole-tone scale made famous by Debussy; the pentatonic (five-tone) scale used for Oriental effects, since it is found in Oriental music; the chromatic scale made up exclusively of semi-tones. But it is the forty-eight scales of the major and minor keys which give us the basic vocabulary that the greatest composers have used in writing their masterworks.

The heart of music is rhythm and tempo.

Walter Damrosch once concocted a picturesque metaphor which distinguishes vividly the two terms of rhythm and tempo. Tempo, he said, is the traffic cop who regulates the flow of traffic; and the flow of traffic is rhythm. Tempo, in short, is the indication at the top of a composition that tells us how fast or how slowly a composition is to be played: Andante, Allegro, Largo, Presto, etc.

Rhythm is the arrangement of long notes and short notes, accented and unaccented notes, according to a repeated pattern. Someone put it well when he said that rhythm is the melody of the monotone. In any event, rhythm is the heartbeat of a musical work; without it, a piece of music cannot live or breathe.

At the beginning of every piece of music is a time signature: a fraction indicating the number of beats to a measure. The most fre-quently used signature—consequently it is known as "common time" —is $\frac{4}{4}$. Strictly speaking, the symbol $\frac{4}{4}$ means that there are four quarter notes to each bar. Actually, you can use full notes, half notes, quarter notes, eighth notes. Specifically, $\frac{4}{4}$ means four beats to a measure. Waltz time ($\frac{3}{4}$) has three beats to a measure; and march time ($\frac{2}{4}$) two beats. Time signatures are also designated in terms of eighth notes, as, for example, $\frac{3}{8}$, $\frac{6}{8}$, $\frac{12}{8}$, etc.

We come now to the brains, or the mind, of a musical work—its harmony and counterpoint.

Harmony is the science of arranging notes into chords of usually three or four notes. A chord of three notes, separated from each other by the interval of a third, is a triad; if the triad is built on the first note of the scale, it is called a tonic triad. A four-note chord is a seventh chord. A chord is constructed by using the interval of a third. Taking the C major scale as an example, the tonic triad is made up of the notes C,E,G, while the seventh chord is C,E,G,F. You can add variety to these chords by a process known as inversion: taking the bottom note of the chord and placing it an octave higher. When you do this (C,E,G becomes E,G,C) there is an interval of a third between the first two tones and an interval of a sixth between the first and third notes—for this reason, this first inversion is known as the $\frac{6}{3}$ chord. A $\frac{6}{4}$ chord is a second inversion, since by taking the new bottom note and raising it an octave higher (G,C,E) there is an interval of a fourth between the first two notes and an interval of a sixth between the first and third notes. We have gone into this explanation—which, of course, is only a smattering of harmonic lore—to point out the most functional chords in music: the tonic triad; the subdominant triad, in other words, a triad built on the fourth note of the scale; the dominant triad, or a triad built on the fifth note of the scale; the $\frac{6}{3}$ chord; the $\frac{6}{4}$ chord. With this elementary equipment it is possible to provide melodies with a very agreeable and serviceable harmonic background.

When a singer or a violinist is accompanied on the piano the artist is being provided with a harmonic accompaniment. In a piece for piano you will often find the melody in the right hand and the harmonic background in the left. A melody, without its harmony, lacks support—depth, color, richness.

In harmony it is a single melody, and its accompaniment, that is being emphasized. In counterpoint, several melodies are emphasized simultaneously. When two, three, or more different melodies are played or sung together with an agreeable effect we have counterpoint. But it is also possible to produce counterpoint by using a single tune, through a technique known as imitation. The best example of this is a round like "Three Blind Mice," or "Frère Jacques." In these two songs, the melody is begun by one voice; at the conclusion of the first phrase the first voice continues with the melody while a second voice begins it; at the end of the second phrase, a third voice enters with the same melody while the other two voices go on with their tune; and so forth. The most advanced, the most complex, the most significant artistic adaptation of this principle is found in the fugue, which will be discussed in a later chapter.

A human body must have a skeleton; and so must music. The skeleton of a musical work is its form. A composer does not write his music in a free and haphazard flow of ideas and sounds. He subjects himself to the rigid discipline of a structural pattern. The symphony, the concerto, the oratorio, the sonata are among the larger forms in music; the song, minuet, rondo, scherzo are among the shorter forms. These are the molds into which composers pour their ideas.

A knowledge of the form of a piece of music is the road map to its topography. Probably no other musical information is more serviceable to a layman in allowing him to dissect and understand a work. The basic forms of music, and the most characteristic works written within these forms throughout the years, will be discussed comprehensively in later sections.

# 2

# A Chronological Table of the Great Composers
### An Explanation of Leading Epochs and Schools in Music History

## THE POLYPHONIC ERA: 1200-1650

The contrapuntal style prevalent during the Polyphonic Era consisted in the simultaneous flow of several different melodies, each melody being independent and of equal importance. The polyphonic style was embodied in choral works, usually for four or five parts (or "voices"), but sometimes for more than that. This music was originally for unaccompanied voices (a cappella), and its first principal forms were the mass and the motet in church music and the madrigal in secular music.

*Gothic Period (1200-1550):* The first and primitive techniques and forms of polyphonic music were developed. This music is known as the *Ars Antiqua*—Ancient Art.

*Ars Nova (14th century):* New techniques of rhythm and melody brought increasing expressiveness and feeling to polyphony and paved the way for the first important schools of polyphonic music. To distinguish this new music from its more primitive predecessor, it is known as the *Ars Nova*—New Art.

*First Important Polyphonic Schools (15th and 16th centuries):*
Schools of polyphonic composers appeared in the Netherlands, in
Venice and in Rome which developed an inchoate musical art into a
vibrant one.

NETHERLAND (OR FLEMISH) SCHOOL

15TH CENTURY

Dufay (1400–1474)          Josquin des Prés (c. 1445–1521)
Orlando di Lasso (1532–1594)

VENETIAN SCHOOL

16TH CENTURY

Willaert (c. 1488–1562)    Giovanni Gabrieli (c. 1557–c. 1612)

ROMAN SCHOOL

16TH CENTURY

Palestrina (c. 1525–1594)          Victoria (c. 1548–1611)

*Secular Polyphonic Music (16th century):*
Monteverdi (1567–1643)            Morley (1557–1603)
Byrd (1543–1623)                  Gibbons (1583–1625)

*Baroque Period: Church Music (17th and early 18th centuries):*
During the Baroque Period the forms became more elaborate; greater
attention was paid to dramatic effect; contrapuntal choruses were
combined with arias, duets, and quartets; choral music was accompanied by instruments. Major new church forms were developed including the oratorio, the passion, and the cantata.

Carissimi (1605–1674)             J. S. Bach (1685–1750)
Schütz (1585–1672)                Handel (1685–1759)

# THE BIRTH OF HOMOPHONIC MUSIC: 17th Century

The homophonic style emphasized the *single* melody with a harmonic accompaniment. This style made possible the emergence of
the opera and the art-song. Early instrumental music for organ, clavier,
and violin now appeared.

*Baroque Period: Secular Music (17th and early 18th centuries):*

OPERA

Monteverdi (1567–1643)            Lully (1632–1687)
Purcell (1659–1695)

ORGAN

Sweelinck (1562–1621)          Frescobaldi (1583–1643)
Buxtehude (1637–1707)          Froberger (1616–1667)
              J. S. Bach (1685–1750)

CLAVIER

Couperin le Grand (1668–1733)          J. S. Bach (1685–1750)
Domenico Scarlatti (1685–1757)          Handel (1685–1759)

VIOLIN

Corelli (1653–1713)          Tartini (1692–1770)
Vivaldi (1678–1741)          J. S. Bach (1685–1750)

ART-SONG

Purcell (1659–1695)          J. S. Bach (1685–1750)

## THE CLASSICAL PERIOD: 18th and early 19th Centuries

During the Classical Period, instrumental music (whose spine was the homophonic style) achieved a dominant position, replacing choral polyphonic music. Forms originating in the preceding era were developed and finally crystallized: the sonata, the concerto, the overture. New forms acquired significance: the symphony, the string quartet. The Classical Period emphasized correctness and lucidity of structure, precision, exactness, objectivity and restraint. Rules of procedure were usually more important than freedom of expression. The rococo style, characterized by its delicacy and courtly grace, prevailed. In the opera composers sought a more intimate relationship between music and drama, seeking greater dramatic truth in their musical writing.

INSTRUMENTAL MUSIC

K. P. E. Bach (1714–1788)          Boccherini (1743–1805)
Johann Stamitz (1717–1757)          Mozart (1756–1791)
Haydn (1732–1809)          Beethoven (1770–1827),
                                                    first phase

OPERA

Rameau (1683–1764)          Gluck (1714–1787)
              Pergolesi (1710–1736)

## THE ROMANTIC PERIOD: 19th Century

The Romantic Period gave precedence to emotion and subjective feelings over traditional procedures. Melody was emphasized; harmony became more expressive; rhythm was varied; and instrumentation grew richer and more brilliant as composers sought increasingly to make music more articulate. The older forms of the symphony, sonata, concerto, etc., became more supple and flexible. Newer forms emerged: smaller pieces for the piano and the violin; new orchestral media, such as the concert overture and the symphonic poem. In opera, the Italian School which glorified *bel canto*—"beautiful song" —was pitted against the German School which emphasized dramatic values and gave considerable importance to the orchestra. The German School culminated with the "Music of the Future," the term which Wagner gave to his concept of the music drama. A French lyric theatre was also established.

### INSTRUMENTAL MUSIC

Beethoven (1770–1827), middle and last phase

Berlioz (1803–1869)

Schubert (1797–1828)

Schumann (1810–1856)

Mendelssohn (1809–1847)

Chopin (1810–1849)

Paganini (1782–1840)

Liszt (1811–1886)

Lalo (1823–1892)

Brahms (1833–1897)

Chausson (1855–1899)

Vieuxtemps (1820–1881)

Wieniawski (1835–1880)

Sarasate (1844–1908)

Bruch (1838–1920)

K. Goldmark (1830–1915)

Franck (1822–1890)

### ART-SONG

Schubert (1797–1828)

Schumann (1810–1856)

Brahms (1833–1897)

Franck (1822–1890)

Fauré (1845–1924)

Richard Strauss (1864–1949)

Hugo Wolf (1860–1903)

### OPERA

Weber (1786–1826)

Cherubini (1760–1842)

Donizetti (1797–1848)

Bellini (1801–1835)

Rossini (1792–1868)

Verdi (1813–1901)

Bizet (1838–1875)

Gounod (1818–1893)

Massenet (1842–1912)

Thomas (1811–1896)

Offenbach (1819–1880)

Ponchielli (1834–1886)

Meyerbeer (1791–1864)                    Wagner (1813–1883)
Halévy (1799–1862)                       Humperdinck (1854–1921)

*Realism and Naturalism:* The Romantic Movement saw an increasing tendency to make music interpret the outside world realistically; to introduce Naturalism into opera; to model melody after the patterns of speech.

Mussorgsky (1839–1881)                   Leoncavallo (1858–1919)
Charpentier (1860–    )                   Mascagni (1863–1945)
                   Puccini (1858–1924)

*Neo-Romanticism:* During the closing years of the Romantic Period, a new movement emerged influenced by Wagner and the Romantics. This movement inspired the use of massive symphonic structures and overladen orchestration; programmatic writing was given preference to absolute music; mysticism and philosophic concepts were introduced.

Bruckner (1824–1896)                     Scriabin (1872–1915)
Mahler (1860–1911)                       Richard Strauss (1864–1949),
                                                     first phase

*Nationalism:* The Romantic Movement encouraged the birth of national schools of music. Composers derived their melodies from folk songs and dances in an attempt to produce music that was inspired by their country's culture, history, and backgrounds.

Glinka (1804–1857)                       Liadov (1855–1914)
"The Russian Five": Balakirev (1837–1910); Borodin (1833–
1887); Cui (1835–1918); Mussorgsky (1839–1881); Rimsky-
Korsakov (1844–1908)                     Smetana (1824–1884)
Tchaikovsky (1840–1893)                  Dvořák (1841–1904)
Grieg (1843–1907)                        Albéniz (1860–1909)

*Ballet:* During the Romantic Period, music written expressly for the ballet achieved artistic significance for the first time.

                   Delibes (1836–1891)
                   Tchaikovsky (1840–1893)


## THE MODERN PERIOD: 20th Century

Reaction against the excesses of the Romantics and the Neo-Romantics—their musical superstructures, their overemotionalism, their extra-musical programs and philosophies—combined with an increasing tendency toward experimentation brought about many new styles, techniques, and idioms. Some contemporary composers carried over the traditions of Romanticism, while others went back to the structures and style of Classicism.

*Impressionism:* Emphasis was placed not on the subject of a piece of music but on the emotions or sensations aroused by the subject. Nuance, light, color, mood, atmosphere gained precedence over form and substance.

Debussy (1862–1918)               Ravel (1875–1937)

Delius (1862–1934)

*Expressionism:* The essence of a musical subject or idea is arrived at through abstraction. The Expressionist avoided a basic key or tonality (atonality). One important technique of the Expressionist School was the twelve-tone system, in which a work was built out of a series of twelve tones, each of equal importance, and according to definite rules.

Schoenberg (1874–1951)

Berg (1885–1935)

*Neo-Classicism:* The return to old classical forms and techniques, at the same time aspiring for purity, economy, and objectivity.

Stravinsky (1882–    ),            Respighi (1879–1936),
later phase                        later phase
Hindemith (1895–    )             Roussel (1869–1937),
                                   later phase

*Dynamism:* The emphasis on primitive rhythms and the dynamic force of primitive music in sophisticated forms.

Stravinsky (1882–    ), earlier phase

Prokofiev (1891–1953)

*Nationalism:*

*Armenia:* Khatchaturian (1903–    )

*Bohemia:* Martinu (1890–    ), Weinberger (1896–    )

*Brazil:* Villa-Lobos (1887–    )

*England:* Vaughan Williams (1872–    )

*Finland:* Sibelius (1865–    )

*Hebrew:* Bloch (1880–    )

*Hungary:* Bartók (1881–1945), Kodály (1882–    ), Dohnányi
(1877–    )

*Mexico:* Chávez (1899–    )

*Moravia:* Janáček (1854–1928)
*Poland:* Szymanowski (1883–1937)
*Rumania:* Enesco (1881–    )
*Spain:* Falla (1876–1946), Turina (1882–1949)
*United States:* Cowell (1897–    ), Ives (1874–1954), Copland
(1900–    )

*Popularism:* As a corollary to nationalistic music there is that which derives its idiom from the techniques and styles of popular music.

| | |
|---|---|
| Villa-Lobos (1887–    ) | Grofé (1892–    ) |
| Gershwin (1898–1937) | Gould (1913–    ) |
| Copland (1900–    ) | |

*Proletarian Music:* The conscious effort to write music for the masses, reflecting the basic interests and ideology of the people. This movement achieved particular significance in the Soviet Union.

| | |
|---|---|
| Shostakovich (1906–    ) | Kabalevsky (1904–    ) |
| Prokofiev (1891–1953) | Miaskovsky (1881–1950) |
| Glière (1875–    ) | |

*Neo-Baroque:* Return to the contrapuntal techniques of the sixteenth and seventeenth centuries.

| | |
|---|---|
| Hindemith (1895–    ) | Harris (1898–    ) |

*Neo-Mysticism:* The combination of a mystical or philosophical program with music that is essentially Romantic and Wagnerian in character.

Scriabin (1872–1915), later phase
Messiaen (1908–    )

*Romanticism:*

| | |
|---|---|
| Saint-Saëns (1835–1921) | Schmitt (1870–    ) |
| Glazunov (1865–1936) | Hanson (1896–    ) |
| Rachmaninoff (1873–1943) | Barber (1910–    ) |

*Realism:*

Richard Strauss (1864–1949), operas in second phase
Respighi (1879–1936), earlier phase

# Brief Biographies of Composers

ALBÉNIZ, ISAAC

Born: Camprodón, province of
Gerona, Spain
May 29, 1860
Died: Cambo-les-Bains, French
Pyrenees
May 18, 1909

Albéniz was a child prodigy at the piano. A love for adventure kept him from formal study for many years, which time he spent in wandering around Spain. At last, an endowment from the King of Spain enabled him to study with François Gevaert in Brussels, and after that with Franz Liszt in Weimar. A turning point in his life came when he met Felipe Pedrell, the scholar who had done intensive research in the field of Spanish folk music. It was Pedrell who fired Albéniz with the ambition of becoming a composer of national Spanish music. For a few years, Albéniz lived in Paris, working on composition. In 1899, he completed a piano piece called *Catalonia* which, in an orchestrated version, was introduced by the Société Nationale de Musique in Paris, launching Albéniz' career as composer.

Albéniz was back in his native land by 1900. Tragedy now followed him: his daughter died; his wife became sick with an incurable disease; he himself suffered illness and pain. Despite the immensity of his misfortunes he was able to work upon and complete his masterwork, the piano suite *Iberia*.

Albéniz' finest works give a vivid and glowing picture of Spain and its people, by successfully exploiting folk idioms. Thus he was the first of the celebrated nationalist Spanish composers (his successors include Manuel de Falla, Turina, and Granados). Besides *Iberia,* Albéniz produced many fine Spanish pieces for the piano, including *Cantos de España* (which includes the celebrated nocturne "Córdoba"); the *Suite Española;* the popular *Tango in D Major;* and *Navarra.*

BACH, JOHANN SEBASTIAN  *Born:* Eisenach, Germany
March 21, 1685
*Died:* Leipzig
July 28, 1750

Bach was left an orphan when he was nine years old. His older brother grudgingly took him into his own household. Peeved that he had another mouth to feed, he treated the boy severely, and did what he could to place obstacles in the way of his development. A position as choirboy in Lüneburg, when Bach was fourteen, freed him from his brother's tyranny. Now able to devote himself to music study without interference, Bach gave himself up passionately to numerous musical pursuits. He studied the organ, clavier, violin, and composition. He made long trips to Hamburg and Celle to listen to musical performances.

In his nineteenth year, he became organist at Arnstadt. He received a month's leave of absence to enable him to visit Lübeck where the celebrated organist and composer, Dietrich Buxtehude, gave performances. So preoccupied did Bach become with the musical activity in Lübeck that he stayed away not one month but three, to the extreme displeasure of his Arnstadt employers.

Bach left Arnstadt for good, in 1707, to become organist in Mühlhausen. There he married his first wife, Maria Barbara, a first cousin. In 1708, he was appointed organist at the Ducal Chapel in Weimar. During this period, Bach devoted himself primarily to the writing of organ music; and it was at this time that he wrote most of his masterworks for that instrument. He also distinguished himself as an organ virtuoso, one of the greatest of his age.

In 1717, Bach was appointed Kapellmeister at Anhalt-Cöthen. In this new post he was required to arrange concerts of instrumental music. For these concerts, Bach wrote a veritable treasury of music for solo instruments and chamber music, including his various concertos. This marked the second great creative period of his life, the period of his orchestral and instrumental works as distinguished from organ and choral music.

Bach married a second time, in 1721, a year after the death of his first wife. To help his second wife, Anna Magdalena, in her study of the clavier, Bach wrote many educational pieces including *Inventions* and the *Little Notebook of Anna Magdalena*. For their child, Wilhelm Friedemann, he also wrote many musical exercises, including the *Well-Tempered Clavier*.

The last creative period in Bach's life began in 1723 when he was appointed cantor of the St. Thomasschule. Here he remained to the end of his days—playing the organ, teaching, training the choir, preparing the church musical services, and above all writing music. It was now that Bach wrote most of his famous religious choral works: the masses, passions, oratorios, cantatas, chorales, etc.

In the closing years of his life, his eyesight failed him. He underwent an operation which, unsuccessful, brought on blindness. This terrible infirmity was followed by still another, that of paralysis. Death relieved him of his sufferings.

Strange to say of a composer who today is considered by many to be the greatest musical creator of all time, Bach was forgotten immediately after his death. For almost a hundred years thereafter most of his masterworks were unpublished, unperformed, and unknown. So little was Bach's music thought of when he died that a bundle of his cantatas sold for $40, while other Bach manuscripts were used as wrapping paper by local merchants. Not until 1829 was a major Bach work performed publicly: at that time Felix Mendelssohn directed a performance of the *Passion According to St. Matthew* in Berlin—the first time this masterwork was heard after Bach's time and outside of Leipzig. Four years after this came a performance of the *Passion According to St. John*. By 1850, the growing consciousness of Bach's greatness led to the formation of the Bach Gesellschaft, whose mission was to recover and publish all of Bach's music. This project took fifty years to complete, and when completed provided the final evidence that here was one of the greatest masters of music. Bach brought the age of polyphony to its glorious culmination, advancing the art and science of counterpoint and developing the forms of music then in use to a stage beyond which no composer could possibly progress. Henceforth, the art of music had to proceed along new directions; and part of Bach's greatness rests in the fact that he, too, had begun traveling in this direction by writing in a homophonic as well as polyphonic style.

Bach wrote numerous choral works, the most famous being the *Passion According to St. Matthew,* the *Passion According to St. John,* the *Mass in B Minor,* the *Christmas Oratorio,* together with numerous church and secular cantatas, magnificats, motets, chorales. His works for the clavier include *The Well-Tempered Clavier,* French and English suites, partitas, the *Italian Concerto,* the *Goldberg Variations,* and the *Chromatic Fantasy and Fugue.* For the orchestra he wrote the six *Brandenburg Concertos,* six suites, and numerous concertos for one, two, three, or four solo instruments and orchestra. He produced an entire library of organ music (toccatas, preludes, and fugues, chorale preludes, the *Passacaglia in C Minor,* etc.); sonatas and suites for violin and piano, and cello and piano; sonatas and partitas for unaccompanied violin, and for unaccompanied cello. There was no facet of music, except that of the opera, that he did not develop and enrich, and to which he did not contribute endurable masterpieces.

BACH, KARL PHILIPP
EMANUEL

*Born:* Weimar, Germany
    March 8, 1714
*Died:* Hamburg, Germany
    December 14, 1788

When people mentioned the name of Bach in the 18th century they were referring to Karl Philipp Emanuel (who at that time was regarded as one of the most famous living composers) and not to his father, Johann Sebastian, by then virtually forgotten by the general world of music.

His father was Karl's only teacher. Though the boy showed exceptional talent, the older Bach planned a career in law for the boy. Karl took up academic study first at the St. Thomasschule in Leipzig and after that at the University at Frankfort-on-the-Oder. But music, with which he had had contact from earliest childhood, continued to play an important part in his life. In Frankfort he founded a choral society which performed some of his earliest works. Later, when he was twenty-four, he decided to become a professional musician. He abandoned both law and the city of Frankfort for Berlin and music. Being a gifted performer on the clavier, Karl played for and deeply impressed the Crown Prince Frederick. When Frederick the Great ascended the throne in 1740 he engaged Bach as his court musician, a post Bach retained until 1767. He played the accompaniments for the flute playing of Frederick the Great, and wrote a great deal of music for the court concerts. At last, Bach longed for another position in a different city. When the Hamburg Kapellmeister Telemann died in 1767, Bach became his successor. Bach remained in Hamburg for the rest of his life, achieving a tremendous reputation for his powers at the clavier, and for the numerous works he wrote for orchestra and solo instruments. His music had a profound influence on his immediate successors, Haydn and Mozart.

Karl Philipp Emanuel Bach is important in music history because he represents the transition from his father to Haydn; or, in other words, he links the age of polyphony to that of homophony. He developed the sonata form, perfected instrumental style, and crystallized the form of the symphony. Some critics like to speak of him as the creator of the modern sonata and symphony, but this is not strictly true. Bach is also famous for an important book on the method of piano playing, *Essay on the True Art of Playing Keyboard Instruments,* published in New York City in a new English translation in 1949.

Bach wrote fifty-two concertos for clavier and orchestra, eighteen symphonies, forty-seven trios, more than two hundred solo pieces for the clavier, and numerous sonatas, oratorios, motets, and other choral works. His *Magnificat in D Major,* in the tradition of his father, is one of his choral masterworks and is still performed. He is also remembered by present-day piano students for his delightful *Solfegietto.*

BARBER, SAMUEL          *Born:* West Chester, Pa.
                        March 9, 1910

Barber is the nephew of Louise Homer, celebrated contralto of the Metropolitan Opera Association during the "golden age." He started music study early. At seven he wrote his first piano pieces, and at twelve he worked as an organist in a West Chester church. He then attended the Curtis Institute where, in 1928, he won the Bearns Prize for composition. He was only twenty-three when the Philadelphia Orchestra introduced *The School for Scandal*. Between 1935 and 1937 he won the Pulitzer Prize twice, and the American Prix de Rome, which enabled him to travel abroad. In Italy he completed the *Symphony in One Movement* which was introduced by the Augusteo Orchestra in Rome, under Molinari, in 1936. A year later, this work became the first American composition played at the Salzburg Festival. Another honor came his way in 1938 when Toscanini and the NBC Symphony introduced two of his orchestral works, the *Essay for Orchestra, No. 1,* and the *Adagio for Strings*. These two remain among Barber's best known compositions. Other works include two symphonies, several concertos; the ballet *Medea;* the *Sonata in E Flat Minor,* for piano; and the *Essay for Orchestra, No. 2*. Barber belongs with the more conservative composers who place considerable emphasis on clarity of structure and development of musical ideas, and whose aim is the production of music rich with poetic content and filled with emotional impulses.

BARTÓK, BÉLA

*Born:* Nagyszentmiklós, Hungary
March 25, 1881
*Died:* New York City
September 26, 1945

Intensely musical as a child, Bartók started composing when he was only nine years old. One year after that he made a public debut as pianist. Music study began intensively in the city of Pressburg, with Erkel and Dohnányi. In 1899, Bartók entered the Royal Hungarian Academy in Budapest, where for the next four years he studied with Thomán and Koessler. While still a student, Bartók wrote several compositions including a symphony, *Kossuth.*

After leaving the Academy in 1903, Bartók earned a meager living by teaching the piano and making arrangements of musical works. In 1907, he was appointed professor of the piano at the Academy. Meanwhile, a major interest began to absorb Bartók's interests: that of Hungarian folk music. He began making trips throughout Hungary, Slovakia and Transylvania gathering folk songs and dances indigenous to each region, putting them down on paper, and making arrangements for them. He unearthed several thousand folk melodies which, up to then, were completely unknown to the rest of the world.

This intensive study of Hungarian folk music influenced his own writing. The folk music he uncovered was far different from the sentimental gypsy tunes which Liszt and Brahms had given the world as authentically Hungarian. The music discovered by Bartók was brutal in its strength, vigorous in its rhythms and strong fibered in its texture. This was the crude and passionate music of a primitive people; the melodies were savage and the harmonies disjointed. These qualities now entered Bartók's writing. His own compositions were now filled with dissonances, unrelated keys, strange modulations, and barbaric rhythms.

Because Bartók's music was so complex, and so primitive in its force, it was not recognized for a long time. His early string quartets and his first piano concertos were occasionally heard, but never with great sympathy and understanding. Meanwhile, Bartók visited the United States in 1927, appearing in performances of his works. This did little to augment his popularity with the general public. In 1940, because of World War II, Bartók returned to this country to settle here permanently.

Between 1940 and his death five years later, Bartók wrote some of his finest and most frequently heard works: the *Concerto for Orchestra;* the *Concerto No. 3,* for piano and orchestra; the *Concerto for Violin and Orchestra.* He now went in for simplification of structure, greater clarity in his writing, and increased emotion in his melodic and harmonic materials.

The last years of Bartók's life were unhappy. He was intensely poor, very sick and usually in pain, neglected and unappreciated. But no sooner had he died of leukemia than recognition came to his music. Only a few months after his death no less than forty-eight performances of his major orchestral works were heard throughout the country, and within a period of eight weeks. Tributes were now paid to his genius, and his place among the most individual and significant composers of the 20th century was accepted. His major works include six string quartets; three concertos for piano and orchestra; the *Concerto for Violin and Orchestra;* the *Concerto for Orchestra; Music for Strings, Percussion and Celesta;* and the *Mikrokosmos Suite,* for piano.

BEETHOVEN, LUDWIG VAN *Born:* Bonn, Germany
December 16, 1770
*Died:* Vienna
March 26, 1827

    Beethoven's childhood in the little Rhine town of Bonn was unhappy. His father, a court musician, was a drunkard who spent most of his money on liquor and made his home sordid with drunken scenes. When Ludwig began to show interest in and talent for music, this drunkard was suddenly fired with the ambition of developing him into a Mozart-like prodigy. He acquired a local piano teacher, Pfeiffer, and, with the tyranny of a despot, kept his son at the piano hour after hour. His cruelty and relentless drive, however, did not smother Ludwig's own passion for music, or arrest his natural development. As a pupil of the court organist Neefe, he made such progress that the eleven-year-old boy was described by his teacher as another Mozart. Beethoven became Neefe's assistant, as court organist, when he was only thirteen. So great was the boy's talent that the Elector of Cologne provided him with funds to travel to Vienna to come into contact with its diversified musical life and to play for the great Mozart. Beethoven played for the master in Vienna who, at first, did not appear impressed by what he heard. But when Beethoven improvised, first on his own themes and then upon themes given him by the master, Mozart was convinced of his genius. "You will some day make a big noise in the world," he told Beethoven.

    Beethoven's visit to Vienna was abruptly terminated after two months by the news of his mother's illness. He came back to Bonn in time to be at her side when she died. Her death was a blow, for she had been closest to him and from her he had received the tenderness and affection he needed. Her death made life at home more difficult than ever, as his father grew more dissolute in his drinking and more irresponsible. Young Beethoven helped support his household by playing in the court orchestra, giving lessons to the children of nobility, and playing the piano. He also did some composing; many in Bonn spoke well of his gifts and prophesied a promising future for him.

    Haydn, passing through Bonn in 1790 on his way to London, heard a Beethoven mass performed in the Bonn church. "He is a man of great talent," Haydn said. Returning to Vienna from London,

Haydn interrupted his trip at Bonn to meet Beethoven personally. Beethoven showed him some of his compositions which impressed Haydn greatly. "You must come to Vienna to study with me," the master said.

It was primarily to study with Haydn that Beethoven paid a second visit to Vienna, in 1792. Strange to report, teacher and pupil did not get along well. Haydn was impatient with Beethoven's uncouth manners and with his sublime disregard for the rules of harmony. Beethoven found Haydn too fussy, too academic, and too firmly rooted in tradition. Before long they parted. Beethoven sought out another teacher, Albrechstberger, but this was no change for the better. Beethoven finally decided that he had had enough of formal instruction; he wanted to make his way in Vienna's musical world.

Letters of introduction from Count Waldstein in Bonn opened up for him the doors of some of Vienna's leading nobility: those of Prince Lichnowsky, Prince Lobkowitz, and Baron von Swieten. In the salons of Vienna's great, Beethoven played and taught the piano, and introduced his compositions. He did not lack for appreciation—this speaks volumes for the musical perception of these noblemen. For young Beethoven was already asserting his independence in his use of harmony and form, and his music was ahead of its time. Nor was the personality of the composer more palatable than his music. He was crude in manner, so sensitive that the slightest affront aroused his violent temper, so conscious of his powers that he considered himself the equal of noblemen and often said so. He was not easy to get along with. But these noblemen tolerated his boorish manners, disregarded his ill-tempered remarks, soothed his sensitive nature, because they admired his music and suspected that he was a genius.

In March, 1795, Beethoven made his first public appearance in Vienna, introducing a new piano concerto (the *Second,* in B flat major), and improvising. He created a sensation. The darling of nobility had now become an idol of the Viennese music public as well.

After 1795, Beethoven changed and grew as a composer. He was freeing himself from the rigid classical structures of Haydn and Mozart. Beginning with the *Sonata Pathétique,* for piano, and the *First Symphony* he was finding new avenues of musical expression through enriched harmonies and expressive melodies.

But as the giant was about to release his strength, tragedy descended.

Early in 1801, Beethoven recognized signs that he was growing deaf. "Sorrowful resignation," he wrote at this time, "in this must I find refuge." Sensitive about his infirmity, he pathetically tried to conceal his oncoming deafness; but he had to give up playing the piano in public and to keep himself aloof from all except intimate friends.

Deafness brought on a period of terrible despair; at the beginning, at any rate, he was incapable of finding refuge in resignation. His despair was expressed in a document called the *Heiligenstadt Testament,* written in 1802. Deafness also sent him to composition with a new fever and passion. Removed from people, he sought communion with the spirit. Deaf to the sounds of music, he sought to put down on paper the sounds he heard within him. One masterwork after another left his pen, works like the *Waldstein* and *Appassionata Sonatas* for the piano; the *Eroica Symphony;* the *Kreutzer Sonata,* for violin and piano. The apprenticeship was over. Beethoven was now in his second creative period, the period of giant achievement.

In 1805, Beethoven's only opera *Fidelio* was produced in Vienna. It came at an inappropriate time: Vienna was then occupied by invading French troops. It was a failure. A revival, one year later, was successful and would have known a long and prosperous run but for Beethoven's uncontrollable temper and unreasonableness. Suspecting that the box office was cheating him of deserved royalties, he impulsively withdrew his opera.

This incident was one of many to point to his explosive nature and increasing sensitivity. Yet his patrons and friends were uniquely sympathetic, aware of his immense powers, and suspecting the Titanic struggles going on within him. When he flew in a rage at his dearest friends (and frequently over a trifle), insulting and abusing them, they quietly accepted the attacks and waited for him to come to his senses.

Withdrawing more and more from society, because of his deafness, Beethoven found solace in nature—and in his music. He worked hard on his compositions—writing, revising, and still revising. To put down on paper the torrential sounds storming in his head and heart was a Herculean task to which he gave himself unsparingly. He knew his own greatness. "With whom need I be afraid of measuring my strength?" he asked proudly. He knew he was opening up new horizons for music—and knowing this he was proud, even arrogant; impatient, even intolerant.

As he kept on extending the dimensions of musical structure, and increasing the poetic expressiveness of his means, he produced masterworks in the forms of symphony, concerto, sonata, and string quartet. And he became a world figure. During the Congress of Vienna, when the nobility and royalty of Europe streamed to the Austrian capital, Beethoven was the object of great attention and admiration.

In 1826, while visiting his brother, Beethoven caught cold. Pneumonia set in, and after that jaundice and dropsy. Confined to bed as an invalid, Beethoven was cheered by the many wonderful gifts sent him from different parts of Europe: a complete edition of Handel; a cash gift of $500; a case of Rhine wine. But he was a very sick man. On March 23, 1827, he signed his will; one day later he submitted peacefully to the last Sacrament; and a day after that he lapsed into unconsciousness. He died in the late afternoon of March 26. All Vienna mourned his passing. Thousands lined the streets of Vienna on March 29 to watch his body carried to its final resting place.

No composer, not even Bach, played such a historic role in music as Beethoven. It is only necessary to compare the *Eroica* and *Ninth Symphonies,* the *Appassionata* and *Hammerklavier Sonatas* and the *String Quartet in C Sharp Minor* (op. 131) with similar works by Haydn and Mozart to realize how formidably music had grown with him. The prodigious development of the symphony, sonata, concerto, and string quartet with Beethoven is discussed in detail in the later sections of this book devoted to these forms.

Beethoven's most important orchestral works include the nine symphonies, five concertos for piano and orchestra, the *Concerto for Violin and Orchestra,* and the overtures to *Egmont, Coriolon,* and *Fidelio.* His works also embrace thirty-two sonatas for piano, ten sonatas for violin and piano, five sonatas for cello and piano, sixteen string quartets, the opera *Fidelio,* and the *Missa Solemnis.*

**BELLINI, VINCENZO**          *Born:* Catania, Sicily
                              November 1, 1801
                              *Died:* Paris
                              September 24, 1835

Bellini attended the Naples Conservatory and while still a student he wrote his first opera. In 1826, his opera *Bianca e Fernando* was produced in Naples and was acclaimed. *Il Pirata,* which followed, was so successful at La Scala that it was soon seen in Paris and other European opera houses. With *La Sonnambula,* seen in Milan on March 6, 1831, Bellini created his first masterwork; it was a sensation. One year later came *Norma,* presented by La Scala on December 26, 1831; and four years after that Bellini's last opera, *I Puritani,* was given in Paris. He died of intestinal fever at the premature age of thirty-four. A performance of *I Puritani* took place in Paris on the eve of his funeral; when it ended, singers and instrumentalists joined in a requiem service to the dead composer.

Together with his contemporaries, Donizetti and Rossini, Bellini helped set and establish the traditions of Italian opera. Without changing the existing structure, Bellini was able to produce an original masterwork like *Norma* through the power of his lyrical genius. He had a gift of song equalled by few—his arias are beautifully sculptured, inevitable in structure, aristocratic in style, varied in expression, and capable of fulfilling all the esthetic needs of his dramas. His harmonic and instrumental resources, however, were meager. But as one unnamed critic remarked in this connection: "In the land of the sun, one does not have to wear much clothing."

## BERG, ALBAN

*Born:* Vienna
February 9, 1885
*Died:* Vienna
December 24, 1935

Though Alban Berg was a musical child, and wrote some fine songs when he was only fifteen, he did not take any lessons in music until his early manhood. A meeting with Arnold Schoenberg was instrumental in bringing Berg to the study of music. Schoenberg became Berg's only teacher, and it was not long before Berg began thinking in terms of his teacher's unorthodox atonal style. Such early Berg works as the *Five Orchestral Songs* and the *Three Orchestral Pieces,* both written before 1914, are in the free tonality that characterized Schoenberg's music. Two of the *Five Songs,* introduced in Vienna in 1913, helped to provoke a riot among audiences outraged by this strange and harsh music.

Even more revolutionary is Berg's most famous work, the opera *Wozzeck,* which he began writing in 1914. He had to abandon this project during World War I when he joined the Austrian Army. But when the war ended, he returned to his opera, completing it in 1920. This opera, introduced in Berlin on December 14, 1925, was so iconoclastic in form and style that one German critic wrote he felt as if he were in an insane asylum. *Wozzeck,* despite its unusual technique, was seen throughout Europe, and made Berg an international figure.

Berg did not write many works. All of them are in an atonal style; and beginning with the *Lyric Suite,* in 1926, Berg adopted the Schoenberg twelve-tone technique. Despite the austerity of the idiom, some of these works are truly romantic in feeling and lyrical in content—so much so that Berg is frequently described as the "Romanticist of the Schoenberg School."

In 1935, Berg suffered severe toothaches, but he was too poor to consult a dentist. It is believed that the poisoning that shortened his life was due to this neglect.

Besides *Wozzeck,* Berg wrote a second opera which he left unfinished, *Lulu.* Other works by Berg include the *Lyric Suite* (which exists in two versions, one for string quartet, the other for chamber orchestra); *the Concerto for Violin and Orchestra;* and the *Chamber Concerto,* for piano, violin and thirteen wind instruments.

BERLIOZ, HECTOR          *Born:* La Côte-Saint-André,
                                          France
                                          December 11, 1803
                              *Died:* Paris
                                          March 8, 1869

Though Berlioz' father planned to make his son a physician, the boy drifted naturally to music. He received some lessons on the piano and guitar from a local teacher, and learned harmony and counterpoint from textbooks. In 1821, he went to Paris to proceed with his medical studies, but the first time he was called upon to dissect an animal he fled from the school in horror. Notwithstanding this experience, he continued with his medical studies and received his Bachelor degree in science in 1824. But he had not abandoned music. In 1823, he began studying music with Jean François Lesueur, and during this period wrote an oratorio, *Le Passage de la Mer Rouge,* and an opera, *Estelle et Nemorin.* By 1826, he knew that he was destined for music rather than medicine. He entered the Paris Conservatory, where his teachers included Reicha and Lesueur. While his father had given his reluctant consent for this development, he became increasingly impatient with this son's musical activities. Before long he withdrew his financial support—particularly when Hector's failure to win the Prix de Rome seemed evidence that the young man was not sufficiently gifted. Berlioz now had to shift for himself as best he could. He became a chorus singer at the Théâtre des Nouveautés, a job that paid so miserably that he often went cold and hungry.

It was at this time that he became involved in the greatest love affair of his life. An English Shakespearean company had come to Paris for a series of performances. In the presentation of *Hamlet,* the role of Ophelia was played by an attractive and sensitive artist named Henrietta Smithson. Berlioz attended that performance and from the moment he laid eyes on Henrietta Smithson he fell in love with her. He left the theatre in a daze. In vain did he try to contact her. By many devious means he attempted to attract her attention to his musical talent, but always to no avail. Finally he rented rooms next to hers, only to discover that she was leaving Paris. Realizing that his quest was futile, Berlioz found solace in the friendship of Camille Moke. They became engaged, but some time later (when Berlioz was in Italy) he learned that she had married somebody else during his absence.

Despite his emotional upheaval over his frustrated love for Henrietta, Berlioz found the time to produce two major works. The first of these was a cantata based on eight scenes from *Faust.* The ink hardly dry on this manuscript, Berlioz wrote a second masterwork, and what is undoubtedly his most celebrated composition, the *Symphonie fantastique.* The first performance of the symphony took place in Paris on December 5, 1830. Franz Liszt, who was in the audience, was so profoundly impressed that from then on he became one of Berlioz' most devoted friends.

In 1830 Berlioz, after several unsuccessful attempts, finally won the Prix de Rome. This prize enabled him to spend three years at the Villa Medici in Rome. He was not happy there: uncomfortable with the rigid rules set for Prix de Rome winners, and unsympathetic to Italian food and music.

He was back in Paris in 1832. Soon after his return, he learned that Henrietta Smithson was back in the city. The old flame burned hot within him again. He arranged a special performance of the *Symphonie fantastique* with the hope that his beloved might hear it and thus become more sympathetic to him; she did attend the concert and was impressed with the music and its composer. From then on, it was not too difficult for Berlioz to arrange an interview with her. After this first meeting, a turbulent courtship followed. And on October 3, 1833, they were married.

It was not a happy marriage. Both were too temperamental and too volatile to live contentedly with each other. For a great many years they lived apart. But in spite of their differences, Berlioz always remained tender to her. When, toward the end of her life, she became an invalid, he attended her with supreme affection and sympathy, even though she was continually churly. She died on March 3, 1854.

The first years of Berlioz' marriage to Henrietta were made even more difficult by his poverty. He earned little, certainly not enough to maintain a household. Some release from financial worry came from time to time—as, in 1838, when he received a gift of 20,000 francs from an anonymous admirer of his *Symphonie fantastique*. Several other and later gifts enabled him to give up hack work and to tour Germany as a conductor of his own works, a tour that was eminently successful.

Meanwhile, Berlioz wrote several works of outstanding importance: the symphony *Harold in Italy*, which was commissioned by Paganini; the dramatic symphony, *Romeo and Juliet;* the opera, *Benvenuto Cellini;* and the *Requiem*.

The last years of Berlioz' life were unhappy. He knew that his best days as a composer had ended, and the knowledge filled him with frustration and despair. He had married again, and with no more success than the first time. His health began deteriorating rapidly. He died at his home in Paris on March 8, 1868. His body was brought to its final resting place by some of France's foremost musicians to the accompaniment of one of his works, the funeral music from the *Symphonie funèbre et triomphale*.

Berlioz was the first of the great Romantics in music. His music was far ahead of its time in its freedom of form, expressiveness of musical content, and in the science of orchestration. By bringing new instruments into the orchestra, by making his structures so much more flexible than they had previously been, by opening up new vistas of musical beauty, and by making his music profoundly subjective, he inaugurated a new era for music.

Among his works most frequently heard today are the *Symphonie fantastique, Romeo and Juliet Symphony, Roman Carnival Overture, Harold in Italy,* orchestral excerpts from *The Damnation of Faust,* and the *Requiem.*

BIZET, GEORGES

*Born:* Paris
October 25, 1838
*Died:* Bougival, France
June 3, 1875

Bizet entered the Paris Conservatory in his ninth year. He proved to be an extraordinary student, and won numerous prizes. In 1857, he won the Prix de Rome. After his stay in Italy, he completed an opera, *Les Pêcheurs de perles (Pearl Fishers),* which was produced in Paris in 1863, but with little success. The two operas that followed were hardly better received. A certain measure of recognition came to him in 1872 with his incidental music to Daudet's *L'Arlésienne.* Three years later, on March 3, 1875, his masterwork—the opera *Carmen*—was introduced at the Opéra Comique. While not the complete failure that legend maintains it was, *Carmen* did not at first gather the triumphs it so well deserved. Bizet did not live to see his opera acclaimed as one of the greatest works in the French lyric theatre, a development that began about a decade after his premature death. Besides *Carmen,* Bizet is best known for an early symphony, the two *Arlésienne Suites,* and the *Agnus Dei* which is actually a vocal arrangement of an intermezzo from his incidental music to *L'Arlésienne.*

BLOCH, ERNEST

*Born:* Geneva, Switzerland
July 24, 1880

Bloch began studying music in his fourteenth year: the violin with Rey and composition with Dalcroze. He progressed so rapidly that two years after beginning these studies he wrote a symphony. When he was seventeen, he went to Brussels for additional lessons with Ysaÿe (violin) and Rasse (composition); subsequently he completed his education in Munich with Knorr. Under Knorr's influence, Bloch wrote the *Symphony in C Sharp Minor.* Failure to get this work performed proved so discouraging that he decided to become a business man. He entered his father's store in Geneva as bookkeeper and salesman; but his free hours belonged to composition. He also did some conducting. During this period he wrote an opera, *Macbeth*, which was accepted by the Paris Opéra Comique and introduced on November 30, 1910. Several major French critics considered it an important work. One of them was Romain Rolland who made a special trip to Geneva to talk to and encourage its composer.

In or about 1915, Bloch's music changed character. Up till then he had been primarily influenced by German Romanticism, with occasional digression into Impressionism. From then on he tried to create Hebrew music. His style became Oriental in character, given to strong rhythms, sensuous melodies, expressive harmonies, and brilliant orchestration. It was in this vein that he produced the first of his celebrated works, notably *Schelomo*, the *Two Jewish Poems*, the *Israel Symphony*, and the *Baal Shem Suite*.

Bloch came to this country in 1916 as the conductor of the Maud Allen troupe. He remained here after this organization went into sudden bankruptcy. Performances of his works by major American musical organizations, such as the Boston Symphony Orchestra, the Society of Friends of Music in New York, and the Flonzaley Quartet, helped to bring him to the attention of the American music public. In 1919, Bloch received the Elizabeth Sprague Coolidge Award of $1,000 for his *Suite for Viola and Piano*.

In 1920, Bloch became director of the Cleveland Institute of Music, remaining in the office for five years. During this period he wrote two major works, the *Piano Quintet*, and the *Concerto Grosso for Chamber Orchestra*. In 1925, he transferred his teaching activities to San Francisco, and in 1927 he won the $3,000 award given by the magazine *Musical America* for a symphonic work, with his epic rhapsody, *America*. *America* was introduced by the New York Philharmonic on December 20, 1928, and on the following day was performed by the Boston Symphony, the Chicago Symphony and the San Francisco Symphony Orchestras.

For a while, Bloch lived in seclusion in Switzerland where he completed his *Sacred Service*, for the Hebrew synagogue. Another unmistakably Hebraic work followed, *A Voice for the Wilderness*. Later works by Bloch include the *Concerto for Violin and Orchestra;* the *Concerto symphonique for piano and orchestra;* and the *Second String Quartet* which received the Music Critics Award as the most distinguished new chamber-music work by an American heard during the 1946–47 season; and the *Third String Quartet*.

During the past decade, Bloch has been living at Agate Beach, Oregon, spending some time each summer to teach at the Berkeley University in California. His best works contain a masculine vigor combined with poetic eloquence, intensity of expression and passion.

BORODIN, ALEXANDER     *Born:* St. Petersburg
                                            November 11, 1833
                                      *Died:* St. Petersburg
                                            February 27, 1887

Borodin was exceptionally precocious in music, languages, and the sciences. After studying music with private teachers, he wrote a concerto and a trio when he was only thirteen. Despite this bent for music he did not neglect academic study. He completed preparatory courses for medical school and, in 1850, graduated from the Academy of Medical and Physical Sciences. For two years after this he served in a military hospital, and for three years more he studied in Europe on a government subsidy. He then settled in St. Petersburg to fill a post as professor of chemistry at the Academy.

A meeting with the Russian musician, Balakirev, awakened his one-time love for music. Balakirev urged Borodin to return to composition, inflaming him with his own ideal to create Russian national music. Spurred on, Borodin completed his *First Symphony* in 1867. From this time on, he divided his life between science and music. As a scientist he did important work in botany and chemistry, established medical courses for women, and was an important member of several scientific organizations. As a musician, he worked laboriously on several major works. The most important of these were the tone poem, *In the Steppes of Central Asia* (1880); the *Symphony No. 2 in B Minor* (begun in 1860, but completed eight years later); the *String Quartet No. 2* (1887); and the opera *Prince Igor* (upon which he worked for many years but which he never completed).

His death came suddenly while he was celebrating a carnival in St. Petersburg.

Borodin was a member of that national school of Russian composers known as the "Russian Five," or "Mighty Five." Like the other members of this group, he drew from Russian history and backgrounds for the inspiration and programs for his musical works, and filled these works with melodies and rhythms that have national character. He was at his best when writing for a definite text or story. His pronounced Russian idiom is blended with an Oriental strain that brings to his music an added charm, color, and exotic interest.

BRAHMS, JOHANNES          *Born:* Hamburg, Germany
                                      May 7, 1833
                                *Died:* Vienna
                                      April 3, 1897

Johannes Brahms was born into a household haunted by poverty and misery. The Brahms family lived in the slums of Hamburg. The father was an indigent musician; the mother worked with the needle. Johannes revealed his musical gifts early. As an infant he used to make up his own melodies, and in early childhood he invented a musical notation of his own to put his melodies down on paper. His father engaged a local pianist, Otto Cossel, to give lessons to the child. When Brahms became adept at the piano he earned some sadly needed coins by playing in disreputable public taverns. In his tenth year, he became a pupil of Eduard Marxsen, and it is from this time on that his musical development becomes marked. Three years later, he gave a piano recital, the program of which included one of his own compositions.

His intense poverty made it necessary for him to earn a living through his music. He gave piano lessons, played the piano in saloons, and wrote about one hundred fifty hack compositions. But serious music was not neglected. He managed to write some songs and a piano trio, the latter was given a private performance in 1851.

A meeting with the Hungarian concert violinist, Eduard Reményi, was a turning point. Impressed by Brahms' gifts, Reményi asked the young composer to tour with him as an accompanist. This tour was responsible for bringing Brahms into personal contact with some of Europe's leading musicians: Joseph Joachim, Franz Liszt, and most important of all, Robert and Clara Schumann. Robert Schumann befriended the young man, took him in his household, showered on him affection and appreciation. And in a now-celebrated article in the *Neue Zeitschrift für Musik,* written on October 28, 1853, Schumann singled out the unknown Brahms "to give the highest and most ideal expression to the tendencies of the times." It was thanks to Schumann that Brahms' early piano works were published and Brahms was engaged to appear as pianist in the Gewandhaus in Leipzig.

In 1857, Brahms was appointed music master to the Prince Lippe-Detmold. During this period he wrote his first works for orchestra, two serenades and the *Piano Concerto No. 1*, in D minor. The latter work was introduced by Brahms himself and the Gewandhaus Orchestra in Leipzig on January 22, 1859, and was a failure.

From 1860 through 1863, Brahms led a women's choir in Hamburg. In 1862, he visited Vienna where his *Piano Quartet, op. 25*, was introduced by the Hellmesberger Quartet, with the composer assisting. This was so successful that a Brahms concert was arranged in which his *Piano Quartet, op. 26*, and the *Handel Variations*, for piano, were heard.

Brahms aspired for the musical-director post of the Hamburg Philharmonic Orchestra. When it failed to materialize he decided to settle in Vienna for good. There, for a year, he directed the Singakademie, and earned his living by teaching the piano. In 1872, he became the director of the famous Gesellschaft der Musikfreunde.

All this while he kept on working on major works in which his creative genius was rapidly flowering. He achieved a success of major proportions when his *A German Requiem* was given in Leipzig on February 18, 1869. His first important orchestral work, the *Variations on a Theme of Haydn*, came in 1873; it was received enthusiastically when introduced in Vienna on November 2, 1873. His success was probably influential in making him undertake an even more ambitious orchestral work—his first symphony. For years, his profound admiration for the Beethoven symphonies had been a deterrent to any attempt in that form; and for four years he worked on sketches. At last, in 1876, his *First Symphony* was written—the most important symphony to be written after Beethoven, and surely the greatest first symphony ever produced by anybody. With the *First Symphony* Brahms emerged as Beethoven's legitimate successor in the symphonic field, a position he maintained and solidified with three more masterworks in that form, written between 1877 and 1884.

The remaining years of Brahms' life were comparatively uneventful. Sometimes he went traveling, and made guest appearances as either conductor or pianist. Sometimes he stayed in Vienna. Sometimes he would spend summers in the mountain districts outside Vienna. He continued to produce masterworks in every musical form except the opera, and received international recognition. In 1878, the degree of Doctor of Philosophy was conferred on him by the University of Breslau, and two years later the Emperor of Austria presented him with the Order of Leopold.

Though he loved several women, and none more devotedly and tenderly than Clara Schumann (Robert's widow), he never married. For several decades he lived alone in his comparatively humble quarters in Vienna, brewing his own coffee, eating at modest restaurants, and going in for simple pleasures.

He was attending the funeral of his beloved friend, Clara Schumann, in 1896, when he caught cold. This infection brought on a prolonged illness from which he never recovered. He attended a concert for the last time on March 7, 1897, when Hans Richter directed a performance of his *Fourth Symphony,* and he was given a touching ovation. He died soon after this, of cancer of the liver.

In his music, Brahms preferred an art that was pure, objective, and classical. As far as he himself was concerned, he had no sympathy for the kind of dramatic and programmatic music written by Wagner and Liszt and which was regarded by many as "the music of the future." In Brahms, the classical past fused with the Romanticism of the middle nineteenth century. He had the classicist's respect for tradition and form, but to these he brought a wealth of emotion, feeling, and poetry. His passionate surges, his intensity of speech, his introspective musings are the identifying qualities of his best works. He combined freedom of emotion with the discipline of structure and classical technique, producing an art that was uniquely his.

Brahms' major works for orchestra include four symphonies, the *Variations on a Theme of Haydn,* the *Academic Festival Overture,* the *Tragic Overture,* two concertos for piano and orchestra, the *Concerto for Violin and Orchestra,* and the *Concerto for Violin, Cello and Orchestra.* Among his most famous chamber-music works are three string quartets, two piano quartets, the *Piano Quintet,* the *Clarinet Quintet,* three sonatas for violin and piano, together with various trios, quintets and sextets. His piano works embrace ballades, rhapsodies, capriccios, intermezzos, waltzes, Hungarian dances, three sonatas, the *Variations on a Theme of Handel,* and the *Variations on a Theme of*

*Paganini.* Brahms also wrote numerous songs (among them such favorites as the "Lullaby," the "Sapphic Ode," and the "Four Serious Songs"), together with such choral masterworks as *A German Requiem, The Song of Fate,* and the *Alto Rhapsody.* A more detailed account of his major works will be found in the sections on Chamber Music, Vocal Music, Piano Music, and Symphony.

BRITTEN, BENJAMIN      *Born:* Lowestoft, Suffolk,
                        England
                        November 22, 1913

He was exceptionally precocious, writing a complete oratorio when he was only nine, and by the time he was sixteen having completed a symphony, several piano sonatas, and various other works. His academic schooling took place at Gresham's School, Holt; he studied music with Frank Bridge, and at the Royal College of Music. Britten first achieved note as a composer with performances of several major works at festivals of the International Society of Contemporary Music between 1934 and 1938; the most important of these works was the *Variations on a Theme of Frank Bridge,* for orchestra, heard in 1938. In 1939, Britten visited the United States, and while here he completed several works, the most significant being the *Sinfonia da Requiem.* In this country, Britten was commissioned by the Koussevitzky Foundation to write an opera. He returned to his own country in 1942 and worked on the opera, *Peter Grimes.* Introduced in London on June 8, 1945, *Peter Grimes* was a sensation, and was soon seen in the principal opera houses of the world. His later operas—among them, *The Rape of Lucretia, Albert Herring, Billy Budd, Gloriana,* and *The Turn of the Screw*—established him as one of the leading creative figures in the contemporary musical theatre.

He has produced distinguished works in other media as well, including *A Ceremony of Carols, Les Illuminations,* the *Concerto No. 1 for Piano and Orchestra,* the *Second String Quartet,* the *Young Person's Guide to the Orchestra,* and the *Spring Symphony.* His style is varied. He is at times complex, dissonant and experimental; on other occasions he is polyphonic with a partiality to medieval mysticism. He can be simple and direct and witty; he can also be deeply moving emotionally and poetically atmospheric.

BRUCKNER, ANTON          *Born:* Ansfelden, Austria
                                      September 4, 1824
                         *Died:* Vienna
                                      October 11, 1896

Bruckner was born to a family which had produced school-teachers for generations. He, too, was directed to the teaching profession. However, in preparing for it, he followed his natural inclinations toward music. A cousin taught him the organ and theory. In his thirteenth year Bruckner continued his music study at the St. Florian School, where he remained for four years. After a period at a teachers' preparatory school in Linz, he assumed his first position. He subsequently taught for eight years at St. Florian's, during which time he also devoted himself to playing the organ and to composing.

By 1853, he came to the decision to abandon teaching for music. He went to Vienna for additional study with Sechter. A few years after his arrival in the Austrian capital he became the director of a choral society which introduced one of his works, an *Ave Maria*.

In 1863, Bruckner heard a Wagner music drama for the first time—*Tannhäuser*. From then on he became one of Wagner's most fervent disciples. He went to Munich to hear *Tristan and Isolde*. He met the master there and reverently fell on his knees before him. This humble act of adoration characterized Bruckner's lifelong attitude to Wagner.

In 1868, Bruckner became professor at the Vienna Conservatory. For the next few decades he divided his energies between teaching and composing. Recognition as a composer was slow in coming. Premières of his *Symphony No. 1* and the *Mass in F Minor* were dismal failures. Though depressed by such a reception, Bruckner never lost his self-confidence and continued working on mammoth symphonic and choral works. Not until the 1880's did a measure of appreciation come to him with performances of his *Symphony No. 4* (*Romantic*) and *Seventh Symphony*. His fame now grew in and out of Vienna, and he was the recipient of many honors. In 1891, the University of Vienna conferred on him an honorary degree; and three years later, on the occasion of his seventieth birthday, he was the object of a national celebration.

A simple, humble, and profoundly religious man, Bruckner poured his heart into his music. Within the classical framework of the symphony he created music that is romantic and full of poetic feeling. He wrote nine symphonies, a Requiem, three masses and various other choral works. His music is commented upon in a later section on the Symphony.

## CHABRIER, EMMANUEL

*Born:* Ambert, France
    January 18, 1841
*Died:* Paris
    September 13, 1894

Chabrier's father wanted him to become a lawyer. After completing his law study in Paris, Emmanuel held a government position. Meanwhile he studied music, which had always been a favorite diversion. With music still a hobby, he wrote the scores of two operettas, both of them produced in Paris with moderate success.

The turning point in Chabrier's life was a performance of *Tristan and Isolde,* which stirred him so profoundly that he made a silent vow to dedicate himself henceforth to music, and music alone. He resigned his government position and became an assistant conductor of the Lamoureux Orchestra.

He visited Spain in 1883. So deeply moved was he by its folk songs and dances, that he planned and completed a major orchestral work built out of these materials. That work made Chabrier famous, for it was the rhapsody *España,* introduced in Paris by the Lamoureux Orchestra on November 4, 1883. Besides *España,* Chabrier wrote several operas in which the influence of Wagner is pronounced, the best being *Gwendoline,* and *Le Roi malgré lui.*

During the last years of his life, Chabrier suffered from paralysis; just before his death his mind was affected.

## CHARPENTIER, GUSTAVE

*Born:* Dieuze, Lorraine
    January 25, 1860

His music study took place first at the Lille Conservatory and then at the Paris Conservatory where he won the Prix de Rome. While in Rome, Charpentier completed an orchestral work that is still performed occasionally, *Impressions of Italy.* Soon after returning to Paris he started working on his most famous composition, the opera *Louise.* After a long delay, *Louise* was introduced by the Opéra Comique on

February 2, 1900. It created a sensation and made its composer world famous. Charpentier wrote a second opera, *Julien* (a sequel to *Louise*), but it was a failure. Since then he has written virtually nothing, living for half a century on the reputation established by *Louise* which, by 1935, had been given a thousand times in Paris alone. The fiftieth anniversary of its première was celebrated at the Paris Opéra on February 28, 1950; at that time, the composer—then ninety years old—took over the baton to direct the last scene.

As the first French opera to treat a realistic and contemporary subject with naturalism, *Louise* is a milestone in operatic history.

CHAUSSON, ERNEST          *Born:* Paris
                                  January 21, 1855
                           *Died:* Limay, France
                                  June 10, 1899

Originally intended for the law, Chausson revealed such a pronounced gift for music that he finally decided to become a professional musician. He entered the Paris Conservatory comparatively late, in his twenty-fifth year; but he soon made up for the lost time. His teachers included Massenet and César Franck, the latter having a profound influence upon him. Chausson left the Conservatory to study privately with Franck. In 1878, he published his first work, two songs; but he did not gain recognition until the end of his life. This happened in 1891 with the première of his *Symphony in B Flat Major* which was a major success. The *Poem,* for violin and orchestra, added to his reputation. In these two works Chausson followed the ideals and principles of Franck. He produced abstract music whose single goal was the creation of beautiful sound and personally felt emotions. Chausson also wrote a fine *Concerto for Piano, Violin and String Quartet,* two operas, and several orchestral works.

CHÁVEZ, CARLOS          *Born:* Mexico City
                                  June 13, 1899

Chávez received practically his entire musical training without the benefit of teachers—through reading, memorizing textbooks, and experimenting with the playing of musical instruments. When he started writing music seriously, in his eighteenth year, he followed European models. But at about this time he became acquainted with the folk music of the Mexican Indian, and this discovery changed his artistic destiny. Chávez became so fascinated with this indigenous music of his land that for a long period he lived with the primitive people of different regions, learning to play on their instruments, and memorizing their songs and dances. This intimacy with Mexican-Indian music brought about a transformation in his style. Like the folk music he loved, his own works are filled with barbaric rhythms, sudden contrasts, and unrelated tonalities—several of his works require the use of authentic primitive Mexican instruments. The first of his works in this new style was the ballet, *The New Fire,* written in 1921. Later works include the ballet, *H.P.; Sinfonía de Antígona; Sinfonía India;* and various concertos.

CHOPIN, FRÉDÉRIC
FRANÇOIS

*Born:* Zelazowa Wola, Poland
February 22, 1810
*Died:* Paris
October 17, 1849

As a child, Chopin was continually found at the piano. When he came upon a particularly pleasing melody he would burst into tears. A local teacher, Adalbert Zwyny, began giving Chopin lessons when he was six years old; by the time he was eight, he was able to make a successful public appearance. Chopin's next teacher, and his last one, was Joseph Elsner in Warsaw. Elsner understood Chopin's temperament and catered to it; instead of burdening the boy with rules and exercises he allowed him to grow and develop freely in the direction to which his romantic nature led. It was largely due to Elsner's sympathy that Chopin was able to evolve a personal style of composition almost from the very beginning.

In 1829, Chopin visited Vienna where he gave two successful concerts and where he published his first ambitious work, the *Variations on Mozart's Là ci darem from Don Giovanni,* for piano and orchestra. This visit convinced him he wanted to live and work in foreign capitals. Back in Warsaw, he was restless until he could leave again for Vienna. In 1830, he left Poland for good. At the city of his birth, a cantata was performed in his honor by his teacher, Elsner. When the festivities ended, Elsner presented his pupil with a silver urn containing some Polish earth, so that Chopin might never forget the land of his birth. This little bit of earth was to be Chopin's last direct contact with his native country. Chopin never again returned to Poland; and when he died in Paris this bit of Polish earth was buried with him.

In Vienna, the news reached Chopin that Poland had risen in revolt against Russian domination. His first impulse was to rush back and fight for his country's liberation. But discretion arrested this impulse. He went on to Germany. In Stuttgart, in July of 1831, he heard that Warsaw had been recaptured by the Russians. Inflamed by this news, he expressed his loyalty and patriotic ardor by writing a piece of music —the *Revolutionary Étude*.

He next went to Paris, expecting to remain only a short while, but staying there for the rest of his life. Chopin became acquainted with some of the leading musicians in Paris who arranged for his debut in the French capital on January 25, 1832. It was not successful; Chopin's style of piano playing was too refined and intimate for Parisian tastes. However, in the salons of Paris Chopin became a great favorite. He was now able to command munificent fees as a teacher and as performer for the social elite of the city.

He was also honored as a composer; for all this while Chopin was writing exquisite pieces for the piano to which the Parisian *haut monde* responded enthusiastically. What was particularly liked in his waltzes, nocturnes, études, polonaises, mazurkas, etc., was their sentiment, tenderness, and aristocracy of style. Few realized that these small pieces were also opening up new worlds for piano music. But if a true measure of this music's greatness was still to come, its popularity was immediate. Publishers competed with one another to issue his latest works; the Parisian salons reverberated with enthusiasm whenever Chopin introduced them.

Early in 1837, Chopin met the celebrated French woman novelist who called herself "George Sand." Her masculinity at first repelled him. But he was soon attracted to the brilliance of her mind and the dynamism of her personality. And before he fully realized it himself, he was in love with her. They were opposites in personality and temperament. Their love affair was stormy, and eventually ended in tragedy.

When George Sand's son suddenly fell ill in 1838, she decided to take him to the warmer climate of Majorca. Chopin followed her.

Their life together on the island was miserable from the start. The townspeople were antagonistic to the pair; the weather was unseasonably cold and damp; the food was sometimes inedible. Always delicate in health, Chopin now broke down completely, becoming a victim of nightmares and hemorrhages. An invalid, he had to be carried back to France aboard a freighter. There he was, at last, able to recover his strength and senses. The only happy result of the sordid Majorca experience was the completion of twenty-four magnificent preludes.

Chopin was now at the height of his creative powers. Pampered and adulated in Paris, he produced some of his most ambitious works, including the *Sonata in B Flat Minor,* and the finest of his ballades, impromptus, and fantasias. He kept up a prodigious creative effort for two years, and it sapped his health. His physical decline began again in 1841.

A quarrel brought the relationship of George Sand and Chopin to a sudden end in 1847. From then on his poor health went into complete disintegration, and his spirits were equally broken. Returning from a brief visit to London in 1849, he did not have enough energy to write music or to play the piano; he refused the society of friends. In the closing weeks of his life he was obsessed with the fear that he would be buried alive; he left a note instructing that his body be cut open before he was buried—a wish that was carried out.

Chopin was essentially a composer of miniatures, and it is for this reason that he cannot be put in the class of Bach, Beethoven, or Mozart. But within his limited sphere he was a genius. The vast library of his works for the piano includes sonatas, ballades, études, nocturnes, polonaises, preludes, waltzes, fantasias, mazurkas, impromptus, rondos, scherzos, and variations—the most significant of which are analyzed in the section on Piano Music and its principal forms. The only major works for orchestra are two concertos for the piano; his handful of chamber-music compositions embraces a piano trio, and a sonata for cello and piano.

COPLAND, AARON                    *Born:* Brooklyn, New York
                                   November 14, 1900

After taking piano lessons with local teachers, Copland decided, in his sixteenth year, to become a composer. To realize this ambition he entered the harmony class of Rubin Goldmark and proceeded to write piano pieces and songs that shocked the teacher with their unusual harmonies. In 1931, Copland entered the American School of Music at Fontainebleau in France. Soon after this, he became a private pupil of Nadia Boulanger in Paris, and under her guidance wrote several works. Back in the United States, in 1924, he started working on a symphony for organ and orchestra which Boulanger had asked him to write for her American tour. The symphony was introduced in January 1925 by the New York Symphony Society under Damrosch. It made such a fine impression that Koussevitzky played it in Boston, and henceforth promoted the interests of the young composer. On Koussevitzky's commission, Copland wrote *Music for the Theatre,* his first serious attempt to use a jazz idiom. An even more ambitious work in this style was the *Concerto for Piano and Orchestra* which Copland introduced with the Boston Symphony Orchestra under Koussevitzky in 1927.

Meanwhile a measure of financial stability came to Copland through the award of a Guggenheim Fellowship in 1925 and 1926; it was the first such fellowship awarded to a composer. In 1930, Copland won a $5,000 award of the RCA Victor Company with his *Dance Symphony.* This and subsequent works like the *Piano Variations, Short Symphony* and *Statements* for orchestra, were complex in style and idiom, and not easily assimilable. Feeling that his music had become too esoteric for general consumption, he now decided to make a special effort to simplify his writing and to make it more entertaining and human. His first important work in this direction was the *El Salón México,* for orchestra, still one of his most popular works. First introduced in Mexico City in 1937, and one year after that performed in America over the NBC network by the NBC Symphony Orchestra under Adrian Boult, it was an instantaneous success.

Copland now wrote some music expressly for children: the opera, *The Second Hurricane,* and the *Outdoor Overture.* He went to American folklore and folk-music idioms for his materials and inspiration, producing the ballets, *Rodeo, Billy the Kid,* and *Appalachian Spring.* He wrote music for the movies (*Our Town, The Red Pony*). It is in this simplified and human manner that Copland has produced his finest music to date, music in which an extraordinary compositorial technique is combined with freshness of style and originality of thought. His *Third Symphony*, written in 1946, received the Boston Symphony Award of Merit, and the Music Critics Circle Award. Before that, the *Appalachian Spring* won the Pulitzer Prize. His one-act opera, *Tender Land*, was given by The New York City Opera on April 1, 1954.

CORELLI, ARCANGELO
*Born:* Fusignano, Italy
February 17, 1653
*Died:* Rome
January 8, 1713

Corelli studied the violin with Bassani, and counterpoint with Simonelli. By 1672, his fame as a violin virtuoso was established. He traveled extensively throughout Europe, acclaimed wherever he performed. For a while he served as court violinist to the Elector of Bavaria, and after that he was the director of an opera company in Rome. He soon became a favorite of Roman society, feted and honored by the elite. Cardinal Pietro Ottoboni became his patron. Corelli made the Cardinal's palace his own home, conducting there Monday evening concerts which were among the most significant musical events in Rome. Corelli, however, lived long enough to see himself eclipsed in fame by younger violinists and more popular composers, and this development made him a bitter and melancholy man before his death.

Corelli was a momentous figure in the early history of instrumental music. His pioneer achievements in the early development of the sonata, concerto grosso and chamber music are evaluated in later sections devoted to these forms.

COUPERIN, FRANÇOIS
(LE GRAND)
*Born:* Paris
November 10, 1668
*Died:* Paris
September 12, 1733

Like the family of the Bachs, that of the Couperins produced musicians for several generations. The greatest of the Couperins—and for this reason he is known as *"le grand,"* (the great one)—was the son of the organist at the St. Gervais Church in Paris. Couperin first studied with his father, and after that with Jacques-Denis Thomelin, organist of the King's Chapel. Couperin entered the King's service when he was twenty-five years old. When the post of organist for the Royal Chapel was vacated, a competition was held to determine the candidate, and Couperin won easily. From then on he was a great favorite at the court of Louis XIV. He was music teacher to the princes; personal performer for the king; royal music master to the court. In the last position he wrote many instrumental works performed at the Sunday evening concerts at Versailles. After the death of Louis XIV, Couperin withdrew from the court. He lived in Paris, giving concerts at his home and writing music, up to the time of his death.

He played a decisive role in the early history of French instrumental music. He wrote the first French sonatas for violin, and his works for various instruments laid the groundwork for French chamber music. His most important music is found in the *Pièces de clavecin,* for harpsichord, which is treated more fully in the section on Piano Music.


**DEBUSSY, CLAUDE**        *Born:* Saint-Germain-en-Laye,
near Paris
August 22, 1862
*Died:* Paris
March 25, 1918


Debussy's parents were so poor that, when he was three years old, they had to turn him over to a comparatively well-to-do aunt for support. This was a blessing in disguise, for the aunt was a lover of the arts and in a position to encourage and develop his pronounced musical talent. He was entrusted to a fine piano teacher, Mme. Mauté de Fleurville, who had been Chopin's pupil; and under her guidance the boy made such rapid progress that by the time he was eleven years old he could pass his entrance examinations for the Paris Conservatory.

His teachers at the Conservatory, particularly Marmontel and Durand, did not understand his persistent attempt to explore new melodies and harmonies that defied the laws of the textbook. It took some years before they overcame their prejudice to his adventurous musical nature sufficiently to be able to recognize his exceptional musical gifts. Eventually, they did recognize his marked talent. Debussy was able to win several important prizes. Besides, Marmontel was willing to recommend him for a desirable summer position as pianist, the employer being Mme. Nadejda von Meck, Tchaikovsky's patroness. Debussy traveled with the von Meck family in France, Italy, and Austria in the summer of 1880, and worked at the von Meck estate in Russia in 1881 and 1882.

In 1885, Debussy won the Prix de Rome with the cantata, *L'Enfant prodigue*. He was not happy in Italy, impatient with the rigid discipline at the Villa Medici, and intolerant of Italian food, climate, and music. He left Rome without completing the three-year stay required of Prix de Rome winners. But he did fulfill his obligations by sending back to the academicians the *envois* required of him. The last of these was a cantata, *The Blessed Damozel* (*La Demoiselle élue*) based on the poem by Dante Gabriel Rossetti.

Back in Paris Debussy met many of those who were helping create new artistic movements in Paris, among them the Symbolist poets headed by Mallarmé, and the Impressionist painters, including Manet and Degas. By listening to and absorbing their ideas, Debussy began crystallizing his own thinking on the kind of music he wanted to write: music delicate and rarefied in effect, seeking subtle atmospheres and vague suggestions. At this same time, Debussy became a friend of the eccentric musician, Erik Satie. Satie, the rebel against the large forms and the excessive emotions of the German Romantics, sought to produce a music essentially French in personality—lean, precise, slight in form, economical in means. Satie's ambitions affected Debussy no less strongly than did the esthetic ideas of the Symbolists and the Impressionists.

Now clear as to the kind of music he aimed to write, Debussy turned more passionately than ever to composition. In short order he produced several masterworks which helped establish his reputation and which helped launch musical Impressionism. The first of these was the *Quartet in G Minor,* introduced by the Ysaÿe Quartet on December 29, 1893. This was followed by the orchestral prelude, *The Afternoon of a Faun* (*L'Après-midi d'un faune*), inspired by the poem of Mallarmé. It was heard for the first time at a concert of the Société Nationale de Musique in Paris on December 22, 1894. After that came the *Nocturnes,* for orchestra; and most important of all, the opera, *Pelléas et Mélisande,* after the drama by Maurice Maeterlinck.

The opera made Debussy one of the most celebrated, and contro-versial, figures in French music. Many called him the prophet of the music of the future. Others regarded him as a charlatan. Oblivious to both praise and attack, Debussy continued producing one master-work after another in his individual manner—works for the orchestra, for the piano, and for the voice. Meanwhile, he had married twice. The first time was in 1899 to Rosalie Texier, a dressmaker. Three years later, Debussy left her to marry Emma Bardac, the wife of a banker. There was a child to the second marriage, a daughter whom Debussy playfully nicknamed Chouchou.

The last years of Debussy's life were somber. A victim of cancer, he had to undergo two painful operations which left him effete and in pain. The outbreak of World War I brought on other problems, mostly financial. Notwithstanding his personal sufferings, he continued to write music, though not in the consistently original and inspired vein of his earlier works.

Debussy was the founder of that school of music known as Impres-sionism. He was the master of color, subtle mood, delicate effects, whether writing an opera, orchestral music, or piano pieces. He ar-rived at new effects through the evolution of a new harmonic language exploiting unresolved discords and permitting chords to move freely from a tonal center. He came to exotic melodies through the wide-spread use of the whole-tone scale, which he helped to make famous, as well as other scales. Through these means he evoked a nebulous and dreamlike world of beauty, which no one before him and few since have realized.

Besides his great opera, *Pelléas et Mélisande,* Debussy's master-works include many compositions for orchestra, piano, chamber-music combinations, and voice. His best orchestral works are *La Mer, The Afternoon of a Faun, Nocturnes,* and *Images* (the last including "Ibéria"). He produced a library of piano music including two books of preludes, two books of études, the *Suite bergamasque* (in which is found the famous "Clair de Lune"), arabesques, *Estampes,* two sets of *Images,* and the delightful suite, *Children's Corner.* Among his vocal pieces are "Mandoline," "Paysage sentimental," two series of *Fêtes galantes;* his chamber-music works include the *Quartet in G Minor,* and three sonatas.

DELIBES, LÉO

*Born:* St. Germain-du-Val,
France
February 21, 1836
*Died:* Paris
January 16, 1891

As a child, Delibes sang in the choir of the Madeleine Church in Paris. In his thirteenth year he entered the Paris Conservatory where his teachers included Bazin, Adam, and Benoist. When his schooling ended, Delibes earned his living by playing the organ and the piano. He also began composing seriously, and had an opera produced in Paris in 1855. As a chorusmaster at the Paris Opéra, he was commissioned to write the music for a ballet. With this ballet, *La Source,* presented by the Paris Opéra on November 12, 1866, Delibes proved his individuality for the first time. Subsequent ballets extended his fame and artistic importance. The most important were *Coppélia,* presented at the Paris Opéra on May 25, 1870; and *Sylvia,* first seen at the Opéra on June 14, 1876. Delibes also wrote an immensely successful opera: *Lakmé,* the first performance taking place at the Opéra Comique on April 14, 1883.

In 1881, Delibes became professor of composition at the Paris Conservatory; and in 1884 he was appointed member of the French Institut. He is now regarded as the father of modern ballet music.

DELIUS, FREDERICK

*Born:* Bradford, England
January 29, 1862
*Died:* Grez-sur-Loing, France
June 10, 1934

Delius' father was a prosperous wool merchant who wanted his son to follow in his footsteps. Delius was sent to Germany to study the wool business, and in 1882 he entered the Manchester firm of an uncle. He prevailed on his father to finance for him an altogether different business venture: the raising of oranges in Florida. In 1884, Delius came to the United States, settling in Solano, Florida, to superintend an orange plantation. In this primitive setting he plunged into music study. Convinced, at last, that he was meant for music, he left his plantation, held various minor musical jobs in Jacksonville and in

Virginia; then returned to Europe to enroll in the Leipzig Conservatory. There he met and became a friend of Grieg who prevailed on Delius' father to allow the young man to follow his musical inclinations. Delius then proceeded to Paris where he wrote his first major works, including the *Concerto for Piano and Orchestra* and the fantasy overture, *Over the Hills and Far Away.*

After marrying Jelka Rosen in Paris, Delius settled in the small French town of Grez-sur-Loing. This was his home for the rest of his life. There, after 1900, he started writing those sensitive impressionistic tone poems with which his name is identified.

Appreciation was slow in coming. It came first in Germany in the early 1900's. In England, it arrived largely through the persistent efforts of the conductor, Sir Thomas Beecham. By 1920, with a revival of Delius' opera *A Village Romeo and Juliet,* his significance was accepted throughout the world of music.

His physical disintegration began taking place after 1920. By 1922, he was hopelessly paralyzed; and in 1925 he became blind. Though a complete invalid, he continued creative work by painstakingly dictating his last works note by note to a secretary.

In the winter of 1929, Delius was carried in an invalid's chair to London to attend a week-long festival of his works. He died five years after that.

He is an Impressionist composer best known for his sensitive and poetic symphonic poems. The best of these include *On Hearing the First Cuckoo in Spring, Summer Night on the River, In a Summer Garden,* and *Brigg Fair.* Other significant Delius works include *A Mass of Life, A Song of the High Hills, Sea-Drift,* and *A Village Romeo and Juliet.*

DONIZETTI, GAETANO          *Born:* Bergamo, Italy
                           November 29, 1797
                           *Died:* Bergamo
                           April 8, 1848

The son of a weaver, Donizetti early showed a gift for music. He entered the Naples Conservatory where his first contact with Rossini's operas (in the published scores) aroused his ambition to become an opera composer. After an additional period of study in Bologna with Padre Mattei, Donizetti joined the army. While in uniform he wrote his first opera, *Enrico di Borgogna,* performed in Vienna in 1818. Success came with *Zoraide di Granata,* given in Rome in 1822. After the première performance, the composer was carried away in triumph on the shoulders of his admirers. He also was exempted from all further military duty. Two later operas spread his fame throughout Europe. The first was the comic opera, *L'Elisir d'Amore,* given in Milan in 1832. This was followed by the serious opera, *Lucia di Lammermoor,* introduced at the San Carlo Theatre in Naples on September 26, 1835. By then an international figure, Donizetti went to Paris in 1839 to assist in the production of some of his operas.

In 1842, he completed another of his masterworks, the opera-buffa, *Don Pasquale.* Its première took place in Paris on January 3, 1843. A year later, Donizetti succumbed to hallucinations and depressions. Confined to a mental institution, he was under strict surveillance for three years. Then, after being turned over to the care of his brother, he died suddenly after an attack of paralysis.

Donizetti belonged with the early Italian opera composers—a group that included Rossini and Bellini—who helped establish the operatic traditions to which Italian composers adhered for a generation. He was equally adept in serious and comic styles. He combined an expressive lyricism with a pronounced feeling for both dramatic and comic situations.

DUKAS, PAUL

*Born:* Paris
October 1, 1865
*Died:* Paris
May 17, 1935

Dukas did not begin his formal training in music until his seventeenth year, when he entered the Paris Conservatory. During his seven years at the Conservatory (his teachers included Dubois and Guiraud) he won several important prizes. In 1892, he achieved his first success as a composer with an orchestral overture *Polyeucte,* and followed it with the *Symphony in C Major,* heard in 1896. Only one year later he became famous through a delightful orchestral scherzo, *The Sorcerer's Apprentice* (*L'Apprenti sorcier*), performed with tremendous success at a concert of the Société Nationale de Musique. An opera, *Ariane et Barbe-Bleue* (given by the Opéra Comique in 1907) was another major success. After 1910, Dukas produced little, and most of what he wrote was destroyed just before his death. His music combines workmanship with refinement, poetic thought with sensitive feelings.

After 1909, Dukas held various positions as a teacher of music, including the post of professor at the Paris Conservatory.

DVOŘÁK, ANTONIN    *Born:* Nelahozeves, near Prague,
Bohemia
September 8, 1841
*Died:* Prague
May 1, 1904

The son of a butcher, Dvořák received a thorough musical and academic education in his childhood. He went to Prague in 1857 to attend the Organ School. After graduating in 1860, he became a member of the orchestra at the National Theatre. The next decade or so was spent in intensive study and self-analysis, and in some composition. In 1873, one of his works, *Hymnus* for chorus, was successfully performed in Prague; and two years later his *Symphony in E Flat* won the Austrian State Prize. His growing prestige brought him a commission from the National Theatre for a nationalistic opera. Infected with the Wagnerian virus he produced a stilted and imitative work in the Wagnerian style. Only after he had changed his libretto and completely revised the score did his opera—called *The King and the Collier*—become a success. After being heard in Vienna, it won for its composer a government stipend.

A meeting with Brahms in Vienna was a milestone. Brahms introduced the young composer to the publisher Simrock. Simrock commissioned Dvořák to write an orchestral work based on native Bohemian dances. In 1878, Dvořák's *Slavonic Dances* appeared; and from this time on his fame throughout Europe was secure.

Within the next few years, Dvořák became one of the most famous composers in Europe. In 1890, he received an honorary degree from Cambridge University. Two years later he was invited to the United States to become director of the National Conservatory in New York. During his stay in this country he became vitally interested in the native music of the American Negro and Indian. This music inspired him to write his finest and best loved works: the *Symphony from the New World;* the *American Quartet;* the *Piano Quintet in E Flat Major.*

Dvořák surrendered his directorial post in New York in 1895 to return to his native land. In 1901, he was appointed director of the Prague Conservatory, a position he held up to the time of his death. The last years of his life were marked by bitter disappointments and disintegrating health. He finally succumbed after an apoplectic stroke.

Dvořák was a Romantic composer concerned with producing beautiful sounds within traditional forms. Richly melodic, his music makes a direct appeal to the heart. Most of his works—even those inspired by native American idioms—have an identifiable Slavic personality in the harmonizations and rhythms, and often in the structure of his melodies. But, except for his three *Slavonic Rhapsodies* and the *Slavonic Dances,* the Slavic elements are subservient to the Romantic traditions of Schubert and Brahms.

Besides the works already mentioned, Dvořák wrote two fine concertos, one for the violin, and another for the cello; the *Carnival Overture;* the *Dumky Trio;* many songs (including such favorites as "Songs My Mother Taught Me," and "Cradle Song"); and various pieces for the piano, the most popular being the *Humoresque, op. 101, No. 7.*

ELGAR, SIR EDWARD          *Born:* Broadheath, England
                           June 2, 1857
                           *Died:* Worcester, England
                           February 23, 1934

Elgar was at first destined for the law. He spent three years in London preparing for that career. But he had always been interested in music, and from early childhood had revealed a marked talent for it. He suddenly decided to end his law study and devote himself to music. He returned home and became absorbed with varied musical activities: he played in orchestras and chamber-music groups; substituted for his father as church organist; gave concerts on the violin. All the while, he studied intensively.

In 1885, he succeeded his father as organist of the St. George Cathedral in Worcester. After marrying Caroline Alice Roberts, he settled in London and concentrated on composition. Since city life distracted him, he soon made a move to Malvern where, in the next few years, he produced his first important works, all for chorus. Some of them were successfully performed at various English festivals.

Success came with two major works, and among the finest he was to write. The first was the *Enigma Variations,* for orchestra, introduced in 1899 in London. The second was the oratorio, *The Dream of Gerontius,* heard in 1900 at the Birmingham Festival.

Elgar was soon to become something of a musical laureate of his country. He produced several patriotic works, including the marches, *Pomp and Circumstance,* written in 1901, (the first of which, in D major, has become as intimately associated with the British Empire as "God Save the King"); and the *Ode* for the Coronation of Edward VII. He received many national honors: knighthood in 1904; the title of Master of the King's Musick in 1924; and baronetcy, in 1931.

The death of his wife, in 1920, was such a tragedy that for nine years he could write no music. In 1929, however, when King George V fell seriously ill, Elgar wrote a hymn of prayer for his recovery. His long silence broken, Elgar started working on a new symphony, his third. The symphony was never completed. Compelled to undergo a serious operation in 1934, Elgar never recovered.

He was the last of the English Romantics. He believed in writing sincerely from the heart. He never tried to be original, or to strike for new paths. Above all, he wished to produce beauty of sound and fullness of emotion; and he succeeded with sensitivity and good taste. His most important works, besides those already mentioned, include two symphonies, the *Concerto for Violin and Orchestra,* the *Concerto for Cello and Orchestra,* the concert overtures *Cockaigne* and *In the South, Introduction and Allegro for Strings,* and various chamber-music and choral works.

## ENESCO, GEORGES

*Born:* Dorohoiû, Rumania
August 19, 1881

Enesco was unusually precocious. When he was three years old he acquired a violin on which he learned to play village tunes without any instruction. After learning something about notation from a local musician he started composing, writing several complete sonatas by the time he was seven. In his eighth year he played the piano part of one of these sonatas at a public concert.

His father tried to get him into the Vienna Conservatory, but its director, Hellmesberger, insisted that the boy was too young. When he heard Enesco play the violin, and saw some of his compositions, Hellmesberger changed his mind. He not only admitted him into the Conservatory but had him live in his own home, where the boy heard a great deal of music and could meet some of Vienna's most notable musicians, including Brahms.

After winning several prizes at the Conservatory, Enesco was sent to France to complete his studies at the Paris Conservatory. His teachers, including Fauré and Massenet, considered him a genius. In 1897, there took place in Paris a concert of Enesco's works. One year later, the *Poème roumain* was introduced by the Colonne Orchestra. In 1900, Enesco entered upon a career as concert violinist. By 1910, he won international recognition not only as a violinist and composer but also as conductor. He has since then continued to distinguish himself in all three departments.

Enesco's most popular work is the *Rumanian Rhapsody No. 1 in A Major,* introduced in Paris on February 7, 1908 under the direction of Pablo Casals. In this, and similar works, Enesco combined the spirited rhythms and languorous melodies of Rumanian folk music with remarkable technique. He has written in other styles, too. In his earlier works, including the *First Symphony,* he wrote in the Romantic vein of Brahms; several works beginning with the *Suite No. 2 in C Major,* written in 1915, are neo-classic.

Besides the *Rumanian Rhapsodies,* Enesco's works include five symphonies; three sonatas for violin and piano (the finest being the third, based on popular Rumanian melodies); an opera, *Oedipus;* and various chamber-music compositions.

(DE) FALLA, MANUEL      *Born:* Cadiz, Spain
November 23, 1876
*Died:* Alta Garcia, Argentina
November 14, 1946

Falla began studying music as a child in his native city with his mother and local teachers. He then attended the Madrid Conservatory where he won highest honors as a piano student. His meeting and ripening friendship with Felipe Pedrell, Spanish scholar, was a turning point, for it directed him away from the concert stage to creative work. It was Pedrell, too, who directed Falla to Spanish folk music and convinced him that it could be the basis of an important musical art. Falla soon turned to writing music in a Spanish style. In 1905, he won first prize in a contest sponsored by the Academy of Fine Arts in Madrid for a national opera, with his first major work, *La Vida Breve*.

He went to Paris in 1907, staying there seven years, and becoming enriched by his contact with French music and French musicians. He was back in his native land a few months before World War I. Soon after his return, *La Vida Breve* was performed in Spain with great success. During the next few years, Falla traveled extensively through Spain, absorbing its music, culture, and folklore. These elements were absorbed in his own music. In 1915, he wrote the score for the ballet, *El Amor Brujo,* based on an Andalusian gypsy folk tale. Heard in Madrid on April 15, 1915, it was only moderately successful; but the orchestral suite derived from the score has become Falla's most famous single work. Other important Spanish works followed; including *Nights in the Gardens of Spain (Noches en los jardines de España)* for piano and orchestra; and the ballet, *The Three-Cornered Hat (El Sombrero de tres Picos)*. These works placed Falla at the head of Spanish composers. Spanish folk elements were skilfully synchronized with modern techniques and styles to produce a powerful and original native art, characterized by its sensitive mood pictures, its picturesque atmosphere, and its deep poetic feeling.

Between 1922 and 1939, Falla lived in comparative seclusion in Granada. Unsympathetic to the Franco regime, Falla left Spain in 1939 and settled in South America where he died.

FAURÉ, GABRIEL                    *Born:* Pamiers, France
                                  May 13, 1845
                              *Died:* Paris
                                  November 4, 1924

Fauré studied music at the École Niedermeyer in Paris, where one of his teachers was Camille Saint-Saëns. His schooling over, Fauré earned his living as organist, first in some of the smaller churches in Paris, after that at the Madeleine. He also taught composition at the École Niedermeyer and the Paris Conservatory, becoming director of the Conservatory in 1905. His influence as a teacher was profound: some of France's most famous musicians were his pupils, and were inspired by him, among them Ravel, Aubert, and Schmitt.

Fauré first attracted attention as a composer with a group of songs published in 1865. He continued writing songs for the rest of his life, producing several that are classics in French vocal literature: "Après un rêve," "Sylvie," "Les Roses d'Ispahan," "Soir," etc. He achieved success with his *First Sonata for Violin and Piano* (1876), *First Piano Quartet* (1879), *Ballade,* for piano and orchestra (1881), and most important of all, the *Requiem* (1887).

Fauré's style is pure, refined, and poetic. Though it often uses modern techniques it never abandons the ideal to project a sensitive beauty. Other well-known works by Fauré include the *Second Sonata for Violin and Piano,* the *Second Piano Quartet,* the orchestral suite *Pelléas et Mélisande* (not to be confused with Debussy's opera), the *Second Piano Quintet,* and the *Nocturnes* and *Preludes,* for piano.

During the last twenty years of his life, Fauré suffered deafness. In 1922 he was publicly honored by the government of France. He resigned as director of the Conservatory in 1920, and died four years after that.

FRANCK, CÉSAR        *Born:* Liége, Belgium
                            December 10, 1822
                     *Died:* Paris
                            November 8, 1890

Franck began studying the piano as a child, then entered the Liége Conservatory. In 1837, he became a pupil at the Paris Conservatory, where he was a brilliant student, winning one prize after another. He was summarily removed from the Conservatory by his father, impatient to have him begin his musical career. Back in Belgium, Franck gave several piano recitals and had some of his early compositions performed, but failed to win that success his father had hoped for. Father Franck finally decided that it was wisest, after all, for the young man to return to Paris and get additional musical experiences. Soon after this return to Paris, Franck achieved recognition for the first time when his choral work, *Ruth,* was successfully introduced at the Conservatory in 1846.

After playing the organ at the Notre-Dame-de-Lorette Church, Franck was appointed, in 1858, organist of the Ste. Clotilde. There he spent the happiest years of his life, playing the organ, improvising, composing. In 1872, he became professor of the organ at the Paris Conservatory. Though he produced one masterwork after another, recognition was slow in coming. First performances of two major works—the oratorio, *Rédemption,* and his most important choral work, *Les Béatitudes*—were both failures, largely due to inadequate performances. Even his masterwork, the *Symphony in D Minor,* introduced in Paris in 1889, was a fiasco, described by some critics as "objectionable music."

The first taste of success came in 1890 with a performance of the *String Quartet* which was acclaimed. But it came too late. In May of the same year, Franck, absorbed in thought, was hit by an autobus as he crossed the street. From then on his health deteriorated, and he died the following autumn.

He was one of the most high-minded of French musicians, and in his best music is found a noble spirit. He was at his best in polyphonic music that is calm and introspective. In some of his later works he introduced a technical device known as the "cyclical form," consisting of developing themes out of germinal ideas, and repeating themes from earlier movements in later ones to achieve integration.

Franck's most important works are his *Symphony; Piano Quintet; String Quartet; Sonata for Violin and Piano; Variations symphoniques,* for piano and orchestra; *Les Béatitudes; Prélude, Chorale and Fugue for Piano;* and *Chorales,* for organ.


GERSHWIN, GEORGE          *Born:* Brooklyn, New York
                          September 26, 1898
                          *Died:* Hollywood, California
                          July 11, 1937


As a boy, Gershwin gave no indication that he might some day become a famous composer. His was a typical New York boyhood. He was first guided to music by his friend Maxie Rosenzweig (later a concert violinist under the name of Max Rosen). Gershwin now wanted to study music, and did so when his family acquired a piano.

His first important teacher was Charles Hambitzer who even then recognized that the boy had genius. But though Gershwin took well to his studies and showed interest in the classics, his all-abiding ambition was to write popular songs—but songs exploiting the fullest resources of melody, harmony, and counterpoint. To realize this ambition he acquired a position as song plugger in the publishing house of Remick in Tin Pan Alley. At the same time he continued the serious study of music. When he was eighteen, he wrote his first song, and soon after his nineteenth birthday produced his first smash "hit," "Swanee," made popular by Al Jolson. By the time he passed his twenty-second year he was one of the most successful composers for the Broadway theatre, writing scores for the annual George White *Scandals,* and other productions. But success in Tin Pan Alley did not satisfy him. He still wished to produce important serious music, even if in a popular idiom. His first effort in this direction was a one-act opera, *135th Street,* written for one of the editions of the *Scandals.* It was a failure, and removed after a single performance. But in 1924, his second serious effort made him world-famous. His *Rhapsody in Blue,* written for an all popular-music concert given by Paul Whiteman in Aeolian Hall on February 12, 1924, made Gershwin one of the most successful and highly esteemed of all American composers.

For the remainder of his life, Gershwin continued to follow two paths. He wrote popular music for mass consumption, for the Broadway theatre and the Hollywood screen, music which yielded innumerable song gems with which the name of Gershwin is inevitably associated. One of his shows, *Of Thee I Sing!,* became the first musical comedy to win the Pulitzer Prize. At the same time he continued writing serious music in a popular idiom: the *Piano Concerto in F;* the *Second Rhapsody;* the *Cuban Overture;* piano preludes; the tone poem, *An American in Paris;* and the opera, *Porgy and Bess.*

While working in a Hollywood studio, Gershwin collapsed and was taken to a hospital. He was suffering from a brain tumor. An operation proved unsuccessful and Gershwin died in a Hollywood hospital.

In his serious works, Gershwin had outstanding melodic vitality and a feeling of spontaneity and freshness that more than compensate for an inadequate technique. The best of his larger works have lost none of their wide appeal through the years; and their permanence in the repertory of serious American music seems assured.

## GLAZUNOV, ALEXANDER

*Born:* St. Petersburg
August 10, 1865
*Died:* Paris
March 21, 1936

Glazunov was a musical prodigy who revealed a powerful creative talent at an early age. His first composition was written before he was thirteen; and by the time he was sixteen he had completed a symphony that was extravagantly praised by many leading Russian musicians. In his nineteenth year his fame was established throughout Europe.

His music study took place first with Elenovsky (piano and theory) and then with Rimsky-Korsakov. Glazunov studied with Rimsky-Korsakov only a year and a half when the master told him there was nothing more he could teach him, that the boy was ready for serious creative work.

Glazunov was a conservative composer who preferred classical forms and traditional melodies and harmonies. He had a sound technique and combined it with a pure melodic gift that was always ingratiating. He was a prolific composer producing numerous works in every possible form (except the opera). A few of his works have acquired a permanent place in music by virtue of their charm: the *Concerto in A Minor,* for violin and orchestra; the ballet, *The Seasons;* the orchestral suite, *From the Middle Ages;* the *Fourth* and *Fifth Symphonies.*

Glazunov was also famous as a teacher. In 1899, he became professor of instrumentation at the St. Petersburg Conservatory. Subsequently he became its director. Many leading Russian composers studied under him.

Glazunov remained in Russia even after the Revolution, though he was never sympathetic to Communism. In 1928, he felt he could stay in Russia no longer. He made a new home for himself in Paris where he remained to the end of his life.

## GLINKA, MICHAEL

*Born:* Novospasskoi, Russia
June 1, 1804
*Died:* Berlin
February 15, 1857

Glinka received a thorough education in both academic and musical subjects. Music study took place with John Field, at Böhm, and at the Milan Conservatory. Before adopting music as a profession, he served as a civil employee in the Department of Ways and Communications in Moscow. A trip to Germany, in 1830, stirred a feeling of homesickness which directed his thinking toward national Russian music. Back in Russia, his ideas about nationalism in art were clarified in conversations with such literary men as Pushkin and Gogol. Now fired with the ambition to produce a national Russian opera, Glinka wrote *A Life for the Tsar*, the first Russian opera based on a text built around an incident in Russian history and utilizing elements of Russian folk song. *A Life for the Tsar* was introduced at the Imperial Theatre in St. Petersburg on December 9, 1836. Six years later came a second opera, *Russlan and Ludmilla*, based on a poem by Pushkin. With these two operas, the nationalist movement in music was first launched. These operas were to provide stimulation and inspiration for such later nationalists as the members of the "Russian Five." During the closing years of his life, Glinka traveled extensively throughout Europe. Glinka also wrote two fine works for orchestra which are still occasionally performed—the fantasy, *Kamarinskaya*, and the *Jota Aragonesa*—together with other orchestral, chamber-music, piano, and vocal compositions.

## GLUCK, CHRISTOPH WILLIBALD

*Born:* Erasbach, Bohemia
July 2, 1714
*Died:* Vienna
November 15, 1787

Gluck, who came of peasant stock, received his early musical training from local teachers and in local schools. He then set out for a life of a wandering minstrel, singing in choirs, and playing the violin at fairs. In 1736, he came to Vienna, where the powerful Prince Lobkowitz took an interest in him and gave him employment. At the Lobkowitz palace, Gluck met Prince Melzi who, impressed with the young man's gifts, took him to Italy. Gluck studied there with Sammartini, absorbing the Italian traditions of opera, and writing several works in the accepted Italian manner. Returning to Vienna in 1748, Gluck made his Viennese bow as a composer with an Italian opera,

*Semiramide riconosciuta.* It was a tremendous success. Now famous, Gluck solidified his position with the writing of other Italian operas.

But he was growing increasingly dissatisfied with the Italian style, aspiring to write a new kind of opera—more human, simpler, and with greater dramatic truth. He found allies in the assistant director of the court theatres, Count Giacomo Durazzo, and in the poet Ranieri Calzabigi. The three united against the Italian tradition. Their first collaborative effort was a ballet, *Don Juan.* This was followed by the opera, *Orfeo ed Euridice,* to this day Gluck's best known masterwork. *Orfeo ed Euridice* was introduced in Vienna on October 5, 1762 and was a failure. Only in subsequent performances did this opera become a success. Other operas in a similar style followed: *Alceste* and *Paride ed Elena,* both failures.

Discouraged by his inability to win over the Viennese audiences with his operatic reforms, Gluck left Vienna for Paris in 1773. In Paris, too, he was confronted by a powerful Italian clique, headed by the famous composer of Italian operas, Nicola Piccinni. The new opera Gluck wrote for Paris, *Iphigénie en Aulide,* had to overcome intrigue and cabal before it was performed; once performed, it was a triumph. But Gluck's enemies did not accept their defeat, continuing to attack him and his new way of writing operas. To bring about a decision in this operatic battle, the Paris Opéra commissioned both Gluck and Piccinni to write music for the same text: *Iphigénie en Tauride.* Gluck's opera, which was given first, was a sensation—so much so that Piccinni tried to withdraw his own work from production. The Opéra insisted on going ahead with the performance, and it was a fiasco.

Victorious in Paris, Gluck left the city to return to Vienna. He lived there for the rest of his life, recognized throughout Europe as a master. He died of an apoplectic fit.

Gluck was one of the most important pioneers in the early history of opera; his tremendous contributions are evaluated in a later section on Opera. Through his theories, and their application, he brought to an end the tyranny that the Italian style and artistic indiscretions had exercised over composers everywhere. He helped to usher in a new era, that of the music drama.

**GOULD, MORTON**               *Born:* Richmond Hill, New York
                                    December 10, 1913

Gould was a child prodigy who began writing music when he was only six. He attended the Institute of Musical Art in New York as a scholarship pupil, and completed his studies with Abby Whiteside and Vincent Jones. After that he earned his living by playing the piano, lecturing, and performing in vaudeville houses. In his eighteenth year, he became staff pianist at the Radio City Music Hall; and three years later he conducted his first radio orchestra over W.O.R. He achieved considerable success both as a radio conductor and arranger.

He first attracted attention as a composer when the Philadelphia Orchestra, under Stokowski, presented his *Chorale and Fugue in Jazz,* in 1931. This was an effective tour de force, exploiting a jazz style within a serious and classical musical form. Gould followed this tendency in later works, producing many fine compositions that were serious in intent even though they employed popular or folk styles. His best known works in this manner include: *Foster Gallery, Cowboy Rhapsody, Latin-American Symphonette,* and *Symphony on Marching Songs.* Less dependent on popular idioms are works like the *Spirituals,* for orchestra; *Concerto for Orchestra; Symphony No. 3;* and *A Lincoln Legend.*

GOUNOD, CHARLES   *Born:* Paris
         June 17, 1818
        *Died:* Saint-Cloud, near Paris
         October 18, 1893

Gounod received his first music instruction from his mother, a fine pianist. In 1836 he entered the Paris Conservatory, and three years after that won the Prix de Rome. After returning to Paris from Rome he became organist in a small Parisian church and, in 1851, wrote his first opera, *Sapho,* presented with moderate success by the Opéra. He wrote several more operas, none of them particularly successful, before producing his masterwork, *Faust,* given in Paris on March 19, 1859. At first *Faust* was a failure, but its long and sustained triumph began with a revival at the Opéra on March 3, 1869. Meanwhile, Gounod wrote two more important operas: *Mireille* in 1864 (based on the Provençal poem by Mistral) ; and *Romeo and Juliet,* in 1867. During the Franco-Prussian War, Gounod lived in England where he helped found the Albert Hall Choral Society. In the closing years of his life he lived in or near Paris, dedicating himself to the writing of religious music.

Gounod was a major figure in French lyric opera. The sweetness of his lyricism, the gentleness of his style, and the poetic eloquence of his musical thought made him one of the most successful exponents of French operatic style.


GRIEG, EDVARD                  *Born:* Bergen, Norway
                                    June 15, 1843
                               *Died:* Bergen
                                    September 4, 1907


As a schoolboy, Grieg wrote a set of piano variations which impressed the famous Norwegian violinist, Ole Bull. Bull urged the boy to concentrate on music. In 1858, Grieg entered the Leipzig Conservatory, his teachers there included Reinecke, Moscheles, and Richter. From Leipzig, Grieg went on to Copenhagen where he met and became a friend of Richard Nordraak, a young Norwegian musician and nationalist. The young man infected Grieg with his own patriotic ardor, and with the ambition of writing national music. When, in 1865, Grieg learned of the premature death of his young friend he dedicated himself to carrying on his ideals and aspirations. He founded an orchestra in Christiana (now Oslo) and conducted a successful program of Norwegian music.

In 1867, Grieg married Nina Hagerup, for whom he had previously written his most famous song, "I Love You." Serious composition now engaged him as never before. He completed the *Sonata in F Major for Violin and Piano* which Liszt praised highly, and followed it with the now-famous *Piano Concerto.* "Carry on, my friend," Liszt told Grieg after seeing the score of the concerto. "You have real talent." The concerto was successfully introduced in Oslo in 1870, with Edmund Neupart as soloist.

In 1874, Grieg was back in his native city. It was at this time that Henrik Ibsen, Norway's leading dramatist, asked him to write the incidental music for his play, *Peer Gynt.* The music was heard for the first time on February 24, 1876, in conjunction with the play, and was acclaimed.

Grieg was now the most important Norwegian composer of his time. The government recognized his significance by granting him an annual pension which enabled him to concentrate exclusively on creative work. He bought a home near Bergen to which admirers from all parts of Europe came to pay him homage. Honors were conferred on him in many different countries: Sweden appointed him a member of the Academy; France elected him a member of the Academy of Fine Arts; Cambridge conferred on him an honorary degree; and in Leipzig, his bust was placed in the famous Gewandhaus.

Grieg belonged with the Romantic School. He forged no new paths. Within the accepted forms and with established styles he produced music of deep feeling and great beauty. He is sometimes called the "Chopin of the North," by which is meant that he had something of Chopin's sensitivity, sentiment, and poetic speech within felicitous structures. Much of his music—and some of the best—is molded after the patterns of Norwegian folk songs and dances.

## HALÉVY, JACQUES

*Born:* Paris
May 27, 1799
*Died:* Paris
March 17, 1862

Halévy entered the Paris Conservatory when he was ten; and in the next few years won many prizes, including the Prix de Rome. He wrote his first operas during his stay in Rome. His first opera to be produced was a one-act work, *L'Artisan,* given in Paris in 1827, but it did not attract much attention. His first major success came two years later with *Clari.* His most celebrated work, *La Juive,* was also a phenomenal success when given by the Paris Opéra on February 23, 1834. Though Halévy wrote many operas after *La Juive,* he never duplicated either its success or its high standard of inspiration. Meanwhile, in 1827, he became professor of harmony at the Conservatory, holding this post with distinction for many years. In the closing years of his life, he was affected by disintegrating health and mental disturbances.

## HANDEL, GEORGE FREDERICK

*Born:* Halle, Saxony
February 23, 1685
*Died:* London
April 14, 1759

It is one of the familiar anecdotes of musical biography how Handel's father, a surgeon, opposed his son's musical education, and how the boy secretly stole into the garret late each night to practice on a spinet concealed there. Only when the boy played for a duke and was compensated with gold did the father relax his stern opposition. Handel now studied with local music teachers, but only on the condition that his academic education was not neglected. For three years, he studied the organ, clavier, violin, and composition with Zachau. He made such sensational progress that the Elector of Brandenburg offered to pay for the boy's continued music study in Italy. Handel's father turned down the generous offer. One year later the father died. For a year Handel tried to fulfil his father's wishes by studying law at the University of Halle. But the studies bored him and he decided to abandon them for good. Settling in Hamburg, then the operatic capital of Germany, he played the violin in the opera-house orchestra. In 1705, his first opera, *Almira,* was introduced at the Hamburg Opera and was successful. A second opera, *Nero,* was a failure.

Beginning with 1706, and for the next few years, Handel wandered extensively through Italy writing operas and playing the harpsichord. In both capacities he achieved considerable renown. He then accepted the post of Kapellmeister in Hanover, from which he took a leave of absence in 1710 to attend the première of his opera, *Rinaldo,* in London. *Rinaldo* was a sensation, and its creator the composer of the hour. This success warmed Handel's heart toward London. He was not very long back in Hanover before he started planning to return to England. In 1712, he revisited London and this time remained there for good. He soon became the most popular and successful composer in England, honored wherever he went. His operas were immense successes. There were times when powerful rivals and enemies tried to destroy him, and they were almost successful; but Handel recovered from temporary defeats to become even more popular than he had previously been.

By 1738, Handel had written about forty operas. He now concentrated on a new field of composition, that of the oratorio. In this medium he was to reveal his greatest powers. *Saul* came in 1738; *Israel Egypt* in 1738; and in 1741 his crowning masterwork, the *Messiah.* Other great oratorios followed in a resplendent procession.

Handel began suffering from failing eyesight by 1751. Two years later he was completely blind. Despite this terrible infirmity he kept on writing music, playing the organ, and directing performances of his oratorios. He was conducting a charity concert of the *Messiah* in 1759 when he fainted. Eight days later he died. He is buried in the poets' corner of Westminster Abbey.

Besides writing operas (which are no longer performed) and oratorios, Handel produced many concertos for solo instruments and orchestra, and famous orchestral concerti grossi. He also wrote abundantly for various solo instruments. His music, with that of Bach, represents the culmination of the contrapuntal era. He brought the structure of the oratorio to its highest development and filled it with nobility, majesty, poignancy, and realism which few writers in this form have equalled and none surpassed. Handel's oratorios are discussed further in the section on the Oratorio.

HANSON, HOWARD          *Born:* Wahoo, Nebraska
                                        October 28, 1896

Hanson began his music study with local teachers, at the same time acquiring an academic education. After graduation from the local high school and the School of Music of Luther College, Hanson enrolled at the Institute of Musical Art in New York, where his teachers included James Friskin (piano) and Percy Goetschius (composition). He next attended the Northwestern University from which he received his degree in his nineteenth year. For three years Hanson was professor of theory and composition at the College of the Pacific in San José, California; and for several years after that he was Dean of the Conservatory of Fine Arts. During this period he wrote several small works for orchestra.

In 1921, he won the Prix de Rome which enabled him to live in Rome for the next three years and concentrate on study and composition. When he returned to the United States he was appointed director of the Eastman School of Music in Rochester, N.Y., a position he has held with immense distinction since that time. In addition to his significance as an educator, Hanson has distinguished himself in Rochester as a propagandist for new American music, conducting an annual festival of modern American music for more than two decades.

Hanson first emerged as an important composer in 1922 when his *Nordic Symphony* was introduced by the Augusteo Orchestra in Rome under his own direction. Subsequent works were widely performed in the United States, including the *Romantic Symphony,* the *Third and Fourth Symphonies,* and the opera *Merry Mount,* which was seen at the Metropolitan Opera House on February 10, 1934. The *Fourth Symphony* was the first symphony to win the Pulitzer Prize.

Hanson has the traditionalist's respect for classical form and the long-established procedures of harmony and tonality. He is interested in projecting beauty through expressive lyricism and well-sounding harmonies. He is a romanticist, but one who can hold his emotions in check. He writes with considerable restraint and achieves a quiet and objective beauty.

HARRIS, ROY                              *Born:* Lincoln County, Oklahoma
                                         February 12, 1898

Roy Harris was the offspring of pioneers who helped settle Oklahoma. When he was five, his family moved to San Gabriel Valley, in California, where he lived a solitary life devoted to reading and playing music. In his eighteenth year, Harris acquired a farm of his own. World War I put him in uniform. When the war ended, Harris entered the University of California to study music, earning his living by driving a dairy truck. Later on he became a pupil of Arthur Farwell, under whose guidance Harris wrote his first orchestral work, an Andante, introduced by the New York Philharmonic Orchestra at the Lewisohn Stadium in 1926. Harris then went to Paris on a Guggenheim fellowship. There he studied with Nadia Boulanger and wrote the first works indicating growing creative powers. Back in the United States, Harris completed several other works which had successful performances, notably the *String Sextet,* the *String Quartet No. 2,* and the *Symphony: 1933.* In these works, Harris employed a contrapuntal style suggestive of the sixteenth century in which individual lines move in broad and flexible sweeps. Modern harmonic and rhythmic techniques were not avoided.

With the *Symphony No. 3*—the first symphony by an American to be performed by Toscanini—Harris achieved national significance. This symphony, and subsequent Harris works, were widely performed by most great American orchestras. Commissions came to him from many notable organizations and musicians. Among his most frequently heard later works are the *Folk-Song Symphony,* the *String Quartet No. 3,* the *Seventh Symphony,* and the *Soliloquy and Dance,* for viola and piano.

During World War II, Harris was chief of the music section of the

Office of War Information. As composer-in-residence, he has been associated with several important colleges and universities including Cornell University, Colorado College, Peabody's Teachers College, and the Pennsylvania Women's College.

HAYDN, JOSEPH         *Born:* Rohrau, Austria
                                   March 31, 1732
                          *Died:* Vienna
                                   May 31, 1809

Showing unmistakable musical talent as a child, Haydn was given instruction by a local teacher named Frankh, a severe master who gave the child a sound training at the violin and harpsichord. When the boy was eight he entered the choir school at St. Stephen's Church in Vienna, where he suffered both physical abuse and pedagogical neglect from his master, Reutter. When Haydn's voice broke in his seventeenth year he was summarily dismissed and sent out to shift for himself.

Haydn found temporary lodgings and food at the impoverished home of a casual acquaintance. Before long he was able to find a few pupils and some engagements as violinist, earning enough to keep alive. At the same time, he kept on with his studies.

Haydn's first important position was as accompanist to the then famous singing master, Porpora. Porpora brought Haydn to the notice of several important Viennese noblemen. One of these, Baron von Fürnberg, asked Haydn to help him arrange concerts at his palace. It was for the Baron that Haydn wrote his first string quartet in 1755, as well as some orchestral music. Through the Baron, Haydn met Count Morzin who engaged him as Kapellmeister at his Bohemian estate. Haydn's job was to lead an orchestra and to write music for it, and it was in this capacity that he wrote his first symphony in 1759.

Now more or less financially secure, Haydn was married to Anna Maria Keller. Actually he had been in love with Anna's younger sister, Barbara. But when Barbara suddenly entered a convent, Haydn was induced to accept Anna instead. He was not in love with her; and the marriage was, from the very beginning, unhappy. Anna was a shrew incapable of appreciating her husband. After a few unhappy years they were separated and lived apart for the rest of their lives.

When Count Morzin had to disband his orchestra owing to financial difficulties, Haydn became Kapellmeister for Prince Paul Anton Esterházy, in 1761. He held this post for the greater part of his life, at the same time writing some of his greatest works and achieving a fame that spanned all of Europe.

The next twenty-five years of his life were comparatively uneventful. He led his daily life at the palace of Prince Esterházy, arranging concerts, and writing abundantly.

In 1781, Haydn met Mozart for the first time. Between these two men, so different in age and fame, there arose a friendship marked by a unique sympathy and understanding. Haydn, who recognized Mozart's genius, did what he could to promote his career. In 1785, Mozart affectionately dedicated six string quartets to Haydn, a token of his high esteem.

When Prince Esterházy died in 1790, his successor liquidated the musical forces at his palace. After a quarter of a century, Haydn had to vacate his position as Kapellmeister. At this time, an English impresario, Salomon, invited him to London to direct some orchestral concerts, and to write some new symphonies for these performances. Accepting, Haydn came to London in 1791, scoring a phenomenal success. In 1794, Haydn returned for a second visit and repeated his former triumphs. For these two visits, Haydn produced two sets of six symphonies now known as the "London" or "Salomon" symphonies.

Back in Vienna, Haydn was now the most celebrated musician in Europe. He was still to write his greatest works of all, the oratorios *The Creation* and *The Seasons,* fruits of his old age. He also wrote a national anthem to honor the birthday of Emperor Franz II in 1797 (henceforth to be the Austrian National Anthem), and later incorporated it into his *Emperor Quartet.*

Haydn attended a public concert for the last time in 1808. After that he was confined to his home with sickness and fatigue. The last months of his life were saddened by the occupation of Vienna by the invading French Army.

When Haydn started writing music, the symphony, sonata, and string quartet were in their infancy. It was due to Haydn that they were brought to full development, that the so-called sonata form was finally crystallized, and that harmonic writing and orchestration made notable advances. His symphonies, sonatas, string quartets, and oratorios are dealt with in the later sections on these various forms.

# HINDEMITH, PAUL

*Born:* Hanau, Germany
November 16, 1895

Unable to overcome his father's resistance to his music study, Hindemith ran away from home in his sixteenth year. He supported himself by playing in theatres and café orchestras, saving enough to be able to enter the Hoch Conservatory in Frankfort-on-the-Main. As a student of Sekles and Arnold Mendelssohn he learned his lessons with such rapidity that his teachers soon pronounced him ready for a professional career. For a brief period in 1915 Hindemith served in the German Army. After his demobilization, he became concertmaster of the Frankfort Opera Orchestra. While holding this post he helped found (and played the viola in) the Amar String Quartet which became famous for its performances of modern music.

Hindemith first attracted attention as a composer with chamber-music works played at festivals in Donaueschingen and Salzburg between 1921 and 1923. In 1926, he achieved a major success with the opera *Cardillac*. From that year on, one success followed another until his position as a leading composer in Germany was acknowledged. He also achieved note as a teacher of music at the Berlin Hochschule.

With the rise of the Nazi regime, Hindemith had to leave Germany —particularly after the scandal created by a projected but unrealized première of his opera, *Mathis der Maler,* denounced by the Nazi officials. He went to Turkey on an invitation from that government to help reorganize its musical life. After that he arrived in the United States which he henceforth made his permanent home. He joined the music faculty of Yale University.

Hindemith's musical style is characterized by a skilful and effective use of counterpoint to which is added the most advanced resources of modern harmony and tonality. His best known works include *Mathis der Maler* (known in two versions, as an opera and as a symphony); concertos for various solo instruments and orchestra; the ballet *Saint Francis;* the *Symphony in E Flat Major; Symphonia Serena;* and various major compositions for different chamber-music groups. While still in Germany he wrote many pieces for films, theatres, schools, and so forth, for which the descriptive name of *Gebrauchsmusik* (functional music) was coined.

## HONEGGER, ARTHUR

*Born:* Le Havre, France
March 10, 1892

Honegger, who is of Swiss parentage and citizenship, has lived most of his life in France, where he was born. He first studied music with local teachers. After a brief and unhappy interlude in business, he enrolled in the Zurich Conservatory, and two years after that entered the Paris Conservatory. While a student in Paris he wrote various small works. One of his first works to be performed was a *Toccata and Variations,* for piano, heard in 1916. Honegger continued writing music but did not attract attention until he was grouped with five other young French composers into a school called the "French Six." Honegger was, however, too much of an individualist to belong to any school, and went his own way. His first major success came with an oratorio that was conservative in style and form, *Le Roi David,* in 1921. After that he produced music much more advanced in rhythm, and harmony, the most notable being the provocative *Pacific 231.*

Between the two world wars, Honegger produced many works whose independence and originality made him one of France's most controversial composers. He wrote a work like *Rugby* that describes a soccer game. On the other hand, he wrote an opera like *Judith* inspired by the Bible.

During World War II, Honegger worked for the Resistance forces in Nazi-occupied Paris. He was never personally abused by the Nazis, allowed to devote himself to writing music. One of the most important works written during this period was the *Symphony No. 2,* for strings. Since the war, Honegger has written a few more symphonies which reveal him at his creative best. In these works a pronounced lyricism is combined with mysticism and religious feeling.

## HUMPERDINCK, ENGELBERT

*Born:* Siegburg, Germany
September 1, 1854
*Died:* Berlin
September 27, 1921

He studied music at the Cologne Conservatory with Hiller, Gernsheim, and Jensen. The winning of the Mozart Award enabled him to go to Munich to study with Rheinberger and Lachner. A second prize, the Mendelssohn Award, brought him to Italy. During this trip he met Wagner for the first time. The master prevailed on Humperdinck to go to Bayreuth and help him prepare the première performance of *Parsifal*. Humperdinck now became a passionate Wagnerite, and his musical writing was profoundly influenced by Wagnerian idioms and esthetics. In 1893, Humperdinck wrote *Hänsel und Gretel,* with which he won international recognition after its première in Weimar on December 23, 1893. He also became famous as a teacher, first at the Hoch Conservatory and after that at the Akademische Schule, both in Berlin. He continued writing operas which received major performances, but none of them duplicated the overwhelming success of his delightful fairy-tale opera. He died from an apoplectic stroke.

D'INDY, VINCENT

*Born:* Paris
March 27, 1851
*Died:* Paris
December 2, 1931

D'Indy started music study early, his teachers included Lavignac, Diémer, and Marmontel. When he was nineteen his first publication appeared, *Three Songs Without Words,* for piano. The Franco-Prussian War put him in uniform, and he fought in the defense of Paris. Soon after the war's end, he became a pupil of César Franck who influenced him greatly. Thereafter, d'Indy's idealism and integrity, as well as his manner of writing music, were affected by his intimacy with Franck. With Franck, he helped found the Société Nationale de Musique, which was a major influence in bringing about performances of new works by French composers.

D'Indy first became prominent as a composer with the *Symphony on a French Mountain Air,* written in 1886, and successfully introduced by the Lamoureux Orchestra one year later. His opera *Fervaal,* the *Istar Variations* for orchestra, and the tone poem, *Summer Day on the Mountain* brought him to a commanding position among French composers.

Like Franck, d'Indy wrote music that radiated a kind of spiritual beauty, betraying the nobility of its creator. An extraordinary technical equipment is ever present; but it is the deeply moving beauty—sensitive and gentle—which impresses itself deeply on the listener.

He was also one of France's great teachers. For a period he was professor at the Paris Conservatory, and after that its director. He was also a teacher and director of the Schola Cantorum which he helped organize.

### KABALEVSKY, DIMTRI     Born: St. Petersburg
                                    December 30, 1904

He began playing the piano by ear when he was only six and soon after that wrote little pieces for the piano. Music study began in his fourteenth year at the Scriabin School in Moscow and was completed at the Moscow Conservatory in 1930. He was such an exceptional student at the Conservatory that upon his graduation his name was engraved on an honor plaque in the hall.

Kabalevsky began his professional career as composer with some children's songs. In 1932 he wrote his *First Symphony,* and two years later achieved his first major success with the *Symphony No. 2,* still one of his finest works. Later important compositions include the *Piano Concerto No. 2,* the opera *Colas Breugnon,* the *Fourth Symphony,* and the *Piano Sonatas Nos. 2 and 3.* As one of the leading composers of the Soviet Union he has received many honors including the Order of Merit in 1940 and the Stalin Prize in 1946.

Kabalevsky belongs with the more conservative of Soviet composers. He is partial to classical forms and fills them with well-sounding melodies and harmonies.

### KHATCHATURIAN, ARAM     Born: Tiflis, Armenia
                                    June 6, 1903

Even as a child, Khatchaturian was attracted to the folk songs and dances of his country which later on, as a mature composer, he would adapt and imitate in the writing of major works. Music study began comparatively late. In 1923, he entered the Gniesen Music School in Moscow. His progress was rapid, and he was sent for further study to the Moscow Conservatory. While still a student, he wrote his first works that revealed pronounced talent.

Success came in 1934 with his *Symphony No. 1.* Subsequent works added to his fame: the *Concerto for Piano and Orchestra* (one of his most frequently heard large works); the *Concerto for Violin and Orchestra;* and the ballet *Gayne* (in which is found the popular "Saber Dance"). The *Violin Concerto, Gayne* and the *Symphony No. 2* all won the Stalin Prize.

Khatchaturian develops the melodic and rhythmic ideas of Armenian folk music into serious artistic creations. Like the folk music from which it is derived, his music is colorful, vital, and full-blooded in its lyricism; occasionally it is sentimental.

KODÁLY, ZOLTÁN                    *Born:* Keczkemét, Hungary
                                   December 16, 1882

While Kodály had various contacts with music from childhood on, he did not begin studying seriously until his eighteenth year, when he entered the Budapest Conservatory. At the Conservatory he became a friend of Béla Bartók with whom he was to engage in exploratory trips throughout Hungary and Transylvania in search of native folk music, which they adapted and published. This study of Hungary's folk music had as pronounced an effect on Kodály as it did on Bartók. For like Bartók, Kodály—who had been writing in the styles of Debussy and Brahms—arrived at a new manner which assimilated the brusque rhythms, angular melodies, and repetitious phrases of the Hungarian folk song and dance.

Kodály's first successful work was the *Psalmus Hungaricus,* written in 1923 to commemorate the fiftieth anniversary of the union of Buda and Pest. Two years after this, he completed the opera, *Háry János,* which has since become famous in concert halls as an orchestral suite. Here, and in such later works as *Dances from Galanta* and *Dances of Marosszék,* Kodály uses folk idioms with brilliant effect.

During World War II, Kodály remained in Nazi-occupied Hungary, secretly engaging in anti-Nazi activities. He visited the United States for the first time in 1946 as an official delegate to the Congress of International Confederation of Authors Societies held in Washington, D.C.

LALO, ÉDOUARD                     *Born:* Lille, France
                                   January 27, 1823
                                   *Died:* Paris
                                   April 22, 1892

He attended the Lille Conservatory, and after that the Paris Conservatory. He was not happy at the latter place, its rigid discipline and strict adherence to set rules proving a continual irritant. He abandoned the Conservatory to continue his studies alone, making sufficient progress to be able to write a gifted *Trio* in 1845.

For an eight-year period Lalo was creatively silent. He earned his living by teaching harmony and playing the viola in a string quartet. He resumed composition in 1865 by writing and completing an opera, *Fiesque*. Success came with the *Concerto for Violin and Orchestra*, written in 1874, and introduced by Pablo de Sarasate with outstanding success. One year after that, Sarasate gave the première of a work by which Lalo is best known, the *Symphonie espagnole,* for violin and orchestra.

Lalo also wrote a beautiful opera, *La Roi d'Ys,* based on a Breton legend, and introduced at the Opéra Comique on May 7, 1888. Another major work preceded it: the *Concerto for Cello and Orchestra,* first heard in 1887.

In the closing years of his life, Lalo suffered from paralysis.

LEONCAVALLO, RUGGIERO  *Born:* Naples
                                    March 8, 1858
                             *Died:* Montecatini, near
                                    Florence
                                    August 9, 1919

As a student at the Naples Conservatory, he wrote a gifted cantata. While attending the Bologna University he completed his first opera, *Chatterton*. Disappointed in his inability to get it performed, he embarked on an extensive trip through Europe and the Near East. After this, he settled in Paris where he lived a Bohemian existence, earning his living by playing the piano in cafés and writing popular songs. A meeting with the influential Italian publisher Ricordi brought him a commission to write an opera. He wanted to create a work along Wagnerian lines, and produced the first opera of a trilogy set in the Italian Renaissance, *I Medici*. Since it was a failure, Leoncavallo decided not to continue with this ambitious project; instead he wrote a one-act opera, *Pagliacci,* in the style then made popular by Mascagni's *Cavalleria Rusticana*. Introduced in Milan on May 21, 1892, under Toscanini, it was a sensation. Now a famous composer, Leoncavallo wrote several more operas, the best known of which was *Zaza;* but his fame rests securely on *Pagliacci* alone. *Pagliacci* was an early and important product of the then new school of Italian opera known as *Verismo,* which brought naturalism and contemporary interest to opera.

LIADOV, ANATOL
> *Born:* St. Petersburg
> May 11, 1855
> *Died:* St. Petersburg
> August 28, 1914

The son of a well-known opera conductor, Anatol Liadov was early brought into contact with music. His studies took place at the St. Petersburg Conservatory, where he was a shiftless pupil. He was suspended—a punishment that seemed to bring him to his senses for, after his reinstatement, he headed his classes. Upon his graduation, he wrote a fine orchestral work, *The Bride of Messina.* In 1878, he was appointed professor of harmony and theory at the St. Petersburg Conservatory. Henceforth, he devoted himself not only to composition and teaching but also to conducting and research in the field of folk music. One of his most famous works, *Eight Russian Folk Songs,* is the result of his researches.

Liadov was notoriously lazy as a composer, reluctant to begin a new work, incapable of completing a major project after it was begun. He was at his best in the smaller and more intimate forms: songs, pieces for the piano, and adaptations of Russian folk songs. He wrote several orchestral tone poems, the best being *The Enchanted Lake.*

LISZT, FRANZ
> *Born:* Raiding, Hungary
> October 22, 1811
> *Died:* Bayreuth, Germany
> July 31, 1886

Liszt's father, an army officer, introduced him to the piano. The boy made such progress that in his ninth year he was able to give an impressive public concert and to interest a group of noblemen in financing his education. He went to Vienna where his studies continued with Karl Czerny. After that he traveled to Paris to enter the Paris

Conservatory. Rules of the Conservatory denied admission to foreign students, and Liszt had to study privately with Reicha and Paër. On March 8, 1824, he gave a concert at the Opéra and was a sensation. From then on, he was a favorite of the Parisian salon, idolized wherever he played.

He now aspired to become the greatest living virtuoso of the piano. For two years he went into retirement working slavishly on his scales and exercises. From this intensive period of preparation, he emerged a fabulous technician, one of the greatest masters of the keyboard of his generation. His imperial position among the pianists of his day was unequivocally conceded in 1837 when he entered into a virtuoso "duel" with Thalberg, a popular pianist of the time, and emerged the victor. He toured Europe, the object of adulation wherever he played. It is interesting to note that it is with Liszt that the public solo piano recital as we know it today originated (before Liszt, a pianist appeared with other artists at concerts); and it is also Liszt who originated the tradition of performing on the stage with the profile to the audience, instead of full face.

In 1848, Liszt became Kapellmeister in Weimar. For the next eleven years Liszt devoted himself, selflessly and with the highest artistic integrity, to directing orchestral concerts and operatic performances. Valiantly, he sponsored young and unknown composers, and new works, that could not get a hearing elsewhere.

When Wagner became a political refugee in 1849, he first came to Weimar to visit Liszt. The two had met before this, but it was now that their friendship was sealed. From now on, Liszt was to work passionately to bring recognition to a man whose genius he both recognized and worshiped. Many years later, Liszt was to become Wagner's father-in-law, when his daughter Cosima left her husband, Hans von Bülow, to live with and subsequently marry Wagner.

Intrigues and cabals brought an end to Liszt's musical activities in Weimar in 1859. He now felt himself drawn to the church. In 1865, he was given the honorary title of Abbé, and after that he officially entered the church by submitting to the tonsure and taking the vows of four minor orders.

In 1870, Liszt became director of the Budapest Academy of Music. He was to distinguish himself in still another field of music: teaching. An entire generation of great pianists studied under him and were inspired by him, including Tausig, Hans von Bülow, Emil Sauer, and Moritz Rosenthal.

When the Wagnerian festival was inaugurated in Bayreuth in 1876, Liszt was a familiar figure in that city. He was to make Bayreuth his home for the rest of his life, except for his occasional concert tours. He died there three years after the death of his famous son-in-law.

Liszt wrote more than a thousand works in virtually every form. He had a romantic style, sometimes sentimental or bombastic; and it is his works in this vein that are heard most often. In some of his larger, and less frequently heard, works he is the author of music of breadth, grandeur, and striking originality, as in the *Faust* and *Dante Symphonies,* the *Années de pèlerinage* for the piano, and the oratorio, *Christus.* Besides writing some very popular works—like the tone poem *Les Préludes,* the *Liebestraum* and the *Hungarian Rhapsodies* for piano, and the *Mephisto Waltz,* for orchestra—and some noble and ambitious works, Liszt is significant as a pioneer. To orchestral music he brought the dramatic principles of Wagner, and evolved a new orchestral form henceforth known as the tone poem (or symphonic poem). Liszt's symphonic poems and piano music are surveyed in later sections.

LULLY, JEAN BAPTISTE          *Born:* Florence
                                 November 29, 1632
                              *Died:* Paris
                                 March 22, 1687

Lully's great talent for music attracted the attention of a Parisian nobleman who took him, in his boyhood, to Paris. There, Lully devoted himself to intensive music study. He soon found a post in the orchestra of Louis XIV, where his pronounced talent was recognized. He became a favored musician at court, and an orchestra was organized for him. During this period, Lully wrote many works for performance at court, including thirty ballets. He was the recipient of many honors, including an appointment as "Maître de musique."

In 1669, the Paris Opéra was founded, and three years later Lully became its director. Lully began writing operas. None of them have survived, but they played an important role in the evolution of opera, by establishing the French opera tradition as opposed to the

Italian. Among Lully's best operas are *Amadis, Roland, Acis et Gala-tée,* and *Persée.*

Lully died two months after directing a performance of his *Te Deum,* written to celebrate the recovery of the King from a serious illness. It is believed that Lully's death was caused by gangrene, brought on by the persistent accidental pounding of his walking stick on his foot when, in directing operas, he used it to beat out the time for the performers.

MACDOWELL, EDWARD       *Born:* New York City
                        December 18, 1861
                        *Died:* New York City
                        January 23, 1908

Beginning the study of music in his eighth year with Buitrago, Macdowell made marked advance. He entered the Paris Conservatory when he was fifteen, and studied with Savard and Marmontel. None too happy with the rigid course of study, Macdowell left the Conservatory for Germany, and completed his music study at the Frankfort Conservatory.

He remained in Germany to divide his time between teaching the piano and composition. He completed the *First Piano Concerto* which he played for Franz Liszt who was greatly impressed. On Liszt's recommendation, Macdowell's *Second Modern Suite,* for piano, was published. An orchestral work, *Hamlet and Ophelia,* performed by several important German orchestras, brought him his first success.

In 1888, Macdowell returned to the United States, and earned his living by teaching and playing the piano. He worked intensively on composition. A number of major performances brought him to a leading position among the American composers of that period. In 1893, the Boston Symphony performed *Hamlet and Ophelia.* In 1894, the New York Philharmonic introduced the *Second Piano Concerto,* to this day his finest and most successful composition.

In 1896, Macdowell became professor of music at Columbia University, remaining there for several years. A serious misunderstanding eventually arose between the college authorities and Macdowell over the way a music department should be run. The struggle broke Macdowell's health and spirit. He retired in 1904, a shattered man. In 1905, a nervous breakdown brought about the disintegration of his brain tissues. Up to the time of his death his mind was like that of a child.

In his music, Macdowell made no attempt to strike for new directions. He was steeped in European traditions, and he preferred writing in the Romantic style of the late nineteenth century composers. What he lacked in individuality he often made up for in his fine feeling for beauty and poetry. Besides works already mentioned, Macdowell wrote three ambitious sonatas for the piano (named *Tragica, Eroica,* and *Norse*), an entire library of solo music for the piano, including the *Woodland Sketches* in which are found the ever-popular "To a Wild Rose," and "To a Water Lily."

MAHLER, GUSTAV

*Born:* Kalischt, Bohemia
July 7, 1860
*Died:* Vienna
May 18, 1911

As a child, Mahler was so fascinated by music, and so absorbed with inventing little melodies at the piano, that his father decided to bring him to Vienna to play for Professor Julius Epstein of the Vienna Conservatory. Epstein felt that the boy had talent and arranged for his admission in the Conservatory where Mahler was a brilliant student and won many prizes.

After leaving the Conservatory, Mahler filled several humble posts as conductor. One of his more ambitious assignments, a performance of Mendelssohn's *St. Paul* in Leipzig in 1885, was so impressively carried out that it brought him an engagement as conductor of the Prague Opera. Mahler conducted the operas of Wagner and Mozart with such painstaking devotion that he was soon engaged by the important Pesth Opera. His rise as one of the great conductors of his generation was now rapid, as he passed from one major post to another: from the Pesth Opera to the Hamburg Opera; from the Hamburg Opera to the Vienna Opera, where he was responsible for one of its most luminous epochs of music making; and from the Vienna Opera to the Metropolitan Opera House. He also directed symphonic concerts with the Vienna Philharmonic and the New York Philharmonic Orchestras.

Despite the exacting demands of his conductorial duties on both his time and energy, Mahler was able to write many ambitious musical works. His *First Symphony* was completed in 1889 and was coldly received. Apathy developed into antagonism with the symphonies that followed; audiences and critics were outright hostile. They felt that Mahler was pretentious, trying to make his symphonies embrace metaphysical concepts within Gargantuan structures. They said he was garrulous and bombastic. But Mahler was convinced in the truth of what he was writing, and kept on producing ever larger, ever more profound symphonies, despite their rejection by the public at large. Mahler's most important symphonic works are discussed in the section on the Symphony.

The strain of his conductorial assignments, combined with his struggles with those who did not understand him, brought on a nervous breakdown. He collapsed in 1911 in New York, and was brought back to Vienna to die.

Besides nine symphonies, Mahler wrote several beautiful song cycles for voice and orchestra, including *Das Lied von der Erde* and *Kindertotenlieder;* and many excellent songs for voice and piano.

## MALIPIERO, GIAN        *Born:* Venice
## FRANCESCO                    March 18, 1882

Much of Malipiero's early music study took place while he and his family were traveling throughout Europe over a period of several years, and was completed in the Conservatories of Venice and Bologna. At the latter place, he completed his first orchestral work, *Dai sepolcri.*

In 1902, he started to interest himself in old Italian music. From then on, he did considerable research in this field, and subsequently made monumental editions of the works of the old Italian masters. His own musical style was affected by this interest. It became contrapuntal instead of harmonic, with his melodies assuming the character of recitatives. His music breathed the spirit of the Renaissance, and in some cases his forms were derived from those of old Italian poetry.

Malipiero first became known before World War I when he entered a competition for new works with five compositions and won four prizes. During World War I, he wrote one of his most eloquent works, *Pause del silenzio,* for orchestra, speaking of the horrors of war. After the war, he achieved recognition in the United States by winning the Elizabeth Sprague Coolidge Award of $1,000 for his *Rispetti e Strambotti,* for string quartet.

For many years, Malipiero has been living in the little town of

Asolo, near Venice, devoting himself to research, composing, and some teaching. He lived there through the years of World War II, the war ending with destruction just a few hundred feet away from his villa. Out of the tragedy of World War II came another poignant composition, his fourth symphony entitled *In Memoriam.*

Malipiero has written many works in every possible form, including operas, large choral works, orchestral and chamber-music works, and songs. For many years he taught composition at the Liceo Benedetto Marcello in Venice, and in 1939 he was appointed its director.

## MARTINU, BOHUSLAV
*Born:* Polička, Czechoslovakia
December 8, 1890

He began to study the violin in his sixth year and started composing when he was ten. A few wealthy citizens of Prague raised a fund to send him to the Prague Conservatory, where Martinu remained until his twenty-third year. For a decade after that he played the violin in the Czech Philharmonic, and during this period he wrote his first ambitious works, one of which—the ballet, *Istar*—was successfully presented in Prague in 1922.

In 1923, Martinu went to Paris, his home for the next seventeen years. French music played a decisive role in his development. His writing became refined, economical, controlled in the manner of many French composers. Among the works produced by Martinu in Paris were *Half-Time* (a description of a football match), and *La Bagarre* (a picture of a crowd). The latter was one of Martinu's first works heard in the United States, introduced in 1927 by the Boston Symphony Orchestra under Koussevitzky.

After 1928, Martinu's style underwent another transformation. He abandoned French impressionism, and started writing in a Czech idiom—the idiom and the musical context derived from Czech folk music, art and lore. In this vein, he wrote the opera, *The Miracle of Our Lady;* and the ballet, *Spalicek.*

Since 1941, Martinu has been living in the United States. He has been writing abundantly, producing music that is more neo-classic in style and approach than Czech. He has turned sympathetically to the old concerto-grosso form and in it produced some of his finest works, including numerous concertos for orchestra and for solo instruments and orchestra. He has also written several excellent symphonies. His writing is now marked by a strong feeling for classical form in which expressive ideas are treated with firmness and economy.

MASCAGNI, PIETRO                *Born:* Leghorn, Italy
                                       December 7, 1863
                                *Died:* Rome
                                       August 2, 1945

After a period of study with private teachers, Mascagni wrote a symphony and a cantata which were performed in his native city in 1879 and 1881 respectively. A rich patron provided funds for additional music study. Mascagni entered the Milan Conservatory, but he was not happy there. He deserted the school, and for the next few years earned his living by conducting the performances of a traveling opera company. He finally settled down in Cerignola, got married, and taught the piano and managed a municipal music school. In 1889, he entered a one-act opera contest sponsored by the publisher Sonzogno. That opera, *Cavalleria Rusticana,* won first prize and was introduced at the Costanzi Theatre in Rome on May 18, 1890. It was such a triumph that overnight Mascagni became famous. Wealth and honor came his way as a result of this opera's success.

Among his later operas are *L'Amico Fritz* and *Iris;* both were well received. But Mascagni's fame rests exclusively on his one-act masterpiece. After 1920, Mascagni identified himself intimately with the Fascist regime in Italy. He was appointed director of La Scala in 1926; and in 1935 he wrote *Nerone,* an operatic tribute to Mussolini. During World War II, his fortune was confiscated by the Socialists after the Nazis were driven out of the country. He died in poverty and disrepute.

Mascagni's *Cavalleria Rusticana* inaugurated a new style in Italian opera that is known as *Verismo,* or naturalism.

MASSENET, JULES                 *Born:* Montaud, France
                                       May 12, 1842
                                *Died:* Paris
                                       August 13, 1912

His mother gave him his first piano lessons. In 1851, the family came to Paris where Jules entered the Conservatory. He won numerous prizes, including the Prix de Rome. After his three-year stay in Italy, he returned to Paris and wrote his first opera; it was a failure. Success came first with an oratorio, *Les Erinnyes* (one section of which is the very popular "Élégie"). He became a member of the Legion of Honor; was elected to the Académie des Beaux-Arts; and was appointed professor of composition at the Paris Conservatory. In 1881, Massenet achieved his first triumph in the field of opera with *Hérodiade*. *Manon,* in 1884; *Le Cid,* in 1885; *Werther,* in 1892; and *Thaïs,* in 1894; established him as one of the most significant creators of French lyric opera. After 1900, there took place a deterioration of his creative power. While he wrote numerous works, only two operas gave some suggestion of his former gifts: *Le Jongleur de Notre-Dame* in 1902 and *Don Quichotte,* in 1910.

At his best, Massenet was the creator of elegant music, always refined, restrained, and in the best possible taste. He has a sensitive melodic vein, and a delicate feeling for instrumental and harmonic colors. It is true that he is often sentimental, but he is rarely cloying. He could also be an innovator: in *Manon* he made expressive use, for the first time, of spoken dialogue against an orchestral accompaniment.

MEDTNER, NICOLAS        *Born:* Moscow
                                   January 5, 1880
                         *Died:* London
                                   November 13, 1951

Medtner started writing music before he had learned to read and write. As a boy he founded and directed his own little orchestra which gave regular concerts in his home. When he was twelve, he entered the Moscow Conservatory; his teachers included Arensky and Taneiev. He was an exceptional pupil. One of his student compositions was published; and he received a gold medal for piano playing.

His studies ended, and his professional career began, in 1902. He made many tours as a concert pianist and eventually achieved a worldwide reputation. He also distinguished himself as a teacher of the piano at the Moscow Conservatory.

Unsympathetic to the new Communist regime in Russia, Medtner left his native land in 1921. He lived first in Germany and after that in France, and finally in England which remained his home up to the time of his death. He continued touring the music world as pianist, particularly in performances of his own music.

Medtner wrote many works for the piano. He is best in the small pieces to which he has given picturesque nomenclatures: Fairy Tales, Musical Pictures, Romantic Sketches, and so forth. Sometimes described as the "Russian Brahms," Medtner owed a great debt to German Romanticism of the closing nineteenth century. His music is deeply steeped in Romantic traditions, filled with singable melodies, robust harmonies, and infectious feelings. Sometimes, his pieces are involved in their rhythmic and contrapuntal writing. But they are always emotional and rarely fail to please the listener.

MENDELSSOHN, FELIX    *Born:* Hamburg, Germany
February 3, 1809
*Died:* Leipzig, Germany
November 4, 1847

Felix Mendelssohn was the grandson of Moses Mendelssohn, famous Hebrew philosopher; and the son of Abraham, a prosperous banker. Born into a wealthy household, where culture was deeply rooted, Felix knew few of the struggles and frustrations experienced by many other composers in their youth. He started to study the piano early; and when he showed unusual talent, was warmly encouraged. Ludwig Berger taught him the piano; and he studied theory with Zelter. In his ninth year, Mendelssohn made a successful appearance as concert pianist, and two years later he started composing. When he was thirteen, Mendelssohn visited Goethe who was profoundly impressed by the boy's musical ability. "You will become a very great composer," Goethe told him.

It did not take Mendelssohn long to fulfill Goethe's prophecy. Even as a child, he was writing music all the time; and his works were performed at little musicales held in his home. He was fifteen when he wrote his *First Symphony* and a comic opera, both performed to appreciative audiences. And he was only seventeen when he produced his first masterwork, the *Overture to A Midsummer Night's Dream.*

In 1829, Mendelssohn distinguished himself in another field of musical activity. From boyhood on he had been an admirer of the music of Johann Sebastian Bach, which had suffered neglect since that composer's death. Mendelssohn admired particularly the *Passion According to St. Matthew,* which had not been performed since Bach's time. He decided to introduce this mighty work to the general music public. In 1829, he directed a performance of the *St. Matthew Passion;* it was so successful that it was repeated ten days later. The revival of interest in Bach's music—and his restoration to the position in music he deserved—can be said to date from these Mendelssohn performances.

In this same year of 1829 Mendelssohn visited England, the first of many visits he was to make to that country. He was now appointed member of the London Philharmonic Society. He proceeded to Scotland, a trip that was to inspire him to write such works as the *Fingal's Cave* (or *Hebrides*) *Overture* and the *Scotch Symphony.* His travels brought him to many different parts of Europe before he settled down in Düsseldorf, in 1833, to become its musical director. His next major musical post came two years later when he was appointed conductor of the Gewandhaus Orchestra in Leipzig. He now distinguished himself as one of the greatest conductors of his generation. His performances set a new standard for fastidiousness over details and for musicianship and authority.

In 1837, Mendelssohn married Cécile Jeanrenaud; it was an idyllic marriage. Three years after that, as Kapellmeister for the King of Prussia, he wrote incidental music for *Athalie* and *Antigone,* and the remaining numbers of an orchestral suite for *A Midsummer Night's Dream,* whose overture he had written years earlier. But Mendelssohn was not happy as Kapellmeister, largely because of petty court cabals; he finally received the King's permission to resign. He returned to Leipzig where, in 1843, he entered upon still another field of music. With Robert Schumann and Ferdinand David he helped found the Leipzig Conservatory, devoting himself painstakingly for the next few years to teaching, but without neglecting either conducting or composition.

His many tasks and his complete submersion in each of them overtaxed his sensitive physique. Ill and weak, he nevertheless decided to go to London to direct a performance of his oratorio, *Elijah.* He returned to Leipzig ruined in health, his spirit further shattered by the news that his beloved sister Fanny had died suddenly. He collapsed physically in the fall of 1847 and died the following November.

Mendelssohn was one of the great figures of the Romantic movement in music. Just as he was the true aristocrat in the way he lived and dressed, so was he the aristocrat in what he wrote. Elegance and finesse characterize every page of his music. The form is always clear, beautiful in design and symmetry; the ideas are ever elegant; the workmanship the last word in grace. He was probably at his best in delicate tone paintings of landscapes and seascapes; and incomparable in projecting graceful, fairy-like effects.

His most famous works include three symphonies (*Italian, Scotch,* and *Reformation*); the orchestral suite, *A Midsummer Night's Dream;* the beautiful *Concerto in E Minor,* for violin and orchestra, and one of the most popular in the entire concerto literature; the oratorio, *Elijah;* various works for the piano, including the *Songs Without Words;* and works for chamber-music ensembles. His major works are described in later sections on the Symphony, Suite, Concerto, and Piano Music.


MENOTTI, GIAN-CARLO        *Born:* Cadigliano, Italy
                                          July 7, 1911


He was a child prodigy in Italy, writing his first opera when he was only eleven. In 1928, he came to the United States, henceforth his permanent home. For the next few years he studied at the Curtis Institute. His first opera written in this country was *Amelia Goes to the Ball,* introduced with outstanding success by the Curtis Institute under Fritz Reiner on April 1, 1937. His next opera, *The Old Maid and the Thief,* was commissioned for radio by the N.B.C., which presented it in 1939. *The Island God,* which followed, marked Menotti's debut at the Metropolitan Opera House in 1942; it was a failure. But with *The Medium,* seen in 1946, and *The Telephone,* presented one year after that, Menotti once again met with acclaim. *The Consul,* presented in New York City on March 15, 1950, was his greatest triumph up to then. It won the Pulitzer Prize and the Drama Critics Award. In 1945 Menotti received a grant from the American Academy of Arts and Letters, and in 1946 a Guggenheim Fellowship. He also taught dramatic form and composition at the Curtis Institute for several years. His operas have been extensively performed on Broadway and in this country's professional and amateur opera houses. *The Medium* was made into a motion picture. In 1951 Menotti wrote the first opera created expressly for television, *Amahl and the Night Visitors,* and once again achieved a success of the first magnitude. This was followed by *The Saint of Bleecker Street.* His operas are noteworthy for unanimity of spirit between music and text (he writes his own librettos, after *Amelia Goes to the Ball* all in English). His musical style is eclectic, ranging from the romantic to the modern; and is always remarkable for its dramatic impact, and sure theatrical instincts.

MESSIAEN, OLIVIER                    *Born:* Avignon, France
                                      December 10, 1908

Messiaen's mother is a famous French poet, Cécile Sauvage. One of her best known poems, *L'âme en bourgeon,* was inspired by Olivier's birth. He proved his talent for music early, starting composing when he was seven, and soon after that learning by himself to play the piano. In his eleventh year he entered the Paris Conservatory, where he won many prizes. After finishing his studies, he became organist of the Trinité Church in Paris; in the year of his appointment his *Les Offrandes oubliées,* for orchestra, was performed.

Most of Messiaen's large works are profoundly religious. Messiaen draws his programs from the Scriptures or the Catholic liturgy. Best known are his *L'Ascension,* for orchestra (the text being Christ's prayer to the Holy Father); the *Visions de l'amen,* for two pianos; and the *Vingt regards sur l'enfant Jésus,* for piano.

Besides mysticism and religious fervor, Messiaen's works are characterized by his interest in unusual and complex rhythms. He wrote a ten-movement symphony called *Turangalîla* in which rhythms, cross-rhythms, reversible rhythms, etc., are used with the most telling effect.

During World War II, Messiaen fought in the French Army and was taken prisoner by the Nazis. He wrote a quartet, *For the End of Time,* in the prison camp. In 1949, Messiaen visited the United States and gave a master course in composition at the Berkshire Music Center in Tanglewood, Massachusetts.

Messiaen has identified himself with a school of French composers called "La Jeune France." This group includes Daniel-Lesur, Jolivet, and Baudrier, and is dedicated to the creation of an authentically French art through "sincerity, generosity, and artistic good faith."

MEYERBEER, GIACOMO        *Born:* Berlin
                          September 5, 1791
                          *Died:* Paris
                          May 2, 1864

He was born to wealthy parents. A child prodigy at the piano, Meyerbeer gave several successful concerts in Berlin. He studied the piano with Clementi; and theory with Zelter, Anselm Weber, and Abbé Vogler. His first opera was a failure when introduced in Munich; and his second opera was no more successful than the first. Discouraged, Meyerbeer went to Italy for further study. He began writing operas in the Italian style. His first such work was *Romildo e Costanza,* a huge success when performed in Padua in 1817. He then wrote many Italian operas which put him in the front rank of opera composers of his day.

After a time he settled in Paris. His association with French composers and the French theatre and ballet brought about a radical change in his operatic style. He now assumed the French manner of writing operas: emphasizing dramatic situations, pageantry, and the ballet, instead of lyricism. His first opera in this vein was *Robert le Diable,* presented at the Opéra on November 21, 1831. It was a sensation. *Les Huguenots,* in 1836, made Meyerbeer the most famous opera composer in France, and one who was widely imitated.

For several years, Meyerbeer served as Kapellmeister to the King of Prussia. A leave of absence brought him back to Paris where he wrote *Le Prophète,* another tremendous success when introduced at the Opéra in 1849. Meyerbeer now turned to the writing of comic operas. But his last operatic work was in the style of the serious French operas that had made him famous: *L'Africaine,* generally credited as being his greatest work. He did not live to see it performed. It was introduced at the Opéra on April 28, 1865, almost a year after his death.

Meyerbeer was the first major figure in French opera: he developed the traditions of French opera which were to be served by his successors. He was an important pioneer in another direction as well. With his fine dramatic sense and his emphasis on orchestral writing (for which he had a remarkable aptitude) he was, as Hugo Riemann remarked, "one of the most important steps to Wagner's art."

## MIASKOVSKY, NIKOLAI

*Born:* Novogeorgievsk, Russia
April 20, 1881
*Died:* Moscow
August 9, 1950

Nikolai was first sent to the Cadets School in his native city and then to St. Petersburg to become an engineer. He was graduated in 1899, and entered upon his chosen profession. But music had always been his favorite hobby. In his maturity, he decided to study it intensively. After some harmony lessons with Glière, Miaskovsky became convinced that music, and not engineering, was his field. He abandoned the engineering profession and entered the St. Petersburg Conservatory where his teachers included Liadov and Rimsky-Korsakov. After leaving the Conservatory, Miaskovsky started composing music seriously, attracting attention with a gifted piano sonata. During World War I, he fought in the Russian Army for three years; was wounded and shell-shocked. After the war, he became a professor of composition at the Moscow Conservatory, a post he held almost up to the end of his life. He also wrote numerous works, including twenty-seven symphonies (the best and the most famous being the *Twenty-First*). Many of his later works were inspired by Soviet subjects and ideology.

In 1948, when the Central Committee of the Communist Party condemned many Russian composers for writing cerebral and formalistic music, Miaskovsky was severely criticized for introducing the study of "inharmonious music" in his classes.

## MILHAUD, DARIUS

*Born:* Aix-en-Provence, France
September 4, 1892

He was a student at the Paris Conservatory where his teachers included Vincent d'Indy and Paul Dukas. In 1917, on the invitation of Paul Claudel, the poet-diplomat, he became an attaché at the French legation in Brazil. The popular melodies and rhythms of Brazil, particularly the tango, fascinated him and he wrote several works imitating this popular style, including *Saudades do Brasil*. He also became interested in American jazz, then very popular in Brazil, and adapted that idiom for other works, notably the ballets *Le Boeuf sur le toit* and *La Création du monde*. After returning to his native land, in 1919, he became a famous and provocative composer whose works were widely performed and discussed. Soon after his return to France the critic Collet included his name with those of five other French composers in a school which became famous throughout the world of music as the "French Six."

Milhaud wrote numerous works in many different styles. He employed not only South American and jazz idioms; but in other works he used the most advanced techniques of modern music, particularly polytonality, which he was one of the first to use with outstanding effect. In all his works, he reveals an extraordinary technical skill, a rich vein of melody, and a personal charm.

When war broke out in Europe in 1939, Milhaud came to this country, and joined the music faculty of Mills College in California. Though he returned to France after the war, to reassume a commanding position in French music, he has spent some part of each year in this country teaching.

His extensive library of music includes major works in all forms. His three most important operas—*Christophe Colomb, Maximilien,* and *Bolivar*—have Latin-American backgrounds. He has written many symphonies, string quartets, concertos for solo instruments and orchestra, together with a great number of piano works and songs.

MONTEMEZZI, ITALO        *Born:* Vigasio, Italy
                                                August 4, 1875
                                        *Died:* Verona, Italy
                                                May 15, 1952

Prepared for a career as engineer, he was sent to the Milan University. There he had a change of heart and decided to concentrate on music. After three attempts, he succeeded in entering the Conservatory where his teachers included Saladino and Ferroni, and from which he was graduated with honors. In 1905, his opera *Giovanni Galurese* was introduced successfully in Turin. His second opera was a failure. But his third work, *L'Amore dei Tre Re,* introduced at La Scala on April 10, 1913, won him international fame. *La Nave,* which came five years later, was also a huge success. From 1939 to shortly before his death, Montemezzi lived in California.

## MONTEVERDI, CLAUDIO

*Born:* Cremona, Italy
May, 1567
*Died:* Venice
November 29, 1643

Monteverdi studied theory with Ingegneri, and in 1583 published a remarkable volume of madrigals. In 1589, he was appointed violinist in the court orchestra of the Duke of Mantua. The Duke regarded Monteverdi highly, taking him on his many travels to different parts of Europe. Thus Monteverdi could come into contact with the music of various countries. In France, after hearing the works of the French School, he began writing in the French style. In Flanders, he heard reports about a new musical form evolved in Florence—the opera. He attended a performance of Peri's *Euridice* which impressed him so greatly that he decided to write works in this new medium. In 1605 he published his last book of madrigals—and after that he specialized in the field of opera.

Meanwhile, in 1601, he had become the Maestro di Capella to the house of Gonzaga in Mantua. The marriage of the Duke's son to the Infanta of Savoy, in 1607, led him to write a work befitting the occasion. Thus he completed his first opera, *Orfeo,* heard at wedding ceremonies on February 24, 1607.

Monteverdi's *Orfeo* can be regarded as the first genuine Italian opera. All operas written before then were primitive in style and inchoate in form, consisting of little more than accompanied declamations. With Monteverdi came arias, duets, ensemble numbers; the orchestra was enlarged and given increased importance; and new orchestral effects were invented. Music, with Monteverdi, was made to convey the emotional and dramatic implications of the text.

In 1613, Monteverdi left for Venice to become the Maestro di Cappella of the St. Mark's Cathedral. He continued writing operas which were performed successfully in Venice—among them, *Il Combattimento di Tancredi e Clorinda* (1624) and *L'Incoronazione di Poppea* (1642). It was due to Monteverdi's presence in Venice, and the performances of his operas there, that Venice became at that time the capital of the operatic world.

MOZART, WOLFGANG          *Born:* Salzburg, Austria
AMADEUS                              January 27, 1756
                                 *Died:* Vienna
                                      December 5, 1791

The phenomenal, and probably unprecedented, musical exploits of the child Mozart have often been written about. At the age of three he started producing melodies and pleasing chords at the harpsichord. Study began when he was four; he learned his lessons as quickly as they were taught. By the time he was six, he had written several charming pieces for the harpsichord, and had made an attempt at creating a concerto.

His father, a violinist in the orchestra of the Salzburg Archbishop, decided to exploit the child's prodigious gifts by having him appear in concerts with his eleven-year-old sister, Marianne, also a gifted musician. Wolfgang won the hearts of everybody who heard him play. The royal courts of Vienna, Paris, and London welcomed and acclaimed him. Empress Maria Theresa kissed him and Emperor Francis I called him a "little master-wizard."

The first two tours were such phenomenal successes that, inevitably, others were planned by the ambitious father. Meanwhile, Mozart proceeded to justify all the extravagant things that were said about him. Still a child, he published several fine sonatas for violin and piano in Paris; in London, he wrote three symphonies; in Vienna, he completed his first opera. Perhaps the most publicized of Mozart's boyhood exploits was that which took place in Rome. Each year, Allegri's *Miserere* was performed at the Sistine Chapel. By papal decree, the music was not allowed to be performed elsewhere; and the only existing copy was guarded by the papal choir. The fourteen-year-old Mozart listened to the performance, went back to the hotel room, and wrote down the entire work from memory. When the Pope got news of this fabulous feat, he forgave the child for violating his decree and, a few months later, bestowed on him the Cross of the Order of the Golden Spur.

In 1770, Mozart's opera *Mitridate* was introduced in Milan, and was so successful that many numbers had to be encored and its composer became the idol of the Milanese opera public.

Mozart was now outgrowing the charm of his childhood. As an

adolescent he ceased to have the exciting appeal to audiences that he had had as a child, even though his genius was no less striking. Consequently, ceasing to be a drawing-card, his European travels ended. He was now confined to his home town, Salzburg. The next few years were unhappy. The cloistered atmosphere of a small town had a smothering effect on him. Besides, he failed to gain the appreciation he deserved. Employed by the Archbishop of Salzburg, he was poorly paid and treated like a lackey. He sought escape, and it came in 1777 with a new concert tour. It was not successful. Royal courts, once his playground, were closed to him. Commissions, once so plentiful, were few and far between. He had to return to his native city, a disappointed man.

He knew he could not stay in Salzburg permanently. A brief taste of success with the opera *Idomeneo*—heard in Munich in 1781—convinced him that he must break loose from his ties with Salzburg, and try his fortune in a large city, preferably Vienna. When the Archbishop of Salzburg, who had taken him to Vienna, treated him arrogantly, Mozart flew into a temper which resulted in his dismissal. Mozart was free, at last.

Soon after settling in Vienna, he was commissioned by Emperor Joseph II to write the comic opera *The Abduction from the Seraglio*. The Viennese public, the court, and Vienna's leading musicians liked it immensely. Mozart wrote for Vienna an even greater opera, *The Marriage of Figaro,* four years later, in collaboration with Lorenzo da Ponte. Though intrigues and cabals tried to keep this opera from being performed—and it was performed only because of the intercession of the Emperor himself—it was a triumph.

In 1782, Mozart married Constance Weber. It was, for the most part, a happy marriage, though disturbed by intense poverty, which was not alleviated by the success of his operas. Strange to say, despite his great fame in Vienna, Mozart was unable to procure a well-paying post at the court. The income he received from the performances of his work was hardly enough to provide him and his wife with the basic necessities of life.

But, at least, he was not without recognition. In 1787, he wrote for Prague a new opera, *Don Giovanni,* whose success made him the man of the hour in that city. But *Don Giovanni* brought its composer a mere pittance. Though this masterwork was followed by many others —the three wonderful last symphonies and the operas, *The Magic*

*Flute* and *Così fan tutte*—Mozart failed completely to establish himself financially.

He was depressed by his inability to gain a desirable post, despondent over his poverty, and worst of all broken in health. In 1791, he was approached by a stranger dressed in gray who commissioned him to write a requiem for a patron whose identity had to remain a secret. To Mozart—morbid, hypersensitive and ill—it appeared that the stranger was a messenger from another world urging him to write his own requiem. He worked feverishly to complete the work before it was too late. He was found unconscious at his desk and taken to his bed, which he was never again destined to leave. He died a few hours after he and a few friends sang parts of his *Requiem,* which was left unfinished (it was completed after his death by his pupil, Süssmayer). A crowning irony in the life of a composer who had been so extravagantly idolized in his childhood was the fact that he was buried in a pauper's grave.

Mozart was not only the genius of the Classical Era who prepared the ground for Beethoven, but one of the greatest musicians and creative geniuses who ever lived. He developed and enriched every form of music he employed—the symphony, the sonata, the string quartet, the concerto, the opera—as will be seen in our later discussion of these forms. To the most consummate mastery of technique, the like of which has not been duplicated, he brought the sure instincts, the inexhaustible imagination, the fabulous invention of his incomparable genius. If perfection has ever been achieved in music, it is found in Mozart. His greatest works have an inevitability of structure and style. With it, there is a vast range of emotion: Mozart passes with unerring instincts from satire and boyish laughter to tragedy and human suffering, from levity to majesty and grandeur with equal power. There is this, too, about a Mozart work that is virtually unique: it can be listened to for the first time and enjoyed for its lyricism, buoyancy, charm, and spontaneity; and it can be listened to a hundred times and appreciated for its subtleties and profundities.

The letter "K," together with an identifying number, is usually seen after each of Mozart's works. This is to designate its order in the definitive catalogue of Mozart's works created by Dr. Ludwig Köchel in 1862. Since in Mozart's day opus numbers were not yet in general use, this is the only practical way of identifying each Mozart work.

# MUSSORGSKY, MODEST

*Born:* Karevo, Pskov, Russia
March 21, 1839
*Died:* St. Petersburg
March 28, 1881

The son of wealthy landowners, Mussorgsky was given some musical instruction in his childhood. He was intended for the army, and was sent to the Military School for Ensigns. After his graduation he became a regimental officer. A meeting with the Russian composer, Dargomijsky, in 1857, represents a turning point in his life. Through Dargomijsky, Mussorgsky met Balakirev and Borodin, both of whom awakened his long dormant love for music. In 1858, Mussorgsky resigned his army commission to concentrate on musical activities. He remained self-taught for the most part, guided more by instincts than by carefully studied techniques.

In 1861, when the Russian serfs were liberated and wealthy landowners suffered serious reverses, the Mussorgsky family lost its fortune. Mussorgsky, faced with the problem of earning a living, took a government job (which he detested), and held it practically to the end of his life.

Inspired by the national ideals of his friends Balakirev and Borodin, Mussorgsky became their partner in the school later famous as "The Russian Five." His first important works came between 1864 and 1867, including some peasant songs, and his only significant work for orchestra, the tone poem, *Night on Bald Mountain.* At about this time, Mussorgsky started to evolve theories of his own, apart from those of the other members of the "Five." He wanted to produce melodies that were patterned after the inflections of speech, calling them the "melodies of life." His first experiment in this direction came in 1868 with the one-act opera, *The Marriage.* But the most successful realization of this style is found in his masterwork, the opera *Boris Godunov,* begun in 1868. Because of its unorthodox idiom, the opera was denied a performance for a long time, and when finally presented —on January 27, 1874—was more or less of a failure. Mussorgsky wrote two more operas: *Khovantchina* and *The Fair at Sorochinsk.*

It is quite true that, as his critics have frequently said, Mussorgsky's style is often crude and undisciplined. His lack of proper training is found in his clumsy use of harmony and in his coarse orchestration.

But what he lacked in technique he made up for in creative power. He was the greatest of the "Russian Five," even though the others were more cultured and sophisticated. His music has a strength, individuality, and stout fiber not found in the works of the other Nationalists; its identification with the Russian soil is unmistakable.

Mussorgsky died prematurely at the age of forty-one after an attack of epilepsy. In the last years of his life he succumbed completely to a lifelong weakness for alcohol. After his death, Rimsky-Korsakov and Stassov edited his works to eliminate their stylistic deficiencies. It is the Rimsky-Korsakov version of *Boris Godunov* that has become famous and is still heard most often in our opera houses.

OFFENBACH, JACQUES          *Born:* Cologne, Germany
                                          June 20, 1819
                                    *Died:* Paris
                                          October 4, 1880

The son of a cantor at a Jewish synagogue in Cologne, Offenbach started studying the cello when he was thirteen. In a few months he was able to make a public appearance in his native city in a concert including some of his own pieces. In his fourteenth year, he went to Paris where he made such a profound impression on Cherubini, director of the Paris Conservatory, that the rule forbidding the admittance of foreigners to the Conservatory was waived for his benefit. Offenbach stayed there for four years; part of that time he earned his living by playing in the orchestra of the Opéra Comique.

His first important musical post came in 1849 when he was appointed conductor at the Comédie Française. Six years after that he leased his own theatre, called it the Bouffes Parisiens, and presented his own comic opera, *Les Deux aveugles*. The opera was successful— launching the theatre on its prosperous six-year history, and Offenbach on his fabulous career as the most successful composer of the opéra comique of all time. Many popular Offenbach operettas were seen at the Bouffes Parisiens, including *Orpheus in the Underworld,* in 1858 (his greatest success). Though Offenbach gave up his theatre in 1861, he continued writing his highly popular operettas, producing *La Belle Hélène* in 1864, *Barbe-Bleue* and *La Vie parisienne* in 1866 and *La Grande Duchesse de Gérolstein,* in 1867, among others.

In 1873, he took over the management of another Parisian theatre, the Gaîté. It went into bankruptcy two years later, largely because of Offenbach's extravagance in mounting his plays and his indifference to other excessive expenditures. He became overwhelmed by immense debts, and to meet his obligations he toured the United States in 1877, enjoying a personal triumph wherever he appeared, and earning more than 100,000 francs.

The last years of Offenbach's life were dismal. He suffered from the gout, and for a time was haunted by strange hallucinations. Notwithstanding his suffering, he worked on his most ambitious musical composition, the opera *The Tales of Hoffmann*. He lived long enough to complete it and to realize that he had created his masterwork.

Offenbach was the genius of French comic opera. He was extraordinarily prolific, producing about ninety operettas within a twenty-five year period. His music has spontaneity, gaiety, a personal charm, effervescence, together with the best possible taste; at his best, in *Orpheus in the Underworld* and *La Vie parisienne,* he was truly *sui generis. The Tales of Hoffmann* is a different cosmos; drama and deep feeling replace Offenbach's one-time gaiety, providing testimony that had he chosen the field of serious opera he would have been a master there, too.

## PAGANINI, NICCOLO

*Born:* Genoa
October 27, 1782
*Died:* Nice, Sardinia
(now France)
May 27, 1840

Paganini's father nursed the ambition of exploiting his son as a prodigy of the violin. He drove the boy relentlessly in his violin studies. Though abused, Niccolo made astonishing progress. He was only thirteen when he gave a concert in Genoa that amazed the audience. Now known as the "wonder child," Paganini concertized throughout Italy. His music study proceeded without interruption, first with Servetto and Costa, and after that with Paër.

Between 1801 and 1805, Paganini went into temporary retirement, applying himself assiduously toward developing his virtuosity. He returned to the concert stage in 1805, immediately impressing his audience with his technical wizardry. From this time on he was a sensation wherever he performed. He became an idol—and a myth. In Paris he was called Cagliostro; in Ireland they said he had come to their shores on the Flying Dutchman; in Prague he was suspected of being the original Wandering Jew. His incredible command of the violin, combined with his cadaverous appearance, inspired many to believe that he was the son of the devil.

In 1836, Paganini founded a gambling casino in Paris in which he lost his life savings. Always delicate in health, this disaster ruined it.

Paganini produced an entire library of music for the violin, filled with happy lyrical ideas, and fully exploiting the technical resources of the instrument. He did more to advance the technique of violin playing than any musician before him, introducing effects that were new for that day. His best known work is the volume of twenty-four caprices for unaccompanied violin. Other well-known pieces include the *Witch's Dance, Perpetual Motion,* and the *Carnival of Venice.* His popular *Violin Concerto in D Major* is most often heard in the adaptation of Fritz Kreisler in which only the first movement is utilized.

| | |
|---|---|
| (DA) PALESTRINA, GIOVANNI PERLIUGI | *Born:* Palestrina, near Rome in or about 1524 |
| | *Died:* Rome February 2, 1594 |

Very little is known of the early life of this, the greatest of all polyphonic composers before Bach. Palestrina became organist and choirmaster at the San Agapito Church in Palestrina in 1544. Seven years later, Pope Julius III appointed him Master of the boys' choir at St. Peter's in Rome. In 1554, he published his first volume, masses for four and five voices; this was followed by a book of madrigals. Dismissed from his choir post on the grounds that he had married in 1547, Palestrina became Maestro di Cappella at the St. John Lateran Church in Rome, and in 1561 he assumed a similar post at S. Maria Maggiore. During the latter period the Council of Trent demanded a reform of church music. It has long been said that Palestrina's celebrated *Missa Papae Marcelli* was responsible for bringing about this reform, but this is doubtful. This mass is, however, one of Palestrina's greatest works, placing him at the head of all Italian composers of the time; it was to serve as a model for all later writers of masses.

For a period, beginning with 1569, Palestrina was employed by Cardinal d'Este, for whom he wrote many important choral works including a book of motets. By 1571, he was back in his old post at St. Peter's, which he retained until the end of his life. Indicative of the high station he now occupied was the fact that, in 1575, fifteen hundred singers from the town of Palestrina came to Rome on foot singing his music as they marched. Palestrina was working on a collection of thirty madrigals when he was stricken with a fatal pleurisy.

PERGOLESI, GIOVANNI      *Born:* Jesi, Italy
                                    January 4, 1710
                               *Died:* Pozzuoli, Italy
                                    March 16, 1736

He received instruction on the violin from Santini and Mondini. When he was sixteen, he entered the Naples Conservatory, where his teachers included Durante, Greco, and Feo. He made his bow as composer in 1731 with a sacred drama, presented at the S. Angello Maggiore Monastery. This was such a success that Pergolesi received a commission to write an opera for the Naples court theatre. This opera, *La Salustia,* was presented in 1731; and was followed one year later by another opera, *Ricimero.* His masterpiece came in 1733. It was the comic opera, *La Serva padrona,* successfully produced in Naples. This was a work of historic importance, since it was the first successful opera buffa, and thus established a medium that was henceforth to be used with immense effect by such composers as Donizetti and Rossini. Twenty years after its first performance, *La Serva padrona* was introduced throughout Europe by a company of wandering players and received tumultuous acclaim wherever it was played. In Paris, where it was seen in 1752, it brought a new cult into existence (sponsored by Rousseau, Diderot, and Grimm, among others) which proclaimed it as the true operatic art as opposed to the operas of Rameau.

In 1734, Pergolesi became court musician for the Duke of Maddaloni. He was to write one other masterwork before his premature death, the *Stabat Mater,* completed in illness and pain and with the awareness that he was dying.

## PISTON, WALTER

*Born:* Rockland, Maine
January 20, 1894

He did not begin formal musical study until comparatively late. He was first graduated from the Massachusetts Normal Art School in 1916. It was only then that he began studying the violin and the piano. During World War I, he played the saxophone in a Navy band. After the war, he entered Harvard University, specializing in music; and from 1924 to 1926 he studied with Nadia Boulanger in Paris. Returning to the United States, he joined the music faculty of Harvard University, where he has remained since that time.

His debut as a composer took place in 1928 when the Boston Symphony under Koussevitzky introduced *Symphonic Piece*. Other important performances followed, the most successful being that of the ballet, *The Incredible Flutist*, in 1938. Piston received the Music Critics Award for his *Second Symphony* in 1943, and the Pulitzer Prize for his *Third Symphony* in 1949.

While adhering to traditional structures and styles, Piston does not hesitate to use modern techniques and idioms for calculated effects. He skilfully combines the accepted means with contemporary techniques in a style uniquely his.

## PIZZETTI, ILDEBRANDO

*Born:* Parma
September 20, 1880

Pizzetti's father was a piano teacher. After a period of piano study with his father, Ildebrando entered the Parma Conservatory, in his sixteenth year. He was a brilliant student and even then began writing ambitious works. After graduating, Pizzetti entered upon a teaching career. For many years he was professor of theory and composition at the Florence Conservatory; in 1921, he became director of the Milan Conservatory; after 1936 he taught composition, and for a while was director of the Santa Cecilia Academy in Rome.

Between 1903 and 1909 Pizzetti wrote several orchestral works that were performed. But it is in the field of opera that he has distinguished himself. His first major success came with the opera *Fedra* in 1915. Later operas—*Debora e Jaele* and *Fra Gherardo*—were even more successful. Pizzetti, unlike so many other Italian opera composers, is more concerned with dramatic truth than with *bel canto*. In place of arias, he prefers expressive recitatives; instead of formal harmonic accompaniments, he exploits a rich and varied orchestral fabric which plays an important role in emphasizing dramatic effects. He places great emphasis on the chorus, for which he writes with exceptional polyphonic skill.

Pizzetti's career is divided into three periods, each revealing a different influence. First he was inspired by the writings of Gabriele d'Annunzio, many of whose works he set to music. This was followed by the Biblical period. The third phase was the one in which Pizzetti went to Italian history for his inspiration and subject matter.

Among his best known works, besides those already mentioned, are a beautiful *Sonata for Violin and Piano*, the *Concerto dell' Estate* and *Rondo Veneziano*, both for orchestra; and many poignant songs.

## PONCHIELLI, AMILCARE

*Born:* Paderno Fasolaro, near
Cremona, Italy
September 1, 1834
*Died:* Milan
January 16, 1886

He entered the Milan Conservatory when he was nine years old and remained there for eleven years. While still a student he wrote several operas. In 1856, two years after leaving the Conservatory, he achieved a moderate success with the opera, *I Promesi sposi,* performed in Cremona. For more than a decade after that, Ponchielli earned his living by playing the organ and leading a band; all this while he kept on writing operas. A revival of *I Promesi sposi* was a huge success in 1872; so was a new ballet, *I Lituani,* seen at La Scala in 1874. But his triumph was yet to come. When *La Gioconda* was introduced at La Scala on April 8, 1876, it created a sensation. Ponchielli wrote three more operas after *La Gioconda* but none of them were successful. His last years were spent as Maestro di Cappella at the Bergamo Cathedral.

## POULENC, FRANCIS

*Born:* Paris
January 7, 1899

A few friends, convinced of Poulenc's talent, contributed to pay for his first music lessons. These consisted of piano lessons with

Ricardo Viñes. Except for this and some additional study of composition with Koechlin, Poulenc has been self-taught. For a period,
during World War I, Poulenc served in the French Army. After demobilization, he continued his study by himself and started serious
composition. He first came to note immediately after World War I
when his name was included with five others in a group which became
famous as the "French Six."

In his writing, Poulenc usually prefers small forms, terse statements,
simple harmonies, and often witty suggestions. In this vein he has
produced his first notable works, including the song cycle, *Le Bestiaire*,
in 1918; and the ballet, *Les Biches*, given by the Monte Carlo Ballet
in 1924. In this vein, too, are his most frequently heard orchestral
works, among them the *Concert champêtre*, for harpsichord or piano
and orchestra, written in 1928; and the witty *Concerto for Two Pianos
and Orchestra*, in 1932. Later important works include the poignant
*Sonata in D Minor for Violin and Orchestra*, dedicated to the memory
of Federico Garciá Lorca; the *Sinfonietta*, for orchestra; and numerous
songs. In 1948, Poulenc visited the United States for the first time,
touring the country in joint recitals with the baritone Pierre Bernac.


PROKOFIEV, SERGE          *Born:* Sontsovka, Ukraine
                                           April 23, 1891
                                *Died:* Moscow
                                           March 4, 1953


Long before he entered the St. Petersburg Conservatory at the
age of thirteen, Prokofiev had written a great amount of music, including a symphony, three operas, and a number of works for the piano.
At the Conservatory, where he remained ten years, he was an outstanding student, but also an unorthodox one. He was constantly
experimenting with harmonies and tonalities that defied tradition, and
venturing into the realm of dissonance to shock many of his teachers.
Nevertheless, he was graduated with the highest of honors, including
the much-coveted Rubinstein Prize for his *Second Piano Concerto*.

During World War I, Prokofiev was exempt from the Russian
Army, being the only son of a widow. He plunged into creative work,
and produced the first compositions in which his individual personality
and unique compositorial mannerisms are markedly evident. Among
the best known of these early works are the *Scythian Suite*, for orches-

tra; the ballet *Chout;* the *First Violin Concerto;* and the *Third Piano Concerto.* In all these works, he was the restless explorer after new sounds and effects. More important is the fact that his personality is already pronounced: his flair for satire and grotesquerie, expressed in mocking melodic phrases, tart harmonies, impulsive rhythms, and piquant use of tonality.

In 1918, Prokofiev visited the United States for the first time and was heard in performances of his own works. While in this country he was commissioned by the Chicago Opera to write a new work for that organization. *The Love for Three Oranges* was given by the Chicago Opera in 1921 and was a failure; it was not heard again until more than a quarter-century later, revived by the New York City Opera.

After his American tour, Prokofiev established his home in Paris where he continued writing important works that solidified his position among contemporary composers. One of his most provocative works during this period was the ballet, *The Age of Steel*—his first attempt to express Soviet ideology in his music—presented by the Ballet Russe in Paris in 1927.

In 1933, Prokofiev decided to return to his native land, after an absence of more than a decade. From this time on, he has identified himself completely with Soviet life and ideals; most of his works from that date have either interpreted and glorified Soviet ideologies or derived their inspiration from the Russian past. He has written music for Soviet films which he later adapted into major works, including the *Lieutenant Kije Suite* and the cantata *Alexander Nevsky.* He also wrote functional music, the most important work in this category being his delightful and popular *Peter and the Wolf,* designed to teach children the instruments of the orchestra. After the Nazis invaded the Soviet Union, Prokofiev reflected the impact of the war on the Russian people in several monumental works, including the *Fifth Symphony,* the *Seventh Piano Sonata* (which won the Stalin Prize), and the opera *War and Peace.*

Though he was then one of the greatest and most highly honored of Soviet composers, Prokofiev did not escape official attack when, in 1948, the Soviet authorities took their leading composers severely to task for being too cerebral. The Central Committee of the Communist Party responsible for this indictment also insisted that Soviet composers must return to the writing of music that was pleasing in its melody and counterpoint, and inspired by folk music and lore. Though Prokofiev tried to write this kind of music, it was some time before he was restored to the good graces of the Soviet officials. Eventually, his rehabilitation in Soviet music became complete. He won the Stalin Prize in 1951 for two works, *On Guard for Peace* and *Winter Bonfire*. And his sixtieth birthday, in the same year, was officially celebrated with a special concert of his works in Moscow.

PUCCINI, GIACOMO

*Born:* Lucca, Italy
    December 22, 1858
*Died:* Brussels
    November 29, 1924

Puccini was a descendant of a long line of church musicians. A subsidy by Queen Margherita, supplemented by a contribution from a relative, enabled him to enter the Milan Conservatory in 1880. One of his teachers there was Ponchielli, who urged him to enter a competition for one-act operas sponsored by the publisher Sonzogno. Puccini's opera, *Le Villi*, did not win the prize (he did not even receive honorable mention); but it was good enough to be published and performed in 1884. Puccini's second opera was a failure. But his third opera, *Manon Lescaut*, was a success when introduced in Turin in 1893, and was soon after that seen in London and Paris.

Puccini now wrote his first two masterworks: *La Bohème*, in 1896, and *Tosca*, in 1900. Both operas have become established as staples in the operatic repertory. Puccini acquired a position of first importance among the Italian composers of his generation. He was rich, idolized; he performed throughout the world of music; he was accepted as Verdi's successor.

In 1903, Puccini was seriously hurt in an automobile accident. Despite intense pain, and forced immobility, he worked on a new opera, *Madame Butterfly*. When introduced at La Scala in 1904, *Madame Butterfly* was a fiasco. But after some revision by the composer, and repeated hearings, it became a great favorite with the opera world, and one of Puccini's best loved works.

Puccini visited the United States in 1907 to help supervise the première of *Madame Butterfly*. In this country he was commissioned by the Metropolitan Opera to write a new work. When this opera was completed—*The Girl of the Golden West*—Puccini returned to the United States to attend the première, which took place under Toscanini's direction in 1910. While it was at first a success of major proportions, *The Girl of the Golden West* failed to hold a permanent place in the repertory.

After a hiatus of seven years, Puccini returned to the writing of a new opera, this time in a lighter vein, *La Rondine*. This was followed by a trilogy of one-act operas comprising *Il Tabarro, Suor Angelica,* and *Gianni Schicchi*. His last opera, *Turandot,* was left unfinished but was completed after Puccini's death by Franco Alfano.

A victim of throat cancer, Puccini had to undergo a difficult operation in 1924. The operation was successful, but it was followed by a fatal heart attack.

Puccini was not a creator of grand masterworks in the way Verdi or Wagner were. But he was always able to enchant and delight opera audiences with the beauty and sensitive emotions of his finest works which are treated more fully in the chapter on Opera.

PURCELL, HENRY                    *Born:* London
                                 in or about 1659
                       *Died:* London
                                 November 21, 1695


The son of a famous musician, Purcell was early brought into contact with good music. He became a chorister of the celebrated Chapel Royal in London, and soon after this began writing music. One of his pieces attracted the attention of the King of England who engaged him. In 1675, Purcell became copyist at Westminster Abbey; and when John Blow resigned as principal organist at the Abbey, Purcell succeeded him. During this period, Purcell wrote a set of fantasias for strings which played an important role in the early development of instrumental music. In 1682, Purcell became organist of the Chapel Royal, but three years after that he was back in Westminster Abbey. In 1689, he wrote his masterwork—the opera *Dido and Aeneas*. His success led him to write other works for the stage, including *King Arthur* and *The Fairy Queen*.

His death is believed to have been caused by the strain of overwork. He was the first musician to be buried in Westminster Abbey. An ode in his honor was written by John Dryden.

Purcell was the greatest composer produced by England up to his time; and it is probable that he is the greatest English composer of all time. His historic importance in the early history of English opera and instrumental music is pointed up in later sections. But his importance is not exclusively historic; he was also a sovereign of pure melody, and his best works are filled with poetic and sensitive beauty.

RACHMANINOFF, SERGE        *Born:* Onega, Novgorod
                                      April 1, 1873
                                *Died:* Hollywood, California
                                      March 28, 1943

As a boy, Rachmaninoff was both outstandingly gifted and out-standingly lazy. He loved music passionately, but refused to give to it the application and dedication it needed. He made progress at the St. Petersburg Conservatory only because he had such natural talent that he could absorb his lessons without expending any energy. At first his teachers did not think he would amount to much. But when Rach-maninoff changed to the Moscow Conservatory and came under the influence of Zverev, who understood him and worked with him, Rach-maninoff conquered his tendency toward indolence and worked at his studies. He was one of the most brilliant students at the Conservatory, winning prize after prize. In his nineteenth year he wrote the opera *Aleko,* which was successfully performed by the Moscow Opera. He also achieved fame with his *Prelude in C Sharp Minor* which—despite its fabulous sales—earned virtually little for him because he had neglected to copyright it. By his twenty-fourth birthday, Rachmaninoff had established himself in Russia not only as a composer, but also as a conductor, and concert pianist.

But, despite his increasingly important position in Russian music, he was not to be spared the heartbreak of failure. His first two major works—the *First Symphony* and the *First Piano Concerto*—both failed dismally when introduced. This defeat so upset the composer that he was seized by a stifling depression that brought him to the brink of a nervous breakdown. A physician, Dr. Dahl, effected a cure through the power of autosuggestion. After a period of inactivity, Rachmani-noff returned to composing and produced his most celebrated works, and one of his best: the *Second Piano Concerto,* which Rachmaninoff himself introduced with the Moscow Philharmonic on October 14, 1901. The concerto scored a huge success.

Once again a successful composer, Rachmaninoff produced one

major work after another, including the *Symphony No. 2 in E Minor,* in 1907; and one year later the tone poem, *The Isle of the Dead.* Meanwhile he had achieved recognition throughout Europe as a concert pianist, one of the greatest virtuosos of his day. In 1909, he toured the United States for the first time, appearing extensively as pianist, and repeating in this country his European triumphs. For this first American tour, Rachmaninoff wrote his beautiful *Third Piano Concerto.*

After the Revolution in Russia, Rachmaninoff left his native land for good. He established residence in Switzerland, and subsequently divided his year between that country and the United States. Up to the end of his life, Rachmaninoff continued to function in two capacities—as composer and as concert pianist—and maintained his immense success in both. Among Rachmaninoff's last works are the *Rhapsody on a Theme by Paganini,* completed in Switzerland in 1934; the *Third Symphony* and *Symphonic Dances,* both written in this country, in 1936 and 1940 respectively.

Other works by Rachmaninoff include the *Fourth Piano Concerto,* numerous preludes, moments musicaux, sonatas for the piano, and songs. Rachmaninoff was a traditionalist whose music is emotional (at times sentimental), frequently elegiac, and always expressing beauty through broad and expressive melodies and rich-sounding harmonies. He was never an innovator, his was not an original voice; but his works have unfailing appeal to the heart.

RAMEAU, JEAN PHILIPPE     *Born:* Dijon, France
                                           September 25, 1683
                              *Died:* Paris
                                           September 12, 1764

The son of an organist, Rameau was a precocious child who could play the harpsichord when he was only seven. His father insisted on an academic education and sent him to the Jesuit College. These studies over, Rameau went to Italy in 1701, there to officiate as organist in several churches and to play in town bands. Back in France he filled an organ post first in Avignon, then in Clermont-Ferrand. He then settled in Paris, studying the organ with Louis Marchand, and devouring every book on theory he could find.

Rameau first distinguished himself as a theoretician. In 1723, he published a treatise on modern harmony that is of historic importance. This volume attracted the interest of Monsieur Riche de la Pouplinière, who appointed him conductor of his private orchestra and commissioned him to write music for it. In 1733, Rameau achieved success in opera with *Hippolyte et Aricie;* and four years after that created his masterwork, *Castor and Pollux.*

Despite the success of his operas, Rameau was the victim of bitter feuds and cabals. The followers of Lully accused him of neglecting beautiful melody for the sake of intricate harmonies, of sacrificing pleasing musical sounds for dramatic effect. The climax of this hostility against Rameau was reached in 1752 in what history books call the *"guerre des bouffons"* (see section on the Opera).

Besides his operas, Rameau produced many works for the harpsichord which are described in the Piano section. He also wrote many compositions for various chamber-music ensembles. His music has courtly grace and refinement even when it uses original harmonic and rhythmic effects.

RAVEL, MAURICE            *Born:* Ciboure, France
                          March 7, 1875
                         *Died:* Paris
                          December 28, 1937

Ravel received preliminary instruction in music from **Henri** Ghys and Charles-René. He entered the Paris Conservatory in 1889, staying there for fifteen years. His teachers included Pessard, Gédalge, Charles de Bériot, and (the one who influenced him most) Gabriel Fauré. Ravel was an outstanding pupil. But only Fauré seemed to understand and sympathize with his need to try out new idioms. In his first attempts at composition Ravel imitated Satie, experimenting with novel melodic ideas and dissonant chords. On March 5, 1896, one of these works—*Sites auriculaires*—was performed and was badly received.

Ravel became famous largely because of two musical scandals in which he was involved. The first happened in 1905 over his failure to win the Prix de Rome. By 1905, Ravel had written several distinguished works—including the *Pavane pour une Infante défunte* and *Jeux d'eau,* both for piano; and the *Quartet in F*—and many authorities considered him the most gifted of the younger French composers.

When, in 1905, Ravel failed for the fourth year to win the Prix de Rome, many notable musicians rose to his defense and wrote stinging denunciations of the Conservatory authorities. So bitter did this attack become that Dubois, the director of the Conservatory, had to resign.

The second Ravel scandal took place two years after that, immediately after the première of his satirical song cycle, *Histoires naturelles.* This performance was a failure. Some critics became vitriolic in their attacks on the composer, accusing him outright of plagiarizing Debussy. Others rushed to his defense, pointing out his individuality of style and his personal approaches.

The two conflicts fought in his name succeeded, in any case, to make him famous. But he justified that fame with a succession of remarkable works whose success was both immediate and permanent: The *Rapsodie espagnole,* for orchestra; the charming *Mother Goose Suite;* and, most important of all, the ballet *Daphnis and Chloë,* which he wrote on a commission from Serge Diaghilev for the Ballet Russe, and which that organization introduced in Paris on June 8, 1912.

By the time of World War I, Ravel was generally accepted as the foremost living composer in France. He maintained that position till the end of his life. During the war he served for a while at the front with a motor corps. After the war, he retired to a villa outside Paris, henceforth his home, to work on several major compositions, among them the *Tombeau de Couperin, La Valse,* and most popular of all, *Bolero,* which took the music world by storm. His last important works were two concertos for the piano (one for left hand alone).

In 1928, Ravel visited the United States and appeared in thirty concerts of his own works, either as pianist or conductor. He suffered a minor injury in a taxi in 1932. A few months later, however, he developed startling symptoms, including the loss of muscular coordination which eventually led to paralysis. He had to be operated upon the brain, and he never regained consciousness. He died in a private clinic in Paris.

There are several veins in Ravel's music. One is Spanish—for he never lost a lifelong interest in Spanish song and dance—in this category we find works like *Rapsodie espagnole, Alborada del gracioso,* both for orchestra; and the charming opera, *L'Heure espagnole.* Another vein is that of wit and satire, as in *Histoires naturelles,* the fantasy *L'Enfant et les sortilèges,* and *L'Heure espagnole.* A third is the Viennese waltz which, in *La Valse* and *Valses nobles et sentimentales,* he recreated in his individual way. A fourth is that of fantasy—the fantasy of children and animals—found in *Mother Goose* and in *L'Enfant et les sortilèges*. Still another is impressionistic, as in *Daphnis and Chloë*. But whatever the style, Ravel always wrote with the authority of a master. Elegance was combined with a stunning compositorial technique, inspiration with variety of idiom, to make him unique in twentieth century music.

RESPIGHI, OTTORINO          *Born:* Bologna, Italy
                                       July 9, 1879
                           *Died:* Rome
                                       April 18, 1936

Born to a musical family, Respighi started music study early in life. After being given his first music lessons by his father, Ottorino attended the Bologna Liceo (where his teachers included Martucci and Sarti) and from which he was graduated in 1899. Later study took place in St. Petersburg with Rimsky-Korsakov and in Berlin with Bruch. All this while, he was writing works for orchestra and operas. One of his operas, *Re Enzo,* was produced in Bologna in 1905; an orchestral work, *Notturno,* was performed in New York City in the same year.

Respighi became famous with the symphonic poem, *The Fountains of Rome,* written in 1916, and still one of his finest works. With this, and two later symphonic poems about Rome—*Pines of Rome* in 1924, and *Roman Festivals* in 1929—Respighi showed a remarkable gift for musical pictorialism. But many of his orchestral works were in the neo-classical vein, calling for classical forms of the past and constructed out of old modes and plain chants.

Though he achieved his greatest importance as a composer for orchestra—he was one of the leaders of the school in Italy attempting to bring about a renaissance of symphonic music, after so many years of Italian concentration on opera—he did not neglect the stage. He scored a major success with *Belfagor,* given by La Scala in 1923; and a triumph with *The Sunken Bell,* first seen in Hamburg in 1927, and given by the Metropolitan Opera House in New York in 1932.

Respighi enjoyed a long and successful career as teacher of composition, principally at the Santa Cecilia Academy in Rome, whose director he became in 1924. He visited the United States several times, the first time in the winter of 1925–1926. He died of a heart attack.

| | |
|---|---|
| RIMSKY-KORSAKOV, NICHOLAS | *Born:* Tikhvin, Novgorod<br>March 18, 1844<br>*Died:* St. Petersburg<br>June 21, 1908 |

Rimsky-Korsakov, who was born to an aristocratic family, started playing the piano at six, and began composition at nine. Since his family wanted him to pursue a naval career, he entered the Naval College in St. Petersburg in 1856. At the same time he continued with his musical interests. In 1861, he met Balakirev who aroused in him the ambition to become a composer—and, especially, a composer of Russian national music. However, for three years, Rimsky-Korsakov had to pursue his naval studies outside of Russia, and it was at this time that he started composing seriously, completing his first symphony. Its success, when introduced under Balakirev's direction in St. Petersburg in 1865, encouraged him to write other works. In 1871, he was appointed professor of composition and instrumentation at the St. Petersburg Conservatory. Two years later, he gave up his naval commission and henceforth specialized in music.

He now played a dominant role in Russian music. For more than three decades he was one of Russia's most influential teachers of music. He also conducted numerous concerts at which young composers and new music were continually given a hearing. And he wrote music in many different forms: operas, like *The Snow Maiden, Sadko,* and *The Golden Cockerel* (*Le Coq d'or*); orchestral music, like the *Antar Symphony,* the *Russian Easter Overture,* and most famous of all, the *Scheherezade;* choral music, piano pieces, and songs. In these works the theories of the national school known as the "Russian Five," and of which he was a member, were crystallized. To his beautiful and unmistakably Russian melodies he brought a daring harmony and a phenomenal virtuosity at orchestration.

Because Rimsky-Korsakov expressed dissatisfaction with the way the St. Petersburg Conservatory was run, he was dismissed from the faculty. His dismissal created such a scandal that he was soon restored to his position, and the director was replaced. He remained on the faculty until the end of his life.

ROSSINI, GIOACCHINO     *Born:* Pesaro, Italy
                                                     February 29, 1792
                                             *Died:* Passy, France
                                                     November 13, 1868

Rossini was a very musical child. By the time he was twelve he was already writing promising works. His studies took place at the Bologna Conservatory where he was a brilliant pupil. Soon after leaving the Conservatory he was commissioned to write a one-act opera for Venice. Three years later he achieved his first major success with a serious opera, *Tancredi,* introduced in Venice in 1813. Other successes followed, the most notable being that of *L'Italiana in Algeri.*

In 1813, Rossini became director of the Naples Opera, for which he wrote a new opera each year. His contract allowed him to accept commissions from other theatres. Thus, the Argentina Theatre in Rome, rather than the Naples Opera, had the historic importance of presenting the world première of *The Barber of Seville* on February 5, 1816. The first performance was a fiasco, due partly to a cabal organized by Rossini's enemies in Rome, and largely to a series of unfortunate mishaps during the presentation. The second performance went better, and the third was given an ovation. *The Barber of Seville* now settled down as a solid success and began its triumphant career as the world's greatest opera buffa.

Rossini was now the most celebrated opera composer in Italy, and possibly all Europe. He was outstandingly prolific, producing both comic and serious operas, many of them exceedingly popular. The best included: *La Cenerentola, La Gazza Ladra, Moses,* and *Zelmira.* He traveled extensively—now to Vienna, now to London, now to Paris. Everywhere he was welcomed and acclaimed as a composer of international stature. In Paris, where he settled for an extended period, he served as director of the Théâtre Italien.

Rossini's last opera, *William Tell,* was seen in Paris on August 3, 1829. Though he lived another thirty-nine years (and though, in 1829, he was at the height of his fame and creative power) he was never again to write another opera. Why he should have suddenly lapsed into silence is a mystery never adequately explained. Some say his indolence got the best of him, once he could afford to be idle; others insist that he was envious of the rising fame of competitors; still others suspect that he may have felt that his inspiration had begun to fail him. In any case, the only important work by him after *William Tell* is the *Stabat Mater*. Except for this choral masterwork, he produced only trifles.

For the remainder of his life, Rossini lived in comfort and idleness. Unfortunately, bad health disturbed the normal course of his later life: insomnia followed by neurasthenia and intense pains in the head. He died in France and was buried at the cemetery of Père Lachaise in Paris. Nineteen years later, his remains were removed from Paris to the Santa Croce Church in Florence.

ROUSSEL, ALBERT    *Born:* Turcoing, France
April 5, 1869
*Died:* Royan, France
August 23, 1937

Roussel's first love was not music but the sea. Before he became a composer he completed naval studies at the Brest Naval School and Stanislas College. He then served as midshipman on a gunboat that sailed the Eastern waters to Cochin China. All this time he was dabbling in music. By 1894, he decided to give up the sea for music. He began music study in Paris privately and continued it at the Schola Cantorum. In 1902, he was appointed professor of counterpoint at the Schola Cantorum; and six years after that he completed his first symphony, *Le Poème de la forêt*.

In 1909–10 he returned to the sea, this time as passenger on a boat bound for the East. This Eastern voyage influenced his music, for upon his return he produced many works in which the backgrounds of the East (India particularly) were prominent. One of these was a symphony for chorus and orchestra, *Évocations;* another, the opera-ballet, *Padmavati*. But the East did not completely dominate his musical thinking. In 1913 he wrote the score for a ballet which was one of his outstanding triumphs, *Le Festin de l'Araignée,* based on Fabre's *Studies of Insect Life,* produced in Paris on April 3. The orchestral suite from this score is Roussel's most famous work.

During World War I, he saw action at the front as a driver in a motor division. After the war, Roussel's musical style became simplified, economical, clear, and objective. Two of his finest works are in this idiom: the *Suite in F Major,* introduced by the Boston Symphony under Koussevitzky in 1927; and the *Symphony No. 4,* first performed by the Pasdeloup Orchestra in Paris in 1938.

In 1930, Roussel paid a visit to the United States, where he was commissioned by Serge Koussevitzky to write the *Third Symphony* in commemoration of the fiftieth anniversary of the Boston Symphony.

SAINT-SAËNS, CAMILLE     *Born:* Paris
                                                October 9, 1835
                                         *Died:* Algiers
                                                December 16, 1921

The son of simple peasants, it did not take long for Camille to give evidence of phenomenal talent. He started piano lessons when he was only two-and-a-half; wrote his first compositions and made his debut as pianist at five; and at ten gave a piano recital (which included concertos by Mozart and Beethoven) that was extravagantly praised. He entered the Paris Conservatory in his thirteenth year, after preliminary studies with Stamaty and Maleden. He won many prizes at the Conservatory and impressed his teachers with his brilliance. But, because he was too young, he was denied the Prix de Rome.

After leaving the Conservatory, he became organist at a small Parisian church and, in 1857, organist at the Madeleine. Meanwhile he began achieving some measure of recognition as a composer with two symphonies, the second winning the Prize of the Société Sainte Cécile. A man of boundless energy, Saint-Saëns continued to write prolifically, at the same time pursuing his careers as concert pianist, organist, teacher (at the École Niedermeyer), editor, and theorist. In 1871, he helped organize the Société Nationale de Musique, an important force in bringing about performances of new French music.

His first major works came in 1871: his first tone poem, *Le Rouet d'Omphale;* and his first opera, *La Princesse jaune,* the latter performed by the Opéra Comique in Paris. Among the important works to follow were the *Concerto for Cello and Orchestra* and the tone poem *Phaëton,* in 1873; the tone poem *Danse macabre,* in 1874; and his masterwork, the opera *Samson and Delilah,* first given in Weimar on December 2, 1877, and with immense success, but not incorporated into the repertory of the Paris Opéra until fifteen years later.

Saint-Saëns was an extraordinarily prolific and facile composer. He wrote in every possible form, his opus numbers passing the 150 mark.

He had an extraordinary technique and an ingratiating melodic charm; but he was never particularly original or profound. Much of what he wrote is already dated. His best works—the *Fourth Piano Concerto,* the *Third Symphony,* the *Carnival of Animals,* and *Samson and Delilah* particularly—have seductive beauty, elegant workmanship, and impeccable taste. In 1881, Saint-Saëns was appointed to the Institut de France, an indication of his high station in French music. He traveled extensively up to the end of his life, paying two visits to the United States. He died while on a holiday in Algiers.

SARASATE, PABLO

*Born:* Pamplona, Spain
March 10, 1844
*Died:* Biarritz, France
September 20, 1908

Sarasate was a child prodigy who made his first concert tour as violinist when he was six years old. Intensive study began at the Paris Conservatory in his twelfth year. He won honor after honor and when he reached fifteen was pronounced ready for the concert stage. From this time on, Sarasate performed in all the music centres of the world, achieving world renown with his phenomenal technique and profound musicianship. He received innumerable honors. Many composers, including Lalo, wrote works expressly for his use.

As a composer, Sarasate is best known for his many violin pieces in which Spanish folk melodies and rhythms are used with brilliant effect. Most famous are two malagueñas, the *Jota Aragonesa,* and *Romanza Andalusa.* Gypsy, rather than Spanish, melodies are developed in one of his most popular compositions, the *Zigeunerweisen.*

Sarasate died a rich man at his beautiful villa at Biarritz, a victim of acute bronchitis. He bequeathed his wealth, together with his celebrated instruments, to conservatories in Madrid and Pamplona.

SATIE, ERIK

*Born:* Honfleur, France
March 17, 1866
*Died:* Paris
July 1, 1925

Satie entered the Paris Conservatory in 1883 but stayed there only a single year, impatient with its academic routines. He started at once to write piano pieces in which Debussy's later harmonic writing was foreshadowed and which adopted such unorthodox practices as barless notation. In 1886, he wrote *Ogives,* and followed it with *Sarabandes, Gnossiennes,* and *Gymnopédies.*

Serious musicians refused to take him seriously. For one thing, he earned his living as a hack pianist in Montmartre. For another, as he kept on writing, he exploited whimsy and grotesquerie to excessive lengths. He gave his pieces such outlandish titles as "Flabby Preludes for a Dog" and "Desiccated Embryos," and he provided such startling instructions as "to be played dry as a cuckoo, light as an egg" and "like a nightingale with a toothache." Musical Paris was inclined to consider him a charlatan. But he was actually a powerful and healthy influence in the music of his day. He was rebelling against the German Romantic traditions that exploited huge forms, a big style, and pretentiousness of approach. He was bringing music back to simplicity, economy, restraint, and wit.

Dissatisfied with his technique, Satie decided in his fortieth year to return to study. He entered the Schola Cantorum and became a pupil of Roussel and Vincent d'Indy. He now engaged upon works more ambitious in form than heretofore—though he still remained true to his ideal for precision and terseness. The most important were the jazz ballet, *Parade,* introduced by the Ballet Russe in Paris in 1917; and the lyric drama, *Socrate.*

He exerted a great influence on his contemporaries. Debussy was first given direction by Satie; and Ravel imitated Satie in his first pieces. Satie's principles also had a far-reaching effect on the members of the "French Six." In the early 1920's, Satie was the godfather of still another French musical school, known as the "Arcueilists," and which included Sauguet and Désormière.

SCARLATTI, DOMENICO     *Born:* Naples
                        October 26, 1685
                        *Died:* Madrid
                        July 23, 1757

Domenico's father, Alessandro Scarlatti (1660–1725), was a celebrated composer of Italian operas, who established the Neapolitan

School. Domenico was largely taught by his father; and soon revealed talent in two directions, in playing the harpsichord and in composition. Eventually he established a reputation as performer on the harpsichord that spanned all of Europe. In Rome (which Scarlatti made his home after 1702), Cardinal Ottoboni arranged a "duel" between Scarlatti and Handel to settle the question as to who was superior at the harpsichord. The "duel" was judged to be a draw.

An appointment as staff musician to Queen Marie Casimire of Poland, in 1709, drew him into the theatre. He now wrote numerous operas which were successfully performed. In 1715, Scarlatti became Maestro di Cappella at St. Peter's Cathedral in Rome. During the last twenty-five years of his life he lived in Madrid, serving for much of that time as music master to the royal family. It was during this period in Madrid that he wrote the works with which he achieved his greatest significance: the *Esercizii,* or as they are now called the *Sonatas,* for harpsichord. These works inaugurated a new era in keyboard music, and are described in the section on Piano Music.

SCHMITT, FLORENT          *Born:* Blâmont, France
                                     September 28, 1870

After combining academic study with that of music, Schmitt entered the Paris Conservatory in his nineteenth year. His teachers included Lavignac, Gédalge, and Dubois. Study was temporarily interrupted when Schmitt had to complete a year of military service; it was resumed at the Conservatory with Massenet and Fauré. In 1900 he won the Prix de Rome. During the early part of the twentieth century, Schmitt completed his first major works—and in some respects they are his best: the *Psalm 47; Quintet in B Minor;* and the ballet, *The Tragedy of Salome.* Later works include numerous compositions for orchestra, chorus, and chamber-music groups together with songs and piano pieces. A remarkable craftsman, Schmitt is notable for his aristocratic style and his refinement and grace and deep feeling for tonal beauty.

In 1922, Schmitt became director of the Lyons Conservatory. He held this post for two years. In 1936, he was elected a member of the French Academy.

SCHOENBERG, ARNOLD    *Born:* Vienna
                                    September 13, 1874
                            *Died:* Brentwood, California
                                    July 13, 1951

     Schoenberg began his music study at the Realschule in Vienna and continued it privately with Alexander Zemlinsky (whose sister he later married). Under Zemlinsky's guidance, Schoenberg wrote his first works, which were in a Wagnerian style, the best and most famous being *Verklaerte Nacht.* For a period, he lived in Berlin where he conducted a cabaret orchestra. During this period he began to work on the *Gurre-Lieder,* still a fruit of his Romantic tendencies. In 1903, he returned to Vienna where he devoted himself to teaching as well as composition. From this time on his writing grew increasingly audacious in harmony, tonality, and melody. His style, which became independent of key relationships, was formed between the years of 1909 and 1912 with *Five Pieces for Orchestra; Six Pieces for Piano;* and the song cycle, *Pierrot Lunaire.* From atonality Schoenberg progressed to the twelve-tone technique, an arbitrary style based on twelve definite tones, each equally important, and used according to a set pattern. This technique, first employed in the *Serenade,* was further developed in the *Third and Fourth String Quartets* and in several major orchestral works. Schoenberg here uncovered a new world of sound, frequently strident, ugly, and high-tensioned. When performed, his music inspired one scandal after another. At one Schoenberg concert, in 1913, an actual riot developed between those who considered the music a fraud and those who defended it.

    After World War I, an entire school grew up around Schoenberg. It included Alban Berg, Egon Wellesz, and Anton von Webern who believed in his theories and wrote music in his individual style. In 1933, with the rise of the Nazi government in Germany, Schoenberg decided to leave Europe. He lived in this country from that time till his death, principally in California, devoted to teaching and composition. In some of his later works, Schoenberg occasionally abandoned the twelve-tone system to write music in a definite key signature and aurally agreeable. But most of his works remained in his own style which limits their appeal to the musical *cognoscenti.* His last important works included *Ode to Napoleon, Theme and Variations,* for orchestra, and

*A Survivor from Warsaw.* In 1947, Schoenberg received a Special Award of Merit from the National Institute of Arts and Letters.

SCHUBERT, FRANZ      *Born:* Vienna
January 31, 1797
*Died:* Vienna
November 19, 1828

Schubert was the son of a parish schoolmaster. When Franz was eleven he became a chorister of the Imperial Court Chapel, where he received an intensive musical training. His voice broke, in 1813, and he was compelled to leave the Chapel. He now prepared himself for the teaching profession, completing the necessary preliminary courses before assuming a post in his father's school. But it was the writing of music, and not teaching children, which was ever on Schubert's mind. He left the children pretty much to their own devices, as he sat at his desk scribbling melodies. When the school day ended, he was free to deliver himself entirely to composition, and he would often work through half the night. He seemed unable to contain the music that was within him, it burst from him turbulently. In the year 1815 alone he produced two symphonies, five operas, two masses, choral works, sonatas, and almost one hundred fifty songs. One of these songs was destined to change the history of music. It was the "Erlkönig." With that song, and with another written a year earlier, "Gretchen am Spinnrade," the Romantic German song (the *Lied*) was born.

Schubert tolerated the drudgery of schoolteaching for three years. Then, without any means of support, he gave up his job and embarked on a merry Bohemian life. The friendships that now surrounded him were to remain with him for the rest of his life: the poet, Mayrhofer; the famous singer, Johann Vogl; Spaun, who had been a fellow-student at the Chapel; Schobert and Hüttenbrenner. This was a happy-go-lucky group which enjoyed evening parties, gaiety at the café house, and even mischief-making in the streets of Vienna. When one had money, everybody ate and drank well. When money was scarce they had good times at pleasant social affairs which acquired the name of *Schubertiaden,* or Schubert Evenings.

First he lived with Mayrhofer, and after that with one or another of his friends. It was mostly a pauper's life. Except for a brief summer's post as music teacher at the Esterházy estate in Zelész, Hungary, in

1818, he held no position; earned nothing from his music; had no pupils. He depended on the generosity of his friends, who had implicit faith in his genius and loved him.

Even though his music was neither published nor performed, he kept on writing with amazing fertility—symphonies, operas, songs, chamber music. Being ignored by the world of music did not stem the tide of his creation. But, in 1820, there was a promise of a change of fortune. Two operas of his were given public performances. Unfortunately, both were failures and did nothing to improve Schubert's position. In 1821, the first of his works was published—a group of friends subsidizing the release of some songs, including the "Erlkönig." This publication made very little impression since the songs were generally regarded as too difficult for adequate performance.

These and other failures brought on depression, which was often combined with poor health. An occasional appreciative gesture—such as the appointment as honorary member to the Musikverein in Graz in 1823—was only temporary balm to his stinging wounds. Schubert could not forget that he was unknown and a failure, surviving only because his friends were generous. But in spite of morbidity and poor health, he kept on working, and he kept on producing masterpieces.

Not until the end of his life did there take place a concert devoted mostly to his works—in Vienna on March 26, 1826. For the first time, Schubert's music met with an appreciative response; and Schubert had every right to believe that the tide had, at last, turned in his favor. But it had turned too late. He had been ailing for some time, frequently compelled to enter a hospital. Personal neglect brought about an inevitable physical disintegration. After a walking trip, in the summer of 1828, he started suffering from fainting spells and nausea. Schubert had become a victim of typhus. He died as he had lived—a pauper. His only belongings were some old clothes and his manuscripts. Many of his masterworks were allowed to gather dust in forgotten corners for many years before being rediscovered.

Schubert was the first giant figure in the Romantic period of music. By bringing to music his highly personal feelings, by making it more expressive emotionally than it had ever been, by permitting form a greater elasticity, and by emphasizing beautiful melody, he brought the art of music toward a new day. An appraisal of his songs, symphonies, piano sonatas, and chamber music will be found in later sections of this book.

## SCHUMAN, WILLIAM

*Born:* New York City
August 4, 1910

Schuman first studied privately, and after that at the Malkin School of Music, the Mozarteum in Salzburg, and with Charles Haubiel and Roy Harris. He discarded his first symphony and first string quartet as unworthy. But his *Third Symphony,* introduced by the Boston Symphony under Koussevitzky on October 17, 1941, was a success of the first order and made Schuman known to the general music public. He then wrote a cantata, *A Free Song,* which won the Pulitzer Prize; the *Third String Quartet* (which received the Town Hall League of Composers' Award); and the *Symphony for Strings,* commissioned by the Koussevitzky Foundation. Now recognized as an American composer of major significance, Schuman became the recipient of several other honors and awards. For ten years, beginning with 1935, he taught music at the Sarah Lawrence College. In 1945, he was appointed president of the Juilliard School of Music.

Other significant works include the *Sixth Symphony;* the *Concerto for Violin and Orchestra;* the ballets *Night Journey* and *Undertow.* His style is primarily contrapuntal but has a sensitive atmosphere and a compelling emotion.

## SCHUMANN, ROBERT

*Born:* Zwickau, Germany
June 8, 1810
*Died:* Endenich, Germany
July 29, 1856

Schumann's boyhood enthusiasms included great literature as well as poetry, and for a time he entertained the ambition of becoming a poet. But he was intended for the law, and for this purpose he was sent to Leipzig to begin his studies. There he attended concerts and studied the piano with Friederich Wieck. In an attempt to divorce him from music and to bring him closer to law, his mother sent him from Leipzig to Heidelberg. But a change of scene did not bring about a change of heart in Schumann. He neglected law more than ever until, in 1830, he announced to his mother his irrevocable decision to become a professional musician. He returned to Leipzig, bringing back with him the sketches of his first works, all for piano: *Papillons, Variations on Abegg,* and *Toccata.*

The zeal with which he applied himself to the study of the piano—for his goal was to become a concert pianist—brought about a temporary paralysis of the hand. His dreams of becoming a virtuoso shattered, Schumann decided to concentrate on composition. In preparation for his lifework he spent two years of study with Heinrich Dorn.

Idealistic and ambitious, Schumann now organized a society which he called the Davidsbündler. King David had conquered the Philistines—in the same way Schumann and his young followers would triumph over the Philistines of their art. They would fight to maintain the highest ideals in their art and to smash sham and hypocrisy wherever they were found. To provide themselves with a voice, they founded a music journal, the *Neue Zeitschrift für Musik,* the first issue appearing on April 3, 1844.

A sensitive constitution combined with overwork brought about a nervous collapse in 1833. He suffered fainting fits and melancholia. Creative work provided a measure of relief from his morbidity. It was during this trying emotional period that he completed his first masterworks, all for the piano: the *Études symphoniques* and the *Carnaval.*

It was soon after he had recovered from his neurasthenia that Schumann entered upon the most turbulent period of his life, that of his love affair with Clara, daughter of his teacher, Friederich Wieck.

Clara fell in love with Robert when she was only twelve years old and it was some time before he began noticing her. What first attracted him to her was her phenomenal talent as a pianist; and only later was he drawn to her personally. By the time Clara was sixteen, their love for each other was mutually recognized and accepted. Unfortunately, Clara's father did not look with favor upon the match. He did not want her promising career as virtuoso to be disturbed by marital responsibilities; and he did not regard an indigent composer as a desirable son-in-law. He tried to poison her against Schumann and failing that he did everything in his power—deceit, lies, strategy, and threats —to break up the affair. For a period, Clara was ordered not to see her beloved. The love affair continued nevertheless, sometimes through an exchange of secret letters, sometimes through hurried clandestine meetings. At last, Schumann decided to take action in the law courts. He won his suit, and on September 12, 1840 he finally married Clara.

His happiness now ignited his creative spark and set it aflame. Turning from piano music to songs he produced some of the most beautiful love songs since Schubert. In 1841, he started writing for the orchestra, producing two symphonies. From orchestral music he turned to chamber music, completing the celebrated *Piano Quintet*, the *Piano Quartet*, and three string quartets.

This idyllic period of love and wonderful creation was aborted by an alarming deterioration of his health. He began hearing strange sounds and seeing sights. In one of his irrational moments he tried committing suicide by plunging into the icy waters of the Rhine. Finally, he had to be placed in an asylum; and it was there that he died.

Schumann was the greatest Romantic composer after Schubert. He filled all his works with a wealth of poetry, feeling, and fancy. There are two predominant traits in his music: one is poetic, tender, meditative, and at times even elegiac; the other is stormy and passionate.

He was at his best in the smaller pieces for the piano in which a new inventiveness of piano writing was combined with the most varied reveries and fancies. Since his larger piano works are actually made up of many small pieces they fall into this category. He was also a master of the art song. His piano works and songs—as well as his symphonies and chamber music—are treated in later sections.

SCRIABIN, ALEXANDER        *Born:* Moscow
                             January 6, 1872
                         *Died:* London
                             April 27, 1915

As a child he demonstrated unusual talent for music, and with it an obsession for the piano. But before he concentrated on music study he was directed toward a military career. He entered the Moscow Military School in 1882. Only after he had completed his military studies did he devote himself to music. He now entered the Moscow Conservatory where he won the gold medal for piano playing in 1891 and, as a pupil of Arensky and Taneiev, revealed a marked creative talent.

He left the Conservatory without his diploma and embarked on a career as concert pianist. The powerful publisher Belaiev became interested in him, gave him a profitable publishing contract, and financed his career. Under Belaiev's direction Scriabin made his first extensive tour of Europe and was an immense success. Belaiev also published Scriabin's first sonatas and études. Between 1898 and 1903, Scriabin taught the piano at the Moscow Conservatory, but he was not happy as a teacher and gave up his position with relief. For a while he was financed by a pupil; but in 1908 he found another influential patron in the person of Serge Koussevitzky, the brilliant young conductor, and the director of a publishing house in Moscow. The composer accompanied Koussevitzky and his orchestra on their tour of the Volga in 1910 and appeared in performances of his own *Piano Concerto*. After Koussevitzky had directed the world première of Scriabin's *Prometheus Symphony* they parted company for good—the relationship was from the beginning a conflict of temperaments—but Koussevitzky never relented in his efforts to perform and propagandize the music of Scriabin.

Meanwhile, since the turn of the twentieth century, Scriabin had been interesting himself in mysticism and theosophy. This direction had a profound effect on his music. In 1903 he wrote the symphony, *The Divine Poem*, which tried to trace the evolution of the human spirit from its bondage to old beliefs and pleasures to its ultimate freedom. Four years later he completed *The Poem of Ecstasy*, a paean to creative activity. In *Prometheus*, written in 1910, he described man asserting his Creative Will through a divine spark given him by Prometheus.

From the writing of music endowed with mysticism he progressed to the conception of a Gargantuan concept which he called "The Mystery." He was thinking of a new kind of art which would combine every artistic element known to man. This art would express the evolution of man from the beginning of time to the final cataclysm, which Scriabin believed was inevitable. He saw the emergence of a new age and a new race, and he planned his "Mystery" as the transition from the old day to the new, and the voice of the new civilization. He wanted his "Mystery" to be performed in India in a special globular theatre built for this purpose; and he described his prospective audience as worshipers of a new religion.

He planned his "Mystery" for many years but succeeded in writing only the text and a few musical sketches for a preamble. His premature death, brought about by a skin infection, aborted this fabulous project.

It is not so much in the large work, with its weighty philosophical implications, that Scriabin is most important as a composer, but in his pieces for the piano—his preludes, études and sonatas, described in the later section on Piano Music.

SHOSTAKOVICH, DMITRI     *Born:* Leningrad
                                                    September 25, 1906

His mother began teaching him the piano when he was nine years old. After that he was enrolled at the Glasser Music School in Leningrad. Soon after his entrance he wrote his first piece of music, *Theme and Variations,* for piano. Despite the turmoil attending the Revolution in 1917, Shostakovich continued his studies at both academic and music schools. In 1919, he entered the Leningrad Conservatory where his teachers included Steinberg and Nikolaiev. He proved his rapidly ripening creative talent by writing some excellent preludes and the first of his works to be published, *Three Fantastic Dances.* He was graduated from the Conservatory in 1926. For that occasion he wrote his *First Symphony* which was introduced by the Leningrad Philharmonic under Malko on May 12, 1916. It was an immense success, and was soon after that heard in Moscow, Berlin, and in the United States. It has since become Shostakovich's most famous work. In the next few years Shostakovich wrote two more symphonies; an opera, *The Nose;* and a ballet, *The Age of Gold.* All were failures, though the ballet won first prize in a national competition for a ballet on a Soviet subject. But success returned with *Twenty-Four Preludes,* for piano; the *Piano Concerto;* and the opera, *Lady Macbeth of Mzensk,* which ran for two years to capacity audiences.

This opera inspired the first of several official attacks. Though it had run for two years to the acclaim of both public and critics, it was suddenly singled out by an editorialist in *Pravda* for violent denunciation. A year later, Shostakovich's next major work, the ballet, *The Limpid Stream,* was also denounced officially. For a while, Shostakovich was in disrepute, and it seemed that his day was over. But on November 21, 1937 there took place the première of his *Fifth Symphony* which was a sensation, and his star rose once more. In 1940, with the winning of the Stalin Prize for his *Piano Quintet,* his rehabilitation was complete.

When the Nazis invaded the Soviet Union in 1941, Shostakovich joined the fire-fighting brigade at the Leningrad Conservatory. He wrote several major works inspired by the war. The most widely publicized of these compositions was the *Seventh Symphony,* sometimes called the *Leningrad Symphony* because it purported to describe the effects of the siege of Leningrad on the Soviet people.

Though Shostakovich was by now a public hero, his trials were not over. His *Ninth Symphony,* though liked by critics and audiences, was accused of "ideological weakness" by Soviet officialdom. Much more serious was the condemnation of all his music by the Central Committee of the Communist Party on February 10, 1948, when the works of some of the leading Soviet composers of the time were denounced as too cerebral, too much addicted to modernism, too much enslaved by "bourgeois conventions." Once again Shostakovich was to emerge from disgrace with flying banners. Confessing the error of his ways, he started writing the kind of music that was demanded and produced the oratorio, *The Song of the Forests,* which won the Stalin Prize.

In March, 1949, Shostakovich visited the United States for the first time, a member of a seven-man Soviet delegation attending the Cultural and Scientific Conference for World Peace held in New York. His visit to the United States was suddenly terminated when the State Department revoked his visa and compelled him to return home.

Shostakovich's music has been subjected to a great difference of critical opinion. There are those who regard him as one of the great creative figures of our time, and others who insist that he has been too highly praised. The reason for this difference of opinion is that Shostakovich is sometimes very good, and sometimes very bad—and, on occasion, in the same work. At times he achieves a grandeur of expression and spaciousness of design as in the *Fifth Symphony,* and wit that is a continual source of delight. But at other times he is pompous and synthetic. However, he has an exceptional technique, and when he is at his best a charming lyrical gift and irresistible force and strength. His best symphonies are discussed in the section on the Symphony.

SIBELIUS, JEAN                     *Born:* Tavastehus, Finland
                                   December 8, 1865

Systematic study of the piano was begun when Jean was nine years old, and one year after that he produced his first composition. Academic study was not neglected. In his eleventh year he entered the Finnish Model Lyceum where he was well liked. Music was continued, the study of the violin beginning when he was fifteen. After the Lyceum, Sibelius entered the University of Helsingfors to study law.

But legal studies bored him and he knew, after a year at the University, that he had to dedicate himself to music. He now entered the Music Academy, where his teachers included Ferruccio Busoni (then visiting Finland) and Martin Wegelius. After that, he became a pupil of Albert Becker in Berlin and Karl Goldmark and Robert Fuchs in Vienna. During his prolonged stay in Germany and Austria, he completed an orchestral overture and an octet, both in the Romantic style then popular in Germany.

It was not long before Sibelius stopped imitating the Germans and arrived at his own style. This happened after his return to his native land, and he became inflamed with patriotism and the ideal of writing national music. His first nationalistic work was a five-movement symphonic poem, *Kullervo,* heard in Helsingfors in 1892. It was successful; in its music the Finnish people could identify their own strivings for freedom. His course now charted, Sibelius wrote music that was the voice and the inspiration of his people: *En Saga,* in 1892, and after that the *Karelia Suite,* the *Four Legends* (inspired by the Finnish epic, the *Kalevala;* one of these "legends" is the famous "The Swan of Tuonela"), and a work sometimes described as the most stirring piece of national music ever written, *Finlandia.* These compositions established Sibelius as a major musical figure in his own country, and the spokesman for Finland to the outside world.

Meanwhile, Sibelius married Ainö Jarnefelt, and began earning his living by teaching at the Musical Academy and at the orchestral school of the Philharmonic Society, and by playing the violin in a string quartet. In 1897, he was permanently relieved of the necessity of earning his living by a government stipend providing a regular income.

In 1899, Sibelius completed his *First Symphony.* Between that year and 1924 he wrote seven symphonies from which he emerged as the foremost symphonic composer since Brahms, and the most widely performed and admired symphonist of the twentieth century. These works are described in a later section on the Symphony. (Sibelius' best tone poems are discussed in the section on the Symphonic Poem.)

Sibelius visited the United States in 1914 on an invitation to conduct his works at the Norfolk Music Festival. The period of World War I brought deprivations and hardships. After the war, Sibelius lived in comparative retirement on his estate in Jarvenpää (forty miles' distance from Helsingfors) where his need for solitude and his love of nature were both satisfied. He was now acknowledged to be one of the giant figures in twentieth century music, and a national hero. His seventy-fifth, eightieth, and eighty-fifth birthdays were celebrated throughout the world with tributes befitting a composer who has become a classic in his own lifetime.

Besides the seven symphonies and various orchestral works already commented upon, Sibelius has written a *Concerto for Violin and Orchestra,* a string quartet entitled *Voces Intimae,* several familiar orchestral works including *Tapiola* and *Valse triste,* and some songs and piano pieces.

SMETANA, BEDRICH        *Born:* Litomischl, Bohemia
                                       March 2, 1824
                             *Died:* Prague
                                       May 12, 1884


At the age of five, Smetana played the violin well enough to join a string quartet; before he was seven he made his public debut as pianist and wrote several compositions. Despite these obvious signs of talent, he was given a thorough academic training and was not permitted to specialize in music until his nineteenth year. At that time he settled in Prague for additional music study. This was a period of great hardship and deprivation. Financial security did not come until 1850 when he was appointed concertmaster of an orchestra engaged by Ferdinand I, former Austrian Emperor. Two major works were completed soon after this appointment: the *Triumph Symphonie,* commemorating the marriage of Franz Joseph of Austria; and the *Trio in G Minor,* inspired by the sudden death of his four-year-old daughter. In 1856, Smetana left for Gothenburg, Sweden where, for the next few years, he was active as teacher and conductor. Back in Prague, in 1861, he became infected with nationalistic ardor. It was now that he was fired with the ambition of developing the musical life of his native land. He headed an art society in Prague, opened a new musical school, and directed a choral group. He also aspired to write national music. The most significant of his national works was the folk opera, *The Bartered Bride,* first produced in 1866. Though not at first successful, the opera (after several revisions) subsequently made its composer the spokesman for national Bohemian music. Another famous work in his national style was the tone poem, *The Moldau* (see section on the Symphonic Poem). Smetana also wrote a fine string quartet, *From My Life* (see section on Chamber Music).

Misfortune dogged Smetana's footsteps throughout his life. After the death of his four-year-old daughter his first wife passed away suddenly. Other tragedies came toward the end of his life: deafness in 1874; a nervous breakdown in 1882; insanity in 1884. He died in an insane asylum.

STRAUSS, JOHANN II

*Born:* Vienna
    October 25, 1825
*Died:* Vienna
    June 3, 1899

His father, also named Johann Strauss, was one of Vienna's earliest waltz kings. For some unknown reason, the father tried to keep his son from music, and little Johann had to learn the violin secretly. When the father deserted his family, Johann was able to follow his natural musical inclinations openly by studying the violin, harmony and counterpoint. He made his debut as café-house conductor at Dommayer's Casino on October 15, 1844. The debut was a sensation, and the reputation of the young musician was made. After the death of his father, in 1849, Johann Strauss was without a rival in café-house music. As a conductor, he had a great gift for inspiring his men. And as a composer, he had incomparable melodic and rhythmic gifts. His best waltzes were written after his marriage to Henrietta Treffz in 1864. She was the inspiration for such gems as *The Blue Danube, Artist's Life, Tales from the Vienna Woods,* and *Wine, Women and Song.* It was also owing to her encouragement and urging that he was able to enter a sphere more ambitious than the waltz—notably, the operetta. In 1873 he produced his masterwork, *Die Fledermaus,* and followed it with the *Zigeunerbaron.* When Henrietta died in 1878, Strauss' best works had been written.

Meanwhile, in 1872, Strauss visited the United States to participate in the commemoration of the centenary of American independence. He conducted an orchestra of a thousand instruments and a chorus of a thousand voices in *The Blue Danube* and was given a hero's acclaim.

In 1894, there took place in Vienna a monumental celebration honoring the fiftieth anniversary of his first appearance. He died five years later from bronchitis.

Strauss was a composer of popular music. But he brought such a fertility of ideas, freshness of viewpoint, and aristocratic taste to his music that even serious musicians like Brahms, Verdi and Wagner admired him. He was the voice of Vienna, and of an epoch now dead. Through his music we catch a glimpse of the Vienna of the Hapsburgs.

STRAUSS, RICHARD        *Born:* Munich
                        June 11, 1864
                        *Died:* Garmisch-Partenkirchen,
                        Bavaria
                        September 8, 1949

Richard Strauss was no relation to the waltz king whose biography appears above. His father was a famous horn player who early directed his son to music. Strauss received an intensive musical education with Benno Walter (violin), August Tombo (piano), and F. W. Meyer (harmony and instrumentation). Strauss produced several major works before his eighteenth birthday, and some of them were given important performances. Benno Walter introduced his string quartet, and the celebrated Wagnerian conductor, Hermann Levi, gave the première of his *Symphony in D Minor.*

Strauss attracted the interest and enthusiasm of one of Germany's most powerful musicians, Hans von Bülow, director of the Meiningen Orchestra. This orchestra, under von Bülow, performed several of Strauss' early works for orchestra. Hans von Bülow appointed Strauss as his assistant; and, before long, Strauss succeeded von Bülow as principal conductor.

In his earliest works, Strauss remained true to the German Romantic traditions then in vogue, and frequently wrote in the style of Brahms or Wagner. A change in his style, and in his entire musical outlook, came with his friendship for Alexander Ritter, a musician philosopher. Ritter urged Strauss to carry only Wagner's torch, to turn to dramatic and poetic expression rather than Romanticism; to strive for structural freedom; to abandon objectivity for programmatic writing. Given a new direction and a new set of ideals, Strauss wrote a symphonic fantasy, *Aus Italien,* in 1886. In 1887, he produced his first tone poem, *Macbeth.* Then in a geyser eruption of genius he produced a series of tone poems which established him as the most controversial composer of his time and rocked the musical world with its harmonic and instrumental daring and its musical realism. These works include *Don Juan, Till Eulenspiegel's Merry Pranks, Death and Transfiguration, Thus Spake Zarathustra, A Hero's Life,* and *Don Quixote.* They are ·discussed in the section on the Symphonic Poem.

Before the period of his tone poems, he wrote the first of his wonderful songs. With "Allerseelen" and "Zueignung," written between 1882 and 1883 (four years before the first tone poem) he demonstrated his lyric powers. Then came such masterpieces as "Ständchen," "Cäcilie," "Traum durch die Dämmerung"—and Strauss proved his right to belong with the great composers of Lieder.

His mastery in orchestral and vocal music fully established, Strauss set out to conquer another musical world: opera. His first two operatic attempts were failures. But in 1905 he wrote *Salome.* It was his first masterwork for the stage; and it revived the bitter scandals and controversies that had raged around his name in the 1890's. For, to its contemporaries, *Salome* appeared immoral and decadent. After *Salome,* Strauss wrote *Elektra,* and *Der Rosenkavalier,* two works which must be numbered with the greatest operas of our generation.

By 1914, Strauss was at the height of his fame and genius. Though he wrote many works after 1914, his creative powers disintegrated. He could be adroit, witty, charming and facile, but he had lost the faculty of being powerful and original and inventive. Such triumphs as he was to gather after 1914 came to him as a conductor. He appeared in most of the capitals of Europe and visited the United States twice.

When the Nazis first came to power, Strauss aligned himself with the new masters and held office as President of the Third Reich Music Chamber. But he soon diverged from the principles of his superiors. When they objected to his collaborating with the Jewish writer Stefan Zweig, he resigned his official post and went into retirement at his home in the Bavarian Alps. During World War II, he lived in Switzerland; toward the end of the war he lived at his Bavarian house. After the war, Strauss was invited to London to direct a concert of his works in a Strauss festival. He was wildly acclaimed. He came in for honors again on the occasion of his eighty-fifth birthday. He died soon after that. His last works include several concertos; *Metamorphosen,* for twenty-three solo strings; and the operas *Die Liebe der Danae* and *Capriccio.* In all of his last works he reverted to the Romantic tendencies of his youth.

STRAVINSKY, IGOR                *Born:* Oranienbaum, Russia
                                June 17, 1882

He was the son of a well-known opera singer, who wanted him to become a lawyer. Only after Stravinsky had enrolled at the St. Petersburg University for the advanced study of law did he begin the formal study of harmony. After learning some counterpoint from a textbook, he started composing. He showed these early efforts to Rimsky-Korsakov who, truth to tell, was not greatly impressed. However, when Stravinsky returned to him two years later with a piano sonata, Rimsky-Korsakov urged him to give up law for music. Stravinsky now studied for two years with Rimsky-Korsakov and under his guidance completed a symphony and *Le Faune et la bergère.* These two works, and its immediate successors—*Scherzo fantastique* and *Fireworks*—were publicly performed. The famous impresario of the recently formed Ballet Russe heard the last two works and was fascinated by their original instrumentation. He commissioned Stravinsky to orchestrate some Chopin pieces for a Chopin ballet. Fulfilling this assignment to Diaghilev's satisfaction, Stravinsky was then given his first major assignment: the score for a new ballet with a scenario by Fokine, *The Fire-Bird. The Fire-Bird,* introduced in Paris on January 25, 1910, was such a success that the composer became famous. It was filled not only with striking harmonic, rhythmic and orchestral innovations but with exciting Slavic colors.

His next two ballets for Diaghilev—*Petrushka,* in 1911, and *The Rite of Spring* in 1913—established him as one of the most original and controversial composers of his day. With greater daring than ever, Stravinsky experimented with dissonance, polytonality, and polyrhythms to produce music unique for its elemental power and its irresistible newness.

No sooner did the music world accustom itself to the barbarism of Stravinsky's style than he was to startle it by a radical change of style. This happened after Stravinsky left Russia and set up his home first in Switzerland, then in Paris. Contact with French art and culture brought a changing set of values. Stravinsky was no longer interested in being the iconoclast, the reckless adventurer in search of new sounds. He swung to the opposite direction, aiming to write music as simply, as lucidly, and as clearly as possible, and within crystal-clear forms. The first work in this new manner was *L'Histoire du Soldat,* introduced in Switzerland in 1918. Stravinsky produced many important works in this neo-classical style: the opera-oratorio, *Oedipus Rex;* the *Symphony of Psalms;* several concertos. Once again Stravinsky became a highly controversial figure in music. Those now willing to concede the greatness of his dynamic works before World War I, insisted that his new compositions were formal and desiccated. But others found that Stravinsky had surpassed his earlier masterworks and had reached a classical and objective beauty which represented the highest sphere of his creative art.

Stravinsky visited the United States for the first time in 1925 when he conducted many American orchestras, usually in programs of his works. Just before World War II, he settled permanently in this country and became a citizen. He has written many notable works since coming here including two symphonies; a mass; the ballet *Orpheus;* an opera, *The Rake's Progress;* and the *Cantata on Anonymous Elizabethan Songs.*

SZYMANOWSKI, KAROL          *Born:* Tymoszkowka, Polish
                            Ukraine
                            September 21, 1883
                        *Died:* Lausanne, Switzerland
                            March 28, 1937

A childhood accident that injured his leg permanently made it impossible for Szymanowski to attend schools or participate in children's games. He was taught privately, and forced to keep to himself. After some music study with a local piano teacher, he wrote a set of preludes which became the first of his works to be published. He was then sent to Warsaw for additional study with Noskowski. As Noskowski's pupil, he completed a piano sonata which won first prize in a Chopin contest in Lemberg. He also wrote a *Symphonic Overture* that was performed publicly.

After completing his studies, he went to Berlin where he was affected by the German Romantic style. He started writing in this vein, but soon left Romanticism to produce an exotic kind of music affected by mysticism and Oriental philosophy. His true identity as a composer did not emerge until after he had paid a visit to the Tatras mountain region of Poland. There he heard the folk songs and dances of the

Tatras Mountains which appeared to him as a new and wonderful world. That first contact with Polish folk music convinced him to devote himself henceforth to glorifying in his music the songs and dances of his country. In 1926, he wrote the ballet *Harnasie,* its text based on a legend from the Polish Carpathian Mountains, and the music deriving its stylistic traits from the peasant music of that region. This was followed by the *Stabat Mater,* which combined the polyphonic style of the past with Polish melodies and rhythms. *Stabat Mater* brought Szymanowski his first major success in his own country.

For a while, he was the director of the Warsaw Conservatory, and after that President of the Academy of Music. But, always sickly, he could not hold any position for an extended period. In 1929, he suffered a nervous breakdown and had to go to a sanatorium. He recovered sufficiently to complete two important works: the *Symphonie Concertante,* for piano and orchestra; and the *Second Violin Concerto.* A few years later he had to return to the sanatorium near Lausanne, Switzerland. He died there of laryngeal tuberculosis.

TARTINI, GIUSEPPE       *Born:* Pirano, Italy
                                        April 8, 1692
                         *Died:* Padua, Italy
                                 February 26, 1770

Since he planned a clerical career, he enrolled for religious study at the Oratorio St. Filippo Neri and after that at the Padri delle Scuole. He abandoned his clerical studies for law, entering the University of Padua; but law proved no more palatable. He then began studying the violin and knew he had come upon his life's calling. He became one of the outstanding virtuosos in Europe. He also wrote a considerable amount of music for his instrument, including many sonatas and concertos. In 1713, he completed his masterwork, *The Devil's Trill Sonata.* Tartini was one of the most important of Corelli's successors, a major figure in the early development of Italian instrumental music.

After holding various posts, and establishing his reputation as virtuoso, he became musical leader of the orchestra of the San Antonio Church in Padua in 1721. He lived in Padua for the rest of his life. In 1728, he established there a school of violin-playing that became famous. In the closing years of his life, Tartini suffered from paralysis and a malignant growth on his foot.

TAYLOR, DEEMS          *Born:* New York City
                        December 22, 1885

Taylor received both his academic and his musical education in New York City, the latter with Oscar Coon. After being graduated from New York University he filled various jobs. In 1921, he became music editor of the *New York World,* and for the next few years he distinguished himself for his trenchant criticisms. Two years before this appointment he had made an impressive debut as composer with an orchestral suite, *Through the Looking Glass,* still one of his best works. After completing his opera, *The King's Henchman,* on a commission from the Metropolitan Opera Association—which introduced it on February 17, 1927—Taylor's fame as a composer was established. He resigned from his post as critic to concentrate on composition, completing a second opera for the Metropolitan, *Peter Ibbetson,* among other works. He has been active in many capacities during the past two decades: as editor, writer, master of ceremonies, program commentator, and so forth. He combines erudition with a charming wit and a human approach. In his music, as in everything else he does, he is technically sound and charming to listen to. Later works include the opera *Ramuntcho* and various orchestral works including an *Elegy.*

TCHAIKOVSKY, PETER        *Born:* Votinski, Viatka, Russia
ILITCH                          May 7, 1840
                          *Died:* St. Petersburg
                          November 6, 1893

Though Tchaikovsky showed unusual talent for music as a child, he was intended not for music but for law. Not until toward the completion of his law studies in St. Petersburg was he permitted to begin an intensive preparation in music. His piano teacher was Rudolf Kündinger who, strange to report, insisted that the young man had no particular aptitude for music and should continue in law. When Tchaikovsky's law studies ended, he worked for three years as clerk in the Ministry of Justice. He found himself drawn more and more to music. He undertook the study of theory with Nicolas Zaremba, and orchestration with Anton Rubinstein. He then entered the St. Petersburg Conservatory where he was a conscientious pupil. For his graduating exercise he wrote a cantata based on Schiller's "Ode to Joy" (the same poem Beethoven had set in the *Ninth Symphony*) which won a silver medal. This work impressed Nicholas Rubinstein who, on becoming director of the newly created Moscow Conservatory, appointed Tchaikovsky professor of harmony. This position made Tchaikovsky financially independent and capable of devoting his efforts to composition.

Tchaikovsky's first important works—including his *First Symphony* and his now celebrated orchestral fantasy, *Romeo and Juliet*—were failures when first introduced. This was only a part of his mounting misfortunes. He was in continual terror that his homosexual tendencies would be discovered, and this aberration made him painfully shy, self-conscious and self-centered. Notwithstanding his sexual weakness, he allowed himself to become involved first in an unhappy love affair with the singer Désirée Artôt; and then in a brief and disastrous marriage with Antonina Milinkova. He now became a victim of violent mental depressions; on one occasion he tried to commit suicide in the Neva River. His physician prescribed a change of scene. Tchaikovsky left Russia, traveling extensively in Switzerland and Italy.

His mental and physical suffering did not curtail his production of important music. He completed two more symphonies (the *Second* and *Third*); the *First Piano Concerto;* two string quartets; the orchestral fantasy, *Francesca da Rimini;* and the *Variations on a Rococo Theme,* for cello and orchestra.

While Tchaikovsky was traveling in Switzerland he first became involved in the most amazing episode of his life. Word reached him that a powerful and wealthy Russia patroness, Mme. von Meck, had become so interested in his music that she was ready to make him financially independent through a generous annual pension. This was the beginning of one of the most curious relationships in musical biography. It was conducted exclusively through letters over a period of thirteen years. At times, there were exchanges of sentiments ardent, even passionate. And yet, at the express wish of Mme. von Meck, a personal meeting between the two never took place.

Now liberated from financial problems, Tchaikovsky began writing his greatest works, among them the *Fourth Symphony* (dedicated to his patroness), and the opera, *Eugene Onegin*. Both were outstandingly successful. From this time on, Tchaikovsky's position in Russian music was secure. He became the recipient of many honors, including a government pension.

While on a tour of Europe, Tchaikovsky learned that his patroness had suddenly decided to end the endowment. The loss of this pension did not disturb Tchaikovsky, who was now financially established. But the suspicion that his patroness had grown tired of him, his music, and their relationship, was a crushing blow. He grew increasingly morbid.

In 1891, Tchaikovsky visited the United States and helped to inaugurate the opening of Carnegie Hall in New York. Back in his native land, he completed his last masterwork, a fruit of his mental depression and pessimism—the *Symphonie pathétique*—sometimes regarded as his own requiem. Soon after completing this work, Tchaikovsky drank a glass of unboiled water, a reckless act considering that a cholera epidemic had broken out in St. Petersburg. He contracted the disease which proved fatal.

Tchaikovsky wore his heart on his sleeve in his music. The emotions that surged so tempestuously within him are expressed, and without inhibition, in his greatest works. They are sentimental, sometimes even hysterical. But Tchaikovsky produced a world of melodic and harmonic beauty all his own. He spoke from the heart and to the heart. Those who seek subtlety or profundity in music may dismiss his importance; but all others who are touched by genuine feelings cannot help being moved by his touching pathos and his personal charm.

To the passionate nationalists of the "Russian Five," Tchaikovsky represented a negation of their most sacred principles, largely because Tchaikovsky's music, in its culture and sophistication, made compromises with the music of Western Europe. But Tchaikovsky is, in his way, as intensely national a composer as Mussorgsky or Borodin. His melodies are often derived from Russian folk songs and dances, and his works are always permeated with Slavic colors and personality. His best symphonies are discussed in the section on the Symphony.

THOMAS, AMBROISE *Born:* Metz, France
August 5, 1811
*Died:* Paris
February 12, 1896

Thomas entered the Paris Conservatory in 1828 where, as a pupil of Zimmermann and Dourken, he won several awards. After completing his studies with Lesueur he won the Prix de Rome. In Rome he wrote several works, one of which (*Caprices,* for trio) attracted the interest of Robert Schumann. Back in Paris, in 1836, Thomas completed his first opera, *La Double échelle,* presented at the Opéra Comique in 1837. Several other operas followed, climaxed by Thomas' first success, *Mina,* in 1843. By 1851, he had written eighteen operas, none of which were calculated to bring him permanent fame; one of these was *Raymond,* remembered today exclusively for its overture.

In 1851, Thomas was elected a member of the Institut, and in 1858 he was appointed professor at the Conservatory. In 1866, the Opéra Comique presented *Mignon,* the opera which immortalized him. Within twenty-eight years, Paris saw one thousand performances of this beloved opera. On the occasion of the one thousandth performance, in 1894, Thomas was elevated to the rank of Grand Cross of the Legion of Honor. *Mignon* was followed by another major success, *Hamlet.* Thomas was now the favorite at the court of Napoleon III; and he was appointed director of the Paris Conservatory.

Even in his best operas, Thomas was not a composer of outstanding stature. He was often sentimental or banal; he lacked power and originality. But he did possess a suave and graceful style and could evoke tender feelings. His music is sensitive in style and endowed with warm feeling.

## VAUGHAN WILLIAMS, RALPH

*Born:* Down Ampney, Gloucestershire, England
October 12, 1872

He combined his academic education at Trinity College in Cambridge with music study at the Royal College of Music. After travels in Germany, he held various minor posts as organist and lecturer in London. In or about 1901, he became interested in English folk music, joining the English Folk Song Society, and doing considerable spade-work in unearthing forgotten gems of English folk songs, some of which he provided with new harmonizations and adaptations. His fascination for English folk music affected his creative work in which he started incorporating folk materials, as in the two *Norfolk Rhapsodies,* written in 1905.

Dissatisfied with his technique, Vaughan Williams went to Paris in 1908 and became a pupil of Maurice Ravel. Following this period of study he produced some of his most important works, in which his individual creative personality began to unfold. Among these were the *Fantasia on a Theme of Thomas Tallis* (his most frequently performed orchestral composition), written in 1910; and two symphonies, one of them being the celebrated *A London Symphony.*

During World War I, Vaughan Williams served in the British Army, seeing action in France. The war over, he became a member of the faculty of the Royal College of Music and conductor of the Bach Choir. Numerous works of first importance made him the leading composer of his land: the *Pastoral Symphony,* the oratorio, *Sancta Civitas,* the masque *Job.* Later works include several remarkable symphonies (the *Fourth, Fifth, Sixth,* and *Seventh*), the *Concerto for Oboe and Orchestra,* and the opera *Pilgrim's Progress.*

The greatest single influence on Vaughan Williams has been the English folk song and the style of the Tudor composers. From these he has absorbed the modal writing, the tranquil lyricism, the objective beauty found in most of his works. But his music is also modern in its advanced harmonic and rhythmic thinking.

VERDI, GIUSEPPE
*Born:* Le Roncole, Italy
October 10, 1813
*Died:* Milan
January 27, 1901

Verdi began music study with a local organist, and continued it in nearby Busseto with the organist of its cathedral, Giovanni Provesi. Verdi made notable progress in Busseto. He composed tunes and marches that were played by the town band. The townspeople were so impressed by his talent that they raised a fund to send him to the Milan Conservatory.

He arrived in Milan in 1832, but was turned down at the Conservatory because his background was inadequate. Instead, he studied privately with a well-known opera composer, Vincenzo Lavigna.

When Provesi died, Verdi returned to Busseto hoping to get Provesi's job as organist of the Cathedral. But the post was filled and Verdi had to be content with the post of conductor of the Busseto Philharmonic. He married Margherita, daughter of his one-time patron and friend. Verdi remained in Busseto several years, then returned to Milan with his family and the manuscript of his first opera, *Oberto.* Introduced in Milan on November 17, 1839, it was such a success that

Verdi was commissioned to write three more operas. His next opera, a comedy, was a failure. But the third, *Nabucco,* made Verdi one of the most popular composers in Milan.

His march to greatness began in 1851 with the première of *Rigoletto* in Venice, on March 11. This opera launched Verdi's second creative period; the apprenticeship was over. He was now to produce a succession of operas loved and honored the world over, making him the most famous opera composer of his generation. *Il Trovatore* was given in Rome on January 19, 1853; *La Traviata* in Venice, on March 6, 1853. The operas of this second period were climaxed with *Aïda,* which had been commissioned by the Khedive of Egypt to open a new opera house built to celebrate the construction of the Suez Canal; it received its première performance in Cairo on December 24, 1871, an event of incomparable splendor.

For a brief period, Verdi engaged in politics: he was elected deputy to the first Italian parliament inaugurated by Cavour. He did not like public life, and after holding this post refused to accept any other. He was subsequently appointed Senator by the King of Italy, but this was an exclusively honorary position.

For sixteen years after *Aïda,* Verdi wrote no more for the operatic stage. In this period he completed a string quartet, an *Ave Maria,* and the famous *Manzoni Requiem.* He devoted himself to his farm at Sant' Agata, convinced that he was through as an opera composer. Arrigo Boïto, famous critic, poet, and composer, was able to stir the dying embers of his creative genius by providing him with a forceful libretto based on Shakespeare's *Othello.* Completing *Otello* in 1886, Verdi entered upon the third and last creative period of his life. Its première on February 5, 1887 was a triumph of the first magnitude, as audiences and critics recognized that a new and even greater Verdi had emerged from his long retirement. Verdi wrote one more opera—another masterpiece and another triumph. It was the comedy *Falstaff* (his first comic opera in half a century!) seen at La Scala on February 9, 1893.

Long ill, Verdi was finally stricken by a fatal paralytic stroke in 1901. His passing was mourned by an entire country which realized it had lost one of its great men. For Verdi was not only the greatest opera composer produced by Italy, but one of the giant figures among opera composers everywhere. His artistic career, and his immense contributions, are evaluated in the section on Opera.

## VILLA-LOBOS, HEITOR

*Born:* Rio de Janeiro
March 5, 1887

His father died when Heitor was eleven years old, compelling the boy to shift for himself. He earned a living by playing in restaurant and theatre orchestras. Except for a brief and unsatisfactory period at the National Institute of Music in Rio de Janeiro he was self-taught. In 1912, he went on a journey throughout Brazil to study its folk music. This expedition initiated his lifelong interest in the folk art of his country and influenced his musical style. From this time on, he made a conscious effort to imitate the melodic, rhythmic and tonal idiosyncrasies of Brazilian folk songs and dances. In his many works— he has produced more than a thousand—he has created a national art in which the culture, geography, people and background of his land are interpreted. He has invented two musical forms in which he has produced some of his finest works. One is the Bachiana Brasileira, a suite in which he attempted a fusion of the style of Bach with elements of Brazilian folk music. The other is the Chôros, a kind of street serenade in which popular Brazilian music and traits peculiar to Brazilian and Indian folk music are emphasized.

Villa-Lobos went to Paris in 1923 on a government stipend, staying there for three years. He returned to Paris for a second visit in 1927. When he returned from this second trip, he became an important figure in the musical life of his country. He was appointed director of music education in Rio de Janeiro, in which post he revolutionized the methods of teaching music.

In 1944, Villa-Lobos visited the United States, appearing as conductor of many of our orchestras in programs of his own works. Besides his various Bachianas Brasileiras and Chôros pieces, Villa-Lobos has written numerous works in every possible form. His best works include the symphonic ballet, *Mandu Carara;* various concertos; the symphonic poems, *Madona,* and *Uirapurú;* the *Brazilian Quartet No. 2* (his sixth string quartet); and many songs and piano pieces.

## VIVALDI, ANTONIO

*Born:* Venice
c. 1675
*Died:* Vienna
July 28, 1741

The meager facts that have come down to us about Vivaldi provide little more than a bare outline of his life. He received his earliest music instruction from his father, a violinist in the ducal palace in San Marco, Venice; and afterward from Legrenzi. He was, however, prepared for the church, and was ordained a priest in 1703. He did not neglect musical activities, perfecting himself as a violinist, and writing numerous works. He abandoned his calling as priest in 1709 to teach the violin at a foundling school for girls that later became a fine Conservatory. In 1716 he became its music director. For the orchestra of this school Vivaldi wrote many instrumental works including some of his finest concertos. For three years, Vivaldi served as Kapellmeister to Prince Philip of Hesse in Mantua. Beginning with 1725 he spent a decade traveling throughout Europe and becoming famous as a composer of operas. He went back to his old post with the foundling school in 1735 and became the dominant musical figure in Venice. In 1740, just before his death, he visited Vienna where he remained a few months.

Vivaldi wrote more than four hundred concertos as well as a hundred or so major choral works, forty operas, and numerous instrumental works for small combinations of instruments. He was one of the major figures in the early history of Italian instrumental music, the most significant of Corelli's successors: he established the early sonata and concerto forms and crystallized an instrumental style.

WAGNER, RICHARD            *Born:* Leipzig
                          May 22, 1813
                          *Died:* Venice
                          February 13, 1883

Wagner's first love was literature rather than music. In his eleventh year he wrote a poetic drama inspired by Shakespeare and the Greek tragedies. He came to music study comparatively late. It was a hearing of Beethoven's music that gave him the ambition to become a composer. He struggled through a book on musical theory, and before long music occupied such a dominating role in his life that he neglected his academic study at the Thomasschule and was expelled; he was equally dilatory at the University of Leipzig.

After a six-month period of study with Weinlig, cantor of the Thomasschule, Wagner wrote a symphony which was performed both in Leipzig and in Prague in 1833. He also completed two operas—text as well as music. One of these, *Das Liebesverbot,* was a fiasco when introduced by the Magdeburg Opera on March 28, 1836.

The failuré of his opera was only one of many troubles harassing the young composer. Gambling reverses put him heavily into debt, and his creditors were hounding him. He was involved in troublesome love affairs, one of which (with Minna Planer) culminated in a marriage that Wagner soon regretted. Finally, he suddenly lost a post as conductor of the Magdeburg Opera, when that company was dissolved, leaving him without a means of earning a living. He found other conductorial posts, one in Königsberg, and another in Riga. But, persecuted by his creditors, he had to flee from Riga by way of a smugglers' route.

His destination now was Paris, and he arrived there in 1839. He came with high hopes for the future since he brought with him the score of a new opera, *Rienzi.* But his hopes were punctured as he met indifference everywhere. The poverty he now suffered was so acute that twice he was imprisoned for debt. Only his willingness to do hack work kept him from starvation. It may well be that this rejection by the Parisian public, and his great personal misery, were responsible for shaping him into the ruthless man he was to become, without moral or ethical scruples.

But he kept on working, completing the score of *The Flying Dutchman,* and starting work on *Tannhäuser.* With borrowed funds, Wagner left Paris to attend the première of *Rienzi* in Dresden on October 20, 1842. The opera was immensely successful. The same opera company gave *The Flying Dutchman* on January 2, 1843, but this new opera was a failure; and so was its successor, *Tannhäuser,* when given in Dresden on October 19, 1845.

Between 1843 and 1848, Wagner was Kapellmeister of the Dresden Opera, during which period he completed *Lohengrin.* He lost this position when he became involved in the revolutionary movement in 1848 and had to escape to avoid imprisonment. He lived in exile for the next twelve years, mostly in Switzerland. Thus he was unable to hear the première of *Lohengrin* which Franz Liszt, now a passionate Wagnerite, gave in Weimar on August 28, 1850. By 1860, *Lohengrin* had become the most popular of Wagner's operas, performed extensively throughout Germany.

At about this time, in exile, Wagner started formulating his ideas about opera, rejecting the old and formal traditions, and evolving the concept of the music drama predicated on a synthesis of the arts. To put theory into practice, he started working on a Gargantuan work, a cycle of four music dramas collectively entitled *The Ring of the Nibelungs*. This immense project took him a quarter of a century to complete. He felt that the *Ring* would never be performed because of the taxing demands it made on singers, orchestra men and the opera house. Consequently during this period he wrote some music dramas of more modest scope, but no less exacting in their fulfillment of his new esthetics—*Tristan und Isolde,* and his only comedy, *Die Meistersinger.*

In 1860, Wagner was officially pardoned for his radical activities and allowed to return to Saxony. Soon after his return, he met Ludwig II, young king of Bavaria, henceforth to be his friend and powerful patron. The king's wealth and influence made it possible for Wagner's music dramas to be performed in Munich. *Tristan und Isolde* was presented on June 10, 1865. *Die Meistersinger* followed on June 21, 1868. *The Rhinegold,* the first drama or prologue of the *Ring* cycle, September 22, 1869. The second drama, *The Valkyrie,* was produced on June 26, 1870.

By this time, Wagner's personal and emotional life was growing more secure. He had left Minna for Cosima von Bülow, daughter of Franz Liszt, and wife of his friend, Hans von Bülow. In 1870, after she had borne him a daughter and a son, they were married—a relationship that proved to be immensely sympathetic.

Having completed writing the *Ring,* Wagner was stirred by a new ambition: to build a special theatre, realizing all his innovations about operatic productions, where his monumental cycle could be given. Patrons were found to subscribe to such a venture, and a site was selected in the little Bavarian town of Bayreuth. There, in August 1876, the first Wagnerian festival took place with the first complete performance of the *Ring* cycle, and the world premières of the last two dramas, *Siegfried* and *The Dusk of the Gods*. The event attracted world attention. Hotels were overtaxed. Correspondents and some of the world's foremost musicians attended. Tickets for each performance were at a premium. Though not everybody liked everything he heard and saw —too much of it was new and startling—it was obvious to all that here was an event of major artistic significance.

Wagner wrote one more music drama, the consecrational play, *Parsifal,* first heard at Bayreuth on June 28, 1882. He was vacationing in Venice when he suffered a fatal heart attack. His body was brought back to Bayreuth where it was buried in the garden behind his home, "Wahnfried."

In many ways Wagner was a petty man—vain, immoral, ruthless, unethical, dissolute. But he was a genius, probably one of the greatest that the musical art has produced. Alone, he changed the course of operatic art; influenced his own and succeeding generations as nobody before him or since; and produced a series of work of incomparable grandeur and nobility. His art is discussed in the section on Opera.

WALTON, WILLIAM        *Born:* Oldham, Lancashire, England March 29, 1902

Walton acquired his first musical training from his father, a church musician. Further music study took place at Oxford and privately with Professor Edward J. Dent and Busoni. In 1923, his *String Quartet No. 1* was performed at the International Society for Contemporary Music Festival in Salzburg. Fame came with his provocative and satirical *Façade*, based on abstractionist poems by Edith Sitwell. Since then, Walton has assumed an ever increasingly important position in English music with such works as the orchestral overture *Portsmouth Point*, the cantata *Belshazzar's Feast*, the *Concerto for Violin and Orchestra*, and the *First Symphony*.

Walton's orchestration is brilliant; his rhythms are vibrant; his melodic line long and flexible; and his harmonic and contrapuntal writing detailed and sometimes complex. Technical astuteness is combined with sensitivity of expression and telling emotional content.

During World War II, Walton served in the British Army, functioning in a musical capacity by writing music for documentary films. After the war he wrote the scores for such notable English films as *Hamlet* and *Henry V;* and completed several chamber-music works and the opera *Troilus and Cressida.* He was knighted in 1951.

(VON) WEBER, KARL MARIA        *Born:* Eutin, Oldenburg, Germany November 18, 1786
*Died:* London, June 5, 1826

Born with a disease of the hip which retarded his walking, he was left in delicate health for the rest of his life. When he began to reveal talent for music his father decided to exploit him as a prodigy and drove him to extensive study and practice. After a period of study with Abbé Vogler in Munich, Weber received his first musical appointment—as conductor in Breslau. During this period he sketched an opera and wrote an orchestral overture. He also indulged in a dissolute existence which put him heavily into debt. In 1810, he was falsely accused of stealing money from his employer and was put in prison; this imprisonment, and his subsequent exile, seemed to have a sobering effect on him. He began to work industriously on composition. In 1811, one of his early operas was produced in Munich, followed by the presentation of a second one in Berlin. His reputation grew, and he was engaged as musical director of the Prague Opera in 1813, where he remained for three years. Much more important was his appointment as Kapellmeister of the Dresden Opera in 1817 in which post he distinguished himself as one of the most significant musical directors in Europe.

He now was seized by the ideal of writing authentically German opera, as distinguished from the Italian products he had thus far been creating. His first effort in this new direction was *Der Freischütz,* produced in Berlin on June 18, 1821. It was a sensation, coming in the wake of a wave of nationalism that had swept through Germany. It was seen in Berlin fifty times that season, then scored another major success in Vienna.

Shortly afterward Weber received a commission to write a new opera for Vienna. The result was *Euryanthe.* Though burdened by a stupid and incredible libretto, *Euryanthe* was well received when introduced on October 23, 1823.

Weber wrote his last opera, *Oberon,* on a commission from Covent Garden in London. The opera was cheered when introduced on April 12, 1826, with the composer conducting; this was probably the greatest triumph of his career. But travel to England and the strain of preparing *Oberon* had been too much for him. He suffered a heart attack and died in his sleep.

German Romantic opera was born with Weber. This was one of his salient achievements. Another was that, by filling his music with dramatic truth and placing importance on the orchestra, he was one of

Wagner's major predecessors. Weber's contributions are evaluated in the section on Opera.

His best operas are no longer heard, but they are remembered through their magnificent overtures which are staples in the symphonic repertory, and through one or two arias. Weber is also important in the evolution of the waltz form. His most popular effort in this direction was the *Invitation to the Dance.* Of Weber's numerous symphonic works only the charming *Konzertstück,* for piano and orchestra, is occasionally given.

WOLF, HUGO                   *Born:* Windischgraz, Austria
                             March 13, 1860
                       *Died:* Vienna
                             September 22, 1903

As a boy, he was expelled from academic schools because he showed no interest in subjects other than music. In 1875, he was enrolled in the Vienna Conservatory. There, he was no happier or more receptive to study than he had been before this. He remained two years at the Conservatory—a period of restlessness and dissatisfaction —and was finally ejected when falsely accused of a misdemeanor. Years of poverty and maladjustment followed; but a measure of escape from this duress came through an intensive study of music from text books. Occasionally, he found a job that helped support him, such as rehearsing choruses for operetta performances in Salzburg. In 1884, he acquired his most important position when he was appointed music critic for the *Salonblatt* in Vienna; he was a vigorous and independent critic.

Wolf's first creative efforts included a string quartet and a tone poem, *Penthesilea.* In 1887, he published two volumes of Lieder. One year later, he gave up criticism to specialize in writing songs. In 1888 he produced several volumes, including some of the greatest songs he was to write: the *Mörike Liederbuch,* the *Goethe Liederbuch,* the *Spanisches Liederbuch,* and so on. Many of his wonderful songs were written in the white heat of inspiration.

Suddenly he felt his creative power had been dissipated and that he could write no more. But, by 1892, the old inspiration returned and once again he was productive and prolific, creating, among other works, the *Italienisches Liederbuch* and the opera, *Der Corregidor.*

In 1897, Wolf suddenly lost his mind. He was confined to a private hospital where recovery took place. He left the hospital, affected by a profound melancholia. It was not long before his mind once again lost its balance; at one time he tried to drown himself. Once again committed to a hospital, he now suffered paralysis of the body. He died there of peripneumonia.

Wolf is a worthy successor to the royal line of Lieder composers that began with Schubert. Wolf's songs are discussed in the section on Vocal Music.

# PART TWO

# *Choral and Vocal Music*

# Choral Music

The art of music, as we know it today, can be said to have emerged with the Gothic Period in the twelfth and thirteenth centuries. The music from ancient times up to the twelfth century has so little resemblance in form, style and structure to the art as we know it today that it has virtually no meaning or interest for the average music lover. Even the music of the Gothic Period sounds foreign to our ears and can appeal only to highly esoteric tastes and to scholars. But since some of the techniques and forms basic to the art were first evolved in the Gothic Period, most musical historians prefer to regard this as the first chapter in modern music history.

The Gothic Period marked the beginning of the first of the great epochs in music: the Polyphonic Era. The first great age in music was devoted exclusively to compositions for groups of voices, rather than for instruments. Only late in the Polyphonic Era did instruments engage the interest of composers, but then only to accompany the choral singing. The Polyphonic Era, however, refers specifically to contrapuntal choral music *without* any accompaniment whatsoever (a cappella music).

The earliest of the polyphonic techniques came to being in the Gothic Period. One of these was the organum, which consisted of two melodies. At first these two melodies, in long notes, moved concurrently in intervals of fourths and fifths. But in the twelfth and thirteenth centuries, the second melody consisted of an improvisation, referred to as the "discant" or "diaphony." A further development, the conductus, allowed two or three, or four melodies to move independently of one another, the text being sung only by the tenor voice. The organum and the conductus were developed in France, and its most significant composers were Magister Leonius and Magister Perotinus.

The polyphonic music of the Gothic Period is designated as the *Ars Antiqua*—or the Ancient Art. A new kind of polyphonic art emerged in the fourteenth century, after the publication of a volume by Philippe de Vitry entitled *Ars Nova* (the New Art). One of the outstanding composers of this new music was the French master, Guillaume de Machaut. Ars Nova was distinguished from the music that preceded it by its fresh and new procedures in rhythm and melody, procedures enabling polyphonic music to acquire greater expressiveness and sentiment. The first important forms of choral music, the mass and the motet, were developed.

Polyphony was transformed into a vibrant art by a number of important schools of composers. The first was the Flemish (or Netherland) School in the fifteenth century, founded by Guillermus Dufay; its most important composers were Josquin des Prés, sometimes spoken of as the first great composer in musical history, and Orlando di Lasso. In the sixteenth century, the Venetian School (which included Giovanni Gabrieli and Adrian Willaert) and the Roman School (whose foremost figure was Palestrina) were prominent. With the Venetian School a new richness entered polyphony through the innovation of antiphony—that is, alternate singing of lines of music by two or more choirs placed in different parts of the church. The Roman School brought religious feeling, mysticism, and a beauty to polyphony it had never known before.

With these schools, the science of polyphonic writing passed out of the primitive stage. No longer was the main stress laid on the mechanics of combining melodies into contrapuntal designs. The musical idea and beauty of sound were now of greater concern to the composer. With each succeeding school, from the Flemish through the Roman, the texture of polyphony became richer, more complex, more varied, and more expressive—finally achieving with Palestrina and his Spanish pupil, Tomás Luis de Victoria, nobility, spirituality, religious grandeur together with spaciousness of design. The most important forms used by these composers were the mass and the motet, together with such newer forms as the magnificat and the madrigal.

Most of the music of this period was confined to the church. But there was some music for secular consumption, too. The principal form of secular music was the madrigal. Originally, the madrigal was also a composition for the church. But when it entered the market place it became earthier, livelier, and more rhythmic.

In the seventeenth century, polyphonic music passed from the Gothic to the Baroque Period. Church music paid greater attention to powerful and dramatic effects (the influence of the opera was being felt), stressed ornamental details, and extended and enlarged the forms. Contrapuntal choruses were supplemented by arias, duets, quartets; and all this music was for the first time being accompanied by instruments. Important new forms came into being with and were amplified by Giovanni Carissimi, Dietrich Buxtehude, and Heinrich Schütz. The Baroque Period came to a magnificent culmination with the works of Johann Sebastian Bach and George Frederick Handel.

Later composers sometimes used the Baroque style; and many great composers after Bach and Handel wrote large choral works for the church. In the Classical Period we find Mozart writing masses and the famous *Requiem;* Haydn wrote masses and his two magnificent oratorios, *The Creation* and *The Seasons.* And Beethoven produced one of his unqualified masterworks in the *Missa Solemnis.* The Romantic Era yielded the masses of Schubert, the *Elijah* of Mendelssohn, Brahms' *A German Requiem,* among many other notable works. The modern composer has not neglected choral music, either. Major choral works, many on religious texts, have been written by some of the greatest composers of our time, including Elgar, Stravinsky, Honegger, Hindemith, Prokofiev, Delius, Walton and Vaughan Williams.

But, though the writing of choral music has not been abandoned, its highest point of artistic and structural development was reached with the age of Bach and Handel. After that, the composer directed his most concentrated and serious efforts toward instrumental rather than choral music, on secular rather than liturgical music, and on homophony rather than polyphony.

# *Vocal Music*

Songs are as old as music itself, since singing is the oldest means of musical communication. There has always been the folk song, created not by any one composer but by an entire race of people who sang of their hopes and dreams and frustrations, and who translated story and legend into poem and melody. From time immemorial one generation passed on its songs to the next; and, in the passing, old songs were changed, and new songs were added. Thus a treasury of vocal music sprang up in many different countries, nursed and grown by the people themselves.

Man, then, began singing single tunes of his own fashioning long before the age of polyphony emphasized the technique of combining several different melodies into a single texture. It is then, curious, indeed, to discover that the art song, as distinguished from the folk song—or, in other words, a song created by a composer to a definite poetic text and made up of a single melody and its accompaniment—was comparatively a late development in music. Only after the polyphonic art had been in full flower for several centuries, did the concept of a single melody and accompaniment—as opposed to counterpoint—become crystallized. It was first realized in the seventeenth and early eighteenth centuries within the structure of the opera and the oratorio as arias and recitatives. And only after that was the concept applied to the structure of the art song.

The first of the important influences brought to bear on the art song was the folk song. It was with the latter that we find the strophic structure which, for generations, characterized the art song: several verses set to the same recurrent melody. Many later composers of the art song, from Mozart on, were inspired by and indebted to the idioms and styles of their country's folk music.

The progress of the art song was slow during the Polyphonic Era. Secular song was growing among the minstrels and troubadours in France and England, and the minnesingers and mastersingers in Germany; these singers wrote text as well as music for their ballads of love and heroism.

Toward the end of the sixteenth century, the lute song—or, a song accompanied by lute—was gaining interest. Collections started appearing in different European countries, beginning with 1536. By the end of the century, the greatest of these composers emerged in England: John Dowland, who completed four volumes of Ayres with lute, the first appearing in 1597. Dowland may well be regarded as the first distinguished composer of art song in England. His four volumes, appearing at a time when most English composers were dedicated to the contrapuntal madrigal, represent a historic break with counterpoint and a dramatic advance toward homophony. But if Dowland was the first distinguished composer of the art song in England, Henry Purcell (who came a century later) was the first master of the form. Purcell wrote secular songs collected in *Ayres for the Theatre* and *Orpheus Britannicus,* and church songs many of them found in *Harmonia Sacra.* Here we find a warmth of lyricism and an understanding of the art of setting text to music unique for that time.

In Italy, the song was profoundly influenced by the then evolving opera and oratorio. The emergence of the monodic style (or recitative) in the first operas of Peri and Caccini in the seventeenth century had a profound effect on the slowly evolving song style; so did the emergence of the operatic aria with Monteverdi and Alessandro Scarlatti. In Italy, most of the earliest song composers were also opera composers, and consequently their songs were actually opera arias even when they were designated as a *villanella,* or a *canzonetta.* Such a delightful morsel as "O Bellissimi capelli" by the seventeenth century lutenist and composer, Andrea Falconieri, was termed a villanella; and Alessandro Scarlatti's equally delightful "Che vuole innamorarsi" was a canzonetta; but their indebtedness to the Italian aria of the seventeenth century is unmistakable.

The first major revolution in the history of the art song aimed at freeing itself once and for all from the opera aria. This development took place in Germany in the seventeenth century, and its pioneer was Hans Leo Hassler who wrote numerous secular and church songs. The charm and lightness of touch found in the Italian aria are also in Hassler's songs; but by setting German texts to music, he was setting the stage for the first significant German song composer, Heinrich Albert, a nephew of Heinrich Schütz. In the first half of the seventeenth century, Albert set the German poems of his day to music that had a Germanic character, since it was derived from the German folk song; and thus the German art song was born.

That the art song was not yet considered a significant medium for the composer is proved by the fact that songs represent so negligible a fraction of the output of both Handel and Bach. Handel wrote a few songs, but none of them are of any permanent interest. Johann Sebastian Bach wrote a few songs that have survived, notably "Komm süsser Tod" and "Bist du bei mir," but these are actually cantata arias under another name. The same unimportant role is occupied by the song in Gluck's career. Gluck did not start writing songs until his seventy-third year when he completed seven songs (or odes) to verses by Klopstock. But Gluck—the genius who played such a formidable role in creating a closer bond between words and music in opera—was uninspired and stilted in his attempt to do the same service for the art song.

Haydn, Mozart, and Beethoven all produced art songs, frequently very beautiful ones. But even these giant figures relegated the song to a minor role while concentrating their greatest powers on the larger forms. Haydn's songs suffered mostly from the fact that he generally chose deplorable texts. But he had, of course, a charming lyricism and an ingratiating manner; songs like "My Mother Bids Me Bind My Hair" and "The Sailor's Song" are delightful to listen to even if they are neither particularly original nor inspired. Mozart was much more gifted in songs than was Haydn. Gems like "Das Veilchen" (poem by Goethe) and "An Chloe" have melodic interest together with a classic beauty. Beethoven's best songs have an emotional intensity of melody and an increasing richness in the accompaniment which sets them apart from the classicism of Haydn and Mozart. "Wonne der Wehmut" (Goethe) and "Adelaide" carried the art song to the threshold of Romanticism. But Beethoven made an even greater contribution to songs by extending the structural design. He evolved the song cycle, in which several different songs, united by a similarity of mood or theme, are gathered into a single work. The first song cycle in musical history is Beethoven's *Sechs geistliche Lieder,* and the most important of his song cycles is *An die ferne geliebte.*

The golden age of the art song came comparatively late in musical development: with Franz Schubert in the early part of the nineteenth century. This late development is understandable. The inspiration of any song is its poetic text; the art song could come into its own only with the efflorescence of lyric poetry throughout Europe during the Romantic Era.

Franz Schubert was the first undisputed genius of the art song; in many respects, he was also the greatest. Singlehanded, he created the *Lied,* a term given to the German art song in which words and music become a single entity, a drama in miniature. Without any precedent to guide him—and at the incredible age of seventeen!—he brought a completely new esthetic approach to the form of the song. We find in "Gretchen am Spinnrade," text taken from Goethe's *Faust,* a realism never before encountered within the song: the whirring of the spinning wheel in the accompaniment, now continuing evenly and uninterruptedly, now gaining momentum, and now stopping short as Marguerite's emotions become intense; her ecstasy in recalling a rapturous kiss caught in an abrupt interval. The same kind of realism, but with even greater subtlety of effect and dramatic impact, is found in a song written by Schubert one year later, "Der Erlkönig," text once again by Goethe. The rhythm in the piano reproduces the angry storm; the melody catches the now gentle pleading of the child and the now terror-stricken conflict with the Erlking; a recitative-like melodic phrase, and after that an actual dissonance, catches the anguish of the father in realizing that his child is dead.

"Gretchen am Spinnrade" and "Der Erlkönig" realized with consummate mastery a technique of song-writing known as through-composition (*Durchkomponieren*). Classical songs were usually strophic in construction. But in the Durchkomponieren process, the melody is permitted to change throughout the entire song, and with each new verse, to reflect the changing emotional and dramatic context of the poem. This was, by no means, a technique new with Schubert. It probably originated with Johann Adam Hiller, born half a century before Schubert. But no one employed this method with such a variety of means, wide gamut of effect, and inevitability of structure as Schubert did in these two songs. It is for this reason that the German Lied can be said to have emerged with "Gretchen am Spinnrade" and "Der Erlkönig."

Schubert wrote about six hundred songs. With his incomparable gift of lyricism and with an infallible instinct for finding the precise musical equivalent for every mood and feeling, Schubert realized the artistic potentialities of the song for the first time. His greatest and most popular individual songs include: "Hark, Hark, the Lark," "Die Forelle," "Der Tod und das Mädchen," "Ave Maria," "Wiegenlied," "An die Musik." But some of his most wonderful inspiration is found in monumental song cycles: *Die schöne Müllerin, Die Winterreise*, and *Schwanengesang*. In the first of these three cycles we find such gems as "Ungeduld," and "Wohin"; in the second, "Der Lindenbaum" and "Der Leiermann"; and in the last, "Der Doppelgänger," "Am Meer," and probably the most famous love song ever written, "Serenade."

After Schubert, the great German composers of Lieder—Schumann, Brahms, Wolf, and Richard Strauss—all tried to arrive at an ever closer, more inextricable marriage of words and melody. More and more with each succeeding composer, is the dramatic element emphasized, sometimes at the expense of lyricism; more and more is the lyric line made to serve the demands of the poem until it sometimes becomes almost a recitative when the dramatic expression so requires. We begin to find declamation in a song like Schumann's "Im wunderschönen Monat Mai," in which the closing bar magically suggests the half-answered question in the poem. Unorthodox harmonies, unusual treatment of the voice, and extended writing in the piano are found in other Schumann songs, such as "An meinem Herzen," "Der Nussbaum," and "Widmung" and in the song cycles, *Dichterliebe* and *Frauenliebe und Leben*.

Increasing richness and independence in the piano accompaniment, more marked attempt to emphasize atmosphere and mood, and an increased dramatic force are found in Brahms' greatest Lieder, which include "Der Tod, das ist die kühle Nacht," "Immer leiser wird mein Schlummer," "Die Mainacht," and the "Vier ernste Gesänge." In the ever-popular "Wiegenlied" (Cradle Song) Brahms is a melodist in the Schubertian meaning of that term; but in most of his great songs he is the dramatist rather than the melodist.

The ever-growing tendency to create a miniature drama out of the Lied achieved culmination with the songs of Hugo Wolf. He was profoundly influenced by the esthetics of the Wagnerian music drama, and specific techniques of Wagnerian style. His songs reveal these influences so markedly that Wolf is sometimes called the "Wagner of the Lied." The poems he set to music dictated so rigorously the kind of music he wrote that there are times when Wolf's melodic line passes from declamation to a simulation of actual speech. The essence of the poetic thought made him seek out intervals and modulations new and daring for the period in which he lived. Melody and piano accompaniment—the accompaniment is now the equal partner of the voice in an artistic undertaking—give the musical equivalent of every suggestion of the poem, however subtle or elusive. At last, word and tone are one and indivisible—so much so that it is frequently difficult to understand and appreciate the music without knowing the words. Wolf's greatest songs are gathered in a series of so-called "song-books" (*Liederbuch*): the Spanish Liederbuch and the Italian Liederbuch (so called because the poems are of Spanish or Italian origin), the Mörike, Goethe, Eichendroff, and Keller Liederbücher. Here we come upon such Wolf masterpieces as "Anakreons Grab," "Auch kleine Dinge," "In dem Schatten meiner Locken," "Storchenbotschaft," "Verborgenheit," "Ständchen," and "Verschwiegene Liebe."

Richard Strauss was the last of the great composers of the German Lied. He, too, emphasized the dramatic element—though his lyrical gift is much more pronounced than Wolf's, his style more sensual, and his concept of aural beauty more traditional. Among Strauss' finest songs are: "Traum durch die Dämmerung," "Morgen," "Zueignung," "Ständchen," and "Allersellen." Like Wolf, Strauss was always concerned over the piano accompaniment as a means of increasing the expressiveness of the song; and the piano is frequently as important in the over-all artistic scheme as the voice.

Strauss' best songs were written before 1900. With some German composers after 1900 the search for dramatic truth led to a new kind of melody: the *Sprechstimme* (Speaking Voice) found in songs by Schoenberg and Alban Berg. Melody as such ceased to exist. What we get now is the inflection of everyday speech, exaggerated and emphasized in terms of musical intervals. This is surely as far as melody can go without becoming actual speech.

This innovation is not the innovation of the twentieth century atonalists. It was first realized in Russia with Mussorgsky. The story goes that, one day, Mussorgsky heard a simpleton speak to a girl. His peculiar intonation fascinated Mussorgsky who seemed to hear a new kind of melody in this strange speech. This gave him the idea, and the ideal, to produce melodies following the patterns of speech which he called "melody of life." "With great pains I have achieved a new type of melody evolved from that of speech," he explained. "Some day, all of a sudden, the ineffable song will arise, intelligible to one and all. If I succeed I shall stand as a conqueror in art." In Bohemia, Leos Janáček was inspired by Mussorgsky to create what he, in turn, described as "melodies of the language"—constructed out of the positive elements of speech in the Mussorgsky manner.

The art song developed along different lines in France. The Germans placed emphasis on drama. The French were concerned with subtle effects, delicate suggestions and nuance, atmosphere, refinement. Art songs were written by Hector Berlioz, and after him by Bizet, Gounod, and Massenet. But the first truly important composer of the French art song was César Franck. In "Ave Maria," the nocturne "O fraîche nuit," and "La Procession," we are confronted with the serenity, mysticism, and radiance that we find in Franck's larger works.

Gabriel Fauré was an even more significant contributor to French vocal music, so much so that he is sometimes spoken of as the "French Schubert." The predominant charm of Fauré's best songs lies in the sweetness of the lyricism and the delicacy of the harmony. But there is also a subtle mysticism in a song like "En Prière"; a deep emotional content in "Les Berceaux"; a touch of the exotic in "Les Roses d'Ispahan"; and tragedy in "Au cimetière" and "Prison."

The French art song becomes even more refined, more elusive in emotional content, more delicate in effect, with Claude Debussy. Fantasy and shadow moods give many of his finest songs their individuality. The Debussy masterpieces of song include the two series of *Fêtes galantes,* after poems by Paul Verlaine; "Mandoline";

"Paysage sentimental"; and the *Trois Ballades de Villon*. The influence of Debussy is perceptible in the songs of Maurice Ravel, while that of Franck prevails in the songs of Henri Duparc, one of the most important French song composers after Debussy.

Among other notable contributors to song literature in countries outside Germany and England are Tchaikovsky, Rachmaninoff, and Alexander Gretchaninoff in Russia; Grieg in Norway; Sir Francesco Tosti and Pizzetti in Italy; Bartók and Kodály in Hungary; Falla in Spain; Stephen Foster, John Alden Carpenter, Charles Ives, and Samuel Barber in the United States.

# Basic Forms of Choral and Vocal Music

## ANTHEM

A piece of sacred music for chorus and mixed solo voices based on a text from the Scriptures or the Prayer Book, and found in the Anglican church. It originated in 1662 when Queen Elizabeth demanded the inclusion of hymns and songs in the Prayer Book. The anthem is the English equivalent of the Latin motet, from which it was derived. Originally, anthems were sung by a cappella chorus exclusively. Instrumental accompaniment and the inclusion of solo numbers came with the anthems of William Byrd and Orlando Gibbons, while those of Henry Purcell gave a strong suggestion of the later form by emphasizing solo parts. Handel wrote anthems (the *Chandos Anthems*) in the style of Purcell. After the seventeenth century, the anthem became too stylized for musical significance, though an important attempt to revive its musical importance was made in the nineteenth century by S. S. Wesley.

## ARIA

A song that is part of an opera or oratorio.

In the earliest operas written, the aria was merely a recitative. It was first with Monteverdi that the aria acquired lyrical interest. The melodic nature of the aria was established by Alessandro Scarlatti who popularized the so-called *da capo aria* (three parts, with the third part repeating the first). Aria writing made rapid advances with the Neapolitan composers succeeding Scarlatti, and the individual traits of several different kinds of arias were clarified. There was the *aria cantabile,* a free-flowing and emotional song in which the singer was allowed freedom to improvise ornamental details. There was the *aria di bravura,* which exploited the vocal technique of the song. There was the *aria parlante,* which was closer to declamation than to melody. Italian composers from Bellini and Donizetti through Verdi placed considerable importance on the aria. Verdi abandoned the aria in *Otello,* and so did Wagner in his music dramas, in an effort to make the entire score a cohesive texture.

## AVE MARIA

A prayer in the Roman Catholic church—a hymn to the Virgin Mary—frequently set to music.

Composers have set this prayer either for chorus or for a solo voice. Probably the most famous Ave Maria of all is one by Franz Schubert, for solo voice and piano. Another famous Ave Maria, also for solo voice and piano, was written by Charles Gounod. Gounod wrote his religious melody to the accompaniment of the first prelude in Bach's *Well-Tempered Clavier.*

Most of the great composers of choral music from Palestrina to Bruckner wrote Ave Marias for chorus.

## BERCEUSE

A cradle song or lullaby, a celebrated example being the tender berceuse "Cachés dans cet asile," in Benjamin Godard's opera, *Jocelyn.*

## CANON

A piece of choral music utilizing the contrapuntal technique known as "imitation." One voice begins a melody and continues it while a second voice enters with the same melody, and so on for three, four, or more voices. When a canon returns to the original melody without a break it is known as a *round*. One of the earliest examples of canonic writing is "Sumer Is Icumin In," in the thirteenth century. Popular examples of canon are "Frère Jacques," "Three Blind Mice," and "Row, Row, Row Your Boat."

## CANTATA

Actually, a small oratorio—consequently a work for chorus or soloists, or chorus and soloists, and orchestra on a religious text, but smaller in dimensions than the oratorio.

This form was created by Giacomo Carissimi, who also played an important role in the early development of the oratorio. Carissimi realized that the oratorio was much too elaborate in form, and called for forces too large, for performance in small churches. He reduced the structure and the number of participants required without changing the essential character of the oratorio, creating a form that was more intimate and economical. Carissimi's cantatas were generally in a single movement requiring a single voice and orchestral accompaniment, and combining recitatives with arias (usually three of each).

In the eighteenth century, many composers produced "solo" cantatas, including Alessandro Scarlatti, Pergolesi, and Handel. But Handel, Buxtehude, and Schütz, also wrote cantatas requiring chorus as well as soloist, and sometimes several soloists. Buxtehude and Schütz brought the cantata to a stage of development where it was ready for the hands of its most consummate master: Johann Sebastian Bach.

There are two kinds of cantatas. The first is the *cantata da chiesa,* written for church services. Schütz, Buxtehude, and Johann Sebastian Bach produced their finest cantatas in this category. A second type is the *cantata da camera,* which treated a secular instead of liturgical text. Handel's *Acis and Galatea* and *Alexander's Feast* belong in this group. Bach also wrote secular cantatas, the best known being the *Coffee Cantata, Peasant Cantata,* and *Wedding Cantata.*

Bach was the greatest composer of cantatas, and the most prolific. He produced three hundred church cantatas. In these, the text is a Scriptural lesson for the day, in verse. These cantatas were a part of the Lutheran service at Bach's St. Thomas Church in Leipzig and were heard every Sunday and on certain festival days. Bach's cantatas are generally in several movements (the most usual number is six) and require between twenty minutes and a half hour for performance. They are for different groups: for solo voice and orchestra; for several solo voices and orchestra; for solo voice, chorus, and orchestra; for several solo voices, chorus, and orchestra; or for chorus and orchestra. They usually end in a chorale.

The Bach church cantatas represent a remarkable facet of the composer's personality and genius, and are a veritable horn-of-plenty of musical riches. They are, however, not so well known as they deserve. Written for religious service, they are not often given in the concert auditorium. Fortunately, within the past few years, the recording industry has conducted an intensive campaign to impress Bach's church cantatas on long-playing records; as a result of this activity, the world of Bach's cantatas is no longer *terra incognita,* in the way it was a few decades ago. We now know what Bach scholars have long told us: namely, that the church cantatas are among Bach's most remarkable works, infinitely varied in mood and style and feeling, filled with spiritual devotion and religious exaltation. But, as Charles Sanford Terry pointed out, these cantatas are also fascinating in the way they reveal Bach's personality—"as a man singularly pondering, emotional, and above all controlled by a religious sense as profound as it was simple."

While the average concert goer has little opportunity to hear Bach's church cantatas in their entirety—except on long-playing records—he is familiar with some of their excerpts, popularized through varied transcriptions. The most celebrated are:

"Jesus, Joy of Man's Desiring," a chorale found in *Cantata No. 147, Herz and Mund,* often heard in transcriptions for the piano, for the organ, and for the orchestra.

"Sleepers Awake," a chorus from *Cantata No. 140, Wachet auf,* available in several transcriptions for the orchestra, the most familiar being that by Leopold Stokowski.

The orchestral sinfonia, or arioso, from *Cantata No. 156, Ich steh' mit einem Fuss im Grabe,* transcribed for the organ, for the modern orchestra, and for the violin and piano.

The sinfonia and tenor chorale, "Jesus Christ, the Son of God," from *Cantata No. 4, Christ lag in Todesbanden,* familiar in various orchestral transcriptions.

Bach was less spiritual, earthier, in his secular cantatas. We find Bach in an unfamiliar pose in these works: indulging in witty and satirical moods. The secular cantatas differ from the church cantatas in their abstention from chorales and in their texts.

One of the finest and most amusing of all Bach's secular cantatas is the so-called *Coffee Cantata* (No. 211), text by Christian Friedrich Henrici. This is a satire of the then prevalent tendency among the women of Leipzig to indulge in coffee drinking. The *Coffee Cantata* is virtually a miniature opera buffa. It has three characters: the Narrator (tenor) who tells the story; and Schlendrian (baritone) and Lieschen (soprano) around whom the story revolves. Schlendrian is outraged to find that his daughter, Lieschen, is a coffee addict and insists that she give up the vice. Lieschen refuses to do this even after her father, in punishment, denies her one pleasure after another. When the father finally threatens to prevent her from getting a husband, Lieschen promises to make amends. But she is not serious in her good intentions. When she finds a husband, she says, she will not marry him until he promises her she can drink coffee as often as she wishes. The cantata ends in a characteristically merry vein when the trio philosophizes: "Cats must have their mice and women their coffee!"

Composers of both the Classical and Romantic Periods neglected the cantata. But it has been revived in the twentieth century, with many of the leading composers of our time producing major works in the cantata form.

In *The Wedding* (*Les Noces*), Igor Stravinsky describes a primitive Russian wedding ritual in four scenes or tableaux. In the first the bride is prepared for the wedding; in the second, a similar scene takes place in the groom's home; in the third, groom and bride join each other and leave for the ceremony; the concluding picture describes the wedding festivities. Scored for solo voices, chorus, and an instrumental ensemble including four pianos and a battery of percussion, this cantata is filled with primitive rhythms and melodic fragments. A novel feature is the placement of the solo singers in the orchestra pit with the instrumentalists.

One of Serge Prokofiev's finest works is the cantata *Alexander Nevsky,* which originated as a score for a motion picture. It is for mezzo soprano, chorus, and orchestra. The seven sections tell of the Russian defense of Novgorod, in 1242, against the invading Knights of the Teutonic Order. The hero of this defense was Prince Alexander Nevsky who, at the head of his men, met and defeated the enemy on the frozen waters of Lake Chud.

The English composer William Walton achieved one of his earliest artistic triumphs with the cantata *Belshazzar's Feast,* for baritone, chorus, and orchestra. Osbert Sitwell wrote the poetic text, adapting passages from the Bible beginning with the prophecy of Isaiah and including two Psalms (81 and 137). In its broadness of style and design, *Belshazzar's Feast* goes back to the traditions of Bach and Handel.

Arnold Schoenberg's *Ode to Napoleon* (a setting of Byron's attack on the autocrat and a hymn to liberty in the poem of the same name) introduces the severe style of the twelve-tone system and the austere melodic line of the Sprechstimme into the cantata. Schoenberg wrote a second cantata in which the twelve-tone technique appears: *A Survivor from Warsaw,* a grim picture of a Nazi concentration camp.

## CAROL
### (in French, *Noël;* in German, *Weinachtslied*)

A Christmas song, usually of religious character.

It is believed that the carol was born in the small town of Grecia, near Assisi. There St. Francis built in his church the first Christmas "crib"—a group of figures in a stable depicting the Holy Birth. He urged the community to sing nativity hymns around the crib, and to dance, and thus the carol was created.

Ultimately, the carol was incorporated into the medieval mystery play, performed by wandering players in the town square. Often these carols proved to be the most welcome parts of the entire performance. It has been recorded that in the town of Chester, England, in the fourteenth century, the audience wrecked the stage of the mystery players because they did not sing enough carols. The popularity of these songs became so great that they became the music of the people, virtually folk songs.

The oldest printed carol is "The Boar's Head," a jubilant melody dating from 1521. To this day it is traditional at Queen's College, Oxford, to have this melody sung as an accompaniment for a procession in which the boar's head is carried.

Carols have survived through many different ways. They have been kept alive orally, handed down from one generation to the next. They survived by way of the printed broadside which was hawked on the streets of England for pennies. Some famous carols were rediscovered in a historic tome written in the sixteenth century, but uncovered in 1850. In this volume, a London grocer made a record of the little things he wished to remember, covering the years between 1500 and 1536: recipes, menus, dates of events, riddles and puzzles, hints on breaking horses and brewing beer. He also included poems, and among them many carols. Another important source for carols is a list drawn up by an Englishman named Hone in 1823, comprising eighty-five carols; many of them had long been forgotten, but were then being restored to the world.

Carols are either dramatic, lyric, or narrative. They may be songs of angels, songs about superstitions, or songs of earthier matters. Sometimes old secular melodies were adapted to religious verse; and sometimes the opposite was true, as when Pepusch adapted an old French noël for a drinking song in *The Beggar's Opera*.

French and Italian carols often have a pastoral character. The pastoral association with Christmas survived for a long time. In Naples, shepherds would come down from the hills at Christmas time, piping their pastoral tunes in the streets before the images of the Virgin and the Child. Thus the pastorale has remained an important element of Christmas music and is often in the Yuletide works of Corelli (*Christmas Concerto Grosso*), Bach (*Christmas Oratorio*), and Handel (*Messiah*).

Many Christmas carols are deathless in their beauty. Few musical pieces surpass them in gaiety, spontaneity, cheer, and sheer loveliness. Christmas is still celebrated throughout the world with these songs. The most famous of these is "The First Nowell," of French origin, a melody of incomparable serenity and charm, describing the first evening of Christmas when a star shone brilliantly in the East, pouring its light over Bethlehem where "born is the King of Israel."

Other Christmas carols are also famous. Such lusty tunes as the "Wassail Song" and "Down in Yon Forest" are among the oldest songs known to man, yet their appeal is as vibrant today as it ever was. The "Wassail Song" is a robust drinking tune full of good humor; wassail songs date from pre-Norman, possibly even pre-Christian days. "Down in Yon Forest" is more poetic, it was sung in medieval times by wandering troubadours. Another great favorite, "We've Been Awhile Awandering," strikes a more hearty note; it is intoned by children in masquerade wandering the street, seeking coins from strangers.

Not all Christmas songs are of anonymous authorship. "Good King

Wenceslas" was adapted by a clergyman of the nineteenth century to a secular melody three hundred and fifty years old, "Now the Time of Flowers Is Here." The ever-popular "Adeste Fideles" (Come, All Ye Faithful), one of the greatest melodies in religious music, was written by John Reading, an English organist of the seventeenth century, for his Christmas services in Winchester. And "Silent Night, Holy Night" —perhaps the most celebrated of all Christmas songs—was composed in 1816 by an obscure Austrian organist and schoolmaster, Franz Xavier Gruber.

## CHORALE

A hymn of the German Protestant church which came into being in the sixteenth century during the Reformation. It was introduced by Martin Luther who wanted to encourage congregational singing. He began setting German liturgical texts or Psalms to simple folklike melodies and interpolated these hymns in the church services, having the congregation sing them in unison. Some of Luther's melodies were original; most of them were adaptations of popular tunes of the day. The most famous of Luther's hymns (the melody was original with him) is "Ein fest' Burg ist unser Gott" (Psalm XLVI) which was subsequently adapted and used by many famous composers including Johann Sebastian Bach, Mendelssohn (the *Reformation Symphony*), and Meyerbeer (*Les Huguenots*). The first Luther book of hymns appeared in 1524.

The chorale achieved immense popularity with Germans and became the popular song of the masses in the seventeenth century, not only in the church, but also in the streets and the home. Contrapuntal richness was added to the chorale in the seventeenth century by Samuel Scheidt, Johann Pachelbel, and Buxtehude. The great age of the chorale came with Johann Sebastian Bach, who introduced them into his larger works (cantatas and passions), besides writing them for his services. Bach wrote only thirty or so chorales that were original. More than four hundred others were harmonized by him, the melodies being in general circulation. The chorale ceased to interest composers after Bach's day.

## DA CAPO ARIA

*See:* Aria

## ELEGY

A song of lamentation, generally for a dead person. A popular example is the "Élégie" of Jules Massenet. It was originally an instrumental piece called "Invocation"—a movement from the orchestral suite, *Les Erinnyes*. It gained popularity, apart from this suite—and under the name of "Élégie"—when the composer adapted it for voice with cello and piano accompaniment, and a lyric was written for it by E. Gallet.

## FOLK SONG

The song of the people, the oldest form of musical expression. It differs from the art song in that it was not created by any single composer but by a whole race of people who handed down these songs aurally from generation to generation. These songs are invariably simple in esthetic appeal and direct in emotion, reflecting and expressing local customs, sentiment, thinking, legends, superstitions, etc. A widespread interest in the folk music of different parts of Europe spread in the middle of the nineteenth century and has continued to this very day. Societies and individual scholars have done immense research in many different regions, unearthing their local tunes and dances, putting them down on paper, and frequently dressing them up in traditional harmonies. Many serious composers have been inspired by these indigenous melodies to produce large serious works in which they were either incorporated or imitated.

## FUGUE

*See:* Page 345

## HYMN

A song of religious worship in metrical or stanza form intended for congregational singing.

## LIED

The German term for art song, but an art song in which words and melody are so intimately related that they become a single artistic entity. The Lied is discussed in detail in Chapter 2 of this section.

## MADRIGAL

The madrigal is the secular equivalent of the motet. The madrigal is a musical setting of a poem on a pastoral or amorous or satirical subject. It is contrapuntal in style, for two or more unaccompanied voices.

Madrigals were written as early as the fourteenth century. But both the form and the style were developed by the early polyphonic composers. One of the earliest masters of the madrigal was Adrian Willaert of the Venetian School. It was he who adapted the motet and made a conscious attempt to give a faithful musical representation to his text. The madrigal was further developed in Italy by Orazzio Vecchi and Luca Marenzio in the sixteenth century, and immediately after them by Carlo Gesualdo. It achieved its most advanced stages of technical and artistic development with Palestrina and Monteverdi.

The madrigal then passed on to England, where an English publisher, Nicholas Yonge, issued a volume of the most representative examples of Italian madrigal writing, together with a single piece by an Englishman, in 1588. The Englishman was William Byrd, acknowledged as the founder of the English Madrigal School, the greatest of all the madrigal schools. Byrd's contemporaries and immediate successors—the most important of whom were Thomas Morley and Orlando Gibbons—brought the English madrigal to a point of development from which it could go no further. In England, the madrigal acquired melodic sweetness and tenderness, a feminine charm—together with a suppleness in part writing—it had not known in Italy. And these traits endeared the English madrigal to the entire world. The best examples of English madrigal music include "Sing We and Chant It" and "Now Is the Month of Maying" by Thomas Morley, and "The Silver Swan" and "Fair Is the Rose" by Orlando Gibbons. They are still heard at choral concerts and continue to afford delight to the discriminating music lover.

## MAGNIFICAT

A musical setting of the Song of the Virgin Mary in the Gospel of St. Luke. This is part of the Vesper services in the Roman Catholic church. This form emerged and was favored by the early polyphonic schools. Two of the most celebrated of all magnificats were produced by the Bachs, father and son. Johann Sebastian Bach wrote his stirring magnificat for the services at his church in Leipzig on Christmas Day, 1723. Bach's son, Karl Philipp Emanuel Bach, completed his magnificat a quarter of a century later, in 1749. The work of Karl Philipp Emmanuel Bach is particularly interesting in its successful attempt to combine older contrapuntal methods with the newer homophonic style.

## MASS

The principal ritual of the Roman Catholic liturgy.

For centuries the custom prevailed to sing parts of the mass, the earliest interpolations being plain songs. With the development of polyphonic music, composers of the Netherland School started writing elaborate polyphonic works for unaccompanied chorus to be used as masses. The unaccompanied mass reached its zenith with Palestrina. In the seventeenth century, the mass abandoned its a cappella format and started using instrumental accompaniments, as well as solo and ensemble parts. The mass had by now established its permanent form, comprising five sections: Kyrie, Gloria, Credo, Sanctus and Benedictus, and Agnus Dei.

The crowning work in this form—indeed, one of the crowning choral works in *any* form—is the *Mass in B Minor* by Johann Sebastian Bach. In 1733, Bach tried to get a post as composer in the Saxon Royal Chapel. To prove his ability he sent King Augustus III a portion of a work which he humbly described as a "trifling example of my skill." This so-called "trifle" was nothing less than the first two sections of the *B Minor Mass:* the Kyrie and the Gloria. Five years later, Bach completed the entire mass—sometimes using material he had already incorporated in other works.

Structurally, Bach's mass is one of the most monumental works in all music. There are twenty-four distinct parts within the traditional five sections: fifteen choruses, six arias, and three duets. A complete performance requires three and a half hours. But the mass is outstanding not only because of its mammoth size, but also for its intense religious feeling, mysticism, and grandeur. Bach was not trying to express his own devout feelings in this music. He aspired to build a mighty edifice to the greater glory of God. Subjective feelings gave way to an objective contemplation of the grandeur of the Deity.

It will be noted that Bach stressed the chorus in his *Mass.* It is in the choral passages, much more than in arias and duets, that the tide of Bach's genius swept with the relentless force of an ocean. Beginning with the opening Kyrie, which is worked out with breadth and spaciousness, and concluding with the majestic Dona nobis pacem, the choral pages have the awe-inspiring proportions of a cathedral.

Haydn wrote fourteen masses intended for church services. They have been deplorably neglected by the concert world. Recent recordings have provided testimony to the high quality of their inspiration and to their deserved place with Haydn's greatest works. Haydn's finest masses include the *Lord Nelson Mass,* written in 1798, and believed to have been inspired by the news of Lord Nelson's victory in the Battle of the Nile; and the *Mass in Time of War,* completed two years before that. In these two works, Haydn not only revealed a master's command of counterpoint—the Credo fugue in the *Mass in Time of War* is probably one of the most striking contrapuntal passages in all of Haydn—but also a cogent sense for drama, a refreshing vitality of ideas, and a moving reverence. This, then, is a far different Haydn from the genial, lovable, and witty "papa" of the symphonies.

Mozart's choral literature includes eight large masses and several smaller ones (*Missa Brevis*). Two Mozart masses are masterworks of the first order. The *Coronation Mass,* in C major, was written in 1779 for a small church near Salzburg (the Maria Plain) which, tradition said, had been visited by the Virgin. Mozart's mass commemorated the Virgin's visit. The *Great Mass in C Minor*—Mozart's greatest work for the church—was written because of a personal vow. Mozart had sworn that if and when he brought his beloved Constance back to Salzburg as a bride he would write a mass as an expression of his gratitude. Mozart married Constance in 1782; and he and his bride returned to Salzburg in 1783. By then, Mozart had fulfilled the vow— but only partially, since he had completed only three sections (Kyrie, Gloria, and Sanctus). Other parts were in sketches; still others had not yet been planned. Mozart never did manage to complete the mass; skeptics insist that he was discouraged from completing the work because of a sense of disenchantment with his wife. When the *Great Mass* was performed for the first time (in Vienna on August 25, 1783) Mozart expropriated music from his other religious works to fill out the design. It is in this way that the *Great Mass* is still heard. The level of inspiration throughout the mass is so consistently high that it is difficult to remember that the work was, after all, a patchwork production. The "Et Incarnatus est" passage in the Credo section—which has become independently famous, and is often heard by itself—is surely one of the most moving pages produced by Mozart.

Beethoven was the first great composer to write masses for concert performance rather than for church services. Beethoven's most celebrated choral work, the *Missa Solemnis,* is one of his noblest and mightiest creations. Despite its liturgical text, it is more dramatic than religious. In place of humility and reverence we get passion and strength and a kind of defiant pride.

Beethoven planned the mass to honor the installation of his pupil and patron, the Archduke Rudolph, as Archbishop of Olmütz. He set to work in 1818. But his composition was not yet complete when, in 1820, the installation ceremony took place. Actually, Beethoven did not complete the mass until 1823. For five years he gave himself to this Herculean task without sparing himself, and when it was completed it contained some of his profoundest concepts. But there is emotional intensity in this music, too. Beethoven, himself, recognized this fact by writing on his manuscript: "From the heart—may it go to the heart."

The mass continued to be a favored form for composers writing choral music after Beethoven. Schubert completed six masses, each filled with wonderful lyricism. The best of his masses is that in E flat major which he wrote in the last year of his life. Cherubini, Weber, Rossini, Gounod also wrote excellent masses. Many twentieth century composers produced notable works within this ambitious form, among them Stravinsky, Delius, and Ralph Vaughan Williams.

## MATTINATA

A "morning song," a love song sung under the beloved's window— favored by many Italian song composers. The best known are by Leoncavallo and Tosti.

## MOTET

A musical setting in polyphonic style for unaccompanied voices of a Biblical text, originally in Latin. It is the religious equivalent of the madrigal. This form was greatly favored by the earliest polyphonic schools; it reached full maturity with Palestrina, who completed more than two hundred works in this form. Bach wrote six splendid motets (all to German texts), the most famous being, "Singet dem Herrn."

## NOËL

*See:* Carol

## ORATORIO

An extended work for soloists, chorus, and orchestra on a dramatized Biblical text but given without scenery or costumes.

The oratorio was created at the end of the sixteenth century in the San Girolamo della Carità Church in Rome. Filippo Neri, founder of the Congregation of the Oratorians, felt that the Bible could become more appealing and stimulating for the younger members of his order if parts were set to music and performed during the regular services. He had composers prepare such settings and had them performed after his sermon during the weekday service. Originally, these settings were called *Laudi spirituali,* but after a short time they came to be known as "oratorios," after the congregation in which they were performed. These Laudi spirituali had little resemblance to the oratorio as we know the form today. They made no pretense at being dramatic; the form was fragmentary and inchoate; the style was monotonous. But the groundwork was laid, and the structure of the oratorio could now be erected.

What is sometimes described as the first oratorio appeared in 1600, *La Rappresentazione di anima e di corpo,* by Emilio del Cavalieri. Cavalieri called his work a "spiritual opera," and actually had it performed with costumes and scenery. But since the text is religious, and because it has spaciousness of form and demands the use of soloists, chorus and orchestra, and finally because there is an attempt to vary the style through alternation between recitatives and choral passages, *La Rappresentazione* is really an oratorio.

The first important composer of oratorios was Giacomo Carissimi who produced a long series of such works in the seventeenth century: *Lucifer, Job, The Last Judgment, Abraham and Isaac, Jepthe,* and many others. For the first time, the music of the oratorio acquires a dramatic character; for the first time there is a definite attempt on the part of the composer at lyric writing; for the first time the orchestra assumes importance. The recitative now becomes the spine of the work, carrying on the dramatic action. Carissimi introduced the Narrator to tell the story through these recitatives, a device often found in later oratorios. With Carissimi the chorus is a commentator on all that is happening—and the choral writing is endowed with emotion, force, and theatrical interest.

Carissimi is the transition from the comparative primitive oratorio of Cavalieri to the completely developed form of Handel. Between Carissimi and Handel, several of Carissimi's disciples carried on the traditions of their teacher; the most important of these was Alessandro Scarlatti. None of the oratorios written at this time are a part of the present-day repertory; but they all played a decisive role in preparing the way for Bach and Handel.

The earliest oratorios that are occasionally heard—and, even then, none too frequently—are those by Johann Sebastian Bach. Bach wrote three works which can be termed oratorios. The best known of these is the *Christmas Oratorio;* somewhat less familiar is the *Easter Oratorio.*

The *Christmas Oratorio*—written in 1734—is, strictly speaking, more a series of cantatas than an oratorio. It lacks the dramatic interest and the unity we have come to expect from this form. As a matter of historical fact, Bach did not present the *Christmas Oratorio* as an integrated work. The first part was heard on Christmas Day. The next five parts were performed on five different occasions: on the second and third Christmas days; New Year's Day; the Sunday after New Year's; and the Feast of Epiphany.

The *Easter Oratorio,* written two years later, has more of an oratorio character. Its dramatic action is carried along by a narrative, while the entire work contains sustained dramatic interest.

Both works are in a joyous vein. There are brilliant orchestral effects, vivid and vital choruses, vigorous arias frequently indulging in picturesque effects and giving an over-all feeling of spirited animation. Regrettably, neither oratorio is familiar even to the lover of great choral music. It is true that neither work represents Bach at his greatest. But each contains enough treasures to make for rewarding listening. Parts of each work are often played. In the *Christmas Oratorio* there is the beautiful orchestral Sinfonia prefacing Part II—an exquisite Pastorale filled with radiance and sometimes known as either the "Shepherd's Christmas Music" or the "Pastorale"; there is also the spirited contralto aria, "Prepare Yourself Zion," ("Betreite dich Zion"). In the *Easter Oratorio,* the most celebrated passage is the beautiful Adagio movement that follows immediately after the opening Sinfonia.

George Frederick Handel is the greatest composer of oratorios in music history. It is with him that the oratorio achieved its golden age —and an age that died with him.

Handel wrote his first oratorio, *La Ressurezione,* when he was twenty-three years old. He was traveling in Italy at that time and beginning to make his mark as a composer of Italian operas. But in Rome, where Handel lived in 1708, there existed a papal decree forbidding opera performances; Handel decided to write a religious work in the form and style of Carissimi, whom he admired. And the work he wrote in this vein was successfully given in Rome at the time.

Though Handel kept on writing oratorios, he specialized in Italian opera for many years, and in opera he achieved his spectacular success in England. It was a long time before he poured the full force of his genius into the oratorio form. Several circumstances finally led Handel to abandon the opera and concentrate on the oratorio. For one thing his popularity as an opera composer was on a sharp decline; Handel knew that he would have to cultivate a new field to regain public favor. For another, he was suddenly made conscious of the fact that the oratorio could be as popular with English audiences as the opera. And what made him conscious of this fact was a private performance of one of his oratorios, *Esther*—with a cast of children, and with the benefit of scenery, costumes and a stage production—in 1732. *Esther* was such a huge success that Handel decided to give the same work a public performance with a professional cast. Because English law forbade the presentation of a religious work on the stage, Handel offered *Esther* in a concert version. Once again the enthusiasm was tremendous. Handel decided to write new oratorios for English consumption —consequently with English texts. His first English oratorio was *Deborah,* successfully performed in London in 1733. During the next few years, Handel wrote several more English oratorios—including *Saul* and *Israel in Egypt* in 1739.

His greatest triumph as a composer of oratorios—and his crowning masterwork—came in 1741 with the *Messiah.*

The *Messiah* was written under dramatic circumstances. In 1741, Handel's fortunes in London were at an ebb. Several of his operas had been appalling failures. His rivals united against him and were relentless in their attack. Financial bankruptcy seemed unavoidable. In London, it was said that the once-great Handel was "through."

It was at this decisive moment that Handel received from Ireland (where his reputation was still untarnished) an invitation to go to that country to direct several performances of one of his oratorios for charity.

Handel planned to present in Ireland the world première of a work he had just completed in an unprecedented outburst of inspiration: the *Messiah*. This monumental work—which takes two and a half hours to perform—was written in twenty-four days; never before had he written music with such fever and frenzy. For days he scarcely touched the food put before him; often he did without sleep. Never before had he dedicated himself to a creative task with such complete dedication; no work before this was produced with such emotional upheaval. His servants, at times, found him in a kind of trance. When he completed the "Hallelujah Chorus," tears were streaming down his cheeks. "I did think I did see all Heaven before me and the Great God Himself!" he told his servant. And when the score was written, he pointed to his bulky manuscript and said simply: "I think God has visited me."

The text was adapted from the Scriptures by his friend, Charles Jennens. It was divided into three parts. In the first, the coming of the Messiah is prophesied; in the second, the suffering and death of Christ are described; the concluding part is devoted to the Resurrection. Handel's score consists of fifty musical numbers: recitatives, arias, duets, choruses, and so forth.

The inspiration of the *Messiah* never falters, never lapses, as Handel's music passes from compassion to grief, from spirituality to ecstatic joy. There are joyous and exalted pages such as the florid tenor aria "Every Valley Shall be Exalted," and the soprano arias "O Thou That Tellest Good Tidings to Zion" and "Rejoice Greatly O Daughter of Zion." There are pages of infinite compassion, such as the bass aria "But Who Shall Abide," and the soprano arias "He Shall Feed His Flock" and "How Beautiful the Lamb of God." There is overwhelming pathos in the alto aria "He Was Despised," and the choral "Surely He Hath Borne Our Grief." There is serenity and spiritual radiance in the soprano aria "I Know That My Redeemer Liveth," and in the famous "Pastoral Symphony" for orchestra. And, finally, there is incomparable exaltation in the "Hallelujah Chorus," and the concluding chorus "Worthy Is the Lamb of God" with its cathedral-like, concluding "Amen."

The present practice of having the audience rise during the singing of the "Hallelujah Chorus" originated with the English première of the oratorio in March 1743. King George II, who was present, was so moved by this music that he rose from his seat and remained standing during the chorus; the audience followed their king. Since then it has been customary for audiences everywhere not only to rise during the rendition of this section but even to join in the singing.

The world première of the *Messiah* took place in Dublin on April 13, 1742, after a general rehearsal (attended by the public) on April 8. Critics and audiences were overwhelmed by the majesty of the work —one of the rare instances of a masterwork being appreciated at first hearing. "Words are wanting to express the exquisite delight it afforded the admiring, crowded audience," reported the *Faulkner Journal*. "The sublime, the grand, and the tender adapted to the most elevated and moving words conspired to transport the ravished heart and ear."

This triumph rehabilitated Handel's fame and fortunes. It also left him with no further doubts regarding the popularity of the oratorio among English audiences. Henceforth he directed his creative power through this medium. Oratorio after oratorio left his pen: *Samson, Semele, Hercules, Judas Maccabaeus, Joshua, Solomon, Theodora, Jephtha,* and many others. No other single person was ever again to make such prodigious contributions to oratorio music; no period in oratorio history, before or since, was so fruitful.

Few of Handel's oratorios are given public renditions. Occasionally there are revivals of *Israel in Egypt;* less frequently of *Samson* or *Judas Maccabaeus.* Only the *Messiah* survives, as popular today as it was in Handel's time. If Handel had written only this one work, he would still be the supreme master of the oratorio. For the *Messiah* is not only the greatest oratorio ever written, but one of the most sublime creations in all music.

Joseph Haydn had long had the ambition to write an oratorio in the style of Handel, whom he admired profoundly. Yet, though he wrote music in virtually every form known in his day, he did not produce an oratorio until the closing years of his long life. It was an English impresario, Salomon (the same man who had commissioned him to write twelve symphonies and direct them in London), who prevailed on the master to realize his lifelong ambition. Salomon brought Haydn a text written by an Englishman named Liddell which combined sections from the Genesis of the Bible and Milton's *Paradise Lost,* and told the story of the creation.

Haydn wrote his first oratorio, *The Creation,* in 1797 and 1798 when he was sixty-six years old. He brought to the writing of this work a humility and a devotion he had shown to few other compositions. Being a profoundly religious man, he looked upon the task of setting the story of the Creation as a kind of consecration. "I prayed to God with earnestness that He should enable me to praise Him worthily," Haydn said.

It took him eighteen months to write *The Creation*, music to which he brought his fullest creative powers grown ripe and incomparably fruitful. To his lifelong gift for melody, he now added the ability to create atmosphere, to build up climaxes, to project dramatic incidents, to write programmatically, and to invest his thinking and feeling with a spiritual glow. The overture describes the conversion of chaos into order, of darkness into light, in a tone painting that is remarkable for the period. The oratorio then tells the story of the Creation during six days. With a realism revolutionary for the early nineteenth century, Haydn describes the blinding flash of light that pierced through the darkness with the command "Let There Be Light," and recreates the "furious storms" that lashed the newborn world. But there is more than realism here. There is fresh and buoyant lyricism in pages like the famous aria "Rolling in Foaming Billows" for basso, and the even more celebrated soprano aria "In Verdure Clad," and the tenor aria "In Native Worth." There is genuine inspiration in the way the music captures the mystery and awe of life suddenly throbbing in the soil (the recitative "Be Fruitful All"), and in the atmospheric picture of morning (the orchestral prelude to the third part).

*The Creation* was introduced in Vienna on April 29, 1798, under the composer's direction. Its success was so great that before long choral societies were founded in Austria just to perform it.

Haydn's second and last oratorio—and his last piece of music—was completed three years after *The Creation*. It was *The Seasons*, its text derived from a poem by James Thomson. If the religious man speaks in *The Creation*, it is the lover of nature who is uncovered in *The Seasons*. The score is filled with ebullient music springing from the heart of a man who reacted sensitively to the varied beauties of nature in different seasons. The oratorio begins with Spring and progresses through Summer, Autumn, and Winter. If *The Seasons* is not so consistently inspired as *The Creation*, it nevertheless has many fine pages. The most famous are the choral apostrophe to the vernal season,

"Come Beautiful Spring" and the richly melodic aria for soprano, "O How Pleasant to the Senses."

Though the Romantic Era was a period of decadence for the oratorio, several notable works in the form were produced. Among the more distinguished are Berlioz' *L'Enfance du Christ* (1854), Franck's *Les Béatitudes* (1879), Liszt's *Legend of St. Elizabeth* (1862) and *Christus* (1866) and, most important of all, Mendelssohn's *Elijah* (1845).

Mendelssohn wrote *Elijah* for the Birmingham Festival in England where it received its world première, under the composer's direction on August 26, 1846. It was so successful that eight numbers had to be encored.

The text by Pastor Julius Schubring begins with the prophet's pronouncement of the coming of the drought. The overture comes after this recitative. We then get a recital of Elijah's miracles and his victory over Baal's prophets. In the second part, the prophet suffers at the hands of his enemies, particularly Jezebel, but receives the protection of the Lord and is finally brought to Heaven in a fiery chariot.

Mendelssohn's score combines incomparable lyricism with powerful dramatic effects. The oratorio arises to its greatest eloquence in its realistic translation of Biblical episodes. The score is most noteworthy for some of its beautiful arias: "If With All Your Hearts," "It Is Enough," and "O Rest in the Lord"—surely some of the finest passages of lyric writing in all oratorio music. There are also powerful choruses: "Help Lord, Wilt Thou Destroy Me" in the first part and the double chorus, "Baal We Cry to Thee," in the second.

Since Mendelssohn's *Elijah*, no oratorio has enjoyed such wide appeal and such sustained popularity as *The Dream of Gerontius* by Edward Elgar, written in 1900. It was one of two works that brought the composer his first major success in and out of England (the other work being the *Enigma Variations,* written one year earlier).

*The Dream of Gerontius* is based on the famous poem by Cardinal Newman. It does not follow the structure of the classical oratorio of Handel. It is built out of a series of lyric and dramatic episodes describing the doctrine of Purgatory in the Catholic church. There are no set arias, duets, and choruses. Influenced by Wagner, Elgar tried to create a continuous and uninterrupted flow of musical ideas. *The Dream of Gerontius* is a unified musical concept, in the way that one of the dramas of the Wagnerian *Ring* is, one part blending inextricably into another.

Because Elgar's approach to the oratorio was unique, *The Dream of Gerontius* was not a success at first hearing: at the Birmingham Festival on October 3, 1900. Not until it was repeated at the Lower Rhine Festival, about a year later, did it achieve recognition for the first time. After it was repeated in England, the work began to make a deep impression on the English music public; its poetic beauty, vivid imagery, mysticism, and nobility of concept were recognized and admired. Its place among the most popular oratorios of all time was now assured.

Several interesting oratorios have been written in the twentieth century. The most important are Arthur Honegger's *King David* (1921), and Stravinsky's *Oedipus Rex* (1927). The latter is designated as an opera-oratorio and, consequently, is occasionally performed as an opera and sometimes as an oratorio.

## PART SONG

A song in the contrapuntal style, for three or more voices.

## PASSION

The Passion is an oratorio, with this difference: Its text is always based on the story of the Passion of Christ according to the Gospels. (The meaning of "Passion," in the Biblical sense, is the "suffering of Christ.")

Long before the Passion form was finally evolved, the story of Christ's suffering had been set to music. In the thirteenth and fourteenth centuries mysteries, containing plain songs and choral passages, retold the Christ story. During the same period it was also the practice to present in church the Passion of Christ, with words and music, employing three characters: a Narrator (tenor), Christ (bass), and the Crowd (alto).

The first formal Passions were written by the members of the early polyphonic schools in the fifteenth century. During the German Reformation two important developments took place: The Passion was set to a German text; and the chorale was introduced to allow the congregation to participate in the singing.

It is with Heinrich Schütz in the seventeenth century that the Passion assumes a personality recognizable to us. In the Schütz Passion, the Narrator tells the story. When he comes to the words of Jesus, St. Paul, or the Evangelist, that character speaks for himself either in recitatives or arias. The chorus is used to represent the crowd, and it comments on what takes place. Schütz not only established the form of the Passion but he also introduced into it dramatic and musical interest unknown before him. Influenced by the opera, then arising in Italy, Schütz brought to the Passion oratorio duets and ensemble numbers and filled his music with dramatic force.

The Passion changed little either in structure or style with Johann Sebastian Bach. But he endowed it with unequalled grandeur and nobility.

The two greatest Passions in musical literature are both by Bach: the *Passion According to St. Matthew,* and the *Passion According to St. John.*

The *St. Matthew Passion* is the greatest work of its kind, awe-inspiring in form and overpoweringly eloquent in content. The text was drawn from the 27th and 28th chapters of the Gospel According to St. Matthew, prepared by a postal clerk named Christian Friedrich Henrici. Bach completed his score in 1728, and directed its first performance at the St. Thomas Church in Leipzig on April 15, 1729. From one of Bach's pupils we learn that the work was not well received. "Some high officials and well-born ladies in one of the galleries began to sing the first chorale with great devotion from their books. But as the theatrical music proceeded, they were thrown into the greatest wonderment, saying to each other, 'What does it all mean?' while one lady exclaimed, 'God help us! 'Tis surely an opera-comedy!' "

The *St. Matthew Passion* is in two parts. The first is gentle and introspective; the second, tragic. In this work, Bach emphasizes the suffering of Christ and the immense tragedy of his betrayal. The music abounds with sorrow and compassion. Essentially, the *St. Matthew Passion* is a work of great emotional intensity, as is proved by such affecting arias as "Grief and Pain" for alto, "O Grief There Throbs the Racked and Bleeding Heart" for tenor and chorus, and "My Savior Now Is Dying" for alto. But it is also music of great reverence. Where in all Passions the recitatives of Christ are accompanied by a keyboard instrument, those in *St. Matthew* have an instrumental background (the recitatives of all other characters are still accompanied by a keyboard instrument), endowing them with special spiritual qualities.

The performance of the *St. Matthew Passion* in the Leipzig church under Bach was the last it received in a century. In the 1820's, young Felix Mendelssohn—then not yet twenty years old—was introduced to this work through his teacher, Zelter, who possessed a copy of the manuscript. So moved was Mendelssohn by the magnificence of this music that he set himself the mission of performing it publicly and thus restoring it to the world of music. The second performance of the *St. Matthew Passion,* then, was given under Mendelssohn's direction in Berlin on March 11, 1829. It was an immense success. One of the singers, Eduard Devrient, reported: "I felt the thrill of devotion that ran through me at the most impressive passages was also felt by the listeners, who listened in deadly silence. Never have I felt a holier solemnity vested in a congregation than in the performers and audience that evening."

The *St. John Passion* was written before the *St. Matthew,* in 1722–1723, and was introduced at the St. Thomas Church in Leipzig, under the composer's direction, one year later. It is simpler in design and smaller in scope than its companion; but at its best its eloquence is no less stirring. Where the *St. Matthew* is filled with pain, grief, and pity, the *St. John* is charged with drama. Thus the emphasis in the *St. Matthew* is on arias and duets while that in *St. John* is on stirring choruses. One beautiful aria in *St. John* should be singled out, and is deservedly famous: the aria for contralto, " 'Tis Finished" ("Es ist vollbracht").

The Passion ceased to be a significant musical form after Bach. There are some examples of Passion music in later centuries, but none of these are distinguished. A popular choral work that can be designated as a Passion is *The Crucifixion* of Sir John Stainer, written in 1887. The contemporary Italian church composer, Lorenzo Perosi— one-time musical director of the Sistine Chapel—has written many Passions, but they are rarely heard outside Rome.

## PSALM

A sacred song of praise for solo voice or for chorus. It was the predecessor of the hymn and the chorale. Specifically, the term applies to a setting of one of the one hundred and fifty poems in the Book of Psalms in the Old Testament. There are three types of psalms employed in church music. The antiphonal psalm uses two alternating choruses. The responsorial psalm uses a soloist and a chorus in alternation. The direct psalm uses no alternation.

## REQUIEM

A mass for the dead. It uses the liturgical text of the mass with the omission of the Gloria and Credo sections, and with the interpolation of a Dies Irae and sometimes other sections.

The requiem form was developed in the early history of polyphonic music by such masters as Palestrina and Victoria. The first requiem in musical history still alive in choral repertory is that of Mozart, written in the last year of his life (1791).

Few works of music have such a dramatic history as Mozart's *Requiem*. A stranger, dressed in gray, and masked, came to Mozart's house to commission him to write a requiem. The source of this commission—so insisted the stranger—must remain a dark secret. Many years later it was discovered that the patron was Count von Walsegg who habitually asked composers to write works for him which he would present as his own. But to Mozart, then sick and weary of spirit, it appeared that this messenger was actually a visitor from another world, coming to ask him to write his own requiem before it was too late.

Though it sometimes required superhuman effort for him to work on the requiem—sick as he was with his last fatal illness—Mozart kept on writing, determined to complete the work before his death, which he sensed was imminent. "I know from what I feel that the hour sounds and I am at the point of death," he has been reported to have said at the time. "And so I must finish my funeral song. I must not leave it incomplete."

The requiem remained uppermost in Mozart's mind to the last days of his life. Sick in bed he called his friends near him and asked them to sing with him the Lacrymosa section. In his last stages of unconsciousness he imitated the sound of trumpets; it is believed that he was accompanying himself in the singing of the Tuba mirum part.

He was able to complete most of the work, and what he did not finish was written by his pupil, Süssmayer. Of the fifteen sections, twelve are by Mozart, though in the last few of these Süssmayer had to fill in the instrumentation. The last three sections—Sanctus, Benedictus, and Agnus Dei—are by Süssmayer. There is, however, no decline in inspiration and creative power in these three concluding parts;

it is for this reason that the belief is general that Mozart must have explained to his pupil in minute detail his musical intentions regarding these final pages.

The requiem is one of Mozart's most sublime and most emotionally profound works. A new depth and otherworldly concept enters his writing. In pages like the Lacrymosa and Salve me we are listening to the voice of a genius who has looked at the face of death. There are also many moments of terror and majesty, nobility and grandeur, in this music. The concluding section, Lux Aeterna, repeats the music of the opening Kyrie.

Two splendid requiems were written by French composers of the Romantic Era. The first is that of Berlioz, completed in 1837; the other, by Fauré, in 1887. Both are sensitive in feeling, refined in style, and of sovereign beauty. They afford pleasure to a sophisticated musical taste as a rare cognac does to a gourmet.

But concert audiences everywhere respond much more strongly to requiems of Brahms and Verdi, because they have an emotional appeal that is more direct and immediate.

Brahms called his work *A German Requiem* because, unlike other compositions of this kind, it uses a German instead of a Latin text which Brahms himself prepared from a Lutheran Bible. Brahms began planning his requiem in 1861 as a memorial to his dear friend, Robert Schumann, who had died five years earlier. However, it was his grief at the death of his mother that provided Brahms with the needed inspiration and emotional stimulus to complete the work in 1866; the fifth part, "Ye That Now Are Sorrowful," is generally regarded as Brahms' specific musical tribute to his mother.

When three movements from the requiem were introduced in Vienna on December 1, 1866, the music was severely criticized. However, the first performance of virtually the entire work, which took place in Bremen in 1868, was an immense success.

There are seven sections. Instead of the traditional Latin titles of Requiem, Kyrie, Gloria, Credo, and so forth, the sections have the following headings: "Blessed Are They That Mourn"; "Behold All Flesh"; "Make Me to Know"; "How Lovely Is Thy Dwelling Place"; "Ye That Now Are Sorrowful"; "Here on Earth"; and "Blessed Are the Dead."

Most of the work is suffused with an autumnal melancholy found in such wonderfully tender and poignant pages as "All Flesh Doth Perish as the Grass" and "Lord Make Me to Know What Measure of My Days May Be." But the sorrow is sometimes touched with a soothing solace, as in the beautiful soprano aria "Ye Who Now Sorrow"; and toward the end of the work there is even a feeling of liberation from grief in the exultant chorus, "Now that Death Is Swallowed Up with Victory."

Verdi, master of Italian opera, produced only one major work in a non-dramatic field, and that was his *Requiem*. He wrote it to honor the memory of the Italian novelist, Manzoni, who died in 1873. Completed in 1874, the requiem was introduced at the St. Mark's Cathedral in Milan under the composer's direction. It was triumphantly received and was soon heard throughout Italy, and in many different versions, including one arranged for brass band, and one transcribed for four pianos and chorus.

In the requiem, the master had not altogether abandoned his operatic habits. There are many florid arias, such as the Domine Jesu and Benedictus which belong in the opera house rather than the church; and there are rousing climactic passages, as in the Dies Irae which has a theatrical effect. But Verdi could express deep emotions and profound religious feelings, too. In the opening Requiem and in the Agnus Dei, for example, he reaches a plane of spiritual beauty which immediately places his requiem with the great works in this form. And in several of his fugues, particularly the monumental one that closes the work, he is a master of the contrapuntal technique.

## ROUND

*See:* Canon

## SERENADE

### (in German, *Ständchen;* in Italian, *Serenata*)

An evening song, specifically, a love song sung under a lady's window. Schubert's "Serenade," from the song cycle *Schwanengesang,* is probably the most famous example of this kind of song. Other familiar vocal serenades were written by Brahms, Richard Strauss, and Tosti.

The *serenata* is also a form of vocal composition popular in the eighteenth century; akin to a secular cantata, it is sometimes for soloists, sometimes for chorus, and given a stage presentation.

The serenade, as a form of orchestral music, is discussed on page 404.

## SONG

A short composition for solo voice and accompaniment in which a poem (known as the lyric) is set to music. The song is usually in two or three parts. The two-part song form consists of a melody and a countermelody. In the three-part song form the original melody returns after the countermelody.

The evolution of the song is discussed in Chapter 2 of this section.

## SONG CYCLE

A group of songs which have a common theme or a unifying mood and atmosphere. The first song cycle in music was Beethoven's *Sechs geistliche Lieder*. Other famous cycles include Schubert's *Der Winterreise*, Schumann's *Dichterliebe*, Hugo Wolf's *Italienisches* and *Spanisches Liederbuch*, and Debussy's *Fêtes galantes*.

## SPIRITUAL

A religious song of the American Negro that developed during the period of slavery.

The spiritual was inspired by the condition in which the Negro found himself, transplanted as he was in a new and cruel world where he was despised and abused. The emotional disturbances of the Negro demanded an outlet. Since he was essentially musical, he found that outlet in songs.

Some of the characteristics of rhythm, syncopation, and shifting beats of the spiritual were derived from the music that the Negro had brought with him from Africa. But the spiritual is American, not African, music. It profited from the Negro's contact in this country with European melody and harmony; it was the expression of his experiences and feelings in the New World.

The spiritual developed technical features not found in any other American folk music: the downward progression of some cadences; the lapses from major to minor without modulation; freedom in the use of pitch and rhythm; different melodic decorations found with each repetition of the melody; the frequent injection of notes (usually the flatted third and seventh) foreign to the scale.

The spiritual is a religious song because, in America, the Negro found Christianity and it became for him a solace and a refuge. His intense religious emotions became in turn the emotions of his songs, and to such an extent that very often religion and song became one and the same thing. The spiritual is also a "sorrow song." The Negro was a child of misery: an outcast in a strange land; separated from those he loved; the victim of a master's whip. He expressed the burdens of his heart in his music.

There are three kinds of spirituals. The first utilizes the "call and answer" form which originated in Africa. Usually in fast tempo, these are spirited and passionate melodies, such as "Gimme Dat Ol' Time Religion." The second class is slower and statelier, requiring a long, sustained phrase as the principal melodic subject: "Nobody Knows de Trouble I've Seen." In the third group we find some of the most famous spirituals in the repertory. In place of a long sustained phrase in the melody, the lyric line is composed of sections of rhythmic patterns of a decidedly syncopated nature. A notable example of this last group is "All God's Chillun Got Wings."

The most wonderful spirituals are those that express the Negro's almost childlike concept of God and religion. Religion was his compensation for and escape from physical and mental sufferings, with its promise of a happier life to come. It taught him the nobility of resignation and hope. When the Negro sang of the Crucifixion of Christ, he brought to it his own immense suffering—his own personal everyday crucifixion—as in "Were You There When They Crucified My Lord?" Not all spirituals have the majesty of Crucifixion songs. Some, like "I Know the Lord Laid His Hand on Me," are more dynamic, fuller of animal spirit. Still others—they were, strictly speaking, not spirituals but shouts—are hysterical, barbaric, and aboriginal. Familiar spirituals were transformed into febrile music, throbbing with rhythmic cogency. Frequently, too, new songs were improvised in the delirium of dance and worship. A refrain would be sounded, one voice would then interpolate a line, another voice would contribute another—and thus, in the heat and passion of a religious orgy, a new Negro melody would be born.

## STABAT MATER

A musical setting of the sequence describing the Holy Mother at the Cross sung in the Roman Catholic church before Palm Sunday and on the third Sunday in September. The Stabat Mater was set by the early polyphonists of the Netherland School and by subsequent polyphonic masters. A remarkable setting was made by Pergolesi in the early eighteenth century. Such later masters as Haydn, Rossini, Schubert, Verdi, and Dvořák produced excellent Stabat Maters that are staples in choral literature.

# Basic Works in Choral and Vocal Music

Bach, J. S.: *Christ lag in Todesbanden*, (Cantata No. 4).

Bach, J. S.: *Christmas Oratorio*.

Bach, J. S.: *Mass in B Minor*.

Bach, J. S.: *Passion According to St. Matthew*.

Bach, J. S.: "Singet dem Herrn," (Motet No. 1).

Bach, J. S.: *Wachet auf*, (Cantata No. 140).

Bach, K. P. E.: *Magnificat*.

Beethoven: "Adelaide"; *An die ferne Geliebte*, (song cycle).

Beethoven: *Missa Solemnis*.

Berlioz: *Requiem*.

Brahms: *A German Requiem*.

Brahms: Selected songs: "Immer leiser wird mein Schlummer"; "Die Mainacht"; "Der Tod, das ist die kühle Nacht"; "Vier ernste Gesang."

Debussy: Selected songs: "Fêtes galantes"; "Mandoline"; "Paysage sentimental."

Fauré: Selected songs: "Les Berceaux"; "En Prière"; "Les Roses d'Ispahan"; "En sourdine."

Handel: *Messiah*.

Haydn: *The Creation*.

Honegger: *King David.*

Mendelssohn: *Elijah.*

Monteverdi: "Lagrime d'amante al sepolcro dell' amata," (madrigal).

Mozart: *Great Mass in C Minor.*

Mozart: *Requiem.*

Mozart: Selected songs: "An Chloe"; "Das Veilchen."

Mussorgsky: *Songs and Dances of Death.*

Palestrina: *Missa Papae Marcelli.*

Pergolesi: *Stabat Mater.*

Rachmaninoff: Selected songs: "Lilacs"; "Night Is Mournful."

Ravel: "Trois chansons madécasses."

Rossini: *Stabat Mater.*

Schubert: Selected songs: "Ave Maria"; "Der Erlkönig"; "Die Forelle"; "Gretchen am Spinnrade"; "Hark, Hark the Lark"; "Serenade"; "Der Tod und das Mädchen"; *Die Winterreise,* (song cycle).

Schumann: Selected songs: "Im wunderschönen Monat Mai"; "Der Nussbaum"; "Widmung"; *Dichterliebe,* (song cycle).

Strauss, R.: Selected songs: "Allerseelen"; "Morgen"; "Ständchen"; "Traum durch die Dämmerung"; "Zueignung."

Tchaikovsky: Selected songs: "None but the Lonely Heart"; "Pilgrim's Song"; "Solitude."

Verdi: *Requiem.*

Wolf: Selected songs: "Anakreons Grab"; "Auch kleine Dinge"; "In dem Schatten meiner Locken"; "Storchenbotschaft"; "Verborgenheit."

# PART THREE

## Music for the Stage: The Opera and Ballet

$\sim\!\sim\!\sim\!\sim\!\sim\!\sim\!\sim$ *1* $\sim\!\sim\!\sim\!\sim\!\sim\!\sim$

# This Thing Called Opera

Every once in a while the lament is sounded that the opera is a dying art form. These jeremiads point out three facts: Nobody is writing vital opera any longer; great operas of the past are more museum curiosities than a vibrant element of our culture; opera performances are smothered under the dead weight of obsolete traditions.

There have been unfortunate periods in recent memory when our opera houses appeared to take special pains to prove these contentions. With tired and boring performances, with stage sets and costuming that have long outlived their usefulness, and with a stodgy approach to staging and repertory, these opera companies sounded a death knell for opera as a living art form.

On the other hand there have been other periods in our time when opera has taken a new lease on life, emerging from temporary relapses more robust than previously. During these more vital periods, opera has proved that there is nothing essentially wrong with it that imagination, initiative, and sound talent cannot remedy completely. We then learn this basic truth: Opera possesses as much vitality as its creators and performers are able to endow it.

Every period in music history has seen the emergence of some composer able to rejuvenate the opera form and open up new avenues of expression. Sometimes this was done through the application of a new set of esthetics, techniques, or approaches, as Wagner did in the nineteenth century, and Debussy and Alban Berg in the twentieth. Sometimes this was achieved through a skilful union of old traditions and new concepts of melody or tonality in the manner of Mussorgsky in *Boris Godunov* and Benjamin Britten in *Peter Grimes*. Sometimes opera was revitalized because a composer was able to bring the freshness and vigor of his talent to old forms and techniques, and through the freshness and vigor was able to shape something essentially new. No new trails for opera were blazed by either Puccini or Gian-Carlo Menotti, for example; but both of them arrived at a living musical theatre.

In a radio interview over the Columbia Broadcasting System a few years ago, James Fassett, in a conversation with the Earl of Harewood, contributed an illuminating footnote to this idea. The Earl of Harewood noted that in England opera had been, for many years, in the doldrums. Along came a powerful, stirring, passionately intense and original work like Britten's *Peter Grimes* and the entire English music world was suddenly invigorated. The Earl emphasized that not only can the emergence in England of two major opera companies be directly attributed to Britten's successful opera; but also a new burst of creative activity in the field of opera among English composers.

If, in the creative field, opera is as vital as the composer who creates it, then, by the same token, opera is as vibrant in the field of interpretation as the people who project it. Given unimaginative performances, opera appears to have outlived its capacity to be a living art. But when electrified through a dynamic approach by singer, conductor, stage director, and scenic designer, even the old war horses of opera reveal amazing health, and their impact on audiences remains potent.

Opera cannot die because it is an art form whose esthetics are sound; it has the indestructibility of all great art. There is perhaps no better way of clarifying the esthetic goal of opera than to repeat a well-known aphorism: Music begins where speech ends. Words, at best, often can only suggest the subtleties of emotion evoked by tones. In the same way, the narrative capacity of words to describe and clarify a given situation can be only vaguely approximated in tones. All this is self-evident to the point of being a truism. But this truism explains the basis of opera: to merge the power of music in arousing emotions with the capacity of words to tell a story. Supplementary to each other, words and music bring new dimensions to an artistic work. Richard Wagner put it this way: "I examined the relations of music to poetry and came to the conclusion that the extreme limits of one mark the exact point at which the sphere of the other begins, and that it is therefore the close union of the two that enables us to express most truly and clearly what they cannot express separately."

While words and music are inseparable partners in opera, it is always the music that fills the starring role. It would be impossible to single out a single opera that has survived with a great text but a poor score; on the other hand there are numerous—perhaps too numerous—examples of operas suffering from an execrable libretto yet continuing to delight audiences because of the vigor of the music. Wagner's effort to create a single artistic entity out of drama and music notwithstanding, his mighty dramas have far greater musical significance than literary; and this is as it should be.

Good opera, then, places the stress on music rather than play. And a good operatic score places stress on melody rather than on any dramatic element. The song—the aria—reigns supreme in the opera house, and probably always will. The quality of song varies with different composers—from the singableness of Rossini and Verdi to the realism of Mussorgsky and the declamation of Debussy. Familiarity with the music of Mussorgsky and Debussy has taught us that these composers are also lyrical, though their lyricism has a different character from that of more traditional composers. Wagner may have dispensed completely with the aria form as such, but the greatest moments in his music dramas boast soaring lyrical effusions. Not all the ingenuity in the world on the part of a composer can compensate for weakness in lyricism.

It is only when a composer has fulfilled the basic requirement of opera to be melodious that he can concern himself with the subtleties that make for great opera: dramatic interest; characterization; atmosphere; variety of mood.

If the song is all-important in opera, the singer is also all-important. The conductor, the stage director, and the scenic designer are all indispensable factors in distinguished performances—especially the conductor, whose genius can integrate a performance and make it glow with a hot flame. But the most important single factor in opera is the singing voice. It is, as Paul Bekker once remarked, "the root from which the opera has sprouted and grown. It is the force that carries the opera forward. It is the power that ever anew leads it to completion according to the mode in which the nature of the voice is perceived. . . . The opera is the realization of the potentialities of the singing voice, whose laws it brings to fulfilment, whose possibilities it brings to concrete realization, whose susceptibility to change at the hands of an ever-changing creative process it represents."

The singer is the focal point of every great opera performance. With beauty and virtuosity of voice, musical intelligence, electricity of personality, the singer can invest an opera performance with glamour, excitement, and musical significance. A great and dynamic star can bring to a thrice-familiar opera a new freshness and exhilaration, make that familiar opera an altogether new esthetic experience for the listener. But great opera, of course, cannot subsist on the star alone. Though of lesser importance, the other elements of good opera—acting, staging, scenery and costumes, orchestral performance—are all important. The star system can be—and has been—a virtue turned into a deadly vice when the impresario prefers to ignore or slight the other elements.

The variety of opera performances with different singers, impresarios, stage directors, conductors—and also at different periods of time which bring changing musical and dramatic values—enables a thrice-familiar opera to excite a music lover each time he hears it. An opera becomes something continually new, even though every line of dialogue and every musical phrase is familiar. George R. Marek elaborated on this point by saying: "We can hear certain operas all our life and derive something new from each performance. . . . As we hear these operas again we hear new things in them. Or we hear the old things in a new way. However it may happen, there is a new element present. Great music is a self-renewing pleasure. I believe that the characteristic of newness is a quality that music possesses to a greater degree than do the other arts. Thus, there is no end to the enjoyment of great operas, because music can hardly ever be heard to the end—its entire content can hardly ever be brought to the surface—because each performance is a new performance."

# How Opera Developed

Opera was created for the specific reason of realizing a new kind of artistic expression through the union of words and tones, play and music.

It was created by a group of intellectuals to whom history has given the name of the *Camerata*. The Camerata gathered in or about 1580 in Florence, Italy, to discuss the theatre, literature, and music. Since this was the age of the Renaissance, the discussions inevitably gravitated to the culture of the ancient Greeks and were focused on the classic Greek drama. The Camerata was fired with an ambition: to restore the classic Greek drama. Since music had played a prominent part in Greek drama the Camerata discussed the problem of uniting drama with music. And this was quite a problem in the sixteenth century. For the kind of music then in vogue, both in and out of the church, was contrapuntal. The concept of a single melody for solo voice was not yet arrived at, nor was there yet any instrumental music to speak of. Contrapuntal music, as the Camerata realized only too well, could never serve in the theatre. The theatre stressed the role of the individual; contrapuntal music was expressive of a group or of masses. Besides, by its very nature, contrapuntal music obfuscated the text often to the point of unintelligibility, thereby negating the primary purpose of the drama.

To resolve this problem, the Camerata delved more deeply into the writings of the ancient Greeks. A treatise on music by Aristoxenus insisted that song should be built out of the inflection of human speech. There was also the following statement of Plato: "Let music be first of all language and rhythm, and secondly tone; not, vice-versa."

The Camerata was given the cue for a *new* kind of music: the recitative, a sing-song declamation by a single voice accompanied by musical instruments. It could now set about restoring the Greek play. It selected the classic drama, *Dafne*. One of the members, the poet Rinuccini, prepared the libretto; another member, Jacopo Peri, set the text to musical recitatives. *Dafne*—written in 1594—was described by its authors as a *"dramma per musica"* (drama through music). Though their intention was the revival of Greek drama, their result was something quite different: As the first dramatic work ever to be set *entirely* to music, *Dafne* was actually a new art form; in later years that new art form would acquire the name of "opera."

*Dafne* was a primitive opera, to be sure. A story, bare of action or conflict, concerned Dafne, beloved of Apollo, who was transformed by her mother into a laurel tree as protection from a pursuing god. This tree henceforth became sacred to Apollo. The poetry was recited by the various characters with exaggerated inflections to suggest song; a small orchestra, consisting of lutes and harpsichord, accompanied the song. Occasional variety was provided by brief ballet sequences and by the chanting of a chorus.

All this was a new theatrical experience for the audience gathered at Jacopo Corsi's palace where *Dafne* was first performed and where it was received most enthusiastically. The Camerata felt that it had realized its goal with sufficient success to warrant their undertaking other works in a similar vein. Peri wrote a second work, *Euridice*. Another member of the Camerata, Giulio Caccini, also wrote a *Euridice* as well as other dramas.

The "new music" (*Nuove Musiche*)—so the recitative was described by Caccini—did not have to wait long for its first acknowledged master. He was Claudio Monteverdi who, it can be said, was the first to suggest the artistic possibilities of the new art form. Peri's *Euridice* came to Monteverdi's attention in 1600. Suddenly, Monteverdi—who up to then had been writing madrigals—saw before him a new musical world. On February 24, 1607, there took place, at the royal palace at Mantua, the first performance of Monteverdi's first

opera, his masterpiece, *Orfeo*. It is with *Orfeo* that the long and fruitful history of Italian opera can be said to begin.

There is no point in overstating the case by suggesting that Monteverdi's *Orfeo* is as exciting to present-day audiences as it was in the
early seventeenth century in Mantua. There are recordings of this
opera (and occasional performances) to prove that it has too great a
monotony of color, mood, and emotion to provide sustained interest;
the melody is still too close to speech to touch the heart; the procession
of one number after another is still formal. *Orfeo* suffers from repe-
titiousness. It is not a living experience. Only on rare occasions, in
several poignant arias by Orfeo, does the opera have genuine emotional appeal.

But *Orfeo* was, nevertheless, a milestone; and for the age in which
it was written, it was a phenomenon. Monteverdi, regarded in his
time as a daring modernist, opened up new vistas for the dramma per
musica. Besides recitatives, his work had arias, duets, and trios. There
was an expanded orchestra, and there was emphasis on instrumental
interludes. There was a striving for musical realism through orchestral
color, even dissonance, and there was a gesture toward dramatic effect
through changes of key. At several points there is the recognizable
shadow of the aria as we know it today. These innovations in *Orfeo*
made earlier operas by Peri and Caccini primitive by comparison.

When Monteverdi settled in Venice in 1613 he succeeded in making
that city a new center of Italian operatic activity. It was in Venice
that there was now opened (in 1637) the first public opera house; and
it opened with Francesco Manelli's *Andromeda*. (Before this, operas
had been given in palaces for private audiences, or in public squares
by roving players.) The San Cassiano Theatre, as the new opera house
was called, made provision for foreign as well as Italian nobility in
boxes that were rented annually; the masses gained admission to the
spacious parterre by paying approximately twenty cents.

This opera house became the focal point for the operatic activity in
Venice. Between 1641 and 1649 approximately thirty different dramatic works were heard, written by Monteverdi and his disciples.
Thus there arose the first school of opera composers, the Venetian
School, headed by Monteverdi. His pupil, Francesco Cavalli, became
its most famous composer after Monteverdi himself. With Cavalli, a
greater distinction was made between recitative and aria, the latter
acquiring greater expressiveness, emotional force, and decorated ele-

gance. The orchestra was assigned increasing importance in projecting atmosphere and dramatic effect.

It was with Cavalli, too, that the word *opera* was first used in connection with the new art form. In 1639, Cavalli referred to his *Le Nozze de Tetias* as an *"opera scenica."*

The Venetian School was the first in the history of opera. But the first *major* school was the Neapolitan. In Naples the traditions of Italian opera—adhered to for the ensuing generations of Italian opera composers—were established.

The founder of the Neapolitan School was Alessandro Scarlatti (not to be confused with his son, Domenico, whose specialty was music for the harpsichord). Scarlatti's first opera was heard in Rome in 1679. Three years later, he followed several members of his family who had settled in Naples, and in 1684 he became there a Maestro di Capella. In this office he started presenting his own operas, both at the royal palace, and for Neapolitan audiences at the San Bartolomeo Theatre. So great was his popularity, and so influential did his music become, that the Scarlatti opera became the model for Neapolitan composers to imitate. There then took place an efflorescence of operatic writing and operatic performances in Naples.

With the Neapolitan School, many new elements entered into opera form and style. The most important was the *aria da capo,* a medium for the projection of melodic expressiveness hitherto unknown. Out of the Scarlatti aria da capo emerged the traditional Italian opera aria with its mobile flow of beautiful lyricism to encourage beautiful singing.

In the Scarlatti operas, ensemble singing became a basic element of opera; and the so-called Italian overture was developed, a prototype of operatic overtures for the next generation.

Other traditions, besides musical, were created in Naples: the use of plots and characters drawn from legend or history; the subdivision of the opera into three acts; the emphasis on music rather than play in an effort to glorify the singer and the song.

Consequently, the structure and the form of Italian opera was now fully realized, not only with Scarlatti himself, but with those who followed him and wrote in his style: Durante, Porpora, Jommelli, Galuppi, Piccinni, and even the Saxon-born George Frederick Handel who absorbed the Neapolitan traditions and adhered to them in his own operas.

The operas written by most of the members of the Neapolitan School were primarily serious dramas (*opera seria*). A parallel development was the comic opera (*opera buffa*). Where the serious opera utilized historic or classical characters, the comic variety called upon everyday characters: scheming servants, cuckold husbands, deceiving wives. Where the serious opera became involved in elaborate plots and florid melodies, the comic opera resorted to elementary situations and simple tunes.

The father of the opera buffa was Giovanni Battista Pergolesi. Before his time short comic scenes had often been set to music. These scenes, known as *intermezzi*, were sometimes independent works; sometimes they were parts of actual operas. In 1709, a theatre was opened in Naples to present these little farces, some of them written by Scarlatti himself.

But it was Pergolesi who developed and extended the intermezzo form into the opera buffa. In 1733, Pergolesi presented a new comic opera for the Neapolitan audiences. It was *La Serva padrona*, a work so fresh in its melodies, so spontaneous in its spirit, so ebullient in feeling, and so ingratiatingly witty, that it can still provide delight for the opera lover. There are only three characters (and no ballet or chorus) engaged in the elementary plot. Serpina, maid to Uberto, aspires to become the wife of her master. She contrives a plot, with the assistance of a mute valet, Vespone. Vespone disguises himself as a sea captain, pays court to Serpina, and thereby arouses Uberto's jealousy. At last, Uberto asks Serpina to be his wife.

The levity of the plot is matched by the nimbleness and light touch of the music. The melodies are always tuneful and supple, a continual joy to the ear. Rhythm and tone color contribute to the deft characterizations.

*La Serva padrona* was introduced in Naples on August 28, 1733. It was such a huge success that many Italian composers began writing operatic works in a similar vein. The best of these were Galuppi, Piccinni, and Paisiello, while the finest opera buffa after Pergolesi came in 1792: Cimarosa's *Il Matrimonio segreto*.

The opera buffa style was established long before the end of the century: the contrasts of light and shade; the fleet use of rhythm and staccato figures for coquettish or mischievous moods; the sculptured elegance of the melody; the wit and malice of both music and text; the use of the chattering bass in the orchestra. With Rossini, in the first decades of the nineteenth century, the opera buffa arrived at greatness.

Meanwhile, in 1752, a group of wandering performers brought *La Serva padrona* to different parts of Europe. Everywhere the opera was acclaimed. When heard in Paris, it was such a triumph that many were ready to concede that this was the only true operatic art; that the more serious kind was spurious. A musical war erupted between those who believed in the traditions of serious French opera and those who upheld the comic style; but about this, more will be said later in our discussion of French opera. The French philosopher Jean-Jacques Rousseau was so enchanted with *La Serva padrona* that he wrote *Le Devin du village* in unashamed imitation.

It is but a step from the opera buffa of Pergolesi to the French product in the same genre—the opéra comique, whose parent was Pierre Monsigny. Hearing *La Serva padrona* in 1752 gave Monsigny a mission and a purpose as a composer. But it was some years before he realized that mission. In 1795, however, he completed his first comic opera, *Les Aveux indiscrets*, with which the opéra comique was born.

Grétry, another early composer of the opéra comique once confessed that "my own work is but a continuation of Pergolesi's." Grétry's first highly successful, and highly gifted, comic opera was *Le Tableau parlant*, produced in 1769. He followed this success with three other notable works: *Zémire et Azor*, in 1771; *L'Amant jaloux* in 1778; and *L'Épreuve villageoise*, in 1784.

The form of the opéra comique now passed to that triumvirate which helped to make the form world famous: François Boïeldieu, who wrote *La Dame blanche;* Daniel François Auber, composer of *Fra Diavolo;* and Adolph Adam, best known for *Le Postillon de Longjumeau*. The crowning genius of the opéra comique—Jacques Offenbach, who wrote *Orpheus in the Underworld, La Belle Helène,* and *La Vie parisienne* among many other works—developed out of the soil fertilized by this gifted trio.

It was also the popularity of *La Serva padrona* that helped create the German equivalent of the opera buffa—the *Singspiel*. Johann Adam Hiller was the first important composer of this theatrical form, which was modest and unpretentious, actually little humorous skits set to music. But the form was soon extended by Johann Friedrich Reichardt and was endowed with artistic significance by Mozart, whose German comic operas (including *The Abduction from the Seraglio* and *The Magic Flute*) are its legitimate offspring.

But let us return to serious opera.

French opera, as distinguished from the Italian, was first evolved by an Italian-born composer, Jean-Baptiste Lully. Lully, who had been brought to Paris in his boyhood, became director of the Opera House which had been established in 1669. For this theatre he wrote operas in which a French style was formulated for the first time. His model was, of course, Italian opera. But he placed greater emphasis on the drama; he increased the resources of his musical writing through an enriched harmony and orchestration; he made ballet and grandiose scenes integral elements of the operatic theatre; he denuded arias of their Italian embellishments; and he assigned a new importance to the recitatives, which now were accompanied by the orchestra, instead of by a keyboard instrument.

The Lully opera was developed by the first great French composer of opera: Jean-Philippe Rameau. Because Rameau preferred more expressive and more intricate harmonies than even Lully, because his orchestrations were more complex, and because his melodies were simpler in design, he antagonized many staunch Lullists. Actually, Rameau was proceeding in the same direction as his predecessor; and his operas followed the Lully technique. Rameau completed what Lully had begun: the evolution of an essentially French operatic style. And for this he had to suffer the abuse of all those who remained faithful to the Italian ways.

When Pergolesi's *La Serva padrona* was introduced in Paris, devotees of the Italian opera used that lovable comic opera as the spearhead for their attacks on Rameau. A war (the musical historian refers to it as the *guerre des bouffons*) erupted. On the one side were Diderot, Rousseau, Grimm, and others who pronounced Pergolesi's way of writing operas the only authentic one. On the other side were those siding with Rameau; Voltaire, who belonged to this latter group, wrote that "Rameau has made of music a new art."

Victory for the French opera did not come in Rameau's lifetime. The battle was fought on and off for a number of years. Another major operatic war, with virtually the same issues involved though with different personalities, erupted in Paris in 1775. Ironically enough, the esthetics of French opera, first evolved by an Italian, were to be fully vindicated by another foreigner: Gluck.

In creating a French tradition of opera, neither Lully nor Rameau had been motivated by a desire to reform opera. They were merely adapting French tastes, temperament, and cultural backgrounds to opera. Since these differed from those of the Italians, the operas they wrote were different.

Nor was reform the concern of Henry Purcell when he achieved an authentically English opera with *Dido and Aeneas,* written in or about 1690. He wrote as his English temperament demanded: melodies and ensemble numbers that derived their simplicity and tight-lipped restraint from the English folk song and madrigal. The sense for good theatre was an Elizabethan heritage that Purcell carried on, achieving a wonderful fusion of music and text—the music vivid in pictorial imagery, rich in emotion, sensitive in feeling, contributing suspense and atmosphere to the spoken word.

But reform *was* the ideal of Christoph Willibald Gluck when he set about writing operas that were different from those the Italians were creating and were popularizing throughout all of Europe.

The Italian opera, in Gluck's day, had come upon evil days. Italian composers—and others writing in the Italian manner—competed with one another in the writing of meretricious melodies exploiting the vocal dexterity of the singers. The music of these composers was bombastic, designed to arouse and excite audiences which wanted opera to please the ear, impress the eye, and lull the senses. And the Italian librettists —the most celebrated of whom was Pietro Metastasio, living in Vienna —concurred in this belief. They wrote artificial texts, cluttered with impossible situations, and filled with euphuistic speeches. If the text served to evoke from the composer ornate, meretricious, grandiose, or sentimental music it served its purpose; the play was not expected to have any artistic merit of its own. Consequently, rarely did the Italian opera of the seventeenth and early eighteenth centuries boast a sincerely felt emotion, a profound sentiment expressed forcefully; rarely, too, did the buoyant lyricism have any relationship with the poetry.

It was with operas in the established Italian manner that Gluck first emerged as a successful composer in Vienna. But the Italian style increasingly dissatisfied him, and he became increasingly impatient with the kind of librettos furnished him by Metastasio. He was being driven toward a new ideal: "noble simplicity." The more he thought about it the more did he feel that a closer partnership was needed between music and text; that the singer must be the servant of the music he sings, and not the other way around; that every element of the operatic theatre should be integrated into a unified conception.

He put these ideas clearly and forcefully into words: "When one wishes to keep to the truth, one's style must be adapted to the subject that is being created. The greatest beauties of melody and harmony become imperfections when they are out of place in the whole." And again: "Beauty in the wrong place has not only the disadvantage of losing a great part of its effect but also of injuring the whole by leading the spectator astray." Finally: "Before I work, I try above everything else to forget that I am a musician, and I forget myself in order to see only my characters."

Gluck's ideals found two powerful allies in Vienna. One was Count Giacomo Durazzo, assistant director of the court theatres, who had come to Vienna from Paris in 1732 already fired with the ambition of instituting French reforms in the Viennese theatres. The other was Ranieri Calzabigi, also from Paris; he had come to Vienna in 1761 infected with the spirit of the French Revolution, an ardent believer in the esthetic principles of simplicity, naturalness, and humanity expressed in the writings of Rousseau, Diderot, and Voltaire.

The three were drawn together by a mutual sympathy for the same ideals. They stood ready to pit themselves against the all-powerful, ever-popular Italian School headed by the mighty Metastasio.

Their first shot in the operatic revolution took place on October 17, 1761 with the ballet, *Don Juan*. The scenario, based on Molière's *Le Festin de pierre*, had a French text prepared by Calzabigi; the music was by Gluck. This was Durazzo's first attempt to bring the esthetics of French art into the Viennese theatre.

But what was needed to overthrow the old regime and introduce a new age was not just a ballet, but an opera. And such an opera was not slow in coming. On October 5, 1762, there took place the première of Gluck's *Orfeo ed Euridice;* and with it came the dawn of a new operatic era. The text by Calzabigi and the music by Gluck were the last words in simplicity and human feeling. More important still, never before had there been an opera in which there existed such an intimate relationship between word and song, play and music. Here music served—not the singer or the audience—but exclusively the text.

Though Gluck's *Orfeo* was at first a failure, Gluck was not discouraged. With *Alceste* which followed, his experiments grew bolder. The formal and stilted overture was dispensed with and replaced by an *intrada* (introduction) to set the mood. Arias, choral numbers, orchestral interludes all emphasized, underscored, and interpreted the action, and brought to it new meanings. Ever more passionate grew the striving for simplicity: the "Chorus of the Spirits," incomparable for dramatic force, consisted entirely of a repeated "F"!

*Alceste* was a failure; so was *Paride ed Elena* which succeeded it. "No obstacles shall deter me from making new attempts to achieve my purpose," wrote Gluck with the conviction of a prophet. If Vienna was not receptive to his ideas, then, surely, Paris would. In 1773, Gluck left Vienna to carry on his fight against the Italian opera in a new setting.

But the battle was no less severe in Paris. Some people there resented him because he was a foreigner; others, faithful to the Italian traditions, were unsympathetic to his ideas. When he wrote a new opera for Paris, *Iphigénie en Aulide,* he needed the intervention of Marie Antoinette herself before it was performed. But when it was finally given, on April 18, 1774, it was a triumph.

Gluck's enemies were only temporarily defeated—or so they thought. They mustered their forces for an all-out encounter, bringing to Paris one of the most famous of all Italian composers of that period, Niccola Piccinni, in an effort to offset Gluck's popularity. The rivalry between Piccinni and Gluck culminated when each wrote an opera on the same text—*Iphigénie en Tauride.* Gluck's was a sensation; Piccinni's, a disastrous failure.

Gluck's victory over Piccinni—and his Italian enemies—was now decisive. The Gluck opera, as opposed to the Italian opera, had won unqualified acceptance.

The impact of Gluck's reforms, which was to be felt strongly in German opera, did not by any means destroy the Italian traditions. Some of the abuses perpetrated by the Metastasio school were shed— but only some. Others remained: the excessive importance given to the voice and to the song; the readiness to accept clichés, incongruities of plot, as well as the discursiveness of the dramatic action; the tendency to rely exclusively on the big musical scene or the affecting aria for effect, even when that scene or aria was out of proportion in the general design.

But even within these limitations several Italian composers were able to produce masterworks in both the serious and the comic vein. Because they were musicians of genius, these composers could take stilted situations and sawdust characters and, by bringing to them the sun of wonderful lyricism, managed to bring to their operas the vibrancy of a living art.

One such Italian was Gioacchino Rossini, who wrote both serious and comic operas. The serious operas—the most famous being *William Tell*—have pages of rare beauty, tenderness, and passion. But Rossini's imperial position in Italian opera is due to his comic operas. His masterpiece, *The Barber of Seville,* is the model all later writers of the opera buffa studied and emulated. Here was a forceful and original creator who could strike out boldly in new directions: in the use of the accompanied, instead of spoken, recitative—the spoken recitative had been up to then the practice in opera-buffa writing; in the origin of the so-called "patter" song for comic effect; in the insistence upon written-down, instead of improvised, vocal cadenzas; in the infectious contrasts of gay and slow passages; in the intriguing use of rhythm to suggest mood or character; in the seemingly inexhaustible supply of wonderful lyricism, as effective in comic effects as in tender or sentimental ones.

Like Rossini, Gaetano Donizetti wrote both serious and comic operas. Also like Rossini, he showed flashes of genuine power and melodic genius in his serious works, the most celebrated being *Lucia di Lammermoor.* But it was in the comic style that he produced an unqualified masterwork—*Don Pasquale.*

Vincenzo Bellini, next in line in the royal succession of Italian opera composers, dedicated himself exclusively to serious opera. In works like *Norma* and *I Puritani* he enriched opera with a virtually unrivalled wealth of beautiful lyricism. On that single string he played with the most consummate artistry and virtuosity, using melody to express different shades of emotion, to project dramatic power, to open up new vistas of beauty. His arias—"ample, marvelous, unique," as Ildebrando Pizzetti described them—brought the art of "beautiful song" (bel canto) to its highest development.

The crowning genius of Italian opera appeared four years after Bellini's death, when the première of a new opera took place at La Scala in Milan. That opera, *Oberto,* was the first stage work of a young and then still obscure composer named Giuseppe Verdi. *Oberto,* a tremendous success, officially launched the career of a composer destined to dominate the world of Italian opera for half a century without a rival.

He did not shatter existing conventions. He bent these conventions pliably to his own purposes. Adhering to the formal structure, he took the bricks of arias, duets, ensemble numbers, and choruses and used them to build such noble and integrated edifices as *Rigoletto, La Traviata, Il Trovatore,* and *Aïda.* He, too, liked the big scene and was partial to bel canto. But he had the genius to invest his operas with immense dramatic power and genuine characterizations. And in the closing years of his life he was still capable of opening new horizons for Italian opera: in *Otello* and *Falstaff* he achieved a synthesis of drama and music, and increasing expressive power of song which were new for Italian opera without abandoning its Italian identity.

A significant development in Italian opera after Verdi was the so-called "Verismo" School. Without sacrificing those musical values Italian composers revered, this school insisted on a greater naturalism in the libretto—away from the stuffy costume play of the past, in favor of incidents of everyday conflicts in contemporary settings. Verismo emerged with Pietro Mascagni's *Cavalleria Rusticana* in 1890; gained momentum with Ruggiero Leoncavallo's *Pagliacci,* two years later; and reached its culmination in the lyric works of Giacomo Puccini.

While Puccini was, as he himself said, "a creator of small things," he was the undisputed successor to Verdi in the Italian operatic dynasty. He did not have Verdi's grandeur, nobility, and bigness of scope; but he had a human quality which made his operas a poignant emotional experience for the opera lover. On the debit side, Puccini was sentimental; was too often satisfied with second-rate materials; could not resist the temptation of building a big aria out of proportion to the general design. But these faults are not too important when placed side by side with his positive qualities. He knew the theatre well: could create dramatic effects with telling force, build a climactic scene with overpowering impact, etch characters and limn back-grounds with a subtle stroke. His music is skilful in technique and astute in adapting itself to the requirements of the play. It is filled with a tender vein of melody identifiably his. In *La Bohème, Tosca,* and *Madame Butterfly* he created a world of operatic enchantment which no one since Verdi had been able to duplicate. And as the years passed, his harmonic, rhythmic and tonal resources were enriched—as he assimilated the influences of Verdi, then Wagner, then the Verismo School, then Debussy, then even the twentieth century modernists. What could serve his artistic purpose was used, regardless of the nature of the style or idiom, and became an inextricable part of his writing.

For some time after Rameau, the French were dependent on visiting Italians to create for them the kind of operas they liked to see. Cherubini and Spontini, both of whom enjoyed extended stays in Paris, adapted Italian opera to French tastes. Since the French liked to emphasize stage procedures, Spontini's *La Vestale* and Cherubini's *Médée* paid great attention to the ballet, to scenes of pomp and ceremony, to stunning tableaux. Scenery and costuming grew more and more elaborate, keeping pace with the drama which became complicated with incidents, and melodramatic in presentation. The play, rather than the music, was the thing. People and events were the central point of interest, rather than the melody or ensemble number. The aria—sovereign of the Italian opera—had to take a secondary place.

This tendency of French opera to become a spectacle for the eye reached a culmination with the "grand" opera of Giacomo Meyerbeer. Eugène Scribe's librettos exploited historic plays on a grandiose design. And for all his lyrical genius, Meyerbeer preferred following the lead of his librettist, adapting his music to meet the complex demands of the stage spectacle. One does not go to a Meyerbeer opera expecting subtlety or delicacy, but rather telling effects which rarely fail to arouse excitement: with *Les Huguenots* and *L'Africaine* opera had truly become "grand."

French opera now passed on to where it belonged rightfully: with the French composer. The Gallic temperament saw to it that the vast dimensions of the Meyerbeer opera be reduced, and that a greater economy of means be employed. This does not mean that the French composer did not occasionally build up a climactic scene with a rousing chorus or an impressive pageant. But the French composer placed stress on the emotional or psychological conflicts of his characters, on the dramatic intensity of an expressive recitative, on the eloquence of a mobile but simple song.

With Jacques Halévy, composer of *La Juive,* French opera acquired agility of movement, directness of expression, economy of means both vocally and orchestrally, and detail in characterizations. This tendency away from the grandiose and toward simplicity and precision, away from indulgence in stilted and artificial means toward the expression of human emotions, away from the pompous and the verbose toward refinement and grace, grew more and more pronounced with subsequent French composers: with Charles Gounod in *Faust;* with Jules Massenet in *Manon;* with Georges Bizet in *Carmen.*

Two important developments took place in French opera at the dawn of the twentieth century. With Charpentier's *Louise* the proletarian opera was realized for the first time, as Naturalism (the French counterpart of the Verismo Movement in Italy) intruded boldly. Opera here drew its text from the backgrounds and problems of the working class; and the music—now built out of Parisian street cries, now achieving vigor and dramatic power through realistic recitatives —matched the text in its naturalistic approach.

Another opera proved to be the ultimate realization of the French aim to achieve a harmonious synthesis of music and text. It was Debussy's *Pelléas et Mélisande,* with which Impressionism makes its first appearance in opera. Probably only in France could such an opera have been written, for only the French temperament was able to express such a sensitive feeling for mood, such an exquisite sense for musical symbolism, such a fabulous palette of delicate musical colors, and such ultra-refinement in style.

German composers were even more concerned than the French in the dramatic values in opera. As German opera evolved, text and music were welded together more and more into an inextricable oneness; the music became increasingly articulate and expressive as it interpreted the action, the characters, the emotions, and the psychological overtones. The German composer went one step beyond the French in stripping opera of many of its extra-dramatic trimmings: the ballet, for example. And it also increased the enrichment of harmonic, contrapuntal, and instrumental writing.

What the German opera was subsequently to become was first suggested by Gluck's *Orfeo.* But Gluck's *Orfeo* still had an Italian text. The German opera composers who followed immediately after Gluck all continued using Italian texts exclusively. The first great German composer to use a German text was Mozart, in the *Abduction from the Seraglio.* This is the first great German comic opera; its quicksilver score—scintillating, witty, satiric, and impudent, mirroring every shade of comedy implicit in the play—set a new standard for comic opera.

Before writing *The Seraglio,* Mozart had completed many operas with Italian texts and in the Italian style: *Idomeneo,* for example. The masterworks of Mozart's maturity—*The Marriage of Figaro* and *Don Giovanni*—also had Italian librettos by Lorenzo da Ponte. The pattern might be Italian, but the content was revolutionary in the appropriateness with which music translated the dramatic, emotional, and psychological conflicts of each play.

In one of his last operas, *The Magic Flute,* Mozart returned to a German text; and he also reverted to the Singspiel style he had favored in *The Seraglio.* The magic, symbolism, and nonsense of Emanuel Schikaneder's libretto evoked from Mozart one of his noblest scores, and some of his most lilting folk tunes. Here, at last, we have for the first time the German Romanticist's interest in legend, superstition, and solemnity in the text, and in folk idioms in the music. For this reason, C. Hubert Parry considered *The Magic Flute* the first representative of German national opera. "He infused a degree of dignified and noble sentiment into certain parts of the work which was quite unlike what was to be met with in Italian operas; and in the end, between his music and the mystery of the play, the work became a spontaneous success of a pronounced description, and was taken up eagerly all over Germany." Wagner also regarded *The Magic Flute* as a highly successful example of German national opera, remarking—and possibly with excessive enthusiasm—that "it laid the foundations and exhausted the possibilities of German opera."

With Beethoven's *Fidelio,* the Singspiel flowered into German opera, even though spoken dialogue was still retained. By striving to make opera a vehicle for ideas as well as emotions, by extending the poetic expressiveness of the music, by avoiding all that is extraneous to the essential drama, Beethoven brought German opera to a new stage of musical and dramatic development.

The dominating figure in German opera, in the period between Mozart and Wagner, was Karl Maria von Weber. For many years Weber wrote Italian operas while nursing the ambition to create an authentically German work. Johann Friedrich Kind, who adapted a ghost story by Apel and Laun into an opera libretto called *Der Freischütz,* provided Weber with the means to satisfy that ambition. Kind's libretto combined supernatural and diabolic elements with German traditions, superstitions, and love of landscape. For such a text, Weber wrote a highly atmospheric and dramatic score, leaning heavily all the time on German musical backgrounds and the German folk song. *Der Freischütz,* written in 1821, became the voice of the rising Romantic Movement in Germany.

The dream world in which the Romantics sought escape was further explored by Weber in *Euryanthe* and *Oberon*. These two operas, like the one that preceded them, were touched with love for the German village and landscape, rich in German atmosphere, filled with Germanic ideals. Text and music were an affirmation of the German spirit. The music was all of these things—and much more, too. It suggested styles and techniques soon to become basic with great German opera: the symphonic treatment of the orchestral background; the significance of the recitative; the first tentative use of a leading motive (*Leitmotif*) technique to achieve integration; the striving for a unity of the arts. Weber's operas, consequently, culminated what had first been attempted by Gluck, Mozart, and Beethoven.

The stage was now set for the greatest of all the German musical dramatists: Richard Wagner.

Wagner was inspired by a grandiose vision. He wanted to realize a fusion of the arts—the musical, dramatic, poetic, and scenic—into one superart, and he called that superart a "music drama." To achieve a greater integration of all these arts than would otherwise have been possible, he wrote his own poetic dramas, gave specific instructions for staging, sets, and costumes, besides writing the music. He created his own dramatic form which, once and for all, broke down the artificial barrier separating recitative and aria by utilizing a continuously flowing melody; set numbers, artificial ballets, and superimposed choral passages were abandoned; the technique of the Leitmotif—a leading theme identifying a character, situation, or emotion, returning whenever that character, situation, or emotion appeared in the play—reached its most complex and ultimate development; the orchestra became a central character—commenting, analyzing, explaining, and interpreting what was taking place on the stage; music, through amplified harmony, counterpoint, and instrumentation, achieved unprecedented expressiveness; the drama, while derived from legend or saga, was filled with human values.

Wagner achieved an art form virtually incomparable for spaciousness of design, grandiosity of conception, and majesty of realization. It was an art that overtaxed the capabilities of singers, instrumentalists, and the existing stage. Though he knew that the nineteenth century opera house was inadequate to house his monumental works—indeed, he knew that a special theatre would have to be built for and dedicated to that purpose—he kept on working, never allowing expedience to constrict him. Eventually, he saw the fruition of his dreams in the performance of his mighty music dramas—the four dramas in the *Ring of the Nibelungs* cycle, *Tristan and Isolde, Die Meistersinger,* and *Parsifal*—in a festival theatre in Bayreuth which had been erected for him. He never doubted that dream—fantastic though it had appeared at first to many others—and knew with unwavering conviction that it would eventually be translated into reality.

He absorbed the past and integrated it into his musical thinking: the dramatic truth of Gluck; the subtlety of Mozart; the symphonic language of Beethoven; the orchestral virtuosity of Berlioz; the Romanticism of Weber; the magnificence of Meyerbeer. But he was also an apostle of the future. He opened new worlds for musical writing through his daring and inventiveness in harmony and orchestration. His music was a tidal wave that submerged his generation and that which followed him. Some composers imitated him, and others rebelled violently against him. But they could no more remain apathetic to him, or ignore him, than they could a hurricane.

Once and for all, Wagner shifted the center of operatic activity from Italy to Germany. The form he developed and the style that he crystallized were to serve other composers in the creation of their own masterworks. The debt owed by works like Humperdinck's *Hänsel und Gretel,* Pfitzner's *Palestrina,* and Richard Strauss' *Salome* and *Elektra,* to Wagner is unmistakable.

In another part of the world—Russia—nationalism in opera was seeded, took root, and flowered. The father of the Russian folk opera was Michael Glinka, the first composer aroused by the ideal to write *Russian* music. His initial major effort in this direction was the opera, *A Life for the Tsar.* The text tore a leaf out of Russia's historic past; and the music assimilated melodic and rhythmic materials derived from folk sources. Prosper Merimée said of it in 1840: "It is more than an opera; it is a national epic." But even more successful an attempt at uniting Russian backgrounds and themes with authentically Russian music was Glinka's succeeding opera, *Russlan and Ludmilla.* This is the cornerstone of Russian national music—the cornerstone on which later composers like Balakirev, Rimsky-Korsakov, Borodin, and Mussorgsky were to erect their own musical structures. From Borodin came another vibrant folk opera, *Prince Igor;* and the greatest of all the Russian folk operas was written by Mussorgsky—*Boris Godunov.*

But nationalism was not an exclusively Russian commodity. In other countries too, composers went to the cultural, musical, social, and historical backgrounds of their lands for strength and inspiration. Out of Bohemia came Smetana's *The Bartered Bride;* out of Moravia, Janáček's *Jenufa;* out of Poland, Moniuszko's *Halka.* In our own day, folk operas have been written by Kodály (*Háry János*), Weinberger (*Schwanda the Bagpipeplayer*), Gershwin (*Porgy and Bess*), and Kurt Weill (*Down in the Valley*).

As in all other fields of music, opera was invaded by bold experimentation in the twentieth century. Berg's *Wozzeck* exploited the atonal style; and his later opera, *Lulu,* was constructed out of the twelve-tone technique. Alois Hába wrote an opera in quarter tones (*The Mother*). Operas in a jazz style were written by Hindemith, Krenek, and Kurt Weill in Germany, and by Louis Gruenberg and George Gershwin in this country. In *The Cradle Will Rock,* Marc Blitzstein used opera as a social forum to interpret the economic and social discords of the time.

The most convincing operas of our time—those which have found the widest and most enthusiastic audiences—do not concern themselves primarily with a new idiom, style, or musico-dramatic approach. Composers like Benjamin Britten (in *Peter Grimes* and *Billy Budd*), and Gian-Carlo Menotti (in *The Medium, The Consul,* and *Amahl and the Night Visitors*) took from tradition and the past those things which were still serviceable—including lyricism and emotion—and blended them gracefully with such contemporary techniques and idioms that served their dramatic purposes.

# 3

# The Stories of Famous Operas

In the section that follows, the operas are listed alphabetically. The following is a listing of the same operas by their composers:

Beethoven: *Fidelio*
Bellini: *Norma*
Berg: *Wozzeck*
Bizet: *Carmen*
Britten: *Peter Grimes*
Charpentier: *Louise*
Debussy: *Pelléas et Mélisande*
Delibes: *Lakmé*
Donizetti: *Don Pasquale*
Donizetti: *Lucia di Lammermoor*
Gershwin: *Porgy and Bess*
Giordano: *Andrea Chénier*
Gluck: *Alceste*
Gluck: *Orfeo ed Euridice*
Gounod: *Faust*

Gounod: *Romeo and Juliet*
Halevy: *La Juive*
Hanson: *Merry Mount*
Humperdinck: *Hänsel und Gretel*
Leoncavallo: *Pagliacci*
Mascagni: *Cavalleria Rusticana*
Massenet: *Manon*
Massenet: *Thaïs*
Menotti: *Amahl and the Night Visitors*
Menotti: *Amelia Goes to the Ball*
Menotti: *The Consul*
Menotti: *The Medium*
Menotti: *The Telephone*

217

Meyerbeer: *L'Africaine*

Montemezzi: *Love of Three Kings*

Mozart: *The Abduction from the Seraglio*

Mozart: *Così fan tutte*

Mozart: *Don Giovanni*

Mozart: *The Magic Flute*

Mozart: *The Marriage of Figaro*

Mussorgsky: *Boris Godunov*

Offenbach: *Tales of Hoffmann*

Ponchielli: *La Gioconda*

Puccini: *La Bohème*

Puccini: *Madame Butterfly*

Puccini: *Tosca*

Puccini: *Turandot*

Purcell: *Dido and Aeneas*

Rossini: *The Barber of Seville*

Rossini: *William Tell*

Saint-Saëns: *Samson and Delilah*

Smetana: *The Bartered Bride*

Strauss, R.: *Elektra*

Strauss, R.: *Der Rosenkavalier*

Strauss, R.: *Salome*

Taylor: *The King's Henchman*

Taylor: *Peter Ibbetson*

Thomas: *Mignon*

Verdi: *Aïda*

Verdi: *Falstaff*

Verdi: *Otello*

Verdi: *Rigoletto*

Verdi: *La Traviata*

Verdi: *Il Trovatore*

Weber: *Der Freischütz*

Wagner: *Lohengrin*

Wagner: *Die Meistersinger*

Wagner: *Parsifal*

Wagner: *The Ring of the Nibelungs (The Rhinegold; The Valkyrie; Siegfried; The Dusk of the Gods)*

Wagner: *Tannhäuser*

Wagner: *Tristan und Isolde*

Wolf-Ferrari: *The Secret of Suzanne*

## (THE) ABDUCTION FROM THE SERAGLIO (DIE ENTFÜHRUNG AUS DEM SERAIL).

*Comic opera in three acts, by Wolfgang Amadeus Mozart. Libretto by Gottlieb Stephanie based on the text of Christoph Friedrich Bretzner used in Johann André's opera,* Belmont und Constanze. *First performance: Burgtheater, Vienna, July 16, 1782.*

Constance and her servant Blonda are kidnapped and abducted to the seraglio of the Pasha Selim. He wants to make Constance his favorite, and ardently expresses his love. But Constance rejects him firmly, insisting that no torture can compel her to express a love she does not feel ("Martern aller Arten"). Meanwhile, Constance's beloved, Belmont, arrives to rescue her, at which fortunate development

Blonda expresses her immense joy ("Welche Wonne, welche Lust!").
To facilitate the escape, Belmont gets Selim's overseer drunk, but
the latter still manages to uncover the plot and to bring the culprits
to the august presence of the Pasha. The Pasha is so touched by the
love of these two young people that he frees them (even after he
learns that Belmont is the son of a lifelong enemy), and permits them
to return to their own land. A hymn of praise to the generous Pasha
ends the opera.

## L'AFRICAINE (THE AFRICAN).

*Opera in five acts, by Giacomo Meyerbeer. Libretto by
Eugène Scribe. First performance: Opéra, Paris, April,
28, 1865.*

Though Inez is in love with the explorer Vasco da Gama, her
father insists that she marry Don Pedro. The explorer returns from
an expedition to announce that he has discovered a new land: his
proof being the African Queen, Selika, and her servant, Nelusko,
whom he has brought back with him. Vasco now wants another ship
for a new expedition, but his wish is denied, and he is thrown into
prison.

Don Pedro decides to seek out for himself the new land described
by Vasco—taking with him Inez, Selika, and Nelusko. But Vasco
learns that Nelusko intends to destroy Don Pedro and his ship and,
to save his beloved Inez, he manages to follow Don Pedro and to warn
him of impending danger. His warning goes unheeded. A mighty
storm arises; Nelusko addresses an invocation to the troubled sea
("Adamastor, re dell' onde profonde"). Through Nelusko's maneu-
vers, Don Pedro's ship crashes on a reef; everyone aboard is either
killed or captured. Selika, in love with Vasco, takes him back to her
land, which the explorer ecstatically describes as a paradise ("O para-
diso"). But learning that Inez is still alive, he deserts Selika who,
grief stricken, commits suicide.

## AÏDA.

*Opera in four acts, by Giuseppe Verdi. Libretto by An-
tonio Ghislanzoni, based on a prose sketch of Mariette
Bey, translated into French by Camille du Locle. First
performance: Cairo, Egypt, December 24, 1871.*

Aïda is the slave of Amneris, the daughter of the Egyptian King. Radames, captain of the guard, is madly in love with Aïda; ecstatically he sings a hymn to her beauty ("Celeste Aïda"). His rhapsody is interrupted by the arrival of Amneris who questions him about the object of his great love, hoping that the person is herself. When Aïda enters, the instinctive reactions of Radames and the slave girl to each other betray the truth to the Princess. At this point, the King of Egypt comes to select Radames to head an Egyptian army against invading Ethiopian forces approaching the Nile Valley. Ecstatically Aïda joins in a prayer for Radames' victorious return ("Ritorna vincitor"). But she is torn by an inner conflict, because she is Ethiopian by birth, and—though this fact is not known in Egypt—actually the daughter of the Ethiopian King.

In her boudoir, Amneris is entertained by her Moorish slaves (Dance of the Moorish Slaves). She calls Aïda, and in order to test the extent of her love for Radames, confides to her that the captain has been slain in battle. Aïda's cry of anguish can leave no further room for doubt. Bitterly, Amneris threatens her with death.

Martial music is suddenly heard; the victorious Egyptian army has returned from the war. Outside the city walls there is song, dance, and festivities to honor the returning warriors ("Gloria all' Egitto": Grand March, Chorus, and Ballet Music). Radames aproaches the Egyptian King to be honored. He has brought back with him prisoners of war, one of whom is Aïda's father, disguised in beggar's rags, and recognized by none except Aïda herself. Radames' appeal to the Egyptian King brings freedom to this prisoner, after which the King announces he is ready to offer his daughter Amneris in marriage to Radames.

Some time later, Aïda—having come to the banks of the Nile for a secret rendezvous with Radames—recalls poignantly her happy childhood in her native land ("O patria mia"). Aroused by his love for Aïda, Radames reveals to her military secrets, but is overheard by Amneris who denounces him as a traitor. Aïda manages to escape; Radames gives himself up to the High Priest. Amneris is ready to forgive Radames and to offer him his freedom—but only if he is willing to renounce Aïda for good. Since he refuses to do so, he is tried, found guilty, and sentenced to be buried alive under the temple of the gods. Within the tomb he finds Aïda, ready and willing to share his fate. When Radames realizes that he cannot dissuade Aïda from her inflexible decision to die with him, he joins her in a farewell to the world ("O terra addio"). From the distance is heard the chanting of the priests. Amneris arrives at the temple to pray at the living grave of the one she loved.

## ALCESTE.

*Opera in two acts, by Christoph Willibald Gluck. Libretto by Raniere Calzabigi, adapted from the tragedy of Euripides. First performance: Burgtheater, Vienna, December 26, 1767.*

King Admetos is dying. The High Priest of Apollo announces that the King can be saved only if one of his subjects is willing to die in his place. The King's wife, Alceste, is ready to make this sacrifice. When Apollo consents to accept her, Alceste invokes the gods of the underworld ("Divinités du Styx").

The King recovers. But when he learns that his wife must die in his place, he entreats the gods to accept him again. But Alceste is just as insistent in her pleas that she remain the victim. Entering the gates of Hades, Alceste meets her husband who has come to rescue her. Apollo, impressed by this devotion of husband and wife, restores Alceste to the King; and both return to earth.

## AMAHL AND THE NIGHT VISITORS.

*Opera in one act, by Gian-Carlo Menotti. Libretto by the composer. First performance: NBC–TV, December 24, 1951.*

The Three Wise Men, on their way to the holy Manger in Bethlehem to deliver gifts to the Holy Child, stop off at the hovel of the crippled child, Amahl, and his mother. When the child learns about their mission he asks them to take his crutches as his own gift. When he delivers the crutches he discovers that he has been miraculously cured, and that he can walk again.

## AMELIA GOES TO THE BALL.

*Comic opera in one act, by Gian-Carlo Menotti. Libretto by the composer. First performance: Philadelphia, April 1, 1937.*

In Milan, Amelia is discovered by her husband writing a love-letter. She promises to disclose to him the identity of her lover if, in return, he will take her to the ball. When the husband discovers that his rival is the upstairs neighbor, he rushes out to shoot him. Afraid of missing the ball, Amelia warns her lover, who seeks refuge in her bedroom. He is discovered there by the irate husband who first tries to kill him and then, when the gun fails to function, wants to talk things over with him. Amelia by now is convinced that she will miss the ball. Furious, she breaks a vase over her husband's head, screaming through the window that a burglar has broken into her room. When the police arrive, she points to her lover as the culprit. The lover is taken to jail. The Chief of Police, sympathetic to Amelia's plight, takes her to the ball. The moral of the story—so announces the final chorus—is that when a woman sets her heart on going to the ball, she will most certainly get there.

## L'AMORE DEI TRE RE (THE LOVE OF THREE KINGS).

*Opera in three acts by Italo Montemezzi. Libretto by Sem Benelli. First performance: La Scala, Milan, April, 10, 1913.*

King Archibaldo, who is blind, suspects that his daughter-in-law, Fiora, is unfaithful to her husband, Manfredo. Indeed, with Manfredo away at war, Fiora is making love to Avito. When Manfredo returns, his wife is cold and distant to him, a fact that further convinces the King that his suspicions are well founded.

Fiora promises to wave her scarf in farewell as Manfredo returns to the army. But before she can do this, Avito comes to her. In spite of her intentions, the scarf falls from her hands as she tenderly embraces her beloved. Archibaldo interrupts this love idyll. Avito escapes, but Fiora is strangled to death by the aroused King.

Suddenly Manfredo returns: having seen the scarf fall from Fiora's hand, he suspects something has happened. Bitterly, his father reveals to him that he has killed Fiora because she was unfaithful. Grief-stricken, Manfredo carries the dead body into the castle. In the crypt, Archibaldo puts poison on Fiora's dead lips, hoping thereby to bring deserved punishment on her sinful lover. Thus Avito comes to his doom, for when he comes to the crypt he cannot resist kissing the woman he loves. But, to Archibaldo's horror, Manfredo also becomes a victim when he, too, kisses the dead lips.

## ANDREA CHÉNIER.

*Opera in four acts, by Umberto Giordano. Libretto by Luigi Illica. First performance: La Scala, Milan, March 28, 1896.*

Andrea Chénier is a French poet who lived in Paris in the middle of the nineteenth century. He is a rival of Gérard, the revolutionary leader, for the love of Madeleine. When Chénier meets Madeleine at a secret rendezvous, Gérard follows and challenges the poet to a duel in which he is wounded. Chénier, unsympathetic to the Revolution, is brought to trial and imprisoned. Thus, Gérard sees his rival removed from the scene. But Gérard cannot help recalling Chénier's nobility and poetic talent and realizes that a man such as this could never be a traitor ("Nemico della patria").

Madeleine comes to Gérard to inform him of her mother's death ("La mamma morta") and to offer herself to Gérard in return for sparing Chénier's life. But Gérard is helpless, for the mob is crying for the poet's body. Eager to die with the man she loves, Madeleine bribes the jailor to permit her to replace one of the condemned prisoners. She enters Chénier's cell, where he is putting on paper his last poem ("Come un bel di di maggio"). Both of them die at the guillotine.

## (THE) BARBER OF SEVILLE (IL BARBIERE DI SIVIGLIA).

*Comic opera in two acts, by Gioacchino Rossini. Libretto by Cesare Sterbini, based upon two plays of Beaumarchais. First performance: Argentina Theatre, Rome, February 20, 1816.*

Count Almaviva is in love with Rosina, even though the two of them have not yet been introduced. As he serenades her ("Ecco ridente in cielo"), Figaro, the barber, enters the street obstreperously. He proceeds to tell Almaviva of his gay and active life as a so-called factotum ("Largo al factotum"). The Count enlists Figaro's aid in bringing him to Rosina. Assuming the humble name of Lindoro—he wants Rosina to love him for himself alone, and not for his high station—Almaviva sings to her a second serenade ("Se il mio nome"). Suddenly Bartolo, Rosina's guardian, appears. Hateful to all her suitors, because he wants to marry her himself for her dowery, he orders his servant to admit no one but the music master, Basilio. But Figaro and Almaviva contrive to gain admittance into Rosina's house by having the Count disguise himself as a drunken dragoon who is to be stationed in the Bartolo household. Inside the house, Rosina—reading a letter from "Lindoro"—expresses her profound emotions at his words of love ("Una voce poco fa"). By this time, Bartolo has come to suspect that Almaviva is a possible suitor for Rosina and does what he can to discredit him with abuse and slander ("La calunnia"). When the Count arrives disguised as a soldier, wise Bartolo suspects his true identity and storms off in order to get proof of the authenticity of the dragoon. His brief absence makes it possible for the lovers to exchange tender sentiments. But Bartolo is soon back with a group of soldiers to arrest Almaviva. Secretly, Almaviva reveals his true identity to one of the soldiers and is summarily released, much to Bartolo's amazement.

Almaviva now assumes a second disguise in order to gain entrance into Bartolo's house: that of a music teacher, substituting for the supposedly ailing Basilio. As he enters, he sings a half-mocking, half-satirical greeting to Bartolo ("Pace e gioia"). Meanwhile the real music master is bribed to maintain the story that he is sick.

Wily Bartolo is finally able to convince Rosina of her lover's perfidy, so much so that she is now ready to marry her guardian out of spite. Delighted, Bartolo rushes off to get a notary to draw up a marriage contract. Almaviva, however, succeeds in convincing Rosina of the true state of affairs. When Basilio, in his capacity as notary, comes to marry Bartolo to Rosina he is compelled, at the point of a gun, to marry the Count and Rosina instead. Bartolo returns to find that the marriage has taken place. He accepts this evil fate as gracefully as he can, while Figaro joyfully wishes the married couple happiness.

## (THE) BARTERED BRIDE.

*Comic folk opera in three acts, by Bedřich Smetana. Libretto by Karel Sabina. First performance: National Theatre, Prague, May 30, 1866.*

A feast day is being celebrated in the square of a Bohemian village. Marie and Hans are in love; but Marie is intended by her father for Wenzel, the half-wit son of wealthy Micha. The marriage has been arranged by a broker. The fact that Hans is also Micha's son, by a first marriage, is not known. The broker, eager to have nothing stand in the way of a profitable match, bribes Hans not to marry Marie. Hans willingly accepts the bribe, but on the signed condition that only the son of Micha be permitted to marry Marie. When Marie learns that her beloved Hans has given her up for a bribe, she is heartbroken, and announces her willingness to accept Wenzel. Hans then discloses that he, too, is Micha's son. Since his agreement with the broker clearly specified that only Micha's son can marry Marie he is free to take her as a bride, and keep his bribe.

The folk dances from this opera are particularly famous: the Polka in Act 1; the Furiant in Act 2; and the Dance of the Comedians in Act 3.

## (LA) BOHÈME.

*Opera in four acts, by Giacomo Puccini. Libretto by Giacosa and Illica, based on* Scènes de La Vie de Bohème, *a novel by Henri Murger. First performance: Teatro Reggio, Turin, February 1, 1896.*

The scene is Bohemian Paris; the plot, the shifting emotions in the love affairs of Rodolfo and Mimi, and Marcello and Musetta.

The poet Rodolfo, the philosopher Colline, and the painter Marcello are trying to warm Rodolfo's cold attic by burning one of Rodolfo's unpublished manuscripts. The musician Schaunard bursts into the room, his arms laden with food and fuel: he has just acquired a rich patron. The need for further celebration sends three of the four friends to the Latin Quarter.

Rodolfo, alone, hears a timid knock. Mimi, his neighbor, is at the door, asking for some light for her candle. Suddenly she succumbs to a coughing and fainting spell. Revived, she takes her leave, but returns a moment later because she has lost her key in Rodolfo's attic room. Their search for the lost key is made more difficult when the candle-light goes out. In the darkness, the two of them grope on the floor for the key when the poet comes upon Mimi's little cold hand, which he takes in his own to warm. The poet now tells Mimi about himself, his life, his dreams ("Che gelida manina"). Mimi, too, becomes communicative about her personal life, and her hunger for the warmth of springtime ("Mi chiamano Mimi"). This exchange of confidences inspires tenderness. As the moonlight streams into the attic window, Rodolfo and Mimi exchange ardent words of love ("O soave fanciulla"). Then they go off together to Café Momus to join Rodolfo's friends.

It is Christmas eve. The public square outside the café swarms with vendors, students, waiters, and working girls. Musetta—estranged beloved of Marcello—arrives in the company of a wealthy old man, Alcindoro, and sits at a table near Rodolfo and his friends. Coquettishly she tries to attract the attention of her one-time lover; and, still coquettishly, she tells of the way in which men are fascinated by and attracted to her (Musetta's Waltz: "Quando me'n vo'soletta"). Feigning that her shoe is too tight, Musetta sends Alcindoro to a nearby shoemaker. During his absence, Musetta and Marcello rush into each other's arms with an uncontrolled outburst of true sentiment. Alcindoro is finally left to pay the bill; and the Bohemians carry off Musetta on their shoulders.

Many weeks have passed. Mimi—cold, shivering, and coughing—comes to a gate at the outskirts of the city. She is looking for Marcello to whom she confides that life with Rodolfo has become impossible due to his unreasonable jealousy. When Rodolfo appears he is overcome with remorse and takes Mimi in his arms with pity and tenderness. But Mimi insists that they must go separate ways. Poignantly, Rodolfo and Mimi bid each other farewell ("Addio senza rancor"). But no sooner have they said goodbye than they experience a sudden change of heart and go off together in a renewed rapture of love.

This reconciliation, however, is only temporary. Once again, Rodolfo and Marcello are sad and lonely, for they are once again estranged from their sweethearts. Nostalgically, Rodolfo recalls his happiness with Mimi ("Ah Mimi, tu più"). The arrival of other friends introduces a temporary note of gaiety. But it is rudely shattered when Musetta brings the tidings that Mimi is deathly sick. Tenderly, Mimi is brought into the attic and placed on Rodolfo's bed. The lovers are once again reconciled. Wan and weak, Mimi closes her eyes for some welcome sleep. Schaunard is the first to notice that she is not asleep but dead, and whispers the tragic news to his nearby friends. Rodolfo, who is at the window putting up a cover to contain the light, notices the peculiar behavior of his friends. A glance at Mimi reveals to him the truth. With an overwhelming outburst of grief he cries out Mimi's name and rushes to her bed.

## BORIS GODUNOV.

*Folk opera in three acts, by Modest Mussorgsky. Libretto by the composer after a play by Pushkin. First performance: St. Petersburg, February 8, 1874.*

Boris Godunov, ambitious of becoming Tsar, murders Dimitri, brother and only heir of Tsar Feodor. To conceal his ambition, Boris discreetly retires to a monastery. The people, unaware of his treachery, come to him there to plead that he become their ruler.

In a monastery cell, an old monk tells the novice Gregory of Dimitri's murder. Gregory now is inspired with the idea of spreading the word that Dimitri still lives so that he, Gregory, might appear as Dimitri and avenge the murder. Before he can do this, however, Boris is coronated the new Tsar in a ceremony full of pomp (Coronation Scene).

Gregory's plan slowly begins to unfold. With two companions he comes to an inn at the Lithuanian border. One of them, Varlaam, indulges in a spirited drinking song ("In the Town of Kazaan"). Polish soldiers, having been warned about Gregory, come to the inn to seize him, but they fail to recognize him. Gregory skilfully manages to throw their suspicion on Varlaam as he makes his escape.

During this period Boris is in a state of great mental anguish. He cannot rid his mind of the image of the murdered Dimitri ("I Have Attained the Highest Power"). His anguish is heightened when Prince Shuisky brings him the news that the people are beginning to believe that Dimitri is alive, that they are rallying around his name in rebellion against Boris. The idea now haunts the Tsar that perhaps Dimitri has arisen from the grave ("Ah I Am Suffocating"). The ghost of Dimitri seems to be before him. Boris yields to a fit of panic, falls on his knees, and prays for his salvation.

Gregory now comes to the Polish palace of Marina, who loves him. The guests are dancing a polonaise. When they retire, Marina and Gregory pledge their love for each other. More determined than ever to lead the people to Moscow against Boris, Gregory leaves Marina to rally the people behind him. They follow him through the Forest of

Kromy, singing mocking verses against Boris, and pledging their loyalty to the false Dimitri.

Because of this critical emergency, the Duma is in session at the Kremlin. Boris' mental disturbances have grown. He asks for his son whom he bids a tender farewell ("Farewell My Son, I Am Dying"). The bells toll. Growing weaker by the moment, Boris prays God for mercy, as he points to his son as the new Tsar. He falls dead. The priests and nobility stand by in prayer.

## CARMEN.

*Opéra comique in four acts, by Georges Bizet. Libretto by Meilhac and Halévy, based on the novel of Prosper Mérimée. First performance: Opéra Comique, Paris, March 3, 1875.*

Carmen, a gypsy cigarette girl in Seville, bids for the attention of the guardsman Don José. She sings mockingly of love (Habanera: "L'amour est un oiseau rebelle"). Enraged because he ignores her, she throws a flower at him, which he conceals in a pocket near his heart. A few moments later, a hubbub is heard: Carmen has stabbed another cigarette girl. Seized by dragoons, Carmen makes light of her offense. Coquettishly, she plays for Don José's attention by telling him they will meet soon in a tavern near Seville's encircling walls (Seguidilla: "Près des remparts de Séville"). Now infatuated with this sensual girl, Don José helps her make her escape.

Carmen finds refuge in the tavern on the outskirts of the city. There she is excited by the presence of the famous bullfighter, Escamillo, who tells the admiring throng of the thrills of bullfighting (Toreador Song).

José makes his way to the tavern to be welcomed passionately by Carmen. He now knows he cannot live without her. Tenderly he takes out the flower that Carmen had thrown at him and which he had saved (Flower Song: "La fleur que tu m'avais jetée"). He deserts his uniform to follow Carmen to the den of smugglers in a nearby mountain pass. Carmen's fortune is read in cards and reveals a tragic future (Card Song: "En vain pour éviter"). Her horror is brief; exhilaration returns when she must go off with the smugglers. Don José is left behind alone to guard the camp. Timidly, fearfully, his former sweetheart, Micaëla, gropes her way into the camp; she has come to ask Don José to return to his dying mother. At this point, Escamillo comes in search of Carmen. Realizing that Escamillo is his rival, Don José attacks him, and only the return of smugglers prevents a fatal incident. Escamillo departs with his usual air of bravado, inviting all the smugglers to be his guests at the next bullfight. Don José departs with Micaëla, warning Carmen not to desert him.

A festive crowd has come to Seville to attend the bullfight. Carmen is with Escamillo. To Don José she says she loves him no longer, and remains deaf to his pleas and anguish. When she tries to enter the arena, he kills her with a dagger. The triumphant Escamillo emerges from the arena to find her lying dead, with José nearby, sobbing.

## CAVALLERIA RUSTICANA.

> *Opera in one act, by Pietro Mascagni. Libretto by Targioni-Tozzetti and Menasci, based on a short story by Verga. First performance: Teatro Costanzi, Rome, May 17, 1890.*

Before the rise of the curtain, Turiddu is heard singing a love song to Lola, the wife of Alfio (Siciliana: "O Lola, bianca come fior di spino"). Though Turiddu and Lola are emotionally involved, this does not prevent him from making love to the village girl, Santuzza.

It is Easter morning; the villagers are entering the church. Santuzza, ashamed of her love affair with Turiddu, feels herself unworthy of entering a holy place. She remains outside the church, kneeling and praying. When Alfio arrives, the remorseful Santuzza reveals to him that his wife is having an affair with Turiddu ("Voi lo sapete").

The services over, the townspeople emerge from church (Intermezzo). The atmosphere now is festive. Turiddu sings a rousing drinking song (Brindisi: "Viva il vino"). When Alfio sulks, Turiddu knows that Alfio is aware of the state of affairs. Suddenly Alfio challenges his rival to a duel. With a premonition of death, Turiddu bids his mother farewell ("Addio alla madre"). An outcry from one of the women betrays the fact that Turiddu has been killed by Alfio.

## (THE) CONSUL.

> *Opera in three acts by Gian-Carlo Menotti. Libretto by the composer. First performance: New York City, March 15, 1950.*

The tragedy of Europe in our own times is the subject for Menotti's play with music. The action takes place in an unidentified police state. Magda and her family pathetically try to penetrate the red tape of a consulate to get a visa for a free land. Bureaucracy and the callousness of a totalitarian regime frustrate her efforts; she and her family can find escape only in death.

## COSÌ FAN TUTTE (SO DO THEY ALL).

*Comic opera in two acts, by Wolfgang Amadeus Mozart. Libretto by Lorenzo da Ponte. First performance: Burgtheater, Vienna, January 26, 1790.*

Guglielmo and Ferrando, two officers, try to prove that their sweethearts, Fiordiligi and Dorabella, are faithful to them. The soldiers announce they must leave for military service, expressing their undying love to their sweethearts ("Al fato dan legge quegli occhi vezzosi"). They return disguised as rich Albanians and try to make love to each other's sweetheart. At first Fiordiligi is unbending ("Come scoglio"), but eventually both she and Dorabella succumb. They are willing to marry the wealthy Albanians, and a mock notary appears to perform the necessary ceremony.

A distant roll of drums gives warning to the startled wedding assemblage that the soldiers are returning from service. The "Albanians" rush off hurriedly, and not much later the two officers appear. They seem surprised to find their sweethearts so cold to them and assume a shocked expression when they come upon the false marriage contract. However, all ends well. The girls are penitent, and the soldiers are forgiving. The finale ("Fortunato l'uom") provides the happy philosophy that we should take everything in our stride.

## DIDO AND AENEAS.

*Opera in three acts, by Henry Purcell. Libretto by Nahum Tate, based on the fourth book of Virgil's Aeneid. First performance: Chelsea, London, in or about 1690.*

Aeneas, sailing from devastated Troy, is brought by a storm to the shores of Carthage. There he meets and falls in love with the queen, Dido. The gods, however, are not in favor of their union, since Aeneas is destined to found the Italian nation. He is compelled to leave Carthage. Dido is in anguish ("When I Am Laid in Earth"), and dies of a broken heart.

## DON GIOVANNI.

*"Dramma giocosa" in two acts, by Wolfgang Amadeus Mozart. Libretto by Lorenzo da Ponte based on Bertati's* Don Giovanni. *First performance: National Theatre, Prague, October 29, 1787.*

The action takes place in eighteenth century Seville. Leporello complains that the escapades of his master, Don Giovanni, give him little rest. Don appears, followed by Donna Anna; they exchange angry words. The Commandant—Anna's father—emerges; challenges Don to a duel; and is killed. After Don effects his escape, Donna Anna returns with her betrothed, Don Ottavio, overwhelmed to find her father dead. Don Ottavio swears he will seek vengeance.

But Don Giovanni is not repentant. He is now found outside Seville consoling Donna Elvira, whom he had once deserted. Leporello explains that this one-time desertion was not Don's fault at all, and goes on to give Elvira a gay account of his master's romances ("Madamina, il catalogo"). When Don Giovanni makes his escape, Donna Elvira also becomes inflamed with the desire for vengeance.

At a country place, townspeople are celebrating the marriage of Masetto and Zerlina. Don Giovanni, attracted to the bride, has Leporello draw the attention of the guests while he pays court to her. Zerlina cannot withstand Giovanni's charm ("Là ci darem la mano") and might have run off with him if Donna Elvira had not arrived to uncover Don Giovanni's treachery. When Donna Anna makes her appearance with Don Ottavio, the latter repeats his oath to avenge the death of the Commandant.

Later on, outside Don Giovanni's palace, Masetto scolds Zerlina for flirting with the Don. He wants to send her away forever, but is dissuaded and appeased by Zerlina's coy pleading ("Batti, batti, o bel Masetto"). Don now invites his guests into the palace where they engage in a courtly dance (Minuet), during which Don is able to conduct Zerlina to an adjoining chamber. Suddenly Zerlina's cry for help is heard. Donna Anna, Donna Elvira, and Don Ottavio—all of whom had come to the palace masked—remove their disguise and openly accuse Don Giovanni of treachery and murder. The culprit is callous. With drawn sword he makes his way through the guests and disappears.

He comes in front of Elvira's house, dressed in Leporello's cloak, to serenade Zerlina who is Elvira's guest ("Deh vieni alla finestra"). Leporello, disguised as Don Giovanni, makes love to Elvira. Masetto, still bitter against Giovanni, arrives and, mistaking Don Giovanni for Leporello, is not on his guard and is administered a sound thrashing by the nobleman. Zerlina finds Masetto stretched out, bruised, and sore; but the latter complains that his heart is hurt more grievously than his body.

Still disguised as his master, Leporello appears in the garden of the Commandant's palace to continue his amusing flirtation with Donna Elvira. Only when he is confronted by Donna Anna, Don Ottavio, and Zerlina does he reveal himself. Ottavio repeats his all-abiding ambition to destroy Don Giovanni, and hymns a poignant song of love to the woman he adores ("Il mio tesoro").

Leporello and Don Giovanni stumble against the Commandant's statue. With his customary bravado, Giovanni orders his servant to invite the statue to dinner. To the horror of Leporello, the statue nods assent. Meanwhile, within the Commandant's palace, Don Ottavio begs Anna to forget her sorrows and marry him. Anna confesses she loves him dearly, but she cannot accept him as a husband as long as she is victim to her grief ("Non mi dir").

Within his own palace, Giovanni is having a regal supper, as an orchestra plays for him. Elvira comes to beg Don to mend his ways. Failing in this mission, she makes her departure, only to return suddenly in terror. Investigating the source of her fright, Leporello also returns trembling. The guest of stone—the statue of the Commandant—has come for its dinner engagement. Fearless, the host calmly accepts the guest. The statue seizes Don by the wrist, demanding that he repent his ways once and for all. When Don refuses, a pit of fire opens to consume him.

In an epilogue, Donna Anna, Donna Elvira, Zerlina, Ottavio, Leporello, and Masetto appear to provide a gay commentary to what has happened. Leporello remarks that since Giovanni has been consigned to flames, the vengeance of all concerned has finally been realized.

## DON PASQUALE.

*Opera buffa in three acts, by Gaetano Donizetti. Libretto by the composer and Giacomo Ruffini, based on the libretto of Angelo Anelli for Pavesi's opera* Ser Marc' Antonio. *First performance: Théâtre des Italiens, Paris, January 4, 1843.*

Don Pasquale opposes the love affair of Norina and Ernesto. Dr. Malatesta, in league with the lovers and eager to aid their cause, rhapsodically praises to Pasquale the beauty of an imaginary sister, until Don convinces himself he is in love with her and must marry her sight unseen ("Ah, un foco insolito"). Ernesto, in despair of ever winning Pasquale's consent for the marriage, gives way to his grief ("Sogno soave e casto").

Norina, masquerading as Malatesta's beautiful sister, goes through a mock marriage with Pasquale. From the moment the supposed marriage contract is signed she becomes a shrew who tortures the old man with her temper, her extravagance, her emotional outbursts, and her suspicions about his fidelity. Malatesta is ready to extricate Pasquale out of this terrible predicament by contriving an elaborate scheme. If Pasquale consents to the marriage of Ernesto and Norina and proposes that they live with him, this arrangement might so annoy Norina that she might want to leave him. The ruse works: Norina cries she will leave for good if the young couple lives in their house. This is precisely what Pasquale was waiting for. He offers Ernesto a handsome endowment to marry Norina without delay, and invites them to his house. It is then that Malatesta reveals to Pasquale that Ernesto's Norina and Pasquale's "wife" are one and the same person; that Pasquale's marriage had been a fraud; and that the old man is free. Pasquale is so relieved at this turn of events that he is no longer reluctant to bless the lovers.

## (THE) DUSK OF THE GODS (DIE GÖTTERDÄMMERUNG).
*See:* (THE) RING OF THE NIBELUNGS.

## ELEKTRA.

*Opera in one act, by Richard Strauss. Libretto by Hugo von Hofmannsthal, after the tragedies of Sophocles, Euripides, and Aeschylus. First performance: Hofoper, Dresden, January 25, 1909.*

Elektra, daughter of Klytemnestra, is forced by her mother to live with menials and suffer abuse. Elektra is, however, much more concerned with the knowledge that Klytemnestra was responsible for the murder of King Agamemnon, Elektra's father. Filled with a terrible hate and a burning passion for vengeance, Elektra tells her mother that some day she, too, will be murdered—and by Elektra's now-exiled brother, Orestes.

When the Queen receives the tidings that Orestes is dead, her terror turns to relief. Elektra, too, becomes convinced of the truth of this report, and schemes to kill her mother herself. Suddenly the messenger, who had brought the news of Orestes' death, returns to reveal his true identity; he is none other than Orestes himself.

He enters the palace; and from its halls emerges an agonizing shriek by Klytemnestra. Vengeance has finally taken place. A fierce battle follows between the followers of Klytemnestra and those of Orestes, in which Klytemnestra's second husband, Aegisthus, is killed. Elektra is filled with mad joy that her mother and stepfather have met the doom they deserved. She sings an ecstatic song, goes into a corybantic dance, and then falls to the ground unconscious.

## FALSTAFF.

*Lyric comedy in three acts, by Giuseppe Verdi. Libretto by Arrigo Boïto, based on Shakespeare's* The Merry Wives of Windsor *and* King Henry IV. *First performance: La Scala, Milan, February 9, 1893.*

Falstaff is in sad financial plight. This situation leads him to write two love letters to two of the most respected women in town: Mistress Ford and Mistress Page. A liaison with one of them, he feels, would surely relieve his depleted purse. The two respectable ladies, comparing Falstaff's notes, discover they are virtually duplicates. They decide to play along with Falstaff, and send Dame Quickly to arrange a rendezvous.

Ford, jealous of his wife, has a scheme of his own. He meets Falstaff under the assumed name of "Signor Fontana," and bribes him to plead his cause with Mistress Ford. Falstaff is delighted to do so, since it promises to be profitable, explaining (to Ford's discomfort) that he actually has a rendezvous with the woman in question. When Falstaff retires to get dressed for a meeting with Mistress Ford, Ford bitterly questions woman's fidelity ("È sogno? O realtà?").

Falstaff prepares to speak to Mistress Ford on behalf of his client. Before he progresses very far, the approaching voice of Ford sends him scurrying behind a screen. Ford and several others unsuccessfully search the house for a concealed lover. When they leave, the women hide Falstaff in a laundry basket which, on Ford's precipitous return, they throw out of the window into the river below.

Scrambling clumsily out of the river, Falstaff returns to the inn, disillusioned with women. Dame Quickly returns and has no trouble reviving Falstaff's self-confidence. She has arranged another rendezvous, this time at midnight at Windsor Park, and she advises him to disguise himself as the Black Huntsman.

The woods of Windsor Park and the darkness of midnight conceal the presence of all those who have come to mock Falstaff. One of these, Fenton, disguised as Oberon, sings a pleasing serenade ("Dal labro il canto estasiato"). Falstaff arrives for his love idyll with Mistress Ford. When strange sounds emerge from the woods, Mistress Ford flees. Sure that supernatural powers are abroad, Falstaff falls to the ground in terror. The conspirators enter disguised as fairies, stumble over Falstaff, and give him a resounding beating. Merriment prevails. Delighted that Falstaff has met the fate he deserved, Ford belatedly consents to the marriage of his daughter and Fenton which he had all this time opposed. In a delightful fugue, everybody (including Falstaff) remarks that "all the world's a stage" ("Tutto nel mondo è burla").

FAUST.

> *Opera in five acts, by Charles Gounod. Libretto by Jules Barbier and Michel Carré, based on Goethe's Faust. First performance: Théâtre Lyrique, Paris, March 19, 1859.*

Old Faust, philosopher and alchemist, is tempted to suicide because he has failed to find a meaning to life. Satan—Mephistopheles —comes with a bargain: He is ready to bring Faust wealth and power in return for his soul. But what Faust wants more than these things is youth. The prospect of being young again, and a vision of beautiful Marguerite at her spinning wheel, convince Faust to enter into the bargain with the Devil. He drinks the magic potion that rejuvenates him.

A public square is filled with merrymakers, for it is the day of the village fair. Marguerite's brother, Valentin, is not gay, for he must leave for military service and he is troubled that his orphan sister is left behind unprotected. But Siebel (secretly in love with Marguerite) promises to keep a watchful eye on her. Valentin expresses his tender gratitude ("Avant de quitter ces lieux"). To dispel the momentary gloom, one of the students sings a vulgar song which is interrupted by the arrival of Mephistopheles, and his rendition of a toast to the universal greed for gold ("Le veau d'or"). When Mephistopheles proposes a toast to Marguerite, Valentin becomes furious and attacks him with his sword. But the Devil is protected by a magic circle. Valentin, imitated by the other soldiers, raises the hilt of his sword as if it were a holy cross. The merry spirit is back. The crowd begins singing and dancing an infectious waltz (Kermesse Waltz). Marguerite now approaches, having come from church, and is joined by Faust who offers to accompany her home. Feeling herself unworthy of him, she declines. As she passes on, Faust watches her tenderly. In contrast to this poignant mood, the crowd continues its swirling waltz.

In the garden in front of Marguerite's house Siebel is gathering flowers for her. He sings a love song to her ("Faites lui mes aveux"); but even as he sings, the flowers wither and die in his hands, owing to the powers of Mephistopheles. But the Devil can be thwarted: Siebel puts his hand into a nearby font of holy water, and revives the flowers which he now places at Marguerite's door.

All this time, Faust and Mephistopheles are hiding behind some shrubbery. When Siebel departs, Faust emerges, singing an ecstatic song to Marguerite ("Salut! demeure chaste et pure"). At the same time, Mephistopheles places a casket of jewels near Siebel's flowers. When Marguerite emerges from the house, they disappear. She sits at her spinning wheel, musing about the handsome stranger she has met at the public square ("Il était un roi de Thulé"). Suddenly, she sees the jewels, which she puts on with delirious joy (Jewel Song: "Je ris de me voir"). Later on, after Faust has returned, the two lovers succumb to the spell of the night and the intensity of their passion, and vow devotion to each other. In the distance can be heard Mephistopheles' sardonic laughter.

Time has gone by; Marguerite has been betrayed by Faust. As she sits at her spinning wheel, she laments her fate. But, still in love with Faust, she goes to church to pray both for him and their child. The mocking voice of Mephistopheles interrupts her prayers and sends her distraught out of church. In the public square outside, the soldiers, back from war, raise a rousing hymn to their recent victory (Soldiers' Chorus: "Gloire immortelle de nos aïeux"). Valentin is with them, and it is not long before he discovers what has happened to his sister. When he encounters Mephistopheles under Marguerite's window singing a mocking serenade ("Vous qui faites l'endormie"), he attacks the Devil and is mortally wounded. The townspeople gather to see what has happened, and hear Valentin denounce his sister bitterly. He dies without forgiving her—Marguerite, hysterical, at his side.

Marguerite, who has murdered her child, awaits execution in a prison cell. Mephistopheles and Faust arrive to rescue her. Finding Marguerite asleep Faust sends Mephistopheles away so that he can be alone with her. As she stirs, he gently calls her name, but she is not aware of his presence. Semi-delirious she recalls their tender love idyll in the garden. Mephistopheles returns to hurry Faust in the rescue. Seeing the Devil, Marguerite calls to Heaven for protection. She now has the strength with which to resist both Faust and Mephistopheles ("Alerte, alerte"). Her soul is carried off by angels.

## FIDELIO.

*Opera in two acts, by Ludwig van Beethoven. Libretto by Josef Sonnleithner and Georg Friedrich Treitschke, based on the French play of Jean Nicolas Bouilly, Léonore, ou l'amour conjugal. First performance: Theater-an-der-Wien, Vienna, November 20, 1805.*

Florestan has been unjustly imprisoned by his enemy, Pizarro, governor of the jail near Seville; he is being starved to death in his dark cell. To save him, his wife, Leonore, disguises herself as a young man, assumes the name of Fidelio, and gets a job as assistant to the jailer, Rocco.

Rocco's daughter, Marcellina, falls in love with Fidelio; Jaquino is in love with Marcellina. Fidelio, Marcellina, Jaquino—supplemented by Rocco—touch on this love triangle ("Mir ist so wunderbar").

When Pizarro arrives, Fidelio discovers that Don Fernando, the Prime Minister, is planning to inspect the jail. Fearful that Fernando will find an innocent man in his jail, Pizarro is bent on killing Florestan. This news overwhelms Fidelio ("Abscheulicher! wo eilst du hin?"). She begs Rocco for a glimpse at the prisoners. Rocco yields and has the prisoners emerge from their cells. As they come they sing a paean to their lost freedom ("O welche Lust!"). Eagerly, Fidelio scans their faces; but that of Florestan is not among them. Rocco then promises Fidelio to take her down into the dungeon.

In his cell, chained to the wall, Florestan bemoans his tragic fate, recalling happier days of freedom with his wife ("In des Lebens Frühlingstagen"). Rocco and Fidelio now enter his cell; Fidelio can hardly restrain her emotions on seeing her husband. Methodically, they begin digging Florestan's grave. When Pizarro arrives for the purpose of killing Florestan, Fidelio rushes to her husband's side to protect him from Pizarro's menacing dagger. When Pizarro makes an attempt at destroying both of them, Fidelio menaces him with a pistol.

Suddenly there is heard the sound of trumpets. The Prime Minister has arrived for his inspection. The Prime Minister frees Florestan and reunites him with his wife; Pizarro is imprisoned. Marcellina, now that she knows her beloved Fidelio is a woman, is ready to marry Jaquino. And the prisoners sing a final hymn of praise to Leonore, whose devotion and courage saved her husband from death.

## (DER) FREISCHÜTZ (THE FREE-SHOOTER).

*Opera in three acts, by Karl Maria von Weber. Libretto by Friedrich Kind, based on an old legend told in* Gespensterbuch, *edited by Apel and Laun. First performance: Schauspielhaus, Berlin, June 18, 1821.*

Max, a marksman, is in love with Agathe. He enters a marksman contest, the prize in which is the hand of that lady. When he fails in a preliminary contest he decides to use magic bullets. Meanwhile, at her home, Agathe awaits her beloved, admiring the tranquil night as she gazes out of her window ("Leise, leise"). Max comes to tell her that he must be off for the Wolf's Glen, a haunted spot. There, with the aid of the black huntsman, Zamiel, he fashions the magic bullets. With six of these he hits his target squarely, but with the seventh he hits Agathe who, in her bridal gown, looks like a dove. The gown, however, has magic powers and saves her life. When the discovery is made that Max has used magic bullets, he is sentenced to banishment. A hermit arrives to plead for Max, and does this so eloquently that Max is forgiven.

## (LA) GIOCONDA.

> *Opera in four acts, by Amilcare Ponchielli. Libretto by Arrigo Boïto, based on Victor Hugo's drama,* Angelo, le tyran de Padoue. *First performance: La Scala, Milan, April 8, 1876.*

La Gioconda is a ballad singer in seventeenth-century Venice, who supports her blind mother, La Cieca, by singing in the streets. La Gioconda is loved by Barnaba, a spy of the Inquisition, who, repelled by her, vows revenge. To a loser in a recent regatta, Barnaba whispers maliciously that the defeat was due to the diabolic powers of that "blind witch," La Cieca. Furious, the loser rushes to attack the old woman, who is protected by the Genoan nobleman, Enzo, whose ship has recently docked in Venice. La Cieca also gains the protection of the Grand Duke Alvise, at the behest of his wife Laura. La Cieca expresses her gratitude to Laura by giving her her rosary ("Voce di donna"). Barnaba now hopes to ruin Enzo as well as La Gioconda. Knowing that this nobleman is in love with Laura, Barnaba falsely tells Enzo that Laura plans to visit him on his ship that very night, and then contrives to inform the Grand Duke about this rendezvous.

Barnaba, disguised as a fisherman, arrives at Enzo's ship singing a fisherman's barcarolle ("Ah, pescator affonda l'esca"). In expectation of Laura's arrival, Enzo is intoxicated by the beauty of the night. He sings an ecstatic soliloquy to love ("Cielo e mar"). Laura is conducted to Enzo's ship by Barnaba. When Enzo plans to sail away with her, she becomes filled with remorse. At this point, La Gioconda arrives to condemn Laura for stealing the love of a man she herself adores. Their quarrel becomes intense, and La Gioconda is about to stab Laura when a boat suddenly comes to view. Horrified, Laura realizes her husband has come. Lifting her rosary, she prays for protection. When La Gioconda recognizes the rosary as the one that had belonged to her blind mother, she helps Laura escape. Rather than face capture by the Grand Duke, Enzo orders his sailors to fire upon the approaching vessel.

The Duke plans to avenge his wife's faithlessness by poisoning her. Just as Laura is about to drink the poison, La Gioconda enters, tears the poison from her hands, and substitutes a sleep-inducing potion. When the Duke sees the inert body of his wife he believes her dead, and feels triumphant.

In the ballroom of the Duke's palace, there take place gala festivities, climaxed by a ballet (The Dance of the Hours). The Duke pulls aside the curtains to reveal to his guests the "dead" body of his faithless wife. Enzo, who is one of the guests, rushes at him with a dagger, but is stopped by one of the Duke's men, arrested, and put in Barnaba's charge. Barnaba promises to release Enzo if La Gioconda will give herself to him, which she agrees to do.

La Gioconda has brought Laura to a ruined palace on the lonely island of Guideca, in the Adriatic. Aware that life now has little in store for her, La Gioconda contemplates suicide ("Suicidio!"). Enzo arrives on the island, brought there by La Gioconda who, even at the expense of her own anguish, is willing to unite the lovers. Ecstatic that they are together again, Enzo and Laura go off together. Barnaba now comes to demand his payment from La Gioconda. She makes a pretense of offering herself to him, but as he approaches she kills herself with a dagger. In a fit of rage, Barnaba shouts into her unresponsive ears that only the other day he had strangled her mother.

## (DIE) GÖTTERDÄMMERUNG (THE DUSK OF THE GODS). *See:* (THE) RING OF THE NIBELUNGS.

## HÄNSEL UND GRETEL.

*Fairy opera in three acts, by Engelbert Humperdinck. Libretto by Adelheid Wette based on a Grimm fairy tale. First performance: Hoftheater, Weimar, December 23, 1893.*

There is no food, and Hänsel and Gretel are hungry. To distract her little brother, Gretel teaches him to sing and dance. When the mother returns from her errands, she sends the children into the woods to pick strawberries. They get lost. Night comes, bringing terror. The Sandman lulls the children to sleep with a gentle lullaby ("Der kleine Sandmann bin ich"). After the children say their prayers ("Abends will ich schlafen gehn") the fairies descend to provide a protective ring for them (Dream Pantomime Music). But the children are nonetheless captured by the witch who brings them to her house in order to bake them into gingerbread. She sings her weird incantation ("Hexenritt"). But the children thwart her by shoving her into the hot oven, which crashes into ruin. All the children previously captured by the witch, and transformed by her into gingerbread, are brought back to life. A general celebration ensues in which join the parents of Hänsel and Gretel, who have finally found their lost children.

## (LA) JUIVE (THE JEWESS).

*Opera in five acts, by Jacques Halévy. Libretto by Eugène Scribe. First performance: Opéra, Paris, February 23, 1835.*

In Constance, in 1414, Rachel, daughter of the Jew Eleazar, is loved by Prince Leopold. Leopold presses his suit by disguising himself as Samuel, a humble Jewish painter. The crowd is hostile to Eleazar because he has refused to join the celebrations in honor of Prince Leopold's victory over the Hussites. Only Leopold's intervention saves him from bodily harm.

Rachel invites Prince Leopold—or "Samuel"—to her house for the Passover ceremonies (Passover Scene: "O Dieu, Dieu de nos pères"). It is only then that she discovers his true identity. So great is Rachel's love that she is willing to accept him for what he is—a Christian. When Eleazar's anger is spent he, too, becomes amenable to their marriage. But Leopold suddenly becomes aware of the immense step he is about to take, and rushes out of Eleazar's house crying it is impossible for him to marry a Jewess.

In the great hall of the imperial palace, Rachel bitterly denounces Prince Leopold, startling the assembly by revealing how Leopold had offered to marry her. The Cardinal excommunicates the Prince, consigning him to prison with Eleazar and Rachel. In prison, Rachel regrets her rash act, and is ready to assume full responsibility for what has happened between her and Leopold. In return, the Cardinal offers to pardon both Eleazar and Rachel, but only if they are willing to embrace Christianity. Proudly, Eleazar refuses to do so. He then confides to the Cardinal that the latter's daughter, believed dead in a fire many years ago, is actually living, having been saved by a Jew. But where she is, or with whom, Eleazar would not say, since this is to be his revenge. When the Cardinal leaves, Eleazar muses sadly on the tragic turn of events that forces him to sacrifice the one whom he has raised as his daughter and whom he has come to love ("Rachel, quand du Seigneur").

Eleazar and Rachel are to be boiled in oil. Eleazar tells Rachel there is still time for her to save herself by accepting conversion. But Rachel can be as brave as her father. Before punishment is meted out, the Cardinal implores Eleazar to reveal the whereabouts of his daughter. After Rachel is thrown into the burning oil, Eleazar cries out: "There she is!"

## (THE) KING'S HENCHMAN.

*Opera in three acts, by Deems Taylor. Libretto by Edna St. Vincent Millay. First performance: Metropolitan Opera House, New York, February 17, 1927.*

In tenth century England, Aethelwold and Aelfrida become lovers through the powers of an incantation. But Aelfrida, daughter of the Thane of Devon, is sought by King Eadgar of Wessex, whom she has never met and who has never met her. The King sends Aethelwold, his friend and foster brother, to Devon to fetch Aelfrida. From Devon, Aethelwold sends a message to the King saying that she is too ugly for him; he, then, marries her himself. The King arrives in Devon to see Aelfrida for himself, and sees how beautiful she really is. Aethelwold commits suicide because he has betrayed his friend.

## LAKMÉ.

*Opéra comique in three acts, by Léo Delibes. Libretto by Edmond Gondinet and Philippe Gille based on Pierre Loti's novel, Le Mariage de Loti. First performance: Opéra Comique, Paris, April 14, 1883.*

In India, the Brahmin priest, Nilakantha, tells his worshippers that the day is approaching when the English invaders will be driven from the land. From the nearby temple, Lakmé's voice is heard in prayer ("Blanche dourga").

A small British party—which includes the British officer, Gerald—disregards the order against violating the sanctity of the temple. It breaks down the surrounding fence, and enters the holy grounds to admire the gardens. The sight of Lakmé's jewels so fascinates Gerald that he stops to sketch them, even while the rest of his party leaves. Lakmé appears in the garden, meets Gerald, and they fall in love with each other. She entreats Gerald to leave the grounds, since the penalty for the invasion is death. He leaves, just as Nilakantha returns. The Brahmin priest, noticing the footsteps of a stranger on the ground, vows to destroy the man who thus dared to desecrate the temple.

In search of this violator, Nilakantha comes to the market place, which is festive with a bazaar. He is disguised as a beggar and he has brought Lakmé with him. He commands Lakmé to sing, hoping that her song will tempt the culprit to reveal himself. Lakmé sings an exotic and haunting song (The Bell Song: "Où va la jeune hindoue"). As Nilakantha had hoped, Gerald—overwhelmed by the beauty of Lakmé's singing—rushes toward her and thereby reveals himself. Nilakantha stabs him, and believing him dead, escapes. Lakmé, however, stays behind. Learning that Gerald's wound is not serious, she has her attendants carry him away into the depths of an Indian forest, where she can nurse him back to health.

Lakmé and Gerald are more deeply in love than ever. She goes off to bring Gerald some water from the sacred fountain which will eternalize their love. While she is gone, Gerald's fellow-officer comes to tell him that their regiment has been called back to duty. Lakmé, after her return to Gerald, hears the distant sound of martial fifes and drums. Perceiving Gerald's reaction to this music she knows, suddenly and with finality, that she has lost her loved one forever, that he is about to return to his regiment. Since she cannot live without him, she poisons herself with the deadly sap of a blossom. Nilakantha comes to destroy Gerald, but the dying Lakmé prevents him by saying that she had offered herself as a victim to the gods.

## LOHENGRIN.

*Opera in three acts, by Richard Wagner. Libretto by the composer based on medieval legends. First performance: Weimar, Germany, August 28, 1850.*

In Antwerp, in the tenth century, Elsa of Brabant is falsely accused by Frederick of Telramund and his wife Ortrud of having murdered her brother. King Henry the Fowler decides that Elsa's guilt or innocence must be decided in a duel between her accuser, Telramund, and any champion Elsa might designate. Elsa has had a vision in which a knight in shining armor comes to her defense (Elsa's Dream: "Einsam in trüben Tagen"). When the Herald calls for Elsa's champion to make his appearance, and no one arrives, she sinks on her knees and prays for her deliverer (Elsa's Prayer:. "Du trugest zu ihm meine Klage"). Suddenly a boat drawn by a swan appears; in it is the knight Lohengrin, Elsa's defender. He bids a tender farewell to his swan ("Leb' wohl, leb wohl, mein leiber Schwan"); then offers himself to Elsa as her champion—but only on the condition that she make no effort to uncover his identity. In the duel that follows Lohengrin is victorious over Telramund, and he asks for Elsa's hand in marriage.

In disgrace, Telramund and Ortrud nurse the hope of destroying Elsa and her knight. Ortrud, feigning repentance, is forgiven by Elsa who, ecstatically happy at her forthcoming marriage, gives expression to her rapture ("Euch Lüften die mein Klagen"). Gaining Elsa's confidence, Ortrud works on her to try to identify her mysterious champion by hinting that he might be a black magician who won his victory by foul means. Elsa refuses to break her vow; but the first seeds of suspicion and doubt have been sowed in her mind.

The wedding procession enters the bridal chamber (Wedding March), for it is the wedding day of Elsa and Lohengrin. The guests hail the bride and groom (Bridal Chorus: "Treulich geführt"). When the guests have departed Elsa—now torn by doubts—implores her husband to reveal himself to her. He is hesitant, but Elsa will not be denied. He is about to disclose his identity when Telramund enters, attacks the knight, and is killed. Sadly, the knight turns to his attendants and asks them to attire Elsa in her finest raiment and to bring her before the King. There, Lohengrin plans to tell her who he really is.

At the banks of the Scheldt River, Lohengrin reveals that he is a Knight of the Holy Grail; that he is allowed to absent himself in pursuit of good deeds; that he must always remain anonymous ("In fernem Land"). Once he betrays his identity he must leave for good. Lohengrin bids farewell to Elsa, and returns the way he came, in his swan-drawn boat. But the swan is really Elsa's brother transformed through Ortrud's witchery; and since Ortrud's spell is broken, Elsa's brother returns to human form.

## LOUISE.

*"Musical romance" in four acts, by Gustave Charpentier. Libretto by the composer. First performance: Opéra Comique, Paris, February 2, 1900.*

The parents of Louise are not kindly disposed toward her love affair with the painter, Julien. The father compels her to promise never again to see Julien. At the dressmaker's establishment, where she is employed as a seamstress, Louise is taunted by the other girls for her unhappy state. From below, Julien's voice rises in a serenade ("Dans la cité lointaine"). The girls rush to the window to flirt with him. But Julien's song turns to mockery as he laments the fickleness of woman. Passionately, Louise rushes out of the shop to join him.

The lovers are together, at last, in a little house on the side of Montmartre hill. Louise ecstatically recalls the time when first she surrendered to Julien's love ("Depuis le jour"), and the two lovers exchange rapturous expressions of sentiment. But Louise's mother bursts in upon their happiness with the tragic news that Louise's father is dying. Julien must consent to Louise's visiting her father, but only after her mother has given her word that Louise will be permitted to return to him.

Louise's return home restores her father to health. She now wishes to return to her lover, but her mother—forgetting her promise—refuses to give her permission. The father takes his daughter in his arms and sings to her a tender lullaby in which he nostalgically recalls happy days of the past (Berceuse: "Reste—repose-toi"). Louise is still determined to go back to Julien. Angrily, the father orders her out of the house. When his daughter leaves him, he curses the evil influence of Paris, blaming the city for having ruined his daughter.


(THE) LOVE OF THREE KINGS. *See:* L'AMORE DEI TRE RE.


## LUCIA DI LAMMERMOOR.

*Opera in three acts, by Gaetano Donizetti. Libretto by Salvatore Cammarano, based on* The Bride of Lammermoor, *a novel by Sir Walter Scott. First performance: San Carlo, Naples, September 26, 1835.*


Lucy (Lucia) is in love with Edgar (Edgardo); but her brother, Lord Henry Ashton (Enrico Ashton), objects to the love affair because Edgar is his sworn enemy, and also because he hopes to rehabilitate the dwindling fortunes of the Ashton household through the marriage of his sister to the wealthy Lord Arthur (Arturo) Bucklaw.

Edgar must leave for France. During his absence, Henry intercepts the letters he sends Lucy, and even forges Edgar's handwriting to deliver Lucy a letter saying that he [Edgar] has left her forever. Lucy is finally convinced to accept Lord Bucklaw as her husband. During the marriage ceremony, a stranger enters: it is Edgar, with gun in hand. The six principal characters of the opera express the turmoil of this situation in the famous sextet ("Chi mi frena"). Edgar curses Lucy, because she is so ready to marry another, and her entire household.

Determined to avenge the honor of his household, Henry challenges Edgar to a duel. Meanwhile, within Henry's house, word has come that the bride Lucy has gone mad and has killed her husband. Confirmation comes with Lucy's arrival. She is dressed in white, her hair is loose, her eyes afire. Her wandering mind has convinced her that she is really married to Edgar, whom she entreats never to leave her (Mad Scene). After this passionate outburst she falls into a faint.

Edgar, who cannot forget that Lucy left him for someone else, denounces her bitterly. He suddenly notices that in the distance mourners are leaving Henry's castle. As they approach him, he is told of Lucy's madness. Even as they speak, bells are tolling to announce that

Lucy is dead. Overwhelmed by this news, Edgar kills himself with a dagger.

## MADAME BUTTERFLY.

*Opera in three acts, by Giacomo Puccini. Libretto by Illica and Giacosa based on a play of David Belasco which was, in turn, derived from a short story by John Luther Long. First performance: La Scala, Milan, February 17, 1904.*

Lieutenant Pinkerton of the United States Navy—stationed in Nagasaki, Japan—is about to enter upon a Japanese marriage with the beautiful geisha girl, Cio-Cio-San. The house of the Lieutenant becomes festive as the bride and her relatives arrive for the ceremony. The festivity is momentarily shattered with the intrusion of the bride's uncle, who expresses his rage that his niece should renounce her people and her religion to marry an American. He curses her, and so do the other relatives as they stream out of the house. Deserted by her kin, Cio-Cio-San bursts into tears, but Pinkerton's tenderness soothes her. As night descends, they are in each other's arms, ecstatic with each other's love ("Viene la sera").

Three years pass. Pinkerton has left Japan with the United States fleet. Cio-Cio-San is convinced that he will return to her ("Un bel di"). To the United States consul, Sharpless, she reveals that her little son is also Pinkerton's child, news that fills Sharpless with the dread of impending doom. Suddenly a cannon shot resounds in the harbor. The American fleet has returned to Nagasaki, and with it has come Pinkerton. Feverish with excitement, Cio-Cio-San and her servant dress the house with cherry blossoms ("Tutti i fior"). She herself puts on her wedding dress to await Pinkerton.

Throughout the night, Cio-Cio-San maintains an uninterrupted vigil for him. At last she goes into her chamber for rest. It is only then that Pinkerton arrives—and with him are Sharpless and an American woman who is Pinkerton's legal wife. When Sharpless convinces Pinkerton that he must not see Cio-Cio-San again, he bids a tender farewell to her and her house ("Addio fiorito asil"). Cio-Cio-San, apprised of Pinkerton's arrival, rushes out to greet him—but he is no longer present. Somehow Cio-Cio-San senses the tragic truth. Pinkerton's American wife begs Cio-Cio-San to deliver to her Pinkerton's son.

She is willing to do this, but only if Pinkerton himself makes the request. When Sharpless and Pinkerton's wife leave to deliver this message, Cio-Cio-San takes her child in her arms and bids him goodbye ("Piccolo iddio"). Covering his eyes with bandages, she goes behind a screen and plunges a dagger in her breast. By the time Pinkerton arrives, she is dead. Grief-stricken he takes her in his arms while Sharpless leads away the little boy.

### (THE) MAGIC FLUTE (DIE ZAUBERFLÖTE).

*Opera in two acts, by Wolfgang Amadeus Mozart. Libretto by Emmanuel Schikaneder and Karl Giesecke, based on a tale of Wieland. First performance: Theater auf der Wieden, Vienna, September 30, 1791.*

Tamino, an Egyptian prince, flees from a serpent and is saved by three attendants of the Queen of the Night. Papageno, a birdcatcher, comes on the scene, blowing on the pipes of his flute and confessing gaily that he prefers catching girls to birds ("Der Vogelfänger bin ich ja"). Tamino, believing that it was Papageno who had saved him from the serpent, thanks him effusively. Papageno accepts the gratitude even though he is undeserving of it, and for this offense he is punished by the Queen's attendants: his lips are sealed by a lock. These attendants then show Tamino a picture of Pamina, the daughter of the Queen. Her beauty is so breathtaking that Tamino must sing a hymn to it ("Dies Bildnis ist bezaubernd schön"). The Queen of the Night now informs Tamino that her daughter is the prisoner of a tyrant named Sarastro; that if he—Tamino—will rescue her she will become his bride. Tamino offers his services cheerfully. The Queen provides him with a magic flute which, when played, will protect him from danger. She also instructs Papageno to accompany Tamino, equipping the former with magic chimes for protection.

Pamina is imprisoned in the palace of Sarastro, High Priest of Isis. Papageno penetrates her well-guarded chamber, convinces her to trust him, and conducts her out of the palace.

Meanwhile, Tamino learns from one of the high priests of Isis that Sarastro is no evil tyrant but a man of ideals and virtue. The reason he has imprisoned Pamina will eventually be explained to him. Alone, Tamino is torn with doubts. From the distance come the sounds of

Papageno's magic chimes. Papageno and Pamina have been caught by her guard and his slaves but have been saved by the chimes. With the accompaniment of flourishing trumpets, Sarastro appears. Pamina falls on her knees and confesses that she tried to escape. When the slaves bring in Tamino, Pamina and Tamino rush into each other's arms. Sarastro orders that each of them be covered with veils so that they might undergo some secret rites.

Before the Temple, Sarastro pleads that Tamino be initiated into the final mysteries, explaining that the marriage of Tamino and Pamina is preordained. When the priests consent, Sarastro sings an invocation to the gods, pleading with them to endow the lovers with courage ("O Isis und Osiris").

Tamino and Pamina are now to be subjected to several tests of strength. Tamino must not speak to his beloved; and Papageno must not speak to the beautiful bride selected for him by Sarastro. The Queen's attendants appear to warn Tamino to flee from this place, but he remains silent. Meantime, in the garden of the palace, the Queen of the Night appears before Pamina and orders her to kill Sarastro with a dagger ("Der hölle Rache"). Pamina is horrified by this command. When Sarastro appears, Pamina pleads for her mother. Sarastro replies with dignity and nobility that within these holy halls there is no place for vengeance ("In diesem heil'gen Hallen").

By playing his flute, Tamino invokes Pamina into the hall of the Temple of Probation. She arrives full of love and tenderness. But Tamino must maintain his silence even though Pamina believes he loves her no more. Pamina's grief is immense ("Ach, ich fühls") and she begs for death. Back in her garden Pamina, indeed, tries to kill herself with a dagger, but several pages arrive to convince her that Tamino still loves her.

Before Tamino meets his next test, Pamina is brought to him and they are permitted to embrace each other. Leading her beloved by the hand, Pamina conducts him through fire—as he plays on his magic flute for protection. Then the lovers must pass through water. Their success is hailed by the priests. Meanwhile, Papageno, having lost his sweetheart, decides to hang himself. The pages remind him to use his chimes. When he does, the pages appear with the girl, who falls into his arms.

After the Queen of the Night and her attendants are destroyed by Sarastro, the pages conduct Tamino and Pamina before the High

Priest. He pronounces them ready to serve Isis. The voices of the priests are now heard in praise of Isis and Osiris.

## MANON.

> *Opera in five acts, by Jules Massenet. Libretto by Meilhac and Gille, based on* L'Histoire du Chevalier des Grieux et de Manon Lescaut *by Abbé Prévost. First performance: Opéra Comique, Paris, January 19, 1884.*

Lescaut has come to an inn at Amiens to await a coach bearing his cousin, Manon, and to conduct her to a convent. When she arrives she is sad at the step she is about to take. Her revery is interrupted by the arrival of Chevalier des Grieux, who is instantly struck by her beauty. He makes advances to her, which are not resisted. Recognizing their attraction for each other, the pair decides to flee to Paris.

In Paris, des Grieux writes to his father of his intention to marry Manon. When he leaves to despatch his letter, de Brétigny, a nobleman who has also succumbed to Manon's beauty, comes to convince her that des Grieux' father soon intends taking his son away from her. He urges Manon to go off with him and enjoy life. Manon is tempted by this offer, for de Brétigny has wealth and power. Torn by indecision, she nostalgically recalls the happiness she has known with des Grieux ("Adieu notre petite table"). On his return, des Grieux finds Manon in tears. He tries to cheer her up by confiding to her a dream he has had: a home which they can share ("Le rêve"). There is a knock at the door. When des Grieux opens it, he is abducted by one of his father's men.

Manon and de Brétigny now go off together. They join the merry-makers in a Paris street, which is festive with song and dance (Gavotte: "Obéissons quand leur voix appelle"). Des Grieux' father passes by, greets de Brétigny, and informs him that his son is about to enter priesthood at Saint Sulpice. Manon's old love is awakened, and she rushes off to Saint Sulpice. Within his cell, des Grieux bids the world a touching farewell, as he seeks peace ("Ah! fuyez douce image"). Manon, more beautiful than ever, comes before him. Des Grieux is ready to surrender himself to her again, and to desert priesthood.

They are next found in a gambling room in Paris. Des Grieux' luck is so phenomenal that he is accused of cheating, and the police is called. But des Grieux is rescued by the arrival of his father. Manon, however, is apprehended as a woman of ill repute and sentenced to exile.

Passing on the road to Le Havre and exile, Manon is awaited by her lover, who has bribed an officer so that he might be able to communicate with her. When she arrives, des Grieux begs her to escape with him. But Manon no longer has either the strength or the will. She sinks into his arms and dies.

## (THE) MARRIAGE OF FIGARO (LE NOZZE DI FIGARO).
*Opera buffa in four acts, by Wolfgang Amadeus Mozart. Libretto by Lorenzo da Ponte based on Beaumarchais' Le Mariage de Figaro. First performance: Burgtheater, Vienna, May 1, 1786.*

Figaro, valet of Count Almaviva, is about to marry Susanna, the Countess' lady-in-waiting. The Count has assigned to the pair a room near his own. Susanna does not fail to point out to her betrothed that the proximity of her room to that of the Count is surely no coincidence, since the Count has previously shown that he is attracted to her. Figaro is troubled; but in mock gaiety he insists he can handle his master ("Se vuol ballare").

Bartolo and Marcellina enter and engage in a plot against Figaro which involves his one-time promise to marry Marcellina. They are overheard by Susanna, who emerges from hiding and begins to quarrel with her rival. Cherubino now appears and speaks of his love for the gardener's daughter. With the entrance of the Count, Cherubino hides behind a chair, from which point he witnesses the Count's effort to flirt with Susanna. Basilio's sudden arrival sends the Count scurrying behind the chair, too. Both are discovered. Angrily, the Count orders Cherubino to join his regiment; this tempts Figaro to comment sardonically on Cherubino's future in the army ("Non più andrai").

In her boudoir, the Countess muses about love ("Porgi amor"). Aware that the Count is none too faithful, she concocts a plot with Figaro for the purpose of awakening his love for her: the Count is to discover a love note seemingly despatched to the Countess from her lover; and in the rendezvous that is to be arranged between the Countess and her lover, Susanna is to take the Countess' place. At the same time, Cherubino is to appear in Susanna's clothes. When Cherubino comes, singing of the meaning of love ("Voi che sapete"), he is hurriedly dressed in Susanna's apparel. The sudden entrance of the

Count sends Cherubino scurrying into the closet. By the time the suspicious Count is ready to break down the closet door, Cherubino has managed to flee out of the bedroom window. The Count, then, does not find Cherubino in the closet, but only Susanna. He regrets his suspicions until the gardener appears to complain that somebody has jumped out of the boudoir window and destroyed his flowers. Figaro suddenly announces that he is the culprit. Unfortunately, the gardener has found a piece of paper dropped by the guilty man: it is Cherubino's commission to the Count's regiment. Hastily, Figaro explains that he had Cherubino's commission in his own possession. The troubled waters seem momentarily stilled when Marcellina arrives and demands that Figaro go through with his one-time bargain to marry her.

Somewhat later, the Count threatens Susanna that unless she is agreeable to him he will personally see to it that Figaro marry Marcellina. Susanna makes a pretense of yielding to the Count's coercion, arranging a rendezvous. But the Count is nevertheless bent on punishing Figaro, and orders him either to marry Marcellina or pay damages. During these negotiations it is suddenly discovered that Figaro is actually Marcellina's son. Nothing now stands in the way of Figaro's marriage.

The Countess, still eager to catch her husband in his philandering and to win back his love, recalls her days of happiness with her husband ("Dove sono"). She plans to double for Susanna during the latter's meeting with the Count. Meanwhile, the marriage ceremony uniting Figaro and Susanna takes place.

In the garden, Susanna and the Countess appear in each other's clothes. Cherubino, who has an appointment with the gardener's daughter, sees the Countess and, thinking she is Susanna, kisses her. Matters become more complicated when both the Count and Figaro appear on the scene. The situation is relieved when the Countess and Susanna reveal their true identities and the motive for their disguise. The Count is contrite and begs for forgiveness. The entire group returns into the castle to celebrate Figaro's marriage.

## (THE) MEDIUM.

*Opera in two acts, by Gian-Carlo Menotti. Libretto by the composer. First performance: Columbia University, New York City, May 8, 1946.*

Madame Flora, a fraudulent medium, confesses her deceit to her clients after she has felt a cold, unearthly hand on her throat. She suspects that the mute Toby—whom she has adopted—is out to murder her. Madame Flora turns to drink. In a frightened stupor she fires several shots through one of her cabinets in which Toby is hiding, killing him.

## (DIE) MEISTERSINGER VON NÜRNBERG (THE MASTER-SINGERS OF NUREMBERG).

*Opera in three acts, by Richard Wagner. Libretto by the composer. First performance: Munich, June 21, 1868.*

Walther von Stolzing, a Franconian knight who is a stranger in Nuremberg, learns that Eva's father Pogner is offering her as a bride to the one who wins a song contest; but in this contest only members of the master guild can compete. Walther is determined to enter into the competition and has the apprentice, David, teach him some of the rules. The Mastersingers arrive for a musical test. During this test, Pogner makes his announcement of offering the hand of Eva to the winner of the song contest. Walther now makes a successful bid to be heard at these preliminary proceedings. He explains how he has studied the art of music from nature and the ancient minstrel ("Am stillen Herd"). He now improvises a love song which (as loudly noted by a rival suitor for Eva, Beckmesser) is full of errors. The other Mastersingers are no more appreciative of Walther's gifts. Despite the efforts of the venerable Hans Sachs, the cobbler, to get a tolerant reaction to Walther, the young knight is rudely sent away.

Hans Sachs, however, cannot forget the beauty of Walther's melody. He thinks about it one night as he works at his cobbling in a Nuremberg street. Eva comes and is coquettish toward old Sachs, but the cobbler knows that she is really in love with Walther. When Eva and Walther meet, they decide to elope. Their conversation is momentarily interrupted by the approach of Beckmesser who comes to serenade Eva under her window—and with the song he hopes to win the contest. Sachs does not appreciate Beckmesser's efforts, and rudely interrupts the serenade with a raucous ditty of his own. When Eva's nurse, Magdalena, appears at the window, Beckmesser—thinking that she is Eva—grows more ardent in his song. The townspeople, awakened by his din, look out of their windows. One of them is David who, believing that Beckmesser is serenading the nurse with whom he himself is in love, goes out to administer a sound thrashing to the ardent serenader. Hubbub prevails. In the commotion, Eva and Walther try to elope but are restrained by Sachs. The confusion subsides. A watchman passes the now silent streets to announce that all is well.

David, penitent over the commotion that he has helped to create, enters Hans Sachs' workshop the following morning. Sachs asks him to sing a carol of St. John, since this is the Saint's day. When David departs, Sachs muses philosophically that the entire world is mad ("Wahn, wahn"). Walther now appears to tell Sachs of a wonderful dream he has had in which a song of incomparable beauty came to him. It is the so-called "Prize Song." Sachs is impressed and puts it down on paper. This manuscript is found by Beckmesser who, believing that it is a piece of Sachs' own creation, decides to steal it for his own use at the contest. Eva enters to have her shoes fixed, and hears Walther sing a part of his wonderful song. Magdalena and David are also present, and the four of them join with Sachs in expressing their reaction to the song ("Selig wie die Sonne").

The day of the contest is at hand. A field, on the shores of the river Pegnitz, is gala with crowds, flags, and banners. The apprentices dance with the girls (The Dance of the Apprentices). The Mastersingers march with pomp and ceremony (Procession of the Mastersingers). Beckmesser is the first contestant. Singing from the manuscript which he has stolen, and which he misreads, he grows so confused that his rendition is a fiasco. Sachs then calls on Walther, the true author, to sing the song. The Prize Song ("Morgenlich leuchtend") is acclaimed. Eva is his. The crowd cheers the wise and noble cobbler, Hans Sachs ("Heil Sachs!").

## MERRY MOUNT.

> *Opera in four acts, by Howard Hanson. Libretto by Richard L. Stokes, based on a New England legend. First performance: Metropolitan Opera House, New York, February 10, 1934.*

Bradford, a clergyman, is attracted to Lady Marigold, who is to be married to Gower Lackland. The marriage is interrupted by the arrival of the Puritans. In the ensuing confusion, Bradford abducts

Lady Marigold. Followed by Gower, Bradford attacks and kills him. Exhaustion brings on sleep and dreams. Awakening, Bradford learns that his village has been ravaged by Indians. When the villagers accuse Lady Marigold for their misfortunes, Bradford seizes her and jumps with her through the flames of a burning church.

## MIGNON.

*Opéra comique in three acts, by Ambroise Thomas. Libretto by Carré and Barbier, based on incidents in* Wilhelm Meister, *a novel by Goethe. First performance: Opéra Comique, Paris, November 17, 1866.*

Lothario, a nobleman who has lost his memory through grief, comes to the courtyard of a German inn, which is filled with merry makers. Mignon (as a child, she had been stolen by gypsies) is ordered by her master to dance, but she refuses. Both Lothario and a young student named Wilhelm Meister protect her from possible abuse at the hands of her master. Meister is now curious about Mignon's personal history. But all she can tell him is that she comes from a strange and far-distant land ("Connais-tu le pays"). Pitying her, Meister buys her freedom and asks her to accompany him in his travels. When Lothario confides to Mignon that soon he will be off for the south, Mignon speaks nostalgically of the land of songs and swallows ("Légères hirondelles"). Meanwhile, Meister is attracted to the actress Philine, who invites him to attend a party in the castle of a Baron.

In the boudoir of this castle, Philine is applying her make-up, thinking all the while of Meister. He soon enters accompanied by Mignon. Mignon notices with anguish how Meister pays court to the actress. When Philine and Meister leave the boudoir, Mignon tries on one of Philine's gowns, singing a poignant tune about a gypsy lad as she does so (Styrienne: "Je connais un pauvre enfant"). Frédéric, a young nobleman in love with Philine, comes through the boudoir window, singing a light tune as he comes ("Me voici dans son boudoir"). When Wilhelm reenters, he attacks Frédéric with his sword, but Mignon intervenes. Realizing that Mignon's devoted presence is proving embarrassing to him, Meister demands that she leave him for good. Anguished at this rejection, and at Philine's taunts, Mignon removes Philine's gown and puts on her gypsy rags.

Mignon contemplates suicide, but is dissuaded by Lothario. However, she is bent on vengeance, and she expresses the hope that the castle might go up in flames. From out the castle emerge the guests and entertainers. Philine is among them, glowing at her recent performance as the Fairy Queen in *A Midsummer Night's Dream* ("Je suis Titania"). Lothario moves over to Mignon and whispers in her ear that her vengeance has been realized: he himself has set fire to the castle. Philine, not yet realizing that the castle is burning, orders Mignon inside to bring her some flowers. When the alarm is spread that the castle is in flames, Meister rushes inside to rescue Mignon.

Both Lothario and Wilhelm Meister take turns in nursing Mignon back to health. Lothario sings a tender lullaby to her ("De son coeur j'ai calmé la fièvre"). Meister now knows he is in love with Mignon and he expresses his feelings passionately ("Elle ne croyait pas dans sa candeur naïve"). Suddenly, Lothario's memory returns. He now remembers that the castle he has burned is his own; that Mignon is his long-lost daughter.

## NORMA.

*Opera in four acts, by Vincenzo Bellini. Libretto by Felice Romani, based on a tragedy of L. A. Soumet. First performance: La Scala, Milan, December 26, 1831.*

Norma, Druid high priestess, is in love with the Roman proconsul, Pollione, and has violated her vow of chastity by bearing him two children. But Pollione is now in love with Adalgisa, virgin of the temple of Esus. His conscience torments him ("Meco all' altar di Venere"). When Norma enters with several Druids, she implores her subjects not yet to rise against the Roman oppressors, for she is eager to spare the life of Pollione. She prays God for peace ("Casta diva"). Meanwhile, Pollione and Adalgisa plot to elope to Rome. But Adalgisa does not know of Pollione's former tie to Norma. Consequently, she comes to the high priestess to confess her passion for the Roman proconsul. In an uncontrolled rage, Norma reveals that she, too, is in love with Pollione. She curses him and, as atonement for her violation of chastity, plans to kill him, her children, and herself. The sight of her sleeping children frustrates her plan to murder them. She calls to Adalgisa and begs her to care for her little ones, since she is determined to commit suicide. But Adalgisa entreats her and prevails on her not to kill herself ("Mira, o Norma").

Norma now arouses her subjects to war on the Romans. When Pollione is discovered in their midst, he is brought before Norma who sentences him to choose between death or immediate exile. But her love for him gets the upper hand. She is ready to pardon him if he will give up Adalgisa. This Pollione refuses to do. Overwhelmed by her grief, Norma turns to her people, confesses her guilt, and insists upon punishment. This confession has such an effect on Pollione that he begs for the right to die with her. Norma and Pollione meet death in a burning pyre.

## ORFEO ED EURIDICE.

*Opera in four acts, by Christoph Willibald Gluck. Libretto by Raniere Calzabigi. First performance: Burgtheater, Vienna, October 5, 1762.*

Orpheus is stricken with grief at the death of his wife, Eurydice, and mourns at her grave. Touched by this demonstration of grief, Amor tells him he can seek the shade of Eurydice in the other world—but only on the condition that, if he takes Eurydice back to earth with him, he must not look at her face until they reach there.

Orpheus enters the caves of Tartarus where the Furies are engaged in a frenetic dance (Dance of the Furies). They try to frighten him, but with his wonderful song ("Deh placatevi con me!") he moves them to pity, and they permit him to proceed. He next comes to the Elysian Fields, home of the Spirits of the Blessed (Dance of the Blessed Spirits). It is here that Orpheus finds Eurydice, and has her follow him back to earth. Because he refuses to look at her, Eurydice is convinced that Orpheus loves her no longer. Her anguish is so great that Orpheus helplessly turns to look at her. She sinks to the ground—dead. Once again he is overwhelmed with grief, as he realizes that he has again lost Eurydice ("Che farò senza Euridice"). But Amor pities his plight, revives Eurydice, and allows the pair to return to earth.

## OTELLO.

*Opera in four acts, by Giuseppe Verdi. Libretto by Arrigo Boïto, based on the tragedy of Shakespeare. First performance: La Scala, Milan, February 5, 1887.*

Othello, victor over the Turkish fleet, comes to the island of Cyprus, whose Governor he has become. His aide, Iago, is resentful that so high a position has come to Othello and he plots his destruction. He sees to it that Othello's lieutenant, Cassio, gets drunk and that a riot develops. When Othello comes to quiet the disturbance, Cassio is punished by having his command taken from him. Alone with his beautiful wife, Desdemona, Othello recalls how they came to fall in love ("Gia nella notta densa").

Later on, Iago expresses his personal philosophy that God is cruel and fashioned man to be cruel, too ("Credo in un Dio crudel"). Still bent on destroying Othello, Iago fans the latter's jealousy by pointing out to him that Cassio and Desdemona are in consultation—a consultation which Iago has arranged. When Desdemona insists that her conversation with Cassio had been innocent, Othello's suspicions mount. His peace of mind has been shattered, as he realizes only too well ("Ora e per sempre addio"). Iago continues to work on Othello by confiding to him that he has seen Desdemona's handkerchief in Cassio's room—he himself having secreted the handkerchief there. Aroused to a pitch of hysteria, Othello begs Iago to join him in seeking vengeance, and they vow to be indefatigable in their pursuit of justice.

Othello comes to Desdemona asking for her handkerchief. She proffers one, but it is not the one he is seeking, and he sends her to her room for it. Alone he curses his fate that the tragedy of his wife's infidelity should have befallen him ("Dio mi potevi scagliar"). Then, seeing Cassio approaching, he goes in hiding, and hears him brag to Iago about a love affair, which Othello falsely assumes is with Desdemona. When Cassio shows Iago Desdemona's handkerchief which he has mysteriously and inexplicably found in his room, Othello can no longer entertain any doubts. He now is determined to kill his wife. At this point the Venetian ambassador comes to tell Othello he must return to Venice, and Cassio is to replace him. When Othello relays this news to his wife, he suddenly becomes so blinded by his fury that he hurls her to the ground, and then faints with the intensity of his emotions.

Preparing to go to bed, Desdemona tells Iago's wife of a song she had learned as a child (Willow Song: "Salce, salce"). After Iago's wife departs, Desdemona falls on her knees and prays to the Madonna ("Ave Maria"). Othello enters her room, once again to subject her to savage questioning about Cassio. His passion mounts to madness, and he fatally chokes his wife. Only too late does Othello learn of Iago's treachery and Desdemona's innocence. Repentant, Othello kills himself with a dagger.

## PAGLIACCI.

*Opera in two acts, by Ruggiero Leoncavallo. Libretto by the composer. First performance: Teatro dal Verme, Milan, May 21, 1892.*

Before the rise of the curtain, the clown Tonio tells the audience that the play it is about to witness is not merely theatre but a true story with flesh-and-blood actors (Prologue: "Si può?").

The curtain rises on a little Italian village, to which a traveling theatrical troupe comes for an evening performance. While one of the troupers, Canio, is in the inn, his wife Nedda sings a pastoral about the birds in the sky (Ballatella: "Che volo d'augelli"). Tonio tries to make love to her and is slashed by her whip. But Nedda is responsive to the advances of Silvio, a villager. Tonio overhears their exchange of ardent sentiments, and—to avenge his humiliation—he calls to Canio to witness this love scene. Silvio escapes before Canio can identify him. After Canio attempts but fails to kill his wife, he sings of the irony of having to play the role of a clown while his heart is breaking ("Vesti la giubba!").

The show which the troupe gives that evening turns out to be very much like the love triangle taking place in the company. In the show, the triangle involves Punchinello (played by Canio), Columbine (Nedda) and Harlequin (Beppe). When Punchinello asks his wife Columbine for the name of her lover, Canio forgets he is playing a role in the play. Again and again he asks Nedda who her lover is. At last, he seizes a knife and kills her. When Silvio rushes from the audience to the stage to help her, Canio kills him, too; and after that commits suicide. The audience streams on to the stage to seize Canio. His last bitter words are: "The comedy is ended."

## PARSIFAL.

*Consecrational festival drama in three acts, by Richard Wagner. Libretto by the composer based on a medieval legend, and Wolfram von Eschenbach's poem. First performance: Bayreuth, July 26, 1882.*

Gurnemanz, knight of the Holy Grail, tells his young squires about the ailing Amfortas, King of the Knights, who can be cured only by a guileless fool.

Parsifal, bow in hand, comes on the scene, having just killed a wild swan. When Gurnemanz questions him about this act he discovers that the lad is completely innocent of the ways of the world—the guileless fool for whom he is searching. He leads Parsifal to Monsalvat, the hall of the Holy Grail, with the hope that this is the lad destined to cure Amfortas.

The scene shifts to the great hall itself (Transformation Scene) where the knights have come to devote themselves to the Communion service. Amfortas, on a couch, uncovers the Holy Grail, while the knights partake of the Last Supper. Parsifal witnesses this scene, but fails to understand it, and is unmoved. Gurnemanz becomes impatient with his stupidity and sends him on his way.

At his castle, the magician Klingsor arouses Kundry from her sleep and sends her off to seduce Parsifal. Parsifal enters a garden filled with beautiful women. Kundry is with them, transformed into a woman of wondrous beauty. She tries to seduce the boy, and momentarily he shows signs of yielding to her passionate kisses (Magic Garden and Flower Maidens Scene). Intuitively, Parsifal senses that in just such a garden, and under precisely these circumstances, Amfortas was once tempted. Savagely he pushes Kundry aside and curses her. Kundry calls on Klingsor to help her. A magic spear is hurled at Parsifal, but the lad—endowed with new powers—is not hurt; the spear remains suspended in mid-air. Parsifal seizes it. Kundry falls unconscious and the Klingsor castle disintegrates.

Many years later, on Good Friday, Gurnemanz finds Kundry asleep in a thicket at a meadow near the Grail, and rouses her. Parsifal, still in possession of his magic spear, appears. Gurnemanz welcomes him, for he knows now that Parsifal is destined to be Amfortas' savior. Gurnemanz sprinkles water on Parsifal's head while Kundry washes his feet and dries them with her hair. Suddenly, Parsifal notices that the meadow has begun to glow with a kind of spiritual beauty; Gurnemanz explains that it is the spell of Good Friday (The Good Friday Spell). The tolling of bells now summons the knights of the Grail to prayer, and Parsifal assumes the robes of a knight.

In the great hall at Monsalvat, Amfortas is borne on a litter. He suffers grievously from his wounds and despairs of a cure. Parsifal arrives. By touching Amfortas' wounds with his magic spear he cures him. Kundry, absolved of her sins, dies. A white dove flutters over Parsifal's head; the Holy Grail shines with a brilliant light.

## PELLÉAS ET MÉLISANDE.

*Opera in five acts, by Claude Debussy. Libretto (the original dramatic poem) by Maurice Maeterlinck. First performance: Opéra Comique, Paris, April 30, 1902.*

The story takes place in legendary times and in a legendary kingdom.

Golaud, grandson of King Arkel, lost in a forest, comes upon Mélisande, who is weeping. She tells him she has dropped her golden crown in a nearby spring, but does not permit Golaud to retrieve it. As darkness descends, Golaud prevails on Mélisande to follow him to a place of shelter.

Six months later, King Arkel receives a letter from Golaud telling him he has married Mélisande and asking forgiveness for doing so without the King's consent. Pelléas, Golaud's half-brother, comes to the King for permission to visit a dying friend. The King reminds Pelléas that Pelléas' father, who is also ill, requires his attention. He then asks Pelléas to light a signal for Golaud and to await his return home.

Soon after Golaud's return, the castle is surrounded with gloom. Pelléas and Mélisande look out into the sea. She is impressed by Pelléas and she quickly voices her regret when Pelléas confides that on the morrow he must make his departure. Afterwards, they are at the edge of a fountain into which Mélisande drops her wedding ring. Since the ring can never be retrieved, Pelléas urges Mélisande to tell her husband frankly what has happened. At the very moment that Mélisande loses her ring Golaud is thrown from a horse. Later on, in bed with physical injuries, Golaud tenderly embraces his wife, Mélisande, only to notice that she is not wearing her wedding ring. Mélisande improvises an excuse: she has lost it in a grotto near the sea. Golaud insists that Mélisande go out and find it, even though it is night, and he asks Pelléas to accompany her. Within the grotto, Pelléas and Mélisande grope their way in a mock search for the ring. When a beam of moonlight illuminates the place, they notice a group of beggars hiding in a corner. Mélisande is terrified, and Pelléas takes her away.

At a window, in a turret of the castle, Mélisande is combing her beautiful long hair, and singing. Pelléas appears below. Mockingly, Mélisande tells Pelléas he must leave and Pelléas, in all seriousness, informs her he has delayed his departure. Overjoyed at this news, Mélisande extends her hand out of the window for Pelléas to kiss; as she does so, her luxurious hair streams out of the window and covers his face. Pelléas is ecstatic with love.

Suddenly, Golaud appears, and upbraids Pelléas and Mélisande for behaving like children. Golaud then takes Pelléas to the vaults below the castle, to the stagnant pool. Pelléas is frightened; Golaud's actions seem ominous. He is relieved when they emerge from the caverns. Golaud warns him not to indulge in childish games with Mélisande, and reveals that she may soon become a mother.

But Golaud is suspicious of Pelléas. He tries to learn from the child, Yniold, whether Pelléas and Mélisande are having clandestine meetings. When the child becomes evasive, Golaud's suspicions increase. A light now appears in Mélisande's window. Golaud raises the child to look into the window and see if Pelléas is there. When the child reveals that this is, indeed, the case, Golaud is compelled to face the truth.

Pelléas and Mélisande have arranged a midnight meeting at the fountain. When Pelléas leaves the castle, Mélisande is at the side of King Arkel, who is very tender to her. The jealous Golaud appears, sword in hand. In violent rage he drags Mélisande by the hair across the room. Only King Arkel's intervention saves her. Meanwhile, Pelléas is waiting for Mélisande at the fountain. At her approach they rush passionately into each other's arms. Golaud emerges from behind one of the trees. Pelléas and Mélisande can no longer conceal their true feelings. They embrace in Golaud's presence. Golaud kills Pelléas and pursues the terror-stricken Mélisande.

Though Golaud has wounded her, Mélisande gives birth to a child. She lies in bed, Golaud is at her side. Golaud is repentant; but Mélisande cannot and will not deny that she loved Pelléas, but insists that her love was innocent. King Arkel brings to the mother her child. The servants, now entering the room, suddenly fall on their knees for they realize that Mélisande is dead.

## PETER GRIMES.

*Opera in three acts, by Benjamin Britten. Libretto by Montagu Slater, based on* The Borough, *a poem by George Crabbe. First performance: Sadler's Wells, London, June 7, 1946.*

Peter Grimes, a fisherman, though exonerated of the charge of murdering his apprentice, is still looked upon with suspicion by his fellow townspeople. When Grimes engages another apprentice, the townspeople wonder if another murder will soon take place. They march to Grimes' lonely hut to see for themselves. Terrified by the approaching mob, Grimes escapes. When the apprentice accidentally slips and kills himself, Grimes is once again accused of murder. Rather than face the fury of the mob, Grimes goes off in his boat to die in the sea.

## PETER IBBETSON.

*Opera in three acts, by Deems Taylor. Libretto by Constance Collier and the composer, based on the novel of George du Maurier. First performance: Metropolitan Opera House, New York, February 7, 1931.*

Brought up by a cruel uncle, Peter Ibbetson finds escape in dreams. In one of these he returns to the scenes of his childhood, and once again meets his childhood sweetheart, Mary. When Peter kills his uncle and is sentenced to life imprisonment, he returns again to his dreams of childhood and of Mary. While in prison, Peter Ibbetson learns of Mary's death. His own death finally reunites him with his childhood sweetheart.

## PORGY AND BESS.

*Opera in three acts, by George Gershwin. Libretto by DuBose Heyward and Ira Gershwin, based on* Porgy, *a play by DuBose Heyward. First performance: Boston, September 30, 1935.*

It is morning in Catfish Row, in Charleston, South Carolina. A mother is singing a lullaby to her child ("Summertime"). A crap game takes place. During the game, Crown quarrels with and kills Robbins; he escapes before he can be caught. Sportin' Life tries to induce Crown's girl, Bess, to go off with him to New York, but she turns him down. Sportin' Life takes this rejection stoically ("A Woman Is a Sometime Thing"). The crippled Porgy takes Bess into his own house for protection. He is in love with her; living with her brings him joy and contentment ("I Got Plenty of Nuttin' "). Bess also is responsive in this love affair. Bess and Porgy freely express their love for each other ("Bess, You Is My Woman Now").

A picnic lodge brings the inhabitants of Catfish Row to Kittiwah Island. Sportin' Life entertains his friends with an amusing commentary on his skepticism ("It Ain't Necessarily So"). Crown is hiding on the island. He manages to get to Bess and compels her to stay with him. After a few days, ill and delirious, she returns to Porgy; he nurses her back to health. When Crown returns to Catfish Row, Porgy stabs him. While the police are unable to uncover the murderer, they are suspicious of Porgy and take him off to jail. During Porgy's absence, Bess finally succumbs to the persuasion of Sportin' Life and goes off with him to New York. When Porgy is released from jail and returns jubilantly to Catfish Row and to Bess, he learns that she has left him. With broken heart, he steps into his goat cart to follow her.

## RIGOLETTO.

*Opera in four acts, by Giuseppe Verdi. Libretto by Francesco Maria Piave, based on Le Roi s'amuse, a play by Victor Hugo. First performance: Teatro la Fenice, Venice, March 11, 1851.*

During festivities at the ducal palace in Mantua, the Duke confides to a courtier that he is interested in a girl of unknown identity who visits a nearby church regularly. He propounds his cynical philosophy of love ("Questa o quella"). The orchestra strikes up the strains of a minuet. The Duke dances with the beautiful Countess Ceprano, arousing her husband's jealousy. Later on, the Duke reveals to his hunchback jester, Rigoletto, that he would like to get rid of the Count. At this point, Count Monterone, whose daughter had once been abused by the Duke, enters to denounce the roué. When the Duke orders his arrest, and Rigoletto mocks the victim, the Count curses the hunchback.

In a deserted street, Rigoletto soliloquizes about his distaste for his profession as a hireling of the Duke ("Pari siamo"). Rigoletto then enters the courtyard of his house and embraces his daughter, Gilda. Solicitous of her safety, he warns her to remain secluded at home. A noise outside sends Rigoletto scurrying into the street. The Duke, disguised as a student, has come to visit Gilda. He calms Gilda's fears by singing to her a gentle song of love ("E il sol dell' anima"). Tenderly, Gilda begs him to reveal his true identity, but the lover insists he is only an impoverished student. When he departs, Gilda thinks dreamily of her lover ("Caro nome"). A group of masked courtiers come to avenge themselves on Rigoletto for his taunts. Thinking that Gilda is his mistress, they dupe Rigoletto into helping them abduct Gilda; they blindfold him and tell him that they are about to seize Ceprano's wife and bring her to the Duke. When the deed is done, Rigoletto senses that something is wrong. Tearing the blindfold from his eyes, he sees a ladder next to his house and Gilda's scarf in the street. The truth finally dawns on him. Apprehensive, he rushes into his house to find that Gilda is gone.

The courtiers arrive at the ducal palace to amuse the Duke with their story of abducting Rigoletto's "mistress." They find him sad, lamenting his inability to find his beloved Gilda ("Parmi veder le lagrime"). Rigoletto comes hastily to the palace seeking his daughter. His emotions get the best of him; he tries to force his way through the courtiers, crying that Gilda is his daughter. Gilda herself confirms this fact when she emerges from another room. Father and daughter exchange tender words; Gilda tells him of her great love for the Duke ("Tutte le feste"). Just then, Count Monterone passes on his way to be executed, and he hurls a terrible curse at the Duke.

In an effort to disillusion his daughter about the Duke, Rigoletto brings her to a decrepit inn. The Duke is there, disguised as a soldier, drinking wine and singing gaily about woman's fickleness ("La Donna è mobile"). When the Duke makes bold overtures to a gypsy girl, Gilda remarks bitterly on the infidelity of her beloved. At the same time, Rigoletto speaks of his revenge; and the Duke and the gypsy girl continue with their flirtation (Quartet: "Bella figila dell' amore").

Rigoletto sends his daughter off to Verona, for he has a job to do. He engages the hired assassin, Sparafucile, to assassinate the Duke and deliver the body to him in a sack. A storm rages, as Gilda, instead of going to Verona, returns to the inn, drawn back by her love for the

Duke. Sparafucile selects her as his victim, stabs her, and puts her into a sack which he delivers to Rigoletto. Rigoletto is about to hurl the sack into the river when, from a distance, he hears the Duke singing his song about woman's fickleness. Savagely, Rigoletto tears open the sack—to find Gilda inside, dying. With her dying breath she begs for forgiveness. When she dies, Rigoletto realizes bitterly that the curse of Monterone has been fulfilled.

## (THE) RHINEGOLD (DAS RHEINGOLD). *See:* (THE) RING OF THE NIBELUNGS.

## (THE) RING OF THE NIBELUNGS (DER RING DES NIBE-LUNGEN).

> *A cycle of four music dramas, called a "trilogy" because the first music drama is regarded as a Prologue. The four dramas include:* The Rhinegold (*Das Rheingold*), The Valkyrie (*Die Walküre*), Siegfried, *and* The Dusk of the Gods (*Götterdämmerung*). *Music and librettos by Richard Wagner, based on ancient German, Icelandic, and Scandinavian sagas. First complete performance: Bayreuth, August 13, 14, 16, and 17, 1876.*

### I. (THE) RHINEGOLD—(*Vorabend*) *Prologue.*
*First performance: Munich, September 22, 1869.*

Three Rhine maidens guard the gold of the Rhine waters. If this gold were fashioned into a ring, its owner could rule the world; but before such a ring can be forged, the forger must renounce love.

Alberich, a Nibelung, comes to the river banks. Because he is ready to renounce love he is able to seize the gold from the wailing Rhine maidens.

In Valhalla, the abode of the gods, Wotan and his wife Fricka have had a new palace built by the giants Fasolt and Fafner. The giants demand their payment: the goddess Freia. But Wotan cannot bring himself to surrender her. The giants are willing to accept Alberich's ring of gold as a substitute.

The gods descend into the subterranean caverns of Nibelheim to get Alberich's ring. There the Nibelung dwarfs are enslaved by Alberich, who tortures them through the power of the Tarnhelm: a magic cap enabling him to transform himself into any form he wishes. Wotan uses guile to get Alberich to become a tiny toad through the power of the Tarnhelm; thus Wotan can capture him, tie him up, and bring him back to Valhalla. In Valhalla, Alberich is compelled to have his slaves bring up the wealth from the caverns, including the Tarnhelm and the Ring. Finally released, Alberich shrieks a violent curse at the Ring, prophesying doom to whoever possesses it.

Alberich's curse begins to work at once. When the giants return for the treasures they insist that Wotan surrender the Ring. Erda, goddess of Earth, rises to warn Wotan not to give up the treasure, for to do so means inevitable doom (Erda's Warning: "Weiche, Wotan, weiche"). But Wotan does not heed her and throws the Ring to the giants. They struggle over its possession until one of them is killed in the fight.

The gods now enter their new palace (Entrance of the Gods into Valhalla). Below, in the Rhine, the maidens are mourning the loss of their gold.

## II. (THE) VALKYRIE.
*First performance: Munich, June 26, 1870.*

During a storm, Siegmund—weary and haggard—enters Hunding's dwelling, seeking rest. Hunding's wife, Sieglinde, brings him water. After her husband arrives and they sit down to eat, Siegmund tells the story of his life: how, returning with his father from a chase, he found their home burned and his twin sister gone. The recital reveals to Hunding that Siegmund is his enemy; but the laws of hospitality dictate that Siegmund be safe from harm under his roof. When Hunding goes to sleep, Sieglinde shows Siegmund a sword that had been plunged by her father in the trunk of a tree; this sword assures protection to the one who can wrest it from the tree. When Sieglinde adds that the one who gains the sword will also free her from misfortunes, Siegmund embraces her and confidently maintains that he is the man. At this moment, the door of the house swings open. The beauty of a spring night floods the room. Siegmund sings about the magic of springtime ("Winterstürme wichen dem Wonnemond"). Sieglinde replies by confessing her love for Siegmund ("Du bist der Lenz"). Siegmund now draws the sword from the tree. Recognizing Sieglinde as his long-lost twin sister, he embraces her ardently—not as a brother, but as a lover. They run out into the storm determined to remain together forever.

In a wild and rocky pass, the Valkyries are singing their battle cry ("Ho-yo-to-ho"). Brünnhilde, one of the Valkyries, is ordered by her father Wotan to defend Siegmund from the pursuing Hunding. But Wotan's wife, Fricka, is of another mind. She insists that Siegmund must be punished for his unholy love for his sister, and orders Brünnhilde to side with Hunding. The weary lovers—Siegmund and Sieglinde—arrive, and seek rest. A skirmish follows between Siegmund and Hunding. Brünnhilde is unable to resist the temptation to help Siegmund. Wotan intervenes; Siegmund's sword is shattered and he is killed. Brünnhilde then gathers the pieces of the  broken sword and conducts Sieglinde away.

On the summit of a rocky mountain the Valkyries are galloping in the air on their steeds (The Ride of the Valkyries). Brünnhilde has incurred her father's wrath, and her sisters can do nothing to save her. Before Wotan arrives, Brünnhilde sends Sieglinde off into a forest where she is to bear Siegmund's child, destined to become a hero. She also gives Sieglinde pieces of the broken sword which, reforged, will become the weapon to protect the hero.

Wotan now enters to tell Brünnhilde she must be punished for her disobedience. She will be put to sleep on a rock, to be taken by the first man awakening her. But to protect her from anyone save a hero, she is to be encircled in flame; only one stout of heart will have the courage to penetrate the fires. Tenderly, the father bids farewell to the daughter he loves so well (Wotan's Farewell: "Leb' wohl du kühnes, herrliches Kind"). He places her on the rock, kisses her, and puts her into a deep sleep. Fires arise from the ground to surround her with a protective flame (Magic Fire Scene).

## III. SIEGFRIED.
*First performance: Bayreuth, August 16, 1876.*

In his cave, Mime is trying to forge for Siegfried a sword from the broken pieces. But he is unsuccessful: any sword he forges is immediately smashed by Siegfried.

Siegfried enters the cave leading a bear with which he frightens Mime, whom he despises. Siegfried then orders Mime to tell him who he—Siegfried—is and from where he has come. Mime has no choice but to obey, explaining that Siegfried is the son of Siegmund and Sieglinde (both now dead) and that he, Mime, has raised Siegfried. He also tells Siegfried about the broken sword. When Siegfried leaves, Wotan arrives, disguised as the Wanderer. He comes to tell Mime that only he who is without fear can forge the sword and whoever does so will also demand Mime's head. Terrified, Mime awaits Siegfried to find out if the young man is without fear. Siegfried proves himself to be such a man. He also proves that he can forge the sword, which he does vigorously (Forging Song: "Nothung, Nothung"). Now convinced that some day Siegfried will kill him, Mime decides to dispose of the hero. He will send him after the giant Fafner, who is disguising himself as a dragon and guarding the Ring. Should Siegfried be able to kill the "dragon" and capture the Ring, Mime plans to give him a sleeping potion and kill him.

In Fafner's cave in a forest, Alberich is waiting for Siegfried, knowing that the hero is coming to slay the giant. He, too, wants to kill Siegfried so that he might repossess the Ring. Arriving into the forest, Siegfried lies under a tree, listening to the song of the birds (Forest Murmurs). Then, blowing his horn, he takes up his trusted sword and goes forth to fight and kill the dragon. A few drops of the dragon's blood falls on Siegfried's hands. Instinctively, the hero raises his hands to his lips. The taste of the dragon's blood gives him the power to understand the language of the birds, who tell him of the treasure guarded by the "dragon." Siegfried confiscates the Ring. Mime now comes with the sleeping potion, but Siegfried, aware of his intentions, destroys him. Then, guided by a bird, Siegfried proceeds to the rock on which Brünnhilde is sleeping.

In a wild region, Wotan calls to Erda. He informs her that no longer does he fear the destruction of the gods, he is determined to leave the heritage of the world to Siegfried and Brünnhilde. But, first, Wotan must test Siegfried's courage. Confronting Siegfried, who is on his way to Brünnhilde, Wotan poses a few questions which the hero answers. When Wotan blocks Siegfried's path, the hero angrily shatters Wotan's spear and continues toward his destination.

He finally comes to the fire-surrounded rock. Fearlessly, he plunges through the flames and awakens the goddess with a kiss. At once, the awakened Brünnhilde knows that Siegfried is the hero destined to free her. They embrace ecstatically in an overpowering demonstration of love (Love Duet: "Heil, dir Sonne!").

## (THE) DUSK OF THE GODS.
*First performance: Bayreuth, August 17, 1876.*

The daughters of Erda, the three Norns, know that doom is at hand. Spinning the fate of the world, one of the threads breaks.

Siegfried, in search of adventure, bids Brünnhilde farewell. He takes with him the magic cap, Tarnhelm, the sword Nothung, and Brünnhilde's horse; but he leaves his wife the precious Ring. He goes forth on his voyage (Siegfried's Rhine Journey), and comes to the palace of King Gunther. There Hagen, son of Alberich, recognizes him. Intriguing to gain the Ring, he gives Siegfried a love potion which makes the hero fall in love with Gutrune. Now having completely forgotten about the existence of Brünnhilde, Siegfried wants Gutrune as his wife. Gunther consents to the match but on the condition that Siegfried use his powers to penetrate the fires surrounding the Valkyrie rock and bring Brünnhilde to him. Siegfried consents to do so. Disguised as Hagen he returns to the rock and seizes the Ring with which Brünnhilde tries to protect herself. He brings Brünnhilde back to Gunther's palace.

A great feast is prepared in the Hall of King Gunther. When Brünnhilde is brought in, she is overwhelmed to see Siegfried (who is no longer disguised) at the side of Gutrune. She also notices the Ring, seized from her on the Rock, on Siegfried's finger. She questions Siegfried, and is further horrified to discover that he does not appear to know who she is. Enraged, Brünnhilde curses him. Discovering that Siegfried's death is being plotted by Hagen, she does not hesitate to reveal to Hagen Siegfried's fatal weakness: his back. The conspirators rejoice, for they know that now they can destroy the hero.

Gunther, Hagen, and Siegfried go off to hunt. Reaching the banks of the Rhine, Siegfried is urged by the Rhine maidens to relinquish the Ring before it is too late, but he refuses to do so. Gunther and Hagen, catching up with Siegfried, give him a drink that suddenly revives his memory. He recalls how the flight of the bird brought him to Brünnhilde, how he awakened her with a kiss. Two ravens circle over his head, and as Siegfried looks up toward them and listens to their cry of vengeance, Hagen thrusts a spear into his back. Dying, Siegfried bids Brünnhilde farewell ("Brünnhilde, heilige Braut"). The dead body of Siegfried is carried back to the Gunther palace accompanied by funereal music (Siegfried's Death Music).

When Siegfried's body arrives at the palace, Hagen demands the Ring on the dead man's finger. Gunther also wants it. In the ensuing battle, Gunther is killed. When Hagen tries to remove the Ring, Siegfried's hand rises as if to threaten him, terrifying Hagen. Brünnhilde orders a funeral pyre for her husband, and she calls to Loge to set the pyre aflame. The fires flicker and rise. After a dramatic apostrophe ("Starke, schette schichtet mir dort"), Brünnhilde mounts her horse and rides to her death in the flames. The Rhine maidens rise with the tide of the river to snatch the Ring from the dead man's finger and to restore it to the Rhine. Valhalla, in flames, is doomed.

## ROMEO AND JULIET.

*Opera in five acts, by Charles Gounod. Libretto by Barbier and Carré, based on the Shakespeare tragedy. First performance: Théâtre Lyrique, Paris, April 27, 1867.*

A masked ball is being given to honor Juliet of the house of Capulets. She expresses her joy in an infectious waltz ("Je veux vivre dans ce rêve"). Romeo, a Montague, enters masked. Tybalt, Juliet's cousin, recognizes him. A clash is averted through the intervention of Capulet, who allows Romeo to leave peacefully.

Despite the bitter rivalry of their respective houses, Romeo and Juliet are in love. Below Juliet's window, Romeo sings a serenade ("Ah, lève-toi, soleil"). After Juliet emerges, the lovers sing ecstatically of their love for each other. The idyll is interrupted when Juliet's nurse calls to her, but Juliet soon returns to reaffirm her love for Romeo.

They are secretly married in Friar Laurence's cell. Later on, in a street in Verona, Romeo's page provokes a fight by singing an impudent song in front of the house of Capulet. When Romeo arrives, he tries, unsuccessfully, to be a peacemaker. In the ensuing brawl, Romeo's friend, Mercutio, is wounded. To avenge his friend, Romeo kills Tybalt; for this act he must suffer banishment.

About to be exiled, Romeo comes to Juliet's room to bid her farewell. Friar Laurence then comes with sad tidings. Juliet's marriage to Paris has been decided upon by her father and must take place without delay. The Friar gives Juliet a potion which will give her the appearance of death, thus enabling her to evade the marriage and to run off with Romeo. Juliet falls inert in her father's arms after drinking the potion.

Believed dead, she is placed in the Capulet vault. Romeo breaks in for a last glimpse of his wife, singing a hymn to her beauty ("Salut! tombeau sombre et silencieux"). Determined to join his wife in death, Romeo drinks poison. As he is dying he notices that life is returning to Juliet. They embrace and bid each other farewell. It is now Juliet who is determined to join her husband in death, she stabs herself fatally.

## (DER) ROSENKAVALIER (THE ROSE BEARER).

*A "comedy for music" in three acts, by Richard Strauss. Libretto by Hugo von Hofmannsthal. First performance: Dresden, January 26, 1911.*

In her boudoir, Princess von Werdenberg expresses her love for young Octavian. He takes to hiding with the sudden arrival of the Princess' cousin, Baron Ochs. Ochs has come to tell his cousin about his impending marriage to Sophie. When Octavian emerges from hiding he is disguised as a maid. The lecherous Baron proceeds to flirt with "her" and tries to arrange a rendezvous. The Princess attends to the business of her morning interviews with people seeking favors and advice. She is also entertained with music (Italian Serenade: "Di rigori amato"). When all this is completed, the Baron asks his cousin to deliver to his betrothed a silver rose, as is the prevailing custom. After the departure of the Baron, the Princess contemplates the sad truth that she is no longer young and that she cannot possibly hold on to Octavian's love ("Kann ich mich auch an ein Mädel erinnern"). She then sends Octavian to deliver the silver rose to Sophie.

He comes to the house of Faninal, Sophie's father. On presenting the rose to Sophie, they both exchange meaningful glances and it is apparent they have fallen in love with each other on sight. They are hardly able to control themselves from openly revealing their feelings. The Baron intrudes upon them and, realizing what has happened, challenges Octavian to a duel. In this fray, Ochs is slightly wounded, though his bellows of anguish might indicate that he had been murdered. But he is appeased when a note arrives—conveniently arranged by Octavian—in which the rendezvous he had made with his cousin's "maid" is accepted and arranged (Letter Scene and Waltzes: "Herr Kavalier"). Meanwhile, Sophie expresses the determination never to marry Ochs in spite of her father's demands.

Octavian, once again disguised as a maid, comes to a disreputable inn to keep her appointment with Ochs. To harass the Baron, Octavian has arranged a series of pranks. Strange faces peer at Ochs from different parts of the room. A woman enters noisily, with a brood of children, insisting that Ochs is their father. Matters get involved. The police enter to arrest the Baron, but are prevented by the arrival of the Princess. It is then that Octavian takes off his disguise and reveals himself.

Magnanimously, the Princess brings Sophie and Octavian together and gives the young lovers her blessings (Trio: "Hab' mir's gelobt"). After her dignified departure, the young lovers rush into each other's arms ("Ist ein Traum"). The Baron sulks. He has not only lost Sophie, but has also been the object of derision.


SALOME.
   *Opera in one act, by Richard Strauss, Libretto by Oscar Wilde (the poetic play, Salomé), translated into German by Hedwig Lachmann. First performance: Dresden, December 9, 1905.*

There is a banquet in Herod's palace. During the festivities there is heard the voice of John the Baptist proclaiming the coming of the Messiah. Salome orders that John the Baptist be brought before her. The holy man curses Salome's mother, Herodias, and warns Salome not to persist in her dissolute ways. Salome tries to get John the Baptist to kiss her, but is savagely thrust aside. When the King, Herod, arrives, he seeks amusement, and asks Salome to dance for him. She is willing, but demands a reward. After she has gone through her dance (The Dance of the Seven Veils), she asks her price: the head of John the Baptist. Herod yields. The head of the holy man is brought to Salome on a tray. Sensuously, Salome dances before the head and sings to it lustfully ("Ah! Du wolltest mich nicht deinem Mund küssen lassen"). This sight so revolts Herod that he orders Salome's death.

## SAMSON AND DELILAH.

*Opera in three acts, by Camille Saint-Saëns. Libretto by Ferdinand Lemaire based on the Biblical story. First performance: Weimar, December 2, 1877.*

In bondage, the Hebrews are mourning before the Philistine temple. Samson urges them to take heart. When the Philistine Abimelech taunts him, Samson seizes Abimelech's sword and kills him with it. The High Priest demands that the Philistine warriors avenge this death. The Hebrews have now found a leader in Samson. They attack the Philistines and are victorious. They return from the war singing a hymn to victory ("Hymne de joie"). The High Priest and the Philistines disperse at their approach. Out of the temple comes the beautiful Delilah, bearing garlands for the Hebrew victors. She sings to Samson a song of spring ("Printemps qui commence") as the priestesses perform a dance. Samson is bewitched by Delilah's beauty, and entreats Heaven for the strength to resist her allure.

Delilah begs Love to give her the power to win Samson over ("Amour! viens aider ma faiblesse"). When Samson arrives at her house, Delilah wins him over with her beauty and tenderness, wooing him ardently ("Mon coeur s'ouvre à ta voix"). A storm is rising outside, token of impending disaster. With all her seductive wile, Delilah entreats Samson to confide to him the source of his immense strength. As the storm outside increases in intensity, Delilah's pleas and coaxing grow more persuasive. Angrily, she insists that Samson is secretive only because he does not love her. At last, Samson can contain himself no longer; he confides that his strength lies in his hair. Delilah manages to cut off his hair, then calls to the Philistines to take Samson away to his doom.

Shorn of his hair, blind, and a prisoner, Samson turns the Philistine mill, grinding corn, and giving expression to his great misery ("Voici, ma misère, hélas!"). In the distance are heard the voices of his countrymen denouncing him for having betrayed them for a woman.

At the temple of Dagon, the Philistines, headed by their High Priests, are celebrating their victory over Samson and the Hebrews. A wild dance takes place (Bacchanale). After this dance, Samson is dragged in chains into the temple. The morning sacrifice to the god

Dagon takes place. Samson asks to be tied to the two pillars that support the temple roof. There he entreats God for a temporary return of his strength ("Tu permets, ô Dieu d'Israël"). His prayer is answered. As the Philistines are involved in their worship, Samson strains to topple the mighty pillars. The pillars fall, the roof crashes, and all the Philistines—and Samson with them—are destroyed.

## (THE) SECRET OF SUZANNE (IL SEGRETO DI SUSANNA).

*Opera in one act, by Ermanno Wolf-Ferrari. Libretto by Enrico Golisciani. First performance: Hofoper, Munich, December 4, 1909.*

Count Gil is suspicious of his newly married wife, Suzanne, because whenever he comes home he detects the smell of cigarette smoke in his house. He is sure that his wife is entertaining a lover in his absence. As Suzanne grows increasingly evasive to her husband's questioning, his suspicions mount. At the insistence of his wife he goes off to his club. But, instead, he spies on his wife outside through the window. To his amazement he sees his wife take out a cigarette and smoke it. The discovery so delights and relieves him that he rushes back into the house to embrace his wife and join her in a smoke.

## SIEGFRIED. *See:* (THE) RING OF THE NIBELUNGS.

## (THE) TALES OF HOFFMANN (LES CONTES D'HOFFMANN).

*Fantastic opera in prologue, three acts, and epilogue, by Jacques Offenbach. Libretto by Barbier and Carré, based on their play derived from stories by E. T. A. Hoffmann. First performance: Opéra Comique, Paris, February 10, 1881.*

The poet, Hoffmann, is dejected. In a tavern filled with gay students he is asked to sing a song and he complies with the "Ballad of Kleinzach" ("Il était une fois à la cour d'Eisenach"). After this, he goes into praise of beautiful women. The students mock him, saying he must surely be in love. But Hoffmann insists he is through with love. He has experienced three unfortunate affairs, and he proceeds to tell his student-friends about them.

The first was with the mechanical doll, Olympia, created by the scientist Spalanzani and his friend Coppelius. She appears so human that Hoffmann, seeing her from a distance, believes her to be human and falls in love with her. He comes to pay her court, and his love deepens as he listens to her sing (Doll Song: "Les oiseaux dans la charmille"). He confides his feelings to the doll, then invites her to dance with him. The dance becomes so delirious that Hoffmann falls in a faint. When Coppelius destroys Olympia because Spalanzani has paid him with worthless currency, Hoffmann realizes with heartbreak that he had been in love with an inanimate object.

His second affair was with Giulietta in Venice.

Nicklausse, Hoffmann's friend, sings a beautiful barcarolle to Giulietta (Barcarolle: "Belle nuit, ô nuit d'amour"). Hoffmann, who is present, is fascinated by Giulietta without knowing that she is the victim of a magician, Dapertutto. One of the victims of Giulietta's beauty is Schlemil who fights a duel with Hoffmann and is killed. But Giulietta is not meant for Hoffmann. She passes Hoffmann in a gondola, accompanied by the magician, and mocks him.

Hoffmann's last love is Antonina, daughter of Crespel. A victim of consumption, Antonina taxes her health through singing ("Elle a fui, la tourterelle"). Hoffmann learns about her sickness and he begs her never again to sing. But the magician conjures the ghost of Antonina's mother who persuades her to render a song. She sings—and collapses dead in her father's arms.

Having heard his tales of woe, the students urge Hoffmann to forget the past. The Muse of Art comes to console the poet. Finding him asleep, she throws a flower at his feet.


## TANNHÄUSER.

*Opera in three acts, by Richard Wagner. Libretto by the composer. First performance: Dresden, October 19, 1845.*

The minstrel knight, Tannhäuser, has escaped from the world to enjoy sensual pleasures with Venus on the Venusberg. A bacchanale takes place (Venusberg Music), after which Tannhäuser sings an ecstatic song of love to Venus ("Dir töne Lob"). But Tannhäuser is weary of sensual joys, and he entreats Venus to permit him to return to his own world. Venus yields.

The scene changes to a valley, in which Tannhäuser suddenly finds himself. Pilgrims enroute to Rome pass by, singing as they go (Pilgrims' Chorus). Then a group of minstrel knights arrive. Recognizing Tannhäuser as one of their own, they urge him to rejoin them at the Wartburg. Wolfram, one of these knights, reminds Tannhäuser of Elizabeth—and it is the thought of Elizabeth that sends Tannhäuser back to join his fellow knights.

In the hall of the minstrels, Elizabeth raises a hymn of praise to the Wartburg ("Dich teure Halle"). The knights arrive, and march into the hall for a song contest soon to take place; the winner is to get Elizabeth's hand (March of the Guests). The first contestant is Wolfram who sings of pure and unselfish love ("Blick ich umher"). Tannhäuser, the next contestant, sings of the carnal love he knew on the Venusberg. The knights are shocked; they draw their swords and rush at him. Only Elizabeth's intervention saves him. Tannhäuser repents his dissolute ways. Hearing the distant strains of the Pilgrims' Chorus, he decides to go to Rome to ask the Pope for forgiveness.

In the Valley of the Wartburg, Elizabeth waits for Tannhäuser's return from Rome. When she does not see him among the band of pilgrims just returned from the Holy City, she prays to the Holy Virgin (Elizabeth's Prayer: "Allmächt'ge, Jungfrau"). Wolfram asks Elizabeth if he may accompany her back to the Wartburg, but she declines. Night falls. Thinking of Elizabeth, with whom he is in love, Wolfram sings an ode (Ode to the Evening Star: "O du mein holder Abendstern"). No sooner does he finish his song than Tannhäuser arrives—weary and ragged. He has not been pardoned, for the Pope has said that pardon will come only when the staff in the Pope's hands sprouts leaves (Rome Narrative). Having failed in his mission, Tannhäuser wants to return to Venus. Only when Wolfram brings up the name of Elizabeth does Tannhäuser change his mind.

A group of mourners arrive carrying a bier. It is the body of Elizabeth who has died. Tannhäuser, having now lost the will to live, dies at Elizabeth's side. And he dies without learning that pilgrims from Rome have arrived with incredible tidings: the staff of the Pope has sprouted leaves.

## (THE) TELEPHONE.

*Opera in one act, by Gian-Carlo Menotti. Libretto by
the composer. First performance: Heckscher Theatre,
New York, February 18, 1947.*

In vain does Ben try to propose to Lucy. He is always being interrupted by the ringing of the telephone. At last, he rushes to the corner drugstore. He proposes to Lucy by telephone—and is accepted.

## THAÏS.

*Opera in three acts, by Jules Massenet. Libretto by
Louis Gallet, based on the novel of Anatole France.
First performance: Opéra, Paris, March 16, 1894.*

In Egypt, in the early Christian era, the monk Athanaël is troubled by the evil existing in the city of Alexandria. He sees in a dream the beautiful courtesan Thaïs as she appears in a theatre before enthusiastic audiences. Athanaël is now fired with the mission of saving Thaïs.

When Athanaël arrives in Alexandria, his friend Nicias is amused at hearing Athanaël's mission, since he—Nicias—has been paying court to Thaïs. But he is willing to help an old friend and dresses him in attractive garb to make him more presentable for Thaïs. When she comes and is told that Athanaël is here to save her soul, she replies cynically that her only interest is in—living.

In the luxurious setting of her home, Thaïs expresses weariness at her way of life ("Ah je suis seule, seule enfin!"). She wonders if she will always be beautiful, and seeks assurances from her mirror (Mirror Song: "Dis-moi que je suis belle"). Athanaël arrives to speak to her of the spirit. In vain does Thaïs try to win him over with her beauty. He leaves declaring he will wait for her at the threshold, confident she will want to atone. As the curtain falls, the music of the well-known "Meditation" is played to symbolize Thaïs' conversion to religion.

Repentant, Thaïs comes to Athanaël seeking salvation. She is ready to leave everything behind her, except a little statue of Eros which she wishes placed in some monastery as a symbol of eternal love. But the monk smashes Eros, just as he would smash every symbol of Thaïs' wanton life. Now quietly acquiescent, Thaïs follows Athanaël back into her own house where Nicias is host to an abandoned revel. Nicias' friends are incensed at Athanaël for having taken Thaïs away from them. They rush to attack him, but Nicias saves the monk by throwing gold coins around. As the crowd scrambles for the gold, Athanaël and Thaïs effect their escape.

At an oasis in the desert, to which Thaïs has come in her journey with Athanaël, she is tortured by thirst and fatigue. Athanaël permits her to rest, bathes her feet, and gives her fruit. She is happy to be led to a nearby convent, for she has found peace of heart.

At the cenobite dwelling near the Nile, Athanaël confesses to a fellow-monk that though he has saved Thaïs' soul he has lost his own. His dreams are haunted by her. In one of these he sees her dying in a convent. He is driven by his anxiety to visit her convent where he learns that Thaïs is, indeed, on her deathbed. He entreats her to come back with him to Alexandria, for he wants to enjoy with her the pleasures of life. But Thaïs has found salvation. She tells him of the gates of Heaven opening up for her ("Te souvient-il du lumineux voyage"). When she dies, Athanaël succumbs to a terrible grief.

## TOSCA.

*Opera in three acts, by Giacomo Puccini. Libretto by Giacosa and Illica, based on the drama of Victorien Sardou. First performance: Teatro Costanzi, Rome, January 4, 1900.*

The painter Cavaradossi comes daily to the Church Sant' Andrea della Valle in Rome to paint—using one of the worshipers as his model. He himself is in love with the celebrated singer Tosca. Removing her picture from his bosom he rhapsodizes over her heavenly beauty ("Recondita armonia").

Angelotti, a political prisoner recently escaped from jail, appears to ask Cavaradossi's help. The fugitive disappears when Tosca arrives that evening to make an appointment with the painter. When she goes, Cavaradossi is able to help Angelotti. Scarpia, chief of police, arrives to search for the fugitive. The church services begin ("Te Deum"). Though he is on bended knee, Scarpia is not concerned with worship; he is plotting Cavaradossi's destruction so that he can have Tosca for himself.

Cavaradossi is brought to Scarpia, but refuses to divulge Angelotti's hiding place. The police chief consigns him to the torture chamber. Tosca, summoned by Scarpia, learns that her lover is in the next room; and hears his cries of torture. Unable to bear Cavaradossi's suffering, she reveals to Scarpia Angelotti's hiding place. But this news assumes secondary importance when Scarpia learns that Napoleon has just won a major victory. Cavaradossi, released from the tortures, emits a cry of joy at this news, for which he is ordered imprisoned and executed.

Scarpia now makes a bid for Tosca's love. In grief and shame she muses how cruel fate has been to her—she who has always given herself to art, charity, love, and prayer ("Vissi d'arte"). Realizing the power of the forces of evil, Tosca is ready to give herself up to Scarpia if he promises to free Cavaradossi. Scarpia consents eagerly, and writes the necessary order for a mock execution. Then, when he rushes passionately to Tosca, she stabs him fatally.

Cavaradossi is about to be executed; he has only a single hour left. He sings a poignant farewell to Tosca ("E lucevan le stelle"). But Tosca is at hand to tell him of Scarpia's death. Cavaradossi is then led to what Tosca believes to be a mock execution. The shots are fired. When the soldiers are gone and Cavaradossi fails to rise, Tosca realizes with anguish that her beloved is dead. She climbs the castle parapet and jumps to her death.

## (LA) TRAVIATA (THE LOST ONE).

*Opera in three acts, by Giuseppe Verdi. Libretto by Francesco Maria Piave, based on* La Dame aux camélias, *a drama by Alexandre Dumas. First performance: Teatro la Fenice, Venice, March 6, 1853.*

In Violetta's festive salon, Alfred Germont is asked by his hostess to sing a drinking song, in which she and the other guests join ("Libiamo, Libiamo"). The guests leave for the adjoining ballroom. Attacked by a sudden fainting spell, Violetta is solicitously looked after by Alfred, who confesses he is in love with her. Violetta protests she is unworthy of such a love ("Un dì felice"), but Alfred grows increasingly ardent. The evening is drawing to a close; the guests take their leave. Alone, Violetta muses about the turn of events: Alfred's expression of love and her own strangely sympathetic reaction ("Ah fors è lui"); her conviction that a new life awaits her ("Sempre libera").

Violetta and Alfred go off to live in a country house near Paris. He is more convinced than ever of his great love for her and expresses his feelings exuberantly ("De' miei bollenti spiriti"). When Alfred learns that Violetta has been selling her jewels to support them he rushes off to Paris to get some money. During his absence, his father arrives to try to break up this illicit affair. He succeeds when he reveals that his daughter is betrothed to a nobleman who threatens to break up the engagement if this scandal in the Germont family persists. Violetta, realizing that her affair with Germont must eventually ruin him, decides sadly to give him up ("Dite alla giovine"). After the elder Germont departs, she writes a farewell letter to her lover. But before she can make her departure Alfred is back. By telling him that she is off to visit his father to beg for his consent to their marriage, she allays his suspicions. But when she is gone, Alfred reads Violetta's note of farewell, and is overwhelmed by the news. His father returns to console him by reminding him of their home in Provence ("Di Provenza il mar"). Alfred, who believes Violetta left him only because she has grown weary of their affair, seeks revenge.

They meet again in Fiora's house in Paris where a gala entertainment takes place. Alfred is busy gambling and is very lucky. Violetta is excited at seeing him, but Alfred ignores her icily and continues gambling. After the guests leave the dining salon, Violetta implores Alfred to leave the house for she senses imminent disaster. Alfred is willing to go—but only if she joins him. Heartbroken, Violetta confesses she is unable to do so because of an oath. Mistaking this oath to be one made to a lover, Alfred summons the guests from their dining to denounce Violetta—contemptuously throwing at her the money he has won.

From this moment on, Violetta comes upon evil days. Dying, her anguish is intensified because Alfred is not with her. Pathetically she bids farewell to the world ("Addio del passato"). At this point, Alfred bursts into her bedroom to take her in his arms and to ask for forgiveness. He has finally learned the truth about Violetta's renunciation, and he wants her to recover her health so that they might once again return to the country house where they had known such happiness ("Parigi, o cara"). But this emotional stress is too much for Violetta; she collapses. The elder Germont arrives with a physician, but it is too late. With a cry, Violetta falls back dead. The elder Germont laments that he has been the cause for so much unhappiness to both Violetta and his son.

## TRISTAN UND ISOLDE.

*Music drama in three acts, by Richard Wagner. Libretto by the composer. First performance: Hofoper, Munich, June 10, 1865.*

The action takes place in legendary times. Tristan and Isolde are sailing from Ireland to Cornwall. Tristan is bringing Isolde from her native Ireland as a bride to his uncle, King Mark. But, in spite of herself, Isolde realizes she is in love with Tristan. Realizing she can never have Tristan, she decides to give him a death potion, and drink it with him. But her attendant, Brangäne, prepares a love potion instead. When Tristan and Isolde drink it all barriers between them are broken. They rush into each other's arms as the ship nears the shores of Cornwall.

Despite this love, Isolde must marry King Mark. The King, suspecting that Isolde is unfaithful to him, goes off on a hunting trip, intending to return unexpectedly and uncover the truth. Although Brangäne reveals this strategy to Isolde, the latter turns a deaf ear. She calls to Tristan. In the castle garden they surrender themselves helplessly to their passion (*Liebesnacht:* "O sink hernieder Nacht der Liebe"). As Brangäne intones a warning ("Habet acht") Kurwenal, Tristan's servant, bursts in to say that the King has come back. Even before his message is told, the King arrives with his courtier Melot. The King is saddened by the treachery of his nephew, and gives expression to his grief. But Melot rushes at Tristan with drawn sword and wounds him.

Tristan is brought by Kurwenal to Tristan's castle in Brittany. Kurwenal has sent for Isolde, and impatiently he scans the horizon for a glimpse of her arriving boat. She arrives—but it is too late. Tristan welcomes her ecstatically, then falls dead in her arms. Isolde has been followed by King Mark—come to forgive the lovers. But Kurwenal has not forgotten that Melot was responsible for his master's death. He engages Melot in a duel and kills him; then Melot's soldiers destroy Kurwenal. Isolde dies beside her lover (*Liebestod:* "Mild und Leise").

# (IL) TROVATORE (THE TROUBADOUR).

*Opera in four acts, by Giuseppe Verdi. Libretto by Sal-vatore Cammarano, based on a play by Antonio García Guitiérrez. First performance: Teatro Apollo, Rome, January 19, 1853.*

Ferrando, captain of the guard for Count di Luna, tells his men how a gypsy was burned as a witch by the Count's father; the gypsy's daughter, in vengeance, stole the Count's younger brother and probably had him burned to death.

In the palace gardens, Leonora confides to her attendant, Inez, of a mysterious lover—a troubadour—who has been serenading her ("Tacea la notte placida"). Inez warns her lady not to think of the mysterious lover. When the ladies leave, Count di Luna—himself in love with Leonora—arrives. Suddenly the song of the troubadour is heard. Leonora rushes in and, mistaking the Count for the unknown troubadour, rushes into his arms. The light of the moon reveals her mistake and outlines the form of the troubadour in the distant shadows. Leonora now goes to him. The enraged Count challenges the troubadour to a duel—the latter's identity is now revealed as Manrico, head of an enemy army.

The gypsy Azucena and her son Manrico are sitting near a fire in a gypsy camp. The gypsies, at work, lustily sing as they strike hammers on anvils (The Anvil Chorus: "Chi del gitano i giorni abbella"). When the work is ended, Azucena succumbs to revery. She recalls how her mother had been burned as a witch ("Stride la vampa"). Manrico listens with fascination, for Azucena's story suggests that he is not actually her son. But Azucena is evasive to his questions, changing the subject abruptly by telling him how once, when he had been wounded in a battle with Count di Luna's men, she had nursed him back to health. It is then that Manrico tells the gypsy woman how he has recently fought a duel with the Count; how some mysterious force kept him from killing his enemy. This news infuriates Azucena who urges Manrico never to forget that the Count must be destroyed.

A soldier arrives to recall Manrico to his troops and to inform him that Leonora is about to enter a convent because she thinks him dead. The news sends Manrico off to the convent. But he has been preceded by Count di Luna and his men, come to abduct Leonora before she assumes her vows. The prospect of having Leonora for himself inspires a glow of happiness in the Count ("Il balen del suo sorriso"). Soon the nuns emerge to conduct Leonora to the chapel. The Count's men rush to seize her. Manrico and his men also appear on the scene, clash with the enemy, and are victorious. Manrico takes Leonora off to Castellor.

The men of Count di Luna come to Castellor to attack Manrico, singing a stirring war song as they come (Soldiers' Chorus: "Squilli, echeggi la tromba"). Meanwhile, Azucena is brought to Count di Luna, accused of being a spy. While questioning her, the Count discovers that Manrico is her son and that the gypsy was responsible for the abduction and possible murder of the Count's younger brother. The Count orders her death.

In a hall adjoining the chapel of Castellor, Manrico and Leonora prepare to be married. Manrico soothes her with gentle words ("Ah si ben mio"). As the lovers are about to enter the chapel, one of Manrico's men informs him that Azucena has been sentenced to death. Bitterly, Manrico vows vengeance ("Di quella pira") and rushes off to save her.

He is captured by Count di Luna's men and is imprisoned. Leonora comes to the prison wall, wishing poignantly that her love were wings able to lift her up into his cell ("D'amor sull' ali rosee"). From the tower comes the sound of voices—praying to Heaven that the one about to die achieves salvation; above these voices, Manrico is heard imploring Leonora not to forget him; Leonora herself gives expression to her own grief (Miserere: "Ah che la morta ognora"). When the Count comes, Leonora makes a bargain with him. She is ready to offer herself to the Count in exchange for Manrico's freedom. After the Count gives his consent, she secretly takes poison.

Within the cell, Manrico tries to soothe Azucena, who is terrified by the flames awaiting her. She suddenly recalls calmer days in the mountains ("Ah nostri monti"), and after that is lulled to sleep by Manrico. Leonora arrives with the news that soon Manrico will be free. But when Manrico learns the price Leonora paid for his freedom he bitterly accuses her of having betrayed him. Hardly has he voiced his bitter condemnation than Leonora sinks to the ground, dying. Manrico now begs Leonora to forgive him. When the Count enters the cell, Leonora tells him with her dying words that she prefers death to life with him. Enraged, the Count orders Manrico's death, and forces Azucena to watch the death scene from the window. Half-crazed by the sight, the gypsy woman finally reveals the bitter truth to the Count: Manrico, now dead, is his long-lost brother. She falls dead, and the Count is left to his terrible remorse.

## TURANDOT.

*Opera in three acts, by Giacomo Puccini. Libretto by Adami and Simoni, based on a "fiaba" by Gozzi. First performance: La Scala, Milan, April 25, 1926.*

In Peking, in legendary times, the Princess Turandot promises to marry anybody who can answer three riddles; but he who fails must forfeit his life. The Prince Calaf, in love with Turandot, accepts the challenge, despite the tearful pleas of the slave girl, Liù, who loves him devotedly ("Signore ascolta"). Calaf consoles her ("Non piangere Liù"), but remains unshaken in his purpose. Appearing in disguise, he succeeds in answering Turandot's riddles. When the Princess begs him to relieve her of her promise and to give up his life, Calaf consents— but only if she succeeds in discovering who he really is. Liù is tortured by the Princess' men, but she refuses to provide the answer, and dies. At last, Calaf himself answers Turandot's question. But she no longer asks for his death. She loves him, and accepts him as her husband.

## (THE) VALKYRIE (DIE WALKÜRE). *See:* (THE) RING OF THE NIBELUNGS.

## WILLIAM TELL (GUILLAUME TELL).

*Opera in four acts, by Gioacchino Rossini. Libretto by de Jouy and Bis, based on a play by Schiller. First performance: Opéra, Paris, August 3, 1829.*

William Tell, a Swiss patriot, is oppressed by the despotic rule of Governor Gessler. When a fellow patriot, Arnold, confesses he loves Gessler's daughter, Mathilde, Tell is furious, demanding that his friend help him overthrow the tyrant.

A festive ceremony in the mountains is disturbed by the sound of horns announcing the presence of Gessler's hunting party. Suddenly the shepherd Leuthold comes seeking help. Leuthold has killed one of Gessler's soldiers and is being sought by Gessler. William Tell offers to help the fugitive. When soldiers arrive to seize Leuthold, they learn that he has escaped. Enraged that Leuthold has eluded them, the soldiers seize as captive Arnold's father, Melcthal.

In a forest, Mathilde sings idyllically how she prefers the simple life with Arnold to wealth and luxury ("Sombre forêt"). Arnold has followed her to the forest. United, the two lovers speak their love for each other and curse the destiny that keeps them apart. When Tell arrives, Arnold is told that his father has been killed by Gessler. From this moment on, Arnold is a member of the conspiracy to destroy the tyrant. The rebels gather in a hidden wood to plot Gessler's destruction and to be inspired by a passionate speech by Tell.

Later on, Arnold and Mathilde have a secret rendezvous in a ruined chapel. Arnold tells his beloved about his father's death, and of his determination to seek vengeance. Tenderly he bids her farewell ("Pour notre amour"). Mathilde promises him that she will remain faithful.

In an open market place, Gessler addresses his people, urging them to celebrate the centenary of Austrian rule with song and dance. The captain of the guards notices that William Tell and his son do not pay the proper homage to the Governor. Tell is arrested, but before he can be brought before the Governor he is able to instruct his son to return home and tell his mother to light beacons on the mountain tops. Gessler hopes to humiliate the patriot by ordering him to split an apple on his son's head with bow and arrow. With a prayer, Tell takes aim and hits his mark squarely. When Tell confesses to Gessler that, had he missed his mark he would have aimed a second arrow at Gessler's heart, the Governor demands his immediate incarceration.

Meanwhile, Arnold returns to his father's house and recalls his happiness there ("Asile héréditaire"). His people arrive, informing him of Tell's arrest, and demanding revenge.

Mathilde arrives at William Tell's house to reveal to Tell's wife that he has escaped and is now on Lake of Lucerne. A storm is brewing. Tell's son calls out the patriots, who are joined by Tell himself. When Gessler appears on a nearby height, Tell kills him with bow and arrow. The patriots rejoice that the despot now is dead. But even better news is at hand: the castle has fallen and Switzerland is free. The patriots lift their voices in a mighty paean to freedom.

WOZZECK.

*Opera in three acts, by Alban Berg. Libretto by the
composer adapted from the drama of Georg Büchner.
First performance: State Opera, Berlin, December 14,
1925.*

Wozzeck, a poor, downtrodden soldier, discovers that his sweetheart Marie has been unfaithful to him with a drummer. When Wozzeck complains to the drummer, he is beaten soundly. Bent on vengeance, Wozzeck murders Marie near a pond. His bloody knife falls in
the waters. Later on, when he tries to retrieve the knife, he drowns.

$$\sim\!\sim\!\sim\!\sim\!\sim\!\sim\ 4\ \sim\!\sim\!\sim\!\sim\!\sim\!\sim$$

# Twenty-five Basic Operas

Bizet: *Carmen.*

Debussy: *Pelléas et Mélisande.*

Donizetti: *Lucia di Lammer-moor.*

Gluck: *Orfeo ed Euridice.*

Gounod: *Faust.*

Leoncavallo: *Pagliacci.*

Mascagni: *Cavalleria Rusti-cana.*

Massenet: *Manon.*

Mozart: *Don Giovanni.*

Mozart: *The Marriage of Figaro.*

Mussorgsky: *Boris Godunov.*

Offenbach: *The Tales of Hoff-mann.*

Puccini: *La Bohème.*

Puccini: *Madame Butterfly.*

Rossini: *The Barber of Seville.*

Smetana: *The Bartered Bride.*

Strauss, R.: *Der Rosenkavalier.*

Strauss, R.: *Salome.*

Verdi: *Aïda.*

Verdi: *Falstaff.*

Verdi: *Rigoletto.*

Verdi: *La Traviata.*

Wagner: *Die Meistersinger.*

Wagner: *Tristan und Isolde.*

Wagner: *The Valkyrie.*

# Music for Ballets

It is not within the scope of this volume to trace the history of the ballet. But so much fine music has been written directly for the ballet, and so many other excellent musical compositions have been adapted for it, that the subject should not be ignored. Our purpose will be to comment briefly on the music rather than on the evolution of the ballet.

The ballet—the dance as a spectacle, as differentiated from all other kinds of dances—originated and developed in the royal court of France. The first "modern" ballet was the *Comique de la reyne,* presented at Versailles in 1581 to celebrate the marriage of the Duc de Joyeuse to the sister of Henry II. In the next thirty years, more than eighty lavish ballet productions were given at court. After that, the ballet flourished with Louis XIV, himself such an enthusiast that he appeared in several productions. It was at his court in Versailles that a composer of major stature was recruited to write ballet music: Jean Baptiste Lully. Lully's ballet scores were made up of minuets (then first coming into vogue), gavottes, bourrées, gigues, and so forth. In 1661, Louis XIV gave a new status to the ballet by founding the Royal Academy of Music and Dancing, with Lully as its director.

With the death of Louis XIV, ballet productions ceased at Versailles. The ballet now passed to Paris and enjoyed particular importance within the operatic theatre. Lully, and after him Rameau, gave such prominence to ballet sequences in their operas that a tradition was established in French opera continuing for many years. Ballets were also used by Gluck, and sometimes by Mozart, in their operas.

Ballet was also seen as independent theatrical productions in Paris. *Pomone,* with music by Cambert, was such an immense success in 1671 that it had an eight-month run to crowded houses.

There was further development in the ballet in the eighteenth century. Great dancers appeared to extend the technique of dancing and to make many important innovations. No less important were the reforms advocated by the ballet master Noverre: a return to classical simplicity and beauty and a departure from stilted conventions and ornateness; emphasis on the art of the pantomime, and avoidance of virtuosity for its own sake. He was such a major figure in the dance world of his day that Garrick called him "the Shakespeare of the Dance." Noverre was an important collaborator of several great opera composers, notably Gluck (in *Iphigénie en Tauride*) and Mozart (in *Les Petits riens*).

Reforms advocated by Noverre were assimilated into the ballet after the French Revolution. The first great age of the ballet was at hand with such performers as Marie Taglioni, Carlotta Grisi, and Fanny Elssler.

But music, for many years, remained the stepchild of ballet. It was first in the middle of the nineteenth century, with Léo Delibes, that music for the ballet acquired artistic significance in its own right. Delibes, who wrote the scores for *Coppelia* and *Sylvia,* brought for the first time such a wealth of melodic and harmonic invention, symphonic breadth, and freshness of approach to ballet music that it was capable of providing the listener pleasure independently of the dance spectacle. "In a class of composition which until then had been neglected," wrote the French critic, Jean Poueigh, "he brought an elevation and vigor of style, a fullness of forms, and a richness of instrumentation unknown before him. . . . He introduced symphonic music into the ballet, at the same time remaining truly French and preserving in choreographic music that nimble elegance, that caressing grace, that spiritual vivacity, which are like wings of the dance."

In another country, virtually at the same time, another composer was bringing unprecedented importance to ballet music: Peter Ilitch

Tchaikovsky. In 1875, the Moscow Opera commissioned Tchaikovsky to write the music for a ballet. He wrote the score for *The Swan Lake* which has classic beauty, personal charm, fresh lyricism, and ingratiating appeal. Tchaikovsky wrote two other fine ballet scores—*Sleeping Beauty* and the *Nutcracker Suite*—which gave further testimony that a serious composer could find the ballet a significant medium for his creative gifts.

The serious composer, writing original music for the ballet, received powerful encouragement from another Russian—the fabulous impresario, Serge Diaghilev, founder and director of the Ballet Russe. In his ambition to reveal to the rest of Europe the finest examples of Russian ballet art, Diaghilev founded the Ballet Russe in 1909. Fokine was ballet master; and the principal dancers included Karsavina, Pavlova, and Nijinsky. A true dilettante, Diaghilev realized that great ballet is much more than just great dancing. In his productions he enlisted the services of world-famous artists to create costumes and scenery; he engaged the most gifted composers he could find to write new music for his productions.

Diaghilev helped create an incomparable era of ballet music. It was for him that Stravinsky (unknown when Diaghilev first engaged him) wrote the music for *The Fire-Bird, Petrushka,* and *The Rite of Spring,* the works that made him the most exciting new figure in contemporary music. For Diaghilev, Ravel wrote *Daphnis and Chloë;* Manuel de Falla, *The Three-Cornered Hat;* Prokofiev, *Chout* and *The Age of Steel;* Satie, *Parade;* Hindemith, *St. Francis;* Poulenc, *Les Biches;* and so forth. The ballet, consequently, was now a major source of inspiration for the contemporary composer. An integral part of modern music belongs to the dance.

The ballet attracted the attention of important composers throughout the world. The emergence of important companies helped bring these composers commissions to write new scores—and, in some cases, to produce their finest works. Among the significant works written expressly for various dance groups are the following: Ravel's *Bolero;* Prokofiev's *Le fils prodigue* and *Cinderella;* Stravinsky's *Card Party;* Copland's *Appalachian Spring* and *Billy the Kid;* Gould's *Interplay;* Bernstein's *Fancy Free;* Schuman's *Undertow;* Piston's *The Incredible Flutist;* Khatchaturian's *Gayne;* Milhaud's *Le Boeuf sur le Toit* and *La Création du monde;* Pierné's *Cydalise;* Shostakovich's *The Age of*

*Gold;* Szymanowski's *Harnasie;* Villa-Lobos' *Mandu-Carara;* and many, many others.

It is important to note, too, that many new ballets have adapted existing musical works, and with considerable artistic success. Among the important works thus utilized are: Rimsky-Korsakov's *Scheherezade;* Balakirev's *Thamar;* Berlioz' *Symphonie fantastique;* Beethoven's *Seventh Symphony;* Bizet's *First Symphony;* Debussy's *Afternoon of a Faun;* Weber's *Invitation to the Dance;* Saint-Saëns' *The Swan;* Gershwin's *Rhapsody in Blue* and *American in Paris;* Schumann's *Carnival;* Arnold Schoenberg's *Verklaerte Nacht;* and so forth.

The following is a list of ballets in the repertory of leading companies whose music was derived from existing compositions: *The Age of Anxiety* (Bernstein's *Symphony No. 2*); *À la français* (Françaix' *Serenade for Orchestra*); *Assembly Ball* (Bizet's *Symphony in C major*); *Bluebeard* (Offenbach's *Barbe-bleue*); *Bourrée fantasque* (Chabrier's *Marche joyeuse*); *La Boutique fantasque* (pieces by Rossini); *The Cage* (Stravinsky's *Concerto in D Major,* for strings); *Capriccio espagnol* (Rimsky-Korsakov's *Capriccio espagnol*); *Carmen* (suite from Bizet's *Carmen*); *Clock Symphony* (Haydn's *Clock Symphony*); *Con Amore* (Rossini's overtures); *Concerto* (Chopin's *Concerto No. 2*); *Concerto Barocco* (Bach's *Concerto for Two Violins*); *Designs with Strings* (Tchaikovsky's *Trio in A Minor*); *Don Juan* (Richard Strauss' *Don Juan*); *The Elves* (Mendelssohn's *Overture to A Midsummer Night's Dream* and the *Concerto for Violin*); *Ensayo sinfonico* (Brahms' *Variations on a Theme by Haydn*); *Fanfare* (Britten's *A Young Person's Guide to the Orchestra*); *The Five Gifts* (Dohnányi's *Variations on a Nursery Theme*); *The Four Temperaments* (Hindemith's *Theme with Variations According to the Four Temperaments*); *Gala Performance* (Prokofiev's *Classical Symphony*); *La Gloire* (Beethoven's overtures); *Good-Humored Ladies* (Scarlatti's sonatas); *Graduation Ball* (Johann Strauss' waltzes); *Illuminations* (Britten's *Les Illuminations*); *Jinx* (Britten's *Variations on a Theme by Frank Bridge*); *Job* (Vaughan Williams' *Job*); *Lady of Camelias* (Verdi's *La Traviata*); *Lilac Garden* (Chausson's *Poème*); *Mother Goose Suite* (Ravel's *Mother Goose Suite*); *Metamorphoses* (Hindemith's *Symphonic Metamorphoses*); *Pas d'action* (Wagner's *Tristan und Isolde*); *Les Patineurs* (waltzes by Meyerbeer); *Picnic at Tintagel* (Bax' *Garden of Fand*); *Pied Piper* (Copland's *Concerto for Clarinet*); *Pillar of Fire* (Schoenberg's *Verklaerte Nacht*); *Pineapple*

*Doll* (the Gilbert and Sullivan comic operas) ; *Prince Igor* (the Polovt-sian Dances from Borodin's *Prince Igor*) ; *The Prospect Before Us* (works by Boyce) ; *Romeo and Juliet* (selected works by Delius) ; *Scheherezade* (Rimsky-Korsakov's *Scheherezade*) ; *Schumann Con-certo* (Schumann's *Piano Concerto*) ; *Scotch Symphony* (Mendels-sohn's *Scotch Symphony*) ; *Scuola di Ballo* (selected works by Boccherini) ; *Le Spectre de la Rose* (Weber's *Invitation to the Dance*) ; *Les Sylphides* (selected works by Chopin) ; *Symphonic Var-iations* (Franck's *Variations symphoniques*) ; *Symphonie Concertante* (Mozart's *Symphonie Concertante*) ; *Symphony in C* (Bizet's *Sym-phony in C Major*) ; *Theme and Variations* (Tchaikovsky's *Suite No. 3 for Strings*) ; *Till Eulenspiegel* (Richard Strauss' *Till Eulenspiegel*) ; *Wise Virgins* (selected works by Bach) ; *Young Man and Death* (Bach's *Passacaglia in C Minor*).

# 6

## Scenarios of Twenty-five Famous Ballets

In the section that follows, the ballets are listed alphabetically. The following is a listing of the same ballets by their composers:

Adam: *Giselle.*
Borodin: *Prince Igor.*
Chopin: *Les Sylphides.*
Copland: *Appalachian Spring.*
Copland: *Billy the Kid.*
Debussy: *Afternoon of a Faun.*
Delibes: *Coppelia.*
Falla: *El Amor Brujo.*
Falla: *The Three-Cornered Hat.*
Glazunov: *The Seasons.*
Glazunov: *Raymonda.*
Glière: *The Red Poppy.*

Khatchaturian: *Gayne.*
Milhaud: *Le Boeuf sur le toit.*
Ravel: *Daphnis and Chloë.*
Ravel: *La Valse.*
Schumann: *Carnival.*
Strauss, J.: *Le Beau Danube.*
Stravinsky: *Card Party.*
Stravinsky: *The Fire-Bird.*
Stravinsky: *Petrushka.*
Stravinsky: *The Rite of Spring.*
Tchaikovsky: *Sleeping Beauty.*
Tchaikovsky: *Swan Lake.*
Weber: *Le Spectre de la Rose.*

AFTERNOON OF A FAUN (L'APRÈS-MIDI D'UN FAUNE).
*Book by Vaslav Nijinsky. Music: Debussy's* Afternoon of a Faun. *First performance: The Ballet Russe, Théâtre du Châtelet, Paris, May 29, 1912.*

A faun lies dreaming at a hillside playing his flute. A group of nymphs appears down the hill. The faun goes toward them, and they flee. But they soon return; when the faun tries to woo them, they escape again. But one returns and joins the faun. Sudden fear sends her scurrying away, leaving her scarf in his hand. The faun takes up the scarf and carries it back to the hillside where he caresses it.

## (EL) AMOR BRUJO (LOVE, THE SORCERER).
*Book by Gregorio Martinez Sierra. Original music by Manuel de Falla. First performance: Teatro de Lara, Madrid, April 15, 1915.*

The gypsy girl, Candela, falls in love with the gypsy lad, Carmelo. The ghost of Candela's dead husband comes to haunt her. Candela arranges for the beautiful gypsy, Lucia, to flirt with the ghost. The ghost is so taken with Lucia's beauty and seductiveness that he leaves Candela alone to pursue her love affair.

## APPALACHIAN SPRING.
*Book by Martha Graham. Original music by Aaron Copland. First performance: Library of Congress, Washington, D.C., October 30, 1944.*

In the Pennsylvania hills, in the early part of the last century, a Pioneer celebration is held to honor the marriage of a farmer. He and his bride look to the future apprehensively, but a neighbor brings confidence with a recital of his own experiences. A revivalist and his followers remind the couple of strange vagaries of fate. The couple is left alone in its new home, confident of the future.

## (L') APRÈS-MIDI D'UN FAUNE. *See:* (THE) AFTERNOON OF A FAUN.

## (LE) BEAU DANUBE (THE BEAUTIFUL BLUE DANUBE).
*Book by Leonide Massine. Music: Johann Strauss' The Blue Danube Waltz. First performance: Monte Carlo Theatre, April 15, 1933.*

In the Prater, in 1860, it is a holiday and gaiety prevails among different groups: children, milliners, salesmen, a young hussar and his girl. A strolling troupe arrives. Its dancer recognizes the hussar as a former lover and tries to win back his affection. The hussar's girl prevents further developments and urges her parents to give their blessing to her marriage with the hussar.

## BILLY THE KID.

*Book by Lincoln Kirstein. Original music by Aaron Copland. First performance: The Ballet Caravan, Chicago, October 16, 1938.*

The composer's own summary of the scenario follows:

"The first scene is a frontier town. Familiar figures amble by. Cowboys saunter, some on horseback, others with their lassos. Some Mexican women do a jarabo, which is interrupted by a fight between two drunks. Attracted by the gathering crowd, Billy is seen for the first time as a boy of twelve, with his mother. The brawl turns ugly, guns are drawn, and in some unaccountable way Billy's mother is killed. Without an instant's hesitation, in cold fury, Billy draws a knife from a cowhand's sheath and stabs his mother's slayers. His short but famous career has begun.

"In swift succession we see episodes of Billy's later life. At night, under the stars, in a quiet card game with his outlaw friends. Hunted by a posse led by his former friend, Pat Garrett, Billy is pursued. A running gun battle ensues. Billy is captured. A drunken celebration takes place. Billy in prison is, of course, followed by one of Billy's legendary escapes. Tired and worn in the desert, Billy rests with his girl. Starting from a deep sleep, he senses movement in the shadows. The posse has finally caught up with him. It is the end."

## (LE) BOEUF SUR LE TOIT (THE NOTHING-DOING BAR).

*Book by Jean Cocteau. Original music by Darius Milhaud. First performance: Paris, February 21, 1920.*

The Nothing-Doing Bar is crowded with a strange assortment of guests. There is a Negro dwarf, a bookie, a huge Negro boxer, a woman with paper hair, and a fashionable lady.

During a crap game, the fashionable lady takes the dwarf over her shoulder and carries him into the billiard room. When the boxer makes a play for one of the women, he is knocked out by the bookie. There is heard the sound of a police whistle. Since this is the era of Prohibition, and the place is America, the bartender removes all traces of liquor and hangs a sign reading: "Only Milk Served Here." The policeman, who enters, seems satisfied that the law is being obeyed. In going through a dance he is decapitated by the fall of a huge ceiling fan. The bartender presents the policeman's head to the fashionable lady who dances around it. All the principal characters leave. When the dwarf balks at paying his check, the bartender replaces the head of the policeman on its body. Revived, the policeman gives the dwarf his check, which is now two feet long.

## CARD PARTY (JEU DE CARTES).

*Book by Malaieff and Stravinsky. Original music by Igor Stravinsky. First performance: The American Ballet, Metropolitan Opera House, New York, April 27, 1937.*

The composer's summary of the scenario follows:

"The characters in the ballet are the cards in a game of poker, disputed between several players on the green baize table of a gaming house. At each deal the situation is complicated by the endless guile of the perfidious Joker, who believes himself invincible because of his ability to become any desired card. During the first deal one of the players is beaten, but the other two remain with even 'straights,' although one of them holds the Joker. In the second deal, the hand which holds the Joker is victorious, thanks to four Aces, who easily beat four Queens. Now comes the third deal. The action grows more and more acute. This time it is a struggle between three 'flushes.' Although at first victorious over one adversary, the Joker, strutting at the head of a sequence of Spades, is beaten by a 'royal flush' in Hearts. This puts an end to his malice and knavery."

## CARNIVAL (CARNAVAL).

*Book by Michel Fokine. Music: Robert Schumann's Carnival, for piano, arranged for orchestra by Glazunov. First performance: Pavlova Hall, St. Petersburg, 1910.*

Three girls are being pursued by their lovers. Other couples enter, dancing a waltz. Chiarina and Estrella arrive and vanish, followed by their admirers. We now see the head of Pierrot, peering furtively; he is flapping his long sleeves. When Harlequin arrives, Pierrot mocks him. Harlequin leaves in anger. In swift succession come Eusebius, Estrella and Florestan, and a coquette to whom Florestan is expressing his love. Gaily they depart in each other's arms, while Eusebius and Chiarana perform a dance. Papillon, watched by Pierrot, now flits across the stage. Pierrot pursues her, tries to catch her with his cap, but finds her elusive. Chiarana and her two friends waltz merrily as Florestan goes in search of Estrella. They try to stop him but he is too nimble. Chiarana beckons to one of her friends and embraces her. Colombine and Harlequin return, both gay in spirit. They kiss. He asks her to run off with him, but she politely turns him down. Pantalon comes with pompous strides, twirling his moustache. Colombine plays coyly with him and resists him when he becomes attentive. Instead, she introduces him to Harlequin who mocks the enraged Pantalon. Colombine comes after Pantalon and soothes him with a kiss. After Harlequin, Colombine, and Pantalon go through a dance, Colombine pays attention to Harlequin who gazes on her adoringly. Suddenly the room is filled with merrymakers who offer congratulations to Colombine and Harlequin. There is joyful dancing. Harlequin cannot resist the temptation of being mischievous; he ties together the sleeves of Pantalon and Pierrot. As they free themselves, the entire assemblage gathers cheerfully and admiringly around Harlequin and Colombine.

## COPPELIA.

*Book by Nuitter and A. Saint-Léon. Original music by Léo Delibes. First performance: Opéra, Paris, May 25, 1870.*

Frantz is in love with a doll whom he believes to be a human being, the daughter of the doll-maker Coppelius. When he discovers she is an inanimate object, he urges Coppelius to use magic in bringing her to life. But when the doll becomes human she gets out of control. Frantz, then, is happy to forget her and to return to his original sweetheart.

## DAPHNIS AND CHLOË.

*Book by Michel Fokine. Original music by Maurice Ravel. First performance: The Ballet Russe, Théâtre du Châtelet, Paris, June 8, 1912.*

Daphnis, asleep at the side of a grotto, dreams that Pan saves Chloë in memory of his own beloved, the nymph Syrinx. Imitating Pan and Syrinx, Daphnis makes a pipe from reeds and begins playing for Chloë, who dances ecstatically, then falls into his arms. A general dance follows among the nymphs and shepherdesses in a general festivity.

## (THE) FIRE-BIRD (L'OISEAU DE FEU).

*Book by Michel Fokine. Original music by Igor Stravinsky. First performance: The Ballet Russe, Opéra, Paris, June 25, 1910.*

The story is based on an old Russian legend. The Fire-Bird is captured by Ivan Tsarevitch. In return for its release, the bird gives Ivan one of its feathers. Suddenly a castle comes into view. Nearby, thirteen girls play with golden apples; they are under the magic spell of the dread Kastcheï. Ivan conquers the Kastcheï; breaks his spell; and releases the maidens from their slavery. One of them becomes his bride.

## GAYNE.

*Book by K. N. Derzhavin. Original music by Aram Khatchaturian. First performance: Kirov Theatre, Molotov, December 9, 1942.*

In a collective farm, Giko proves himself a traitor by joining a band of smugglers. He sets fire to his own farm and attempts to murder his wife, Gayaneh, and their daughter. Kazakov, in love with Gayaneh, saves her, and when Giko is punished, marries her.

## GISELLE.

*Book by Vernoy de Saint Georges, Gautier, and Coralli.*

*Original music by Adolphe Adam. First performance:
Opéra, Paris, June 28, 1841.*

The peasant girl, Giselle, loves and is loved by Albrecht, a prince disguised as a peasant. In her dreams, Giselle sees her loved one married to a noblewoman; but Albrecht assures her that he is a peasant and is in love only with her. A hunting party of noblemen and noble ladies arrives. In their midst is Bathilde, the daughter of a prince. When the peasant Hilarion, who loves Giselle, proves to her that Albrecht is a prince in disguise, Giselle recognizes Bathilde as the lady of her tortured dreams. Realizing she must lose her loved one, Giselle loses the will to live. She stabs herself to death with Albrecht's sword.

With a flash of lightning the scene changes to a forest on the bank of a pool. It is midnight, the hour when nymphs and spirits come to life. The hunters flee in terror. The apparitions dance in the moonlight. Their Queen announces that a new sister has come to join them. She waves a wand over the fresh grave of Giselle. She emerges from her tomb and becomes one of the spirits. Meanwhile, Albrecht arrives to grieve at the grave of his loved one. The Queen orders Giselle to dance for Albrecht to entice him into the circle of nymphs. In spite of herself, Giselle follows the command. But hardly has Albrecht been enticed when the hour of four begins to strike. The nymphs and spirits disappear. Giselle returns to her grave. Albrecht takes some flowers from the grave, kisses them, and swoons with grief.

JEU DE CARTES. *See:* CARD PARTY.

(LE) LAC DES CYGNES. *See:* SWAN LAKE.

LOVE, THE SORCERER. *See:* (EL) AMOR BRUJO.

(THE) NOTHING-DOING BAR. *See:* (LE) BOEUF SUR LE TOIT.

PETRUSHKA.
   *Book by Benois and Stravinsky. Original music by Igor
   Stravinsky. First performance: The Ballet Russe,
   Théâtre du Châtelet, Paris, June 13, 1911.*

The scenario has been summarized as follows by Philip Hale: "Petrushka is a sort of Polichinelle, a poor hero always suffering from the cruelty of the police and every kind of wrong and unjust persecution. This represents symbolically the whole tragedy in the existence of the Russian people, suffering under despotism and injustice. The scene is laid in the midst of the Russian carnival: the streets are lined with booths, in one of which Petrushka plays a kind of humorous role. He is killed, but he appears again as a ghost on the roof of the booth to frighten his enemy, his old employer, an allusion to the despotic rule of Russia."

## PRINCE IGOR.

*Choreography by Michel Fokine. Music: Borodin's "Polovtsian Dances" from the opera* Prince Igor. *First performance: The Ballet Russe, Théâtre du Châtelet, Paris, May 18, 1909.*

The ballet has no plot but consists of a series of dances—slow and sensual by the women, barbaric and ferocious by the men. These dances take place in a Polovtsian camp at dawn. First we see the women rising languorously from the ground, weaving their bodies slowly. The chief of the Polovtsians begins a corybantic. Inspired by him, his lieutenants imitate him. The women return with their sinuous dance. They arouse the warriors who come in stamping and begin a wild orgy. Four youths emerge to engage the maidens in a passionate dance. They encircle the chief. At last, all the others join in a demoniac outburst as the ballet ends.

## RAYMONDA.

*Book by Lydia Pashkova and Marius Petipa. Original music by Alexander Glazunov. First performance: Maryinsky Theatre, St. Petersburg, January 19, 1898.*

Raymonda's birthday is being celebrated in a castle in medieval Hungary. The guests participate in a waltz, and remain undisturbed when Raymonda's aunt warns them that the statue of the White Lady will punish anyone bringing dishonor to her great household. A messenger arrives to inform Raymonda that her fiancé, Jean de Brienne, will return from the wars the following day. But he is preceded by the Saracen knight, Aberdam, who tries to win Raymonda and, failing to do so, wishes to abduct her.

The statue of the White Lady leads Raymonda into the garden. There Raymonda sees a vision of her beloved and after that one of Aberdam. The sight of Aberdam terrifies her, and she faints with fright. She is carried back into the castle.

The festivities continue. In vain does Raymonda plead with her aunt to send Aberdam away. Aberdam entertains the assemblage with performances by his men, and after that orders wine for all. When revelry is at its height, Aberdam instructs his men to abduct Raymonda. But before this can be done, Jean de Brienne arrives in the company of the King of Hungary. Jean is about to destroy Aberdam, but the King insists they must meet in combat. Aided by the powers of the statue of the White Lady, Jean kills Aberdam. The festivities now celebrate the forthcoming marriage of Jean de Brienne and Raymonda.

## (THE) RED POPPY.

*Book by M. T. Kurillko. Original music by Reinhold Glière. First performance: Bolshoi Theatre, Moscow, June 14, 1927.*

Chinese coolies are being exploited in a Chinese port. A Soviet ship comes to the harbor, and a series of dances for sailors of different nationalities follows. The port commander, angered at the Soviet sailors, tries to kill their captain. A Chinese woman, Tai-Hao, is in love with the Soviet captain, and is fired with the ambition to fight for the freedom of her oppressed people. When she uncovers a plot to poison the captain she is able to thwart it. The port commander shoots and kills her. Dying, she urges her people to continue fighting for their liberty, giving them a flower symbolic of freedom: a red poppy.

## (THE) RITE OF SPRING (LE SACRE DU PRINTEMPS).

*Book by Roerich and Stravinsky. Original music by Igor Stravinsky. First performance: The Ballet Russe, Théâtre des Champs Elysées, Paris, May 29, 1913.*

The scenario, which has no plot or specific program, is concerned with a pagan ritual in Russia. It is spring; the earth is reborn. A series of ceremonials follows. In the last, a young girl becomes the victim of a sacrifice, and she dances herself to death.

## (THE) SEASONS.

*Book by Petipa. Original music by Alexander Glazunov.*
*First performance: Hermitage Theatre, St. Petersburg,*
*February 23, 1900.*

The scenario interprets the four seasons of the year, beginning with Winter, who is at play with his companions, Ice, Hail, and Snow. When two gnomes set afire some faggots, Winter disappears. Spring arrives, escorted by Zephyr, Bird, and Flowers; they dance joyfully. We next see Summer, represented by a cornfield in which the flowers dance till they become weary. The Corn Spirit dances with the Naiads. Satyr and Fauns arrive to kidnap the Corn Spirit but fail when Zephyr comes to his rescue. The last scene is Autumn, in which Bacchantes dance under falling leaves. He is joined by all the other seasons.

## SLEEPING BEAUTY.

*Book by Petipa and Vsevolozhsky, based on the famous*
*fairy tale by Perrault. Original music by Peter Ilitch*
*Tchaikovsky. First performance: Maryinsky Theatre,*
*St. Petersburg, January 15, 1890.*

The fairy tale from which this scenario was derived is familiar, telling of the beautiful princess who is awakened from her prolonged slumber by the kiss of Prince Charming, who marries her.

The last act of this ballet was adapted into another well-known ballet by the Ballet Russe—*Aurora's Wedding.*

## (EL) SOMBRERO DE TRES PICOS. *See:* (THE) THREE-CORNERED HAT.

## (LE) SPECTRE DE LA ROSE.

*Book by J. L. Vaudoyer. Music: Weber's Invitation to*
*the Dance. First performance: Monte Carlo Theatre,*
*April 19, 1911.*

A young girl holds a rose in her hand. She kisses it, then looks at it reflectively. Falling into an armchair, she sinks into a deep sleep. Through the window comes her lover, dancing with abandon. He approaches her, and she joins him in a waltz. The music ends. She is back in her chair, and her lover disappears through the window. She awakens, looks about her quizzically, and realizes that she has been dreaming. Sadly she picks up the rose that has fallen from her hands, pressing it to her lips.

## SWAN LAKE (LE LAC DES CYGNES).

*Book by Begitchev and Geltzer. Original music by Peter Ilitch Tchaikovsky. First performance: Maryinsky Theatre, St. Petersburg, February 8, 1895.*

A celebration is held to honor the coming of age of Prince Siegfried. When swans pass overhead, a hunt is proposed, to which Siegfried agrees.

At the side of a lake, a group of swans appears, one of them wearing a crown. At midnight they return to their original human form. Siegfried, who sees them in their human form, falls in love with their queen, Odette. He invites her to a ball at which he wishes to choose her as his bride. But Odette explains that this is impossible until the magic spell of the enchanter Rotbart—a spell that makes her swan— is broken. At dawn, the girls once again become swans and glide away across the lake.

At Siegfried's ball, the guests arrive and the festivities begin. One of the guests has been made by Rotbart to look like Odette. Odette's spirit, beating at one of the windows of the castle, warns Siegfried of the deception. Magician and the false Odette vanish, and Siegfried goes in search of his beloved. He finds her again at the side of the lake. Rotbart brings on a terrible storm. Siegfried expresses the wish of dying with the one he loves. This self-sacrifice breaks the magic spell, and the swans become human again permanently.

## (LES) SYLPHIDES.

*Choreography by Michel Fokine. Music adapted from the piano works of Chopin including: Nocturne, op. 32, no. 2; Waltz, op. 70, no. 1; Mazurka, op. 33, no. 3; Mazurka, op. 67, no. 3; Prelude, op. 28, no. 7; Waltz, op. 64, no. 2; Waltz, op. 18, no. 1. First performance: The Ballet Russe, Théâtre du Châtelet, Paris, June 2, 1909.*

It is nighttime at a sylvan glade. On one side are the gray ruins of a monastery; in the background are the outlines of a tomb. The dancers, in silvery wings, go through various dances; then they, and the somber scene, disappear into mist.

## (THE) THREE-CORNERED HAT (EL SOMBRERO DE TRES PICOS).

*Book by Martinez Sierra. Original music by Manuel de Falla. First performance: Alhambra Theatre, London, July 22, 1919.*

A governor (who wears as badge of office a three-cornered hat) is in love with the miller's wife. He sees to it that the miller gets arrested so that he might make love to her. But she proves elusive, and she coquettishly avoids his outstretched hands until he stumbles into a nearby stream. Drenched, he is forced to remove his clothes and wait in bed until they dry. By then, the miller has managed to leave his prison and come home. Seeing the governor in his bed he hastily replaces the governor's clothes with his own. Gaily he departs, leaving a note saying that the governor's wife is every bit as desirable as his own.

## (LA) VALSE.

*Book by B. Nijinska. Music: Ravel's La Valse. First performance: Opéra, Paris, 1929.*

A ballroom, in the Third Empire period, is almost empty. Several ladies, seated on a settee, rise and begin to waltz. Suddenly other dancers come into view, going through the motions of a waltz. On a second stage, other dancers are seen in a distance. There is a kind of counterpoint of motion between the two groups of dancers.

# PART FOUR

*Music for Solo Instruments*
*and*
*For Chamber-Music Groups*

# *The Organ*

When the Camerata in sixteenth century Florence evolved the "New Music" (*Nuove musiche*)—that is, single-voiced declamation as distinguished from several-voiced polyphony—it succeeded in creating something more than just opera. It also helped bring about the development of instrumental music. For by emphasizing a single melody, the New Music provided a style that was adaptable for instrumental writing.

The first important musical instrument to engage composers was the organ.

Organ music had been written before New Music changed the course of musical history. Sixteenth-century contrapuntists—among them the Gabrielis and Sweelinck—adapted the polyphonic style of choral music to the organ. The concept of instrumental music as something different from choral music—paying greater attention to a single melody, rhythm, color, and nuance—was not reached until after the new age of homophony had been introduced.

The first important composer to achieve an instrumental style, to free music from the so-called "vocal tyranny," was Girolamo Frescobaldi, in the early seventeenth century. It was with Frescobaldi that such important organ forms as the toccata, partita, and fugue were fully crystallized. Frescobaldi was also one of the first composers to bring clarity of outline to these forms, to fill his music with human feeling, to emphasize the melodic character of his works.

Frescobaldi's immediate successors in the writing of organ music were Samuel Scheidt (who helped create modern organ notation) and Johann Schein (who imported the Italian organ style of Frescobaldi into Germany).

It was in Germany that there arose, in the seventeenth century, the dominating figure in organ music before Johann Sebastian Bach. He was Dietrich Buxtehude. It is a familiar story that Bach, in his twentieth year, made the two-hundred-mile trip from Arnstadt to Lübeck just to hear Buxtehude play the organ and come into contact with his music. The influence of Buxtehude on Bach was incalculable. The organ forms in which Bach produced so many remarkable works were inherited directly from Buxtehude, who had brought these forms to their highest point of structural development up to that time. The forms Frescobaldi had used were extended and amplified, while others —like the passacaglia, chaconne, and chorale-prelude—were established. Indeed, so astute a critic as Alfred Einstein once remarked that the Bach passacaglias would have never been written if Buxtehude had not previously produced works in that form.

In the province of organ music, Buxtehude towered over his predecessors and contemporaries by placing less emphasis on technique and virtuosity and more on creative power. His attention to detail, the subtlety of his decorative treatment, his contrasts of color and mood, his impressive climaxes, the originality of his harmony, and the expressiveness of his melodies, were elements new to the organ music of that period, bringing altogether new artistic significance to the established organ forms. No wonder, then, that the English critic, A. Eaglefield Hull, wrote: "As John the Baptist was to Christ, so was . . . Buxtehude to Bach."

Undoubtedly, the greatest single figure in the entire history of organ music is Johann Sebastian Bach. He was a remarkable virtuoso, unparalleled in his gift for improvisation; and he knew the secrets of his instrument as only a great performer does. For his instrument he wrote many toccatas, preludes, fugues, chaconnes, passacaglias, fantasias, and so forth. This music represents the richest contribution to organ literature ever made by a single person. All the forms he touched were brought to their ultimate development; when Bach was through with them they had exhausted their structural possibilities. The science of writing for the organ—the full exploitation of dynamics, colors, and technique—was created. Most important of all, no one before Bach— not even Buxtehude—could bring to organ music such a majesty and grandeur of expression, such a unique creative originality, such inexhaustible invention, and such beauty and drama.

Bach is the Mt. Everest of organ music: beyond this summit no man can climb. Consequently, after Bach, organ music went into a decline—even though, at intermittent periods, composers turned to this instrument. Haydn and Beethoven avoided the organ completely. Mozart, when he wrote for the organ, usually combined it with strings or with the orchestra. In German Romantic literature, the organ was a stepchild of such masters as Schumann, Mendelssohn, Liszt, and Brahms. Later German Romanticists—such as Joseph Rheinberger and Max Reger—produced many works for organ; but in these works there is more artifice than art, more science than poetry, more skill than imagination.

The French Romanticists were more successful than the Germans. César Franck wrote few works more elevated in thought, nobler in concept, more spiritual in feeling than the *Three Chorales* completed in the last year of his life. Franck comes closest to inheriting the mantle of the great Johann Sebastian, not only as a composer for the organ, but also as a performer. The story is told that when Franz Liszt heard Franck improvise at the Madeleine Church in Paris, he muttered under his breath that Bach had just returned to life. But even Franck wrote comparatively little for his beloved instrument, and could hardly be regarded as a success in restoring the organ to its one-time imperial position in the world of music.

Camille Saint-Saëns, another splendid organist, was one of the most prolific composers of all time; but Saint-Saëns produced only seven opus numbers for that instrument. Other Frenchmen—notably, Alexandre Guilmant, Charles-Marie Widor, and Louis Vierné—were far more prolific, and their works are frequently heard at organ recitals. But these are creative figures of comparatively small stature. Nor have more recent composers anywhere found the organ creatively stimulating.

The great age of organ music had passed with Bach.

# 2

## *The Piano*

The earliest music for the piano was written for keyboard instruments producing tone qualities different from those of the present-day piano.

The piano, as we know it today, was invented in the eighteenth century by a Florentine instrument maker, Cristofori. Before then, we had instruments which can be regarded as the ancestors of the piano: virginal, clavichord, and the harpsichord. All these were controlled by a hammer action different from that found in the piano. In the virginal and harpsichord the strings were plucked by quills; in the clavichord, the strings were struck by brass wedges. All these instruments had a small, thin tone, and were incapable of sustaining sound.

For a long time before Cristofori, instrument makers realized that a richer and more resonant tone could be produced if the strings were struck by hammers. But early experiments in this direction failed to produce a hammer action in which the hammer sprang back instantly, allowing the strings to vibrate. It was Cristofori who was the first to solve this problem. He called his invention a *"gravicembalo col piano e forte,"* a name which, when shortened, introduced the word "piano" into the musical dictionary. By 1720, Cristofori had developed a four-octave instrument in which the force of the hammer on the strings

312

could be controlled by the force of the finger on the key. The soft, bell-like tinkle of the virginal, harpsichord, and clavichord made way for the more forceful, richer, and resonant tone of the piano.

But it is the soft, bell-like tinkle of the virginal, harpsichord, and clavichord that we find in the earliest music for the "piano." (For convenience alone, we shall henceforth often refer to all the early keyboard instruments as pianos.)

The first important school of composers of piano music is found in England in the seventeenth century. Several important collections of music for the virginal appeared in England in the first two decades of the seventeenth century, among them the *Fitzwilliam Book* and the *Parthenia*. Here we find represented such distinguished composers of English church music and madrigals as Tallis, Byrd, Morley, Gibbons, and Bull. The kind of music these composers wrote for virginals usually consisted of such popular dances as the pavane, or the galliard, or the gigue. At times, composers prefaced one of these dances with a short prelude, virtuoso in character. At other times, these composers combined two or more dances to provide contrast of mood, as in the delightful "Earl of Salisbury" by William Byrd.

These delightful miniatures for the virginal explored, for the first time, a technique of writing for a keyboard instrument other than the organ. And in coupling two or more dances into a single work, this early virginal literature provided the basis for the later suite form. Other forms utilized by the early English piano composers included fantasias (a form brought over from organ music), and a form introduced from Spain, variations.

For about half a century after this virginal music was published, piano music suffered neglect at the hands of composers. But in the middle of the seventeenth century there was an awakened interest in the piano. In France, Jacques de Champion Chambonnières, a distinguished harpsichordist, published two volumes of music for the harpsichord. The importance of these publications rests both on the fact that they marked a revival of interest in the piano and that they helped establish one of the basic forms of harpsichord music—the suite.

This activity in France by Chambonnières was paralleled in England by Henry Purcell, who found the harpsichord a grateful medium for his genius. Purcell's suites mark another step forward for the suite form. These and other harpsichord pieces did much to increase both the technical resources and the expressiveness of the instrument.

Since the early organ composers used to do much of their practicing on the harpsichord, it was inevitable that they write music for the latter instrument. Also, since these men were essentially organ composers, it was equally inescapable that they adapt organ forms for the harpsichord. Thus we find Frescobaldi producing toccatas and partitas for the harpsichord. We also find that his pupil, Johann Jakob Froberger, wrote similar pieces for the harpsichord, as well as many suites. Froberger, who was born in Stuttgart, must be regarded as one of the earliest successful composers of piano music in Germany.

It is in Germany that we encounter a major phase in the evolution of early piano music. It is encountered with Johann Kuhnau, the immediate predecessor of Johann Sebastian Bach at the St. Thomas Church in Leipzig. Kuhnau published his first harpsichord suites in 1689. They represent a sharp and permanent break with the music thus far written for that instrument by the organ composers. The old forms of organ music are completely superseded by the newer form of the suite; an essential harpsichord style—delicate, refined, crystal-clear—replaced the organ style. Kuhnau was the first German composer to understand that the harpsichord could be the source of great music, and to help evolve a technique capable of producing such music.

Kuhnau was also the pioneer in the use of the word "sonata" in conjunction with a piece of music for the piano. (Kuhnau's sonatas are discussed in greater detail in the section analyzing the growth and evolution of the sonata.)

For the further development of piano music we must once again cross the Rhine back into France. François Couperin le Grand is the father of French piano music. He evolved a style and technique of his own; he drew from the harpsichord new sound qualities and effects that increased its dynamics and varied its colors.

Couperin wrote four volumes, collectively entitled *Pièces de clavecin*. There is nothing like these pieces in the harpsichord literature of the seventeenth and early eighteenth centuries. They are unique for structural perfection, variety of style, aptness of musical expression, and flexibility of technique. Many of these pieces are programmatic, descriptive of bees and gnats and butterflies, reapers and grape-gatherers, jugglers, gossip, and court life. "La Favorite" (a chaconne) describes the pomp of the court of the Roi Soleil. The suite *Les Folies françaises* (a theme and variations) tries to find in music the equivalent between a mood or character trait and a color: modesty (rose); ardor (scarlet); hope (green); loyalty (blue); languor (violet); jealousy (dark gray); frenzy (black).

Couperin provides us with a cross-section of eighteenth century court life in France by interpreting pictures, suggestions, customs, incidents, and objects of his period. More important, however, is the fact that Couperin was the first French composer to understand both the strength and the limitations of the harpsichord, and to cater to them. He extended the horizon of piano music by enriching harmonic writing, bringing fullness to the lyric line, and introducing a variety of rhythm never before realized.

The next important landmark in piano music is—Domenico Scarlatti.

Domenico Scarlatti (who should not be confused with his father, Alessandro, genius of Neapolitan opera) was one of the outstanding harpsichord virtuosos of his time. So phenomenal was his technique that some of his contemporaries were convinced that it stemmed from supernatural powers. "He is possessed of the devil," they would say. It is, then, to be expected that he should know the instrument intimately and comprehensively; that in writing for it he should be able to make it speak more flexibly than heretofore. Since he also had immense creative powers, he could combine his immense knowledge of his instrument with subtlety of expression—with an incomparable charm, beauty, wit, and grace.

Scarlatti wrote numerous pieces. He himself designated them as "exercises" (*esercizi*), but today we refer to them as "sonatas." The term "exercise" is certainly more appropriate since these delightful and picturesque items are essentially brief pictorial or emotional excursions rather than examples of sonata writing.

The modern age of piano playing is inaugurated with these Scarlatti pieces. They exploited new techniques of all kinds: runs, arpeggios, crossing of hands, shakes, leaps across the keyboard, and so forth. Never before, not even with Couperin, had the harpsichord been so articulate.

We have now come to the age of Handel and Bach—an age that made formidable advances in the technique of piano playing and in the style of piano writing. But this advance is much more noticeable in Bach than in Handel. Handel's literature for the piano—sixteen suites, two chaconnes, six fugues—is not representative of his genius, nor was the development of piano music influenced by it. (This library, however, does include a charming, and still highly popular, composition known as *The Harmonious Blacksmith*.)

But the piano music of Johann Sebastian Bach is a new world. Here, as in all other media, Bach brought the full measure of his genius. He produced several concertos with orchestra, six partitas, and such mighty creations as the *Well-Tempered Clavier,* the *Goldberg Variations, Chromatic Fantasy and Fugue,* and the *French* and *English Suites*—to this day, among the greatest works written for the piano. The soaring flights of tone, the dramatic surges of sound, the majesty of thought and grandeur of feeling, the inevitability of the structural logic, the incomparable skill in the contrapuntal writing which made Bach's organ music unique are also found in this piano literature. To compare such music with morsels by Scarlatti and Couperin—however charming and historically significant those morsels may be—is to place a cathedral at the side of a basilica.

The creative strength found in Bach's piano music brought to this medium an altogether new artistic significance. Henceforth, the piano would cease to be a stepchild of music, but, on the contrary, would engage the most serious attention and efforts of the greatest composers. Bach's piano music also changed and revolutionized the art of music by establishing (in *The Well-Tempered Clavier*) a new system of keyboard tuning. This work, which consists of forty-eight preludes and fugues, each in a different key of the major and minor scales, proved the efficacy of a method, new in Bach's day: that of dividing the octave into twelve equal notes, a system finally producing the forty-eight scales as we know them now.

The Classical Period in piano music entered with one of Bach's sons—Karl Philipp Emanuel. He, and his immediate successors—Haydn and Mozart—introduced a new style of piano music: the *galant* style, calling for grace, delicacy, refinement, and aristocratic polish. With their many sonatas, concertos and other sundry works for the piano, Bach, Haydn and Mozart brought to piano music a mastery of classical form together with a felicitousness of expression and a development of harmonic and rhythmic means which marked a golden age. In their hands, the piano proved to be one of the most expressive and artistically rewarding of all musical instruments.

It was during their lifetime that the piano—as distinguished from the harpsichord and clavichord—was invented and came into general use. The piano music of Bach was still intended for the harpsichord and clavichord; consequently it is still delicate in sonority and of an almost fragile delicacy. With Mozart's piano music there comes increasing vigor of style and a greater richness of texture indicating that Mozart was beginning to think in terms of the new piano rather than the old harpsichord. The clarity and the precision are, however, reminders of the older instrument.

It is with Beethoven that the piano replaced the harpsichord and clavichord completely and permanently.

It was surely a fortuitous development that the piano should have been perfected when Beethoven was writing his keyboard music. His ungovernable temperament, the leonine strength of his personality, and his forceful language would surely have found both the harpsichord and clavichord unsatisfactory for the kind of music he *had* to write: rich in dynamics, vigorous in its chord construction, powerful in sonority, passionate and dramatic in its sweep of sound. Beethoven's genius called for a sturdier instrument than the harpsichord, and he found it in Cristoforo's piano.

The right man, then, came at the right time. Beethoven understood the new instrument, and fully recognized its musical possibilities. Restlessly, up to the end of his life, he experimented with the new colors, sonorities, and dynamics of which the piano was capable. He uncovered sounds—and in the last sonatas these sounds were of almost orchestral texture—which no one suspected the piano could produce. At the same time he enlarged classical forms to such proportions that they seemed to burst out of the constrictions set by tradition. A new breadth, a new spaciousness were brought to piano writing. All this was but the means to an end: the end being music of nobility, profundity, and intensity.

By his increasing impatience with the limitations imposed upon the sonata and concerto by classical tradition, and by his indefatigable search for full freedom of artistic expression, Beethoven represents the transition from the classicism of Haydn and Mozart to the romanticism of Schubert, Schumann, Mendelssohn, Chopin, and Brahms.

The necessity of writing as they pleased—as their heart and consciences dictated rather than the rule of the textbook—governed the piano music of the Romantics. They embraced a new concept of form. When they wrote sonatas and concertos they made the structure a humble servant of the idea, instead of the other way around. They also evolved new forms which allowed them to move with greater freedom.

The smaller forms gain significance with Franz Schubert. Schubert wrote impromptus and moments musicaux, self-sufficient miniatures, each a perfect jewel. Schubert's successors followed his example. Some of the greatest music ever written for the piano was created within the small forms: Mendelssohn's *Songs Without Words;* Schumann's novelettes, romances, arabesques; Chopin's nocturnes, waltzes, études, preludes, and so forth; Brahms' rhapsodies, intermezzi, capriccios, and ballades. Schumann also created a form all his own, by taking a great many of these miniatures and connecting and integrating them into a single complex work through a central poetic idea. Such major creations as *Carnival, Fantasiestücke,* and *Kreisleriana* are made up of many small pieces so skilfully joined together that the many pieces become a single, inextricable unity.

More and more fluid does piano style become with each successive Romantic composer, while with Mendelssohn piano virtuosity is glorified for its own sake for the first time.

The greatest of these Romantics was Frédéric Chopin. One could say more: He was the greatest composer for the piano of all time. He was the only major composer in music history to specialize in piano music. Of his less than two hundred works, one hundred and sixty-nine are for solo piano, and a few others are for piano and orchestra. None of his works dispenses with the piano altogether.

Here was a composer who, from the beginning, knew his greatness and his limitations. He knew he was not at ease writing for any medium other than the piano; consequently he never wrote a symphony, an opera, choral or vocal works, and very little chamber music. He realized that he was not adept at instrumentation; for this reason only a scattered handful of his works requires an orchestral accompaniment. He was uncomfortable in the larger forms: he who was so prolific produced only two concertos and three sonatas, the remainder of his immense library comprising small items in various forms.

To piano technique Chopin brought a new gamut of colors, an increased range of dynamics, greater resiliency and fluidity. At the same time piano style was enriched with a new variety of expression, of atmosphere and mood, together with deeper poetic ideas and richer romantic feelings. His structures were always tailor-made for the thought and mood he was trying to project. His writing never departed from good taste and aristocratic breeding. As Franz Liszt once wrote, in Chopin's music we "meet with beauties of the highest kind, expressions entirely new, and harmonic material original as it is thoughtful. In his compositions boldness is always justified; richness, often exuberance, never interferes with clearness; singularity never degenerates into the uncouth and the fantastic; the sculpturing is never disordered; the luxury of ornament never overloads the chaste tenderness of the principal lines. Daring, brilliant, attractive, they disguise their profundity under so many charms that it is with difficulty we free ourselves sufficiently from their magical enthrallment to judge coldly their theoretical value."

His world was more limited than that of Bach, Mozart, Beethoven, or Wagner. But it was *his* world, and within it he was truly incomparable.

The outstanding figures in piano music after Chopin include Franz Liszt, Brahms, Debussy, and Scriabin. Liszt wrote études, ballades, legends, liebesträume, *Années de pélérinages* (three sets of tone pictures inspired by his travels), and various transcriptions. We find here a dazzling, almost spell-binding, virtuosity not even encountered in Chopin, together with an orchestral sonority, and a new exactness in musical notation. Brahms combined his respect for classical form with Romantic passion and at times profundity of thought or excursions into whimsy. Debussy did more to advance piano technique and style than any composer since Chopin. By bringing Impressionism to the keyboard (and through his exploitation of such new devices as the whole-tone scale) he uncovered new resonances and hues. The quintessence of his art is found in his two books of *Preludes,* the *Suite bergamasque,* and two sets of piano *Images*—particularly in such celebrated pieces as "The Girl with the Flaxen Hair," and "The Engulfed Cathedral" from the first book of *Preludes,* and the nostalgic and atmospheric "Clair de lune" from *Suite bergamasque.* Scriabin began his career as composer by writing piano music in the style of Chopin; but he ended up by producing pieces of extreme individuality. His originality arose from his increasing bent for mysticism which filled him with a grandiose ambition to express a world philosophy in music. Thus from the romanticism of his early études, preludes, and sonatas, he progressed to music weighed down by mysticism and philosophic thought. At the same time, he showed increasing partiality for strange effects in melody, unusual harmonies and progressions (built out of the so-called "mystic chord," made up of intervals of the fourth), and an amorphous form. His last preludes and sonatas are rambling in construction and elusive in thought. But his piano works up to op. 30 are exquisite pieces, poetic in thought, sensitive in mood, delicate in construction. They are among the finest examples of Romantic piano music.

In the twentieth century composers like Béla Bartók, Paul Hindemith, and Charles Ives went beyond Scriabin in the use of daring harmonic and rhythmic combinations and startling percussive effects. Others introduced completely new techniques. Henry Cowell was the exponent of "tone clusters"—chords made up of simultaneous seconds and produced by banging a fist, forearm, or palm on the keyboard. (Charles Ives anticipated Cowell by calling for the use of a ruler in some passages of the *Concord Piano Sonata*.) Still others tried changing the very structure of the piano. Hans Barth devised a quarter-tone piano and wrote for it a new library of music utilizing quarter-tone intervals instead of half-tones. John Cage created the "prepared piano" and also wrote special music for it; a "prepared piano" is one in which dampers of metal, wood, rubber, felt, and other materials are stuffed between the strings in carefully measured positions to produce new tone qualities.

But experimentation is only a single facet of twentieth-century piano music. Many composers progressed along more traditional lines to write music more concerned with content than with technique and means, more interested in the projection of beauty and emotion than with novelty. In this category we find Rachmaninoff, Nicolas Medtner, Prokofiev, and most important of all, Maurice Ravel. These composers combined the fullest resources of piano technique with deep feeling, poetic imagination, and frequently a remarkable ability at descriptive writing. These composers have reaped a rich harvest of piano music which indicates that the soil is still extremely fertile.

# 3

## *The Violin*

In the sixteenth century there was also instrumental music for a variety of stringed instruments called "viols." These viols were the antecedents of the violin, viola, cello, and double-bass. The viols differed from our present strings in several important respects. The viols had flat, instead of convex, backs, and sloping, instead of round, shoulders. They had a heavy and mellow instead of a brilliant and sonorous tone. They had more strings than four. And none of the old viols were held under the chin (as the violin and viola are today), but either between knees or legs.

The most important members of the old viola family were: the treble viol (later to become the violin); the viola da braccia (evolved into the viola); the viola da gamba (subsequently the cello); and the violone (the double-bass in later years). The viol family had several other members, but they have passed out of existence and have no descendants.

The "chest of viols"—as this group of instruments was called in the sixteenth century—was in popular use for over a century. Even while the newer instruments—the violin, viola, and cello—were being evolved and coming upon the musical scene, the viols retained their popularity. Indeed, the newer instruments were for a long time regarded with some contempt, because their tone was considered too piercing and brilliant; during all of the sixteenth century, and part of the seventeenth, composers were much more partial to the older instruments. Not until a family of instrument makers, the Amatis, built remarkable violins, violas, and cellos in the early seventeenth century, did these instruments begin to acquire a respected status in musical society.

The first known piece of music for the solo violin was Carlo Farina's "Capriccio stravagante," written in 1627. This rather novel piece of music imitated sounding fifes, barking dogs, beating drums, and strumming guitars. New technical effects were introduced, such as trills and double-stops.

But though "Capriccio stravagante" is the first solo work for the violin, that instrument had been used seventeen years earlier with striking artistic and revolutionary effect by Claudio Monteverdi in his opera *Orfeo*. It was Monteverdi who was the first to use successfully such basic violin techniques as the tremolo, portamento, and pizzicato.

The history of violin music, and the history of violin playing, really began with Arcangelo Corelli in the middle of the seventeenth century. Corelli was the first violin virtuoso. Contemporary accounts are rich with descriptions of his playing, of its fire and beauty, even of the physical transformations which took place in his face as he performed. Some of his contemporaries, remembering that his first name was Arcangelo, described him as the "archangel of the violin." Others, preferring to ascribe diabolic powers to him, said that he was the "archdevil."

Later authorities of the violin were just as ready to concede his exceptional powers. "Before Corelli," wrote J. B. Cartier, "the art of the violin was completely ignored." "It is Corelli," wrote Paul Stoeving, "who raised the art of fiddling to the dignity of an art." As a performer, Corelli knew his instrument, and it was he who formulated the science of bowing, who introduced chord playing, and who developed sundry other technical devices to extend the horizons of violin playing. This alone would have assured him a permanent place in music history. But more significant than his performances was the music he wrote for the violin—widely published and performed in his own day—which further raised the violin to a virtuoso rank and, at the same time, was an important factor in the early development of instrumental music.

In Corelli's time the art of music was undergoing a revolution, as we have already remarked in previous sections—the revolution being the change from polyphony to homophony. But many composers in Corelli's time were merely translating a vocal style to musical instruments, rather than thinking in terms of the new medium. Corelli was one of the first to recognize the basic fact that writing music for instruments entailed a different approach and style: the singing quality of a melody, and the way it lay naturally for the voice, was no longer a determining factor in writing music. What was all important now were tonality, freedom of modulation, greater flexibility of rhythm, and enrichment of harmony.

Corelli's twelve sonatas for violin and accompanying bass, gathered in *Op. 5*, is the first landmark in violin music. This was a pioneer attempt to produce sonatas for a solo instrument and accompaniment. This was also the first successful realization of an individual style of violin music. These epical works are discussed in greater detail in our analysis of the sonata at the end of this section.

Corelli's sonatas—he also wrote sonatas for two instruments and accompanying bass—had a profound influence on his contemporaries. Henry Purcell, a pioneer in English instrumental music, confessed he was inspired by Corelli to write his first instrumental trios. François Couperin le Grand conceded that his first sonatas were written in emulation of Corelli. "Charmed by the works of Corelli," he wrote in the introduction to his first published instrumental opus, "whose compositions I have loved as long as I lived . . . I attempted to compose one, which I had performed at that very concert where I first heard those of Corelli." An eminent composer of German instrumental music, and one of the earliest—George Telemann—wrote in his autobiography that Corelli was his model.

Corelli's fame inevitably attracted to his home in Rome young violinists from all parts of Italy. They studied with him, then carried away his science and innovations. Many of them—including Francesco Geminiani and Pietro Locatelli—were fine composers themselves, producing much excellent music for the violin. Other successors of Corelli in Italy were also tremendously influential in developing violin technique and enriching the violin repertory. The most famous of these were Antonio Vivaldi, Giuseppe Tartini, Gaetano Pugnani, Giuseppe Torelli, and Giovanni Viotti. The instrument acquired increasing range; the music, greater expressiveness and deeper emotional content.

The best works of some of these composers are still heard at violin recitals and are still capable of bringing enjoyment.

The great day of violin music—just as it was the great day for all other kinds of music—began with Bach and Handel and continued with Haydn, Mozart, and Beethoven. Their various concertos, sonatas, and suites for the violin—and their use of the violin in chamber and orchestral music—were the culminating stage in the artistic evolution of this instrument. The violin was now one of the two great solo instruments in music (the other, of course, being the piano) ; and to it, great composers of the world would write some of their noblest music.

Meanwhile, the science of violin technique was being carefully and methodically formulated. The first to do so was Leopold Mozart (father of Wolfgang Amadeus) who published a *Violin Method* in 1756. After that came the *Forty Etudes* of Rudolf Kreutzer, published in the closing years of the eighteenth century. But no single person did more to increase the technical resources of the violin than the fabulous Italian virtuoso and composer, Niccolo Paganini, in the early nineteenth century. Paganini was the greatest violinist of his generation, and it is also possible he was the greatest violinist music has known. His fantastic technique made him the most worshiped musical figure of his time—not only among the average concert goer but also with such discriminating musicians as Liszt, Schubert, and Meyerbeer. Paganini's concert tours throughout Europe were blazed with triumph. Like Corelli before him, Paganini was said to possess diabolical powers. Some even insisted that he was the son of the Devil—a rumor which his own cadaverous appearance helped to give credence; on one occasion he was compelled to publish letters from his mother as proof that his parents were human.

As a performer and as a composer, Paganini brought altogether new powers to the violin. His concertos and his numerous smaller pieces (the most famous and significant being the twenty-four caprices) are filled with breathtaking feats intended to exploit his own digital dexterity. Ultimately they succeeded in extending the violin's capabilities. No composer before him used harmonics, double and triple stops, left-hand pizzicati, passages in tenths, and so forth, with such dazzling effect. He also endowed the science of bowing with new variety and resiliency.

Modern violin music, and modern violin technique, came with

Paganini's playing and Paganini's music. All his successors were influenced by him. The foremost violinists of the latter part of the nineteenth century—among them Henri Wieniawski, Henri Vieuxtemps, and Pablo de Sarasate—produced a library of virtuoso music for the violin which surely would not have been written in that way if Paganini had never lived. The Romantic violin concerto—in which the virtuosity of the performer is exploited in pyrotechnical music—was also derived from Paganini.

The late Romanticists all produced splendid music for the violin, in both the large and the small forms. Johann Brahms wrote excellent sonatas and a wonderful concerto; Bruch wrote two concertos and the *Scottish Fantasy;* Saint-Saëns' best works for violin include three concertos, several sonatas, and such familiar virtuoso items as the *Havanaise,* and *Introduction and Rondo capriccioso;* Lalo contributed two staples in the repertory, *Symphonie espagnole* and *Poem;* César Franck and Fauré produced notable sonatas.

The violin repertory was further amplified by the distinguished concert violinist, Fritz Kreisler, who produced a library of smaller pieces that are abiding favorites in the repertory: *Caprice Viennois, Schön Rosmarin, Liebesfreud, Liebesleid, Praeludium and Allegro, Sicilienne et Rigaudon, Tambourin chinois,* and many others. And thereby hangs a tale—one of the most fantastic in musical history.

From the beginning of his great career, Kreisler had been performing many pieces for the violin which he said were his transcriptions of the works of such old masters as Vivaldi, Pugnani, Francoeur, Martini, and so forth. These pieces were published, carrying the legend that they had been discovered by Kreisler in European libraries and monasteries and freely adapted by him for the violin. But, in the 1930's, the New York music critic, Olin Downes, tried to trace the source of Kreisler's arrangement of Pugnani's *Praeludium and Allegro.* Downes was then told—and the world of music was informed for the first time— that the piece was original with Kreisler; that most of the other so-called Kreisler "transcriptions" were also original with him. In short, for over thirty years, Kreisler had perpetrated a hoax on the music world that went undetected. The discovery aroused a storm of outrage. But when the storm blew over, Kreisler's reputation remained untarnished; indeed, it was somewhat enhanced, with the realization that such a wealth of violin music was of his own creation.

# *Chamber Music*

Chamber music embraces works for small combinations of instruments: sonatas for a solo instrument and piano; trios; quartets; quintets; sextets; septets; octets.

The term "chamber music" made its first appearance in 1630, in an English publication: Martin Peerson's *Motets, or Grave Chamber Musique.* The word "camera," in the "sonata da camera" form, used by seventeenth-century Italian instrumental composers, also provides an indication that this is chamber music. Besides the sonata da camera, another variety of early chamber music was the old dances and fantasias written for viols.

The volumes of Corelli's sonatas, published between 1680 and 1694, form the foundation upon which rests all later chamber music. The first four volumes are made up of sonatas for two instruments and accompaniment; the fifth volume (as we have already remarked in the preceding chapter on the violin) consists of sonatas for violin and accompaniment. It is not necessary to analyze in detail the structure of Corelli's sonatas for two instruments and accompaniment. Only a single element in his form is of outstanding interest historically: occasionally Corelli used a second theme of contrasting nature to supplement his principal melody, and by doing this he gave the first suggestion in music of the dual-theme construction in the later sonata form.

It is the content of these sonatas that is all important—the variety of their melodic ideas, the sensitivity and naturalness of their modulations, the fluidity of the style, the transparency of the texture, the warmth and beauty of the slow passages.

Corelli, then, pointed the way in the writing of chamber music; composers everywhere followed his lead. In 1693, Tomasso Antonio Vitali published a group of sonatas da chiesa (suites) for two violins, cello and bass. Several decades later, Alessandro Scarlatti wrote two string quartets which, for the first time, used that combination of instruments henceforth to characterize the string quartet—two violins, viola, and a cello; so did Giuseppe Tartini after him. Scarlatti also wrote quartets for various other combinations of instruments, principally flutes and accompaniment. Trios (or as they were first called, trio-sonatas) were written in France by Couperin le Grand; in Germany by Telemann, Buxtehude, Stamitz, Johann Sebastian Bach and Handel; and in England by Purcell.

While string quartets were written before Haydn's time, it was he who was the first to endow them with artistic importance. How far the string quartet progressed with Haydn can be accurately measured by comparing his first works in that form with the last. Haydn wrote his first string quartet in 1755, while he was in the employ of Count von Fürnberg. In short order he produced seventeen other similar works (embracing opp. 1, 2, and 3). These quartets were no different from most of the chamber music written at that time. They were actually little divertimenti, nocturnes, suites, or cassations in five movements (two of them minuets). The lyrical ideas were breezy and slight, and invariably assigned to the first violin. There is no hint here of the later string-quartet form, nor is there much of an effort to assign equal importance to all four instruments.

In 1771, Haydn wrote a set of six quartets (op. 17) in which the four-movement form is the accepted procedure. The first movement is in a quick tempo, and usually in the sonata form; the second is slow and lyrical; the third is a minuet; the fourth, a fast finale. One other fact about these works is noteworthy: the quartet is freed of the tyranny of the first violin, as the composer places importance on the other three instruments.

Having found his medium, Haydn produced, one year later, six more quartets (op. 20), filled with some of his most gracious thoughts and moods. "Perhaps no single or sextuple opus in the history of instrumental music," wrote W. W. Cobbett, "has achieved so much or achieved it so quietly." Haydn was henceforth to use the structure of the quartet with consummate mastery, and to write for the four instruments with a wonderful adjustment of the four parts to one another. The range of his moods and feelings became increasingly wide: he was at turns witty or playful, pensive or tragic, tender or dramatic—and always with disarming charm and personal appeal. He was also to grow increasingly courageous in trying out new ways of saying what was in his heart. In the six quartets written in 1781 (op. 33), he gave new significance to the development section of the first movement, showing how thematic material can be altered and extended to provide changing interest.

Beginning with the set published as op. 50, and written between 1784 and 1787, Haydn produced some of his crowning works in the string-quartet form. The *Quartet in E Flat Major* (op. 50, no. 3) is a miracle of wit and lightness of touch; this is the genial and lovable composer whom history has designated as the kindly "papa" of music. In later quartets profounder depths are plumbed. The *Quartet in D Minor* (op. 76, no. 2) has, in the slow movement, some of the most exalted music ever written by Haydn; this work is generally known as the *Quinten Quartet* because the opening theme of the first movement is made up of fifths. *The Quartet in D Major* (op. 76, no. 5) also has a slow movement of surpassing beauty, so much so that the entire quartet is sometimes referred to as the *Largo Quartet*. The *Quartet in C Major* (op. 76, no. 3) is famous because the theme of the slow movement is the Austrian National Anthem which Haydn had written some years earlier at the request of the Emperor; in this quartet—which appropriately is named the *Emperor*—this theme is subjected to a series of variations.

While Haydn wrote many other chamber-music compositions—duos of all sorts, a quintet, sextet, and so forth—he reserved his noblest materials for the string quartet. This was not strictly true of Mozart who, despite the magnificence of his string-quartet music, was also capable of producing masterworks for other chamber-music combinations, too.

Mozart wrote his first string quartet in 1770. He completed a dozen more between 1772 and 1773 before his full creative power was in evidence. He inherited form and style from Haydn, whom he admired profoundly; the earliest Mozart quartets betray this indebtedness. But as Mozart kept on writing his individuality asserted itself more and more. While he did virtually nothing to advance the form as Haydn crystallized it, he did succeed in filling it with a depth of feeling and thought rarely encountered in Haydn. Also unique was his courageous willingness—determination might be the apter word—to experiment with his harmonic and melodic constructions.

Mozart's greatest quartets are gathered in a set of six, completed between 1782 and 1785, and dedicated to Haydn. Never before was Mozart so complete a master of his means, and so concerned with the poetic or dramatic content. Never before was he so daring in essaying the untried! The opening bar of the *Quartet in C Major* (K. 465) opens with a discord that startled and shocked his contemporaries; to this day, this work is known as the *Dissonant Quartet*. The finale of the *Quartet in G Major* (K. 387) has a sudden excursion from the polyphony of a fugal passage to homophony in a way to electrify the ear. The *Quartet in B Flat Major* (K. 458), known as the *Hunt Quartet* because the opening theme suggests a hunting call, is of such bold invention throughout that even Haydn was puzzled and could only say: "If Mozart wrote it, he must have a good reason to do so."

Mozart wrote twenty-six string quartets. But the literature of Mozart's chamber music contains treasures for various other instrumental combinations. Among his finest works are five string quintets, including the *Quintet in G Minor* (K. 516) which is so poignant a work that it has been described by some as the "quintet of death." Other composers before Mozart had written various compositions for five instruments (mostly divertimenti); but the five-string quintets of Mozart are the first examples of a string-quintet combination—since then, the most popular—of two violins, viola, and two cellos. Mozart also wrote a *Quintet for Clarinet and Strings, in A Major* (K. 581) which is one of his most greatly admired chamber-music works. Mozart produced two splendid piano quartets (piano, violin, viola and cello), of which the first, in G minor (K. 478), has one of his most deeply felt slow movements and a finale of architectural grandeur. There are also two quartets for flute and strings, and a delightful quartet for oboe and strings. Other chamber-music works by Mozart include various duets; various trios; more than forty sonatas for violin and piano (commented upon in the analysis of the sonata in the next section); and so forth.

Beethoven was partial to the string-quartet form, in which he communicated some of his most personal, and subsequently, some of his most imaginative and daring, concepts. Beethoven wrote sixteen string quartets which hold as significant a position in chamber music as his sonatas do in piano literature and his symphonies in orchestral music. These sixteen quartets were written during the entire expanse of Beethoven's creative life: his first quartet was sketched as early as 1795; his last came one year before his death, in 1826. His development as a composer can be clearly traced in the transformation to which the form and content of the string quartet were subjected.

His first quartets, a set of six works (op. 18), were written in the six-year period between 1794 and 1800: they are known as the *Lobkowitz Quartets* because they were dedicated to Prince Lobkowitz, one of Beethoven's patrons. The style and structure are those of Mozart—but with differences. Now and then we get brusque accents, vigorous rhythms, passionate outbursts that reflect Beethoven's virile nature. The tragic accents of some of these pages—the slow movement of the first quartet and the concluding "La Malinconia" of the sixth quartet —are identifiably Beethoven's.

Beginning with the first of the three quartets found in the op. 59 group, Beethoven completely parts company with the past. These works are known as the *Rasoumovsky Quartets,* having been commissioned by and written for Count Rasoumovsky, Russian Ambassador to Austria. Remembering the nationality of his patron, Beethoven interpolated Russian melodies in the first two of these works: in the finale of the first, and in the third movement of the second. But it is not its Russian identity that distinguishes these quartets and sets them sharply apart from all other chamber music of that period. What we have here is an altogether new manner of writing: dramatic contrasts; turbulent emotions; a spiritual radiance in the serener moments; huge designs of the structure, and enlargement of the thematic developments. There is also a subtle unity among the individual movements of each quartet, creating a single monumental drama. The three quartets represent three different moods. The first, in F major, is dramatic; it is unusual structurally in that it employs the sonata form in all four movements. The second, in E minor, is tragic, with a slow movement that is one of the most eloquent pages found in the Beethoven of the middle period; the third, in C major, has a heroic character.

Beethoven wrote several quartets before producing the so-called "last quartets" which are among the most provocative of all his works. In his last four quartets Beethoven arrived at an altogether new concept of form, and a new way of expressing poetic ideas. His language becomes more spiritual, more touched with mysticism, more weighted by profound ideas than ever before—he had found a new kind of music. The structure becomes ever more spacious. The *Quartet in B Flat Major* (op. 130) is in six movements; the *Quartet in C Sharp Minor* (op. 131) is in seven. As Beethoven sought more *Lebensraum* for his thoughts and feelings, his form became so elastic as to be, at times, almost amorphous. Here we find strange modulations, intervals, harmonies—harsh accents and abrupt moods—to startle the imagination. The formal presentation of themes is replaced by a new method in which a fragment of a theme is succeeded by another fragment; the fragments return, are transformed, then are finally built into an inextricable unity. This is a new kind of musical coherence.

It is not easy to comprehend the music of Beethoven's last quartets; for several generations musical authorities spoke disparagingly about them. But as we grow intimate with them, as we are able to follow the flight of Beethoven's subtle thought, we realize that music of greater nobility, depth, and other-worldly concept has not been written. This is music in which is compressed a lifetime of grief and struggle, and in which victory over both is complete. As we listen to the Cavatina of the *B Flat Major Quartet,* to the opening slow fugue of the *C Sharp Minor Quartet,* and to the slow movement of the *F Major Quartet* (op. 135), we find ourselves in the presence of what Wagner once described as a "transcendental calm, which can come only when the heart has found true peace."

Beethoven wrote one more work for string quartet, and this, too, came in his last period. It is the *Grosse-Fugue (Grand Fugue).* Originally, this fugue was the last movement of the *B Flat Major Quartet.* But the publisher considered it too recondite in style and too difficult of performance, and he prevailed on Beethoven to write a different finale for his quartet. The *Grosse-Fugue* was then published as an independent and self-sufficient work (op. 133). It is a great dramatic exhortation, filled with tensions, and creating a powerful momentum from the beginning to the end.

Among Beethoven's other works for other chamber-music combinations, the most celebrated are some of his sonatas for violin and piano and for cello and piano (they are discussed in the next section), and the *Trio in B Flat Major,* op. 97, called the *Archduke,* because it was dedicated to his pupil, the Archduke Rudolph.

Franz Schubert wrote eighteen string quartets which are of uneven quality. But the best are sustained masterworks. Probably no other composer brought such a wealth of melodic beauty into string-quartet music as Franz Schubert did in the *Quartet in A Minor.* The slow movement of this work uses a melody of which Schubert was particularly fond, since it is found in a piano impromptu (op. 142, no. 3) and in one of the entr'actes in *Rosamunde* (B flat minor). It is easy to see why he was so partial to it, since it is one of the most moving and eloquent of his lyric inspirations. The plane of eloquence is sustained throughout the entire slow movement of the quartet, so much so that H. L. Mencken once said that this music was the most convincing proof he could find for the existence of God.

Another of Schubert's masterworks in the string-quartet form is the *Quartet in D Minor,* better known as the *Death and the Maiden Quartet.* In the slow movement, Schubert uses the first part of his song, "Death and the Maiden," and then constructs a series of variations around it. But the feeling of death is prevalent in the other movements, too: in the struggle and defiance of the first movement, in the feverish unrest of the third movement, and in the brief quotation from another Schubert song about death ("Der Erlkönig") in the last.

Schubert wrote two quintets that are unique. One of these is the beloved *Quintet in A Major,* the *Die Forelle,* or *Trout.* This is the first important quintet to use the combination of a piano and strings. The instrumentation is most unusual: the strings include a double-bass with the violin, viola and cello. The number of movements is also unusual— five in place of the traditional four. Once again Schubert quotes himself. This time it is the gay and lovable song, "The Trout" (Die Forelle), which is heard in the fourth movement as the basis of a series of six variations.

Schubert's other celebrated quintet, in the key of C major, also requires an unusual combination of instruments: two violins, viola, and two cellos. It was written in the last year of Schubert's life, and it reflects the intensity of the physical and mental sufferings Schubert experienced at that time. Where the *Die Forelle Quintet* is throughout effervescent and light of heart, the *Quintet in C Major* is profoundly tragic. Even in the scherzo movement—usually in a light vein with other composers—there is a dirge in the middle Trio section which some writers think is Schubert's requiem for himself. But if we are to search for a requiem in this work it is surely found in the Adagio, filled as it is with an impenetrable gloom—one of the most pessimistic utterances in all chamber music.

Schubert also wrote two fine piano trios—B flat and E flat—both in the year of 1827. Both works have beautiful slow movements. That in the *B Flat Major Quartet* is an idyllic and tender melody, while the one in E flat is a funeral march. Schubert's other chamber-music compositions include the highly melodious *Octet,* for two violins, viola, cello, double-bass, clarinet, bassoon, and horn, written in 1824.

Robert Schumann wrote three string quartets in a single year (1842); the best of these is the *Quartet in A Major.* An interesting technical feature in this work is the emphasis on a specific interval, or intervals, in the melodies—the intervals of fourths and fifths in the first movement; fourths, in the second movement; sevenths, in the third movement; and sixths in the finale.

Besides the three string quartets, Schumann wrote a *Piano Quartet in E Flat Major,* and a *Piano Quintet in E Flat* (the last generally considered his greatest chamber-music work). The piano quintet is filled with some of Schumann's most felicitous lyricism, particularly in the slow movement, which resembles a funeral march. There is also some remarkable polyphonic writing in the finale, the crown being a giant fugue built out of main themes from the first and fourth movements.

Mendelssohn's finest chamber-music works—his *String Octet* and his *String Quartet in E Flat Major*—are the creations of his youth. The former was written when he was sixteen; the latter, four years after that. Youthful ardor, exuberance, freshness are the identifying qualities of both works. What it lacks in profundity of thought or feeling it makes up for with grace and tenderness and spontaneity. The familiar "Canzonetta" from the string quartet and the Scherzo from the octet are in Mendelssohn's recognizable fairy-like, diaphanous style.

Mendelssohn's chamber music is a less significant facet of his over-all production. This was not the case with Brahms. It was with his chamber music that Brahms first impressed his genius upon his contemporaries. Two piano quartets written in 1861, and the great *Piano*

*Quintet in F Minor,* are Brahms' first masterworks. Passion and soaring emotion—at other times poetic introspection and an autumnal beauty —are already evident in these early works; and they are qualities which we have come to associate with Brahms. An interesting characteristic of the two piano quartets is the interpolation of Hungarian dance rhythms in the finale of each.

Brahms came comparatively late to the string quartet, completing his first two quartets (C minor and A minor) in 1873. There is greater emotional restraint in these works than in, say, the popular *Piano Quintet.* The *A Minor Quartet,* particularly, is characterized by its sobriety, economy, and reflectiveness. The hot blood of youth has made way for the pensiveness of full maturity. In 1875, Brahms completed his third and last quartet (B flat major) in which the virility of his early chamber-music works is again in evidence, and which has a prevailing mood of gaiety and healthy spirits.

We have mentioned the *Piano Quintet* as one of Brahms' most popular chamber-music works. Another quintet, this time for clarinet and strings, also belongs with Brahms' best known and most frequently heard chamber-music works. The *Clarinet Quintet* (in B minor) was written in the last years of Brahms' life, in 1891. Here too—as in the first two string quartets—there is mellowness and a gentle sadness, moods for which the elegiac voice of the clarinet is particularly appropriate. This is one of Brahms' most melodic works, but the melodies are invariably wistful and reflective.

The prolific library of Brahms' chamber music includes two string quintets, two string sextets, and various trios and sonatas. There is a major point of interest in the *Piano Trio in B Major.* Brahms wrote it originally in 1854 when he was only twenty-one years old. Thirty-seven years later—and at the height of his creative powers—he revised it completely. Both versions of this trio exist, and both are still heard— providing a fascinating study in the development of a genius. The second version is a phenomenon among Brahms' works in that it combines the effusiveness and ardor of youthful writing with the supreme craftsmanship and immaculate taste of maturity.

While the works of Antonín Dvořák are deeply rooted in Bohemian folk music his two best chamber-music works were inspired by American idioms. Both were written during Dvořák's stay in this country, in the year 1893. The *Quartet in F Major,* known as the *American Quartet,* has pleasing melodies whose similarity to plantation songs of the Negro and Spirituals is obvious. The *String Quintet in E Flat Major* has lyrical ideas and rhythms derived from the exotic music of the American Indian; the throb of Indian ceremonial drums is felt in the first and third movements.

Another distinguished Bohemian composer, Bedrich Smetana, produced an autobiographical document in his finest chamber-music composition: the *Quartet in E Minor,* which he himself subtitled "From My Life." This work was written in 1876, two years after the composer knew he was growing deaf. This discovery inspired him to review his life and career—in music. The first movement tells of his early love of art and folk music and his romantic yearnings; the second movement, a polka, describes youth's joys; the slow movement depicts Smetana's love affair with the woman he married; and the finale begins with his exhilaration in discovering Bohemian folk music and allowing it to influence his own writing, and ends with the catastrophe of his deafness.

Though the Russian nationalist composers preferred the opera and orchestral music they made occasional excursions into chamber music. Borodin's *Quartet in D Major*—the finest movement of which is the beautiful Nocturne—is one of the peaks in Russian chamber music. Tchaikovsky's pleasing *Quartet in D Major* is remembered exclusively for its slow movement—the Andante Cantabile, one of the composer's most popular pieces of music.

French chamber music flowered with the late Romantics. The *Piano Quintet in F Minor,* the *String Quartet in D Major,* and the *Sonata for Violin and Piano in A Major* contain the essence of César Franck's style; this is reflective music of incomparable serenity and spiritual beauty. Gabriel Fauré's *Piano Quartet in C Minor* and two piano quintets are in a similar vein. Musical Impressionism entered chamber music with Claude Debussy's only string quartet (G minor), and further unfolded in Ravel's *String Quartet in F Minor,* and Florent Schmitt's *Quintet in B Minor.*

One of the most significant additions to contemporary chamber-music literature was made by the Hungarian composer, Béla Bartók. His six quartets are remarkable for their daring invention of harmony and tonality, originality in writing for the strings, and contrasts in sonority. These quartets also represent the evolution of Bartók's style. An early work, like the *Quartet No. 2 in A Minor* (1917), is in the advanced idiom assumed by Bartók at that period—made up of broken rhythms, dissonant chords, fragmentary melodies, and cogent rhythms. With each succeeding quartet, Bartók showed less and less tendency to indulge in strong and independent statements, and a greater interest in an objective approach and in economical means. His *Quartet No. 6,* written in 1939, is a conscious attempt to arrive at simplicity of style and clarity of structure.

There is even greater iconoclasm in the string quartets of Arnold Schoenberg, apostle of the twelve-tone technique. In his *String Quartet No. 2* (1908), Schoenberg departed from a traditional tonality; in *String Quartet No. 3* (1926) he used the twelve-tone technique in music that is austere and deprived of all emotion. But in his *String Quartet No. 4,* written in 1937, Schoenberg was able to combine the dynamic power of his earlier works with an awareness of the heart; the third movement has great expressive feeling, with a principal melody that has striking resemblance to the traditional Hebraic song, "Kol Nidrei." Schoenberg's most famous chamber-music work, however, is the sextet *Verklaerte Nacht,* which he completed in 1899, but which he subsequently transcribed for string orchestra. Another famous chamber-music work of the Schoenberg school is the *Lyric Suite,* for string quartet, by Alban Berg.

Darius Milhaud also made important contributions to contemporary chamber-music literature. Throughout his life he has written works for the string quartet. The earlier quartets have frequently an intriguing lightness of touch, brevity, and charm. The later quartets are more animated, and often more original. Milhaud embarked on a highly unique experiment with his *String Quartets Nos. 14 and 15.* These two quartets are contrasts in style. Milhaud has planned these works so that they can be played independently, and enjoyed as separate works, or played together simultaneously as an octet.

Many other leading composers of the twentieth century have produced significant works in this field. Shostakovich's *Piano Quintet* (1940) is one of his most human and lyrical works, despite its strictly classical form; it begins with a prelude and fugue, continues with a scherzo, and ends with an intermezzo in a march rhythm. Prokofiev's two string quartets reflect this composer's consistently high standard of inspiration. The second, completed in 1942, is particularly interesting for its use of Caucasian folk songs.

American composers have also produced some of their most notable works for small groups. Among them should be singled out Ernest

Bloch, whose three string quartets and *Piano Quintet* are among the finest in American music. Other distinguished works include Roy Harris' *Quartet No. 3,* and *Piano Quintet;* Quincy Porter's half dozen or so quartets; and Aaron Copland's *Piano Quartet.*

Modern music embraces many other works for chamber-music groups which fall into the formal class of trio, quartet, or quintet, and so forth. In this category we find a remarkable set of seven works which Paul Hindemith wrote early in his career for various groups and which he entitled collectively *Kammermusik* (Chamber Music). In this category we also find compositions like Manuel de Falla's *Concerto for Harpsichord, Flute, Oboe, Clarinet, Violin and Piano;* Ravel's *Introduction and Allegro,* for harp, string quartet, flute, and clarinet; and Turina's *La Oracio del Torero,* for string quartet.

# Basic Forms of Instrumental Music

### ALLEMANDE

*See below:* Suite.

### ARABESQUE

A composition for the piano in which the melody is ornamented. In ancient and Renaissance art an arabesque referred to a fanciful bit of ornamentation. Robert Schumann adapted this term for piano music: His *Arabesque in C Major* is a delicate piece with a highly decorative melodic line, and a poetic epilogue. Debussy wrote two fine arabesques for piano, and some arabesques are found in the piano works of the twentieth-century Russian composer, Nicolas Medtner.

### BAGATELLE

A slight piece for the piano, of brief duration, and unpretentious in its content (see Part Six).

### BALLADE

A composition for the piano, with a narrative character. It is comparatively free in form and improvisatory in style. While most ballades do not have a specific program, they all appear to tell some kind of story through the dramatic character of the music.

The term "ballade" acquired significance in music with Chopin. He wrote four works in that form. Chopin himself explained that his first two ballades, in G minor and F major, were inspired by the poems of the Polish patriot, Adam Mitskeyvich. Some believe that the *G Minor Ballade* recreates *Konrad Volenrod,* which describes the battle between the pagan Lithuanians and the Christian Knights.

Liszt wrote two familiar ballades, for piano, in each of which lyrical and tender themes are contrasted with rhythmic and passionate ones. The *Ballade in B Minor* has dramatic, even theatrical interest. Grieg's famous *Ballade in G Minor* is based on a Norwegian melody and consists of a series of variations. Brahms wrote five ballades, the first of which (D minor) retells the story of the Scottish poem, "Edward." Fauré wrote a poetic and serene ballade, in F sharp minor, for piano solo, and later adapted it for piano and orchestra; it is now most often heard in the latter version.

## BARCAROLLE

A boat song of the Venetian gondoliers. Generally, a barcarolle is a form of vocal music, but it has been successfully adapted as a form of piano music as well. As a piano composition, it has a melody that simulates a Venetian boat song, while the rhythm suggests the gentle sway of a gondola in the water (as, Chopin's *Barcarolle in F Sharp Major*). Mendelssohn's *Songs Without Words* contains two fine barcarolles, each appropriately called "Venetian Boat Song" (G minor and F sharp minor).

## BERCEUSE

A cradle song, or lullaby. Like the barcarolle it is most often a form of vocal music. Several composers have adapted it for the piano where the melodic character of the lullaby or cradle song is simulated in the principal theme. In Chopin's *Berceuse in D Flat Major* we even get the rocking of the cradle in the rhythm.

## BOURRÉE

*See below:* Suite.

## CAPRICCIO

The Italian word for "caprice," discussed below. In writing seven capriccios for the piano, Brahms used the term as a diminutive for "caprice." His pieces are, in short, "little caprices"—light-hearted, gay, and whimsical musical fancies. His second capriccio, in B minor, is particularly well known. Its main melody, in staccato, pursues a kind of butterfly flight, while a contrasting second melody is tranquil.

## CAPRICE

A short piece, quick in tempo, which exploits whimsy or surprise or fanciful ideas through sudden changes of mood or style. It has become a popular form of violin music.

Originally the term "caprice" was used for certain vocal works in the contrapuntal style (sixteenth century)—fugal fantasias. In the seventeenth century, Frescobaldi wrote fugal organ caprices; later organ composers used "caprice" to describe fugues in a comparatively free style. Harpsichord composers used "caprice" interchangeably with "fantasia"—as in some of Johann Sebastian Bach's partitas, and in Karl Philipp Emanuel Bach's *Capriccio on the Departure of a Dear Friend*.

As a violin form, caprice was made famous by Niccolo Paganini who wrote twenty-four such pieces for unaccompanied violin. (Several musicians have written piano accompaniments for the Paganini caprices; and both Liszt and Schumann transcribed some of these caprices for the piano). Paganini made the caprice a kind of étude in which a melody recurs frequently, and in which the virtuosity of the performer is demonstrated through passages of great technical brilliance and dexterity. Paganini's most celebrated caprice is the Twenty-Fourth, where the melody is followed by a series of dazzling variations. The main melody of this *Twenty-Fourth Caprice* was also used by Brahms and Rachmaninoff for major works in the variation form: Brahms' *Variations and Fugue on a Theme of Paganini* (for solo piano), and Rachmaninoff's *Rhapsody on a Theme of Paganini* (for piano and orchestra).

Another popular violin caprice is Fritz Kreisler's *Caprice Viennois*. The caprice is found in the introductory page with its quixotic leaps of intervals, glissandi, and so forth. This caprice prefaces a beautiful melody in double stops which has also become famous as the song, "An Old Story."

It should also be noticed that the form of caprice, or capriccio, has also been used for orchestral music. These works are discussed in the orchestral section.

## CHACONNE

An old, slow folk dance which is believed to be of Spanish origin. As a form of organ music it is characterized by a four-beat theme that is constantly repeated in the bass, while the treble provides variations. The chaconne is virtually the same as the passacaglia; the two terms were used interchangeably by composers of the seventeenth century.

While the chaconne was a form of organ music—and was developed as such by Frescobaldi and Buxtehude—it acquired prominence in other branches of music. Early opera composers (Lully, Rameau, and Gluck) sometimes ended their operas with a chaconne. The chaconne also became one of the movements of the classical suite (*see below:* Suite), and through this avenue it entered harpsichord literature; notable chaconnes for the harpsichord were written by Purcell and Handel. The most famous chaconne in all music is one for unaccompanied violin: the concluding movement of Johann Sebastian Bach's *Partita in D Minor,* where a stately melody is followed by thirty-three variations. Another familiar chaconne for the violin is by the Italian composer, Tommaso Antonio Vitali—the only work of his that has survived.

## CHORALE PRELUDE

A short piece for the organ, in vogue in seventeenth century Germany, in which the performer reveals his skill in contrapuntal improvisation.

The chorale prelude was first developed by Sweelinck in the sixteenth century. The evolution of this form parallels that of most organ music: from Scheidt to Buxtehude, and from Buxtehude to Johann Sebastian Bach. Bach used the chorale prelude as a brief preface to a hymn melody, and it became a kind of fantasia on that melody. Bach completed more than one hundred chorale preludes. The best of these are among his finest pieces for the organ: *Ein' feste Burg, Ich ruf' zu dir, Nun komm der Heiden Heiland,* and *Wir glauben all'.* Forty-five chorale preludes are gathered in the volume called *Orgelbüchelein,* meant for various seasons of the Church calendar—beginning with Advent; continuing with Christmas, New Year's Eve, New Year's Day, through Ascension, Whitsunday, and Trinity Sunday; and ending with The Christian Life.

There are not many examples of chorale-prelude music after Bach's day. A notable exception are the eleven chorale preludes of Brahms, gathered in two volumes, and among that composer's last works (written in 1896, and published as op. 122).

## COURANTE

*See below:* Suite.

## ÉCOSSAISE

A dance, believed to be of Scottish origin, in 2/4 or 3/4 time, introduced into France toward the end of the eighteenth century. As a form of piano music it was used by Beethoven, Chopin, and Schubert.

## ÉTUDE

Strictly speaking, an exercise for the violin, or piano, and so forth, posing a technical problem and serving the pedagogical purpose of helping solve that problem. In this category are found the splendid and widely utilized études of Czerny, Cramer, and Clementi, for the piano, and those of Kreutzer, and Rode, for the violin.

The étude is also a form commanding the serious attention of the composer. Chopin wrote twenty-four études for the piano which began with the premise that the étude is an exercise for the pianist, but ended with the realization that it was capable of becoming the medium for serious art. Individual Chopin études touch on the problem of arpeggios, chromatic scale exercises, syncopation, passages in thirds, sixths, and octaves. But Chopin's creative genius transformed exercise pieces into important music. If the science of contemporary piano technique is formulated in these Chopin études, we also find here a whole gamut of poetic and emotional expression. Because of their musical distinction —apart from their pedagogical value—these pieces are referred to as "concert études" to differentiate them from the Czerny-like étude. Among Chopin's most frequently heard études are the following: the so-called *Revolutionary Étude* (Op. 10, no. 2) in which the composer's patriotism for Poland finds expression; the *Étude in E Major* (op. 10, no. 3), regarded by the composer himself as one of his finest works; the so-called *Black Key Étude* (op. 10, no. 5) which employs the black keys exclusively; and the étude known as *The Butterfly* (op. 25, no. 9), one of Chopin's most gossamer creations.

Liszt wrote many concert études in which the dynamics and technique of the piano are extended and which are either dramatic, poetic, or atmospheric. Liszt's *Paganini Études* (inspired by a visit of Paganini to Paris in 1831) utilize melodic material from the Paganini caprices; the famous *Campanella* is one of these items.

Debussy's *Twelve Études* have opened new horizons for piano colors and dynamics. Each étude poses a different problem. In the first book, there are exercises in thirds, fourths, sixths, octaves, and so forth. In the second book, the problems of chromatic intervals, grace notes, arpeggios, and chords are explored. As in the case of Chopin, technical problems become effective artistic concepts due to Debussy's creative imagination and harmonic daring. The Debussy études are also interesting in that they embody the main characteristics of his individual piano style.

Some of Scriabin's *Twenty-Four Études* betray the influence of Chopin and Brahms. Scriabin, however, interests himself in unusual harmonic progressions and rhythmic patterns. The études in op. 65, and the étude, op. 8, no. 2, are of particular interest—the first group for its new melodic and harmonic resources; the latter étude for its powerful and passionate expression.

Robert Schumann wrote an extended work for the piano employing the étude form: *Études symphoniques.* This extended work is not so much a series of short études as it is a composition in the theme-and-variations form; but each of the twelve variations has an étude-like personality.

## FANTASIA (or FANTAISIE)

A work, flexible in form, allowing for complete freedom in presentation and elaboration of the melodic ideas. Originally, a fantasia utilized the contrapuntal style. The word was first used in a collection by the Spanish contrapuntist, Luis Milan, published in 1536. It is with the early Italian contrapuntists (the Gabrielis, Sweelinck, and so forth) that the form became popular in organ music. The fantasia form was further developed by Frescobaldi and Froberger, both of whom introduced the variation technique which was henceforth to characterize organ fantasias. The apotheosis of this form was realized with Johann Sebastian Bach who sometimes used it to preface a fugue, as in the case of the famous *Fantasia and Fugue in G Minor.* Some later composers wrote organ fantasias, among them Franz Liszt (*Fantasia and Fugue on a chorale from Meyerbeer's Le Prophète*) and Max Reger.

The fantasia form was also used for instruments other than the organ, and for combinations of instruments. Purcell's four-part and five-part fantasias, for strings, are among the most important examples of early instrumental writing. The most unique of these Purcell works is the *Fantasia on One Note* in which the violas sustain the note "C" while other instruments decorate that note with harmonic and melodic arabesques.

The fantasia form was used successfully for the piano. Bach's *Chromatic Fantasy and Fugue* is an early application of the organ fantasia to the piano, and at the same time a successful application of the fantasia form to the chromatic scale. Mozart wrote several fantasias notable for their dramatic effect, and spaciousness of form, as in the *Fantasia in C Minor* (K. 475) which was written in conjunction with the *Sonata in C Minor* (K. 457). Schubert utilized his song "Der Wanderer" as the starting point for an extended *Fantasia in C Major* for solo piano. (But it is best known in the Liszt arrangement for piano and orchestra.) Chopin's *Fantaisie Impromptu in C Sharp Minor* is an interesting amalgamation of the fantasia form and the impromptu. Schumann's *Fantasy in C Major* is one of his monumental creations—in a heroic vein, though ending on a pensive and lyrical note. Brahms designated his set of piano pieces (op. 116) as *"fantasien,"*—though they contained capriccios and intermezzi—probably to emphasize their improvisational character.

The fantasia form, as used in orchestral music, is discussed in the orchestral section.

## FOLIA

A Spanish dance in ¾ time. One of these dance tunes became extremely popular in the seventeenth century and was used by many instrumental composers as the basis for variations: a celebrated example is Corelli's *La Folia,* for violin and piano.

## FORLANE

*See below:* Suite.

## FUGATO

A passage in fugal style.

## FUGHETTA

A little fugue.

## FUGUE

This is the most complex and the most exact of all the organ forms. The fugue represents the most advanced stage of development of a contrapuntal technique found in the early choral pieces, namely the "round" and "canon." In these pieces a single melody is taken up by successive voices to create a polyphonic texture. But in the fugue, the technique follows a set and elaborate pattern. The number of voices—or parts—in a fugue is usually three, four, or five. After the theme is presented by one voice, it is followed by an answer: the same theme a fifth higher or a fourth lower. Together with the answer we get a countersubject in another voice. The third voice then enters with the theme, after which a fourth voice arrives with the answer—and so on. A development section follows, and after that a recapitulation.

The fugue form was developed in the sixteenth and seventeenth centuries by such early organ composers as Sweelinck and Frescobaldi. The early German organ composers—including Froberger and Buxtehude—developed it further. The greatest master of the fugue was Johann Sebastian Bach. His fugues are the last word both in polyphonic skill and variety of thought, for spaciousness of architectonic design and nobility of concept. Bach's fugues for organ are prefaced by fantasias, or toccatas, or preludes. His epic in the fugue form is a work called *The Art of the Fugue,* written in the last year of the composer's life in which the science of fugal writing, on a given theme, is virtually exhausted. It is not known definitely whether Bach intended this work for the organ or for the piano.

The fugue, as a form of organ music, attracted composers after Bach's time, too. Mendelssohn wrote a set of preludes and fugues for organ; so did Saint-Saëns. Schumann wrote six fugues on a theme derived from the name of "B-A-C-H." (In German notation the letter "h" represents B natural; consequently the four letters of Bach's name, translated into tones, can be used as a theme.) Liszt also wrote a fugue on Bach's name. Organ fugues were written by many other composers including Brahms, Reger, and Rheinberger.

The fugue was, of course, not exclusively reserved for the organ. It is found in great choral music—in the passions, masses, requiems of

Haydn, Mozart, Beethoven, Brahms, Verdi, and so forth. Verdi's opera *Falstaff* ends with a vocal fugue. Johann Sebastian Bach wrote many fugues for the clavier, including those in the monumental *Well-Tempered Clavier,* which consists of forty-eight preludes and fugues. Fugues also appear in piano works by Mendelssohn (*Prelude and Fugue in E Minor*) and Brahms (*Variations and Fugue on a Theme of Handel*). Beethoven wrote a *Grosse Fugue* for string quartet; the opening movement of his *Quartet in C Sharp Minor,* op. 131, is a slow fugue. Mozart wrote an effective *Adagio and Fugue,* for strings. There are even interesting examples of fugal writing in contemporary music—notable examples being found in Ernest Bloch's *Concerto Grosso,* for strings (concluding movement), and Roy Harris' *String Quartet No. 3* (which comprises three preludes and fugues).

## GIGUE

*See below:* Suite.

## GAVOTTE

*See below:* Suite.

## HABANERA
### (in French, *Havanaise*)

A song and dance believed to have originated in Africa, but become popular in Spain and in Havana, Cuba. It is in duple rhythm with the first beat dotted. While the most famous of all habaneras in music is the soprano aria in Bizet's opera, *Carmen,* the form is found in instrumental music. Debussy's *La Soirée dans Grenade,* for piano, is a habanera; Chabrier also wrote a fine *Habanera* for the piano. In 1895, Ravel wrote a *Habanera,* for two pianos, which he subsequently orchestrated and included in his *Rapsodie espagnole.* Saint-Saëns' *Havanaise,* for violin and piano (also for violin and orchestra), is familiar.

## HUMORESQUE

A short, and usually slight, piece generally gay or whimsical. Schumann wrote a *Humoresque* for piano which is something of a misnomer since it does not fulfil this specification, actually being a suite. The *Humoresques* of Dvořák are much more characteristic, particularly the highly popular *Humoresque* (op. 101, no. 7), familiar in transcriptions for violin and piano. The fanciful and lively character of Grieg's *Humoresques* is also characteristic. Paderewski's famous *Minuet* was designated by the composer as a "humoresque de concert."

## IMPROMPTU

This piano piece suggests an improvisation, but it is actually an extended song form. The impromptu originated as a musical form in 1822 with the Bohemian composer, Vorisek. It became famous with Schubert, who not only expropriated the term from the Bohemian composer but also some of the Bohemian traits found in Vorisek's pieces: the irregular rhythms, sharp accentuations, and folk character of the melody. Schubert wrote eight impromptus, each being a developed song for the piano. The third impromptu, in B flat major (op. 142), utilizes a melody Schubert was particularly fond of, he utilized it several times in different works. Chopin wrote four impromptus. The last of these, *Fantaisie Impromptu,* is the most famous; its principal melody was used by an American popular song composer for the song hit, "I'm Always Chasing Rainbows." Schumann wrote a set of impromptus on a theme of Clara Wieck (op. 5)—a set of variations.

## INTERMEZZO

As a form of orchestral music, the intermezzo is discussed in the section on Orchestral Music.

In instrumental music, it sometimes appears as a slow transition between two movements (as in Beethoven's *Waldstein Sonata,* for piano).

The composers of the Romantic Era created an independent form which they called "intermezzo": a short piano piece with no specific form but expressing some brief thought. Schumann wrote six intermezzi (op. 4) which are extended songs for the piano. Brahms' eighteen intermezzi for piano are particularly famous. Brahms used this form to express intimate revelations—sometimes elegiac, sometimes stormy, sometimes pensive. The *Intermezzo in E Flat Major* (op. 117, no. 9) is a cradle song inspired by the Scottish ballad, "Lady Anne Bothwell's Lament." The *Intermezzo in B Flat Minor* (op. 117, no. 1) combines a gentle melancholy with restlessness, while the *Intermezzo in E Minor* (op. 119, no. 2) is a love song.

## INVENTION

A musical idea, a short form for the piano popularized by Johann Sebastian Bach (see Part Six).

## LOURE

*See below:* Suite.

## MALAGUEÑA

A Spanish dance from Malaga in which the melody resembles an improvisation. The form has been effectively used by instrumental composers: for the violin, by Pablo de Sarasate; for the piano, by Albéniz and Ernesto Lecuona.

## MARCH

While a march is essentially music for a band or orchestra (see orchestral section), there are many examples of marches for the keyboard. Little marches are found in the harpsichord music of Couperin. Mozart incorporated a "Turkish March" in his *Sonata in A Major.* Schubert wrote a very popular Military March for four hands (op. 41, no. 1), while Chopin's Funeral March in his *Sonata No. 2,* for piano, is the most celebrated of all funeral marches.

## MAZURKA

A Polish national dance which Chopin adapted into a form of piano music. He wrote fifty-five mazurkas.

The Polish dance is characterized by its two or four sections, its triple time, its accentuation on the second or third beat, and its improvisational character. These qualities are found in Chopin's mazurkas.

Within this form Chopin poured his nationalistic ardor. He loved his native land, Poland. Since most of his creative life was spent as an expatriate, he found an outlet for his intense nationalism by writing music in the style of Polish folk dances. Chopin's mazurkas are usually fiery, abandoned, and passionate; but a few of them are poetic and nostalgic. Some highly effective mazurkas for the piano were also written by the twentieth-century Polish composer, Karol Szymanowski, who was greatly influenced by Chopin.

## MINUET

A slow and stately dance of French origin, in triple time. It was extremely popular in European courts up to the eighteenth century. Its great popularity inspired composers everywhere to write music within this form. It is in three sections, the middle part being a trio, and the last part repeating the first. Minuets are found in the old classical suite (see below). They appear as a movement in the classical sonatas and quartets. Beethoven's celebrated *Minuet in G* is the second in a set of six such pieces for the piano, published without opus number in 1796. No less popular is Paderewski's *Menuet à l'antique,* the first of six pieces for the piano collectively entitled *Humoresques de concert* (op. 14).

The minuet, in orchestral music, is commented upon in the orchestral section.

## MOMENT MUSICAL

A form for the piano created by Franz Schubert. It is a brief musical episode, mood, or sentiment expressed in a musical miniature. Ernest Hutcheson admirably described it as a "tidbit for the musical epicure." Schubert wrote six of these pieces (op. 94), the most famous being the *Moment Musical in F Minor* (no. 3).

## MUSETTA

A simple and tender air or dance in $\frac{2}{4}$, $\frac{3}{4}$, or $\frac{6}{8}$ time.

## NOCTURNE

This term originated with orchestral music of the Classical Era. It has a different connotation in Romantic piano literature, where it suggests a romantic and poetic piece of music suggesting the night. The piano form was created by John Field, who preceded Chopin, but whose pieces suggested the style and form perfected by the Polish master. It was Chopin who made the nocturne form famous in music. He wrote twenty of these pieces. Each is usually in three parts (the third section repeating the first). It is filled with poetic, sentimental moods. Probably the most famous of the Chopin nocturnes is the one in E flat major (op. 9, no. 2). This is familiar not only in its original piano version but also in transcriptions for violin and piano, and cello and piano. Another famous Chopin nocturne is the one in A flat major (op. 32, no. 2), used prominently in the ballet *Les Sylphides*.

The nocturne is also found in orchestral music, and is further discussed in that section.

## NONET

A musical composition for nine instruments.

## NOVELETTE

A brief piece for the piano, with no set form, and with a narrative character. It was introduced by Robert Schumann in a set of eight pieces (op. 21). While none of these have a title to provide a clue to the program, each seems to tell a story. Nicolas Medtner also wrote pieces under this name.

## OCTET

A musical composition for eight instruments.

## PARTITA

A term used in early classical music interchangeably with the suite, and like the latter form it consists of a group of old dances (*see below:* Suite). Bach's six partitas for the piano, and three partitas for unaccompanied violin are really suites, and have dance movements.

## PASSACAGLIA

Originally a Spanish dance in slow time, but transformed into a form of organ music by the early Italian organ composers. Structurally, it is so similar to the chaconne (see above) that the two terms have been used interchangeably. Frescobaldi was one of the first masters to write passacaglias for the organ; the form was further developed by Buxtehude; while Johann Sebastian Bach brought it to its ultimate evolution. Bach's *Passacaglia in C Minor* is both the greatest work in that form and one of Bach's crowning creations for the organ. It has also become famous in various transcriptions for symphony orchestra. There are not many examples of passacaglia music after Bach. Beethoven's *Thirty-Two Variations,* for the piano, resembles the passacaglia form; and Brahms resurrected this form for the last movement of his *Fourth Symphony.*

## PASSEPIED

*See below:* Suite.

## PAVANE

A slow, dignified dance in ¾ time usually divided into three parts. It became one of the movements of the classical suite (*see below:* Suite). The form was resurrected by Maurice Ravel for one of his best known pieces for the piano, *Pavane pour une Infante défunte* (also familiar in transcriptions for orchestra, for violin and piano, etc.).

## PERPETUAL MOTION
### (in Italian, *Perpetuum mobile*)

A piece of music, virtuoso in character, trying to suggest continuous motion. It is in very fast tempo, and usually in notes of equal value. Composers for the violin—among them Paganini and Novák—have written perpetual motions for that instrument.

## POLONAISE

A national Polish dance which originated as a court ceremonial, and which achieved popularity outside of Poland in the eighteenth century. It subsequently became a form of music favored by serious composers.

The dance is characterized by its triple time, its two- or three-part form, and its marked syncopations and accents on the half beat. The polonaise entered serious music as a movement of the classical suite (*see below:* Suite). Handel, Mozart, Beethoven, Weber, and Schubert also wrote polonaises. A polonaise is found in Tchaikovsky's opera *Eugene Onegin;* Philine's famous aria, "Je suis Titania" in Act 2 of Thomas' *Mignon* is also a polonaise.

In solo instrumental music, the polonaise was first made popular by Frédéric Chopin. It is believed that he wrote his first polonaise in his twelfth year. In any case, following his natural bent to express his love for his native land by treating its folk dance with serious artistic purpose, Chopin wrote thirteen polonaises; twelve are for solo piano, while the thirteenth (*Introduction and Polonaise*) is for cello and piano. These pieces have two prevailing moods. One is martial; the other, sad and pensive. The so-called *Military Polonaise* is the most famous of these compositions (A major, op. 40, no. 1). Another celebrated polonaise is the *Heroic* (A flat major, op. 53). Both of these are in a stormy, martial vein.

An effective use of the polonaise was made by Henri Wieniawski in a piece for violin and piano—the *Polonaise brillante* in D major.

## PRELUDE

The prelude is essentially a work for orchestra and is described in the orchestral section.

One concept of the orchestral prelude—as a preface to another piece of music—is carried out in instrumental music in Bach's *The Well-Tempered Clavier,* in which each fugue is preceded by a prelude; also in various preludes and fugues for organ by Bach, Mendelssohn, Reger, and others.

The prelude is found in piano music: an independent piece, of brief duration and without any specific form, attempting to portray a mood, a picture, or a passing emotion; when completed it seems to suggest that more is to follow. The prelude became a fixture in piano music with Chopin who wrote twenty-six of them in his most intimate vein. Anton Rubinstein once described the preludes as "Chopin's pearls." Chopin wrote most of them on the island of Majorca where he had come with George Sand during the first year of their strange love affair. But the preludes are not idylls of love, they are often poems of torment. Chopin wrote some of them when he was ill, unhappy, and frequently the victim of strange hallucinations. His temper and mood are reflected in this often dreary and melancholy music.

Each of the twenty-four Chopin preludes is in a different key. One of the best known is the sixth, in B minor, sometimes known as the *Raindrop.* It is said that the beating of the rain on the rooftop gave Chopin his inspiration for this piece which has an inexorably repetitive musical figure throughout. Other familiar preludes include: the fourth in E minor, among the most pensive and poetic of Chopin's pieces (it was played at the composer's funeral); the seventh in A minor, a delicate song; the seventeenth, in A flat major, one of the few gay pieces in this set, filled with sunshine and the song of birds; the twenty-second and twenty-fourth, in G minor and D minor respectively, both stormy and agitated.

Many composers after Chopin wrote preludes that are basic in the piano repertory. Debussy produced twenty-four preludes (published in two volumes). They contain some of his finest inspiration, some of his most delicate and exquisite writing, some of his subtlest effects. Each prelude has a title which, significantly, Debussy placed at the *end* of each composition. Evidently, he did not wish to give the title undue significance; as a matter of fact some of the names were concocted after he had written the music. The first book contains some of Debussy's most popular piano pieces including *La Fille aux cheveux de lin* (The Girl with the Flaxen Hair), a portrait of a girl with the most sensitive lines and colors; *La Cathédrale engloutie* (The Engulfed Cathedral), retelling the old Breton legend of the Cathedral of Ys which comes to sight on clear mornings and then disappears into the depths of the sea. The second book is, on the whole, on a less sustained plane of inspiration, but it also contains a few memorable items, notably *La Puerta del Vino,* a musical description of the Alhambra gate in Granada; and *Ondine,* a picture of a water nymph.

Scriabin wrote eighty-five preludes which fall into three groups. The first, op. 1 to op. 31, reveals the influence of Chopin, and contains pieces that are consistently lyrical, romantic, and poetic. In the preludes from op. 31 to op. 67, the technique becomes more involved, the harmony and rhythm more complex, as the composer persistently strives for subtler nuances of expression. After op. 67, Scriabin's style becomes ultrarefined and rarefied, and his ideas are so detached that it is sometimes difficult to follow the train of his thought.

Rachmaninoff completed twenty-five preludes for the piano. Most of them are so dramatic that they appear to tell a story; but what that story is, each listener must decide for himself. The two most celebrated preludes by Rachmaninoff—indeed, they are among the most popular pieces ever written for the piano—are the *Prelude in C Sharp Minor,* op. 3, no. 2 (with its opening three descending chords sounding the voice of implacable fate), and the *Prelude in G Minor,* op. 32, no. 5, which has a martial character. The first of these two preludes, written in 1892, established Rachmaninoff's fame throughout the world of music while he was still a young man. Because Rachmaninoff failed to copyright the piece, it managed to earn a fortune for various publishers and virtually nothing for its composer.

Another Russian composer, Dmitri Shostakovich, contributed a set of twenty-four preludes for the piano in 1933, and a second set of twenty-four preludes and fugues, for the piano, in 1951. The American composer, Abram Chasins, also wrote twenty-four preludes, for piano.

## QUARTET

A musical composition for four instruments.

Specifically, a quartet is a large work for four instruments which follows the general pattern of the sonata and symphony. It is usually in four movements—the first in sonata form; the second, lyrical and slow, in song form, or a theme and variations; the third, a scherzo; the fourth, a finale in sonata form or rondo form or theme and variations, etc.

The string quartet comprises two violins, viola, and cello. The piano quartet is for piano, violin, viola and cello. There are also quartets for other combinations of instruments, such as oboe and strings, or flute and strings, or four brass instruments, and so on.

For the development of the quartet, see the fourth section in this Part.

## QUINTET

A musical composition for five instruments.

Specifically, a quintet is a large work for five instruments, which follows the pattern of the quartet (described in the preceding entry), sonata and symphony.

The most familiar combination is the piano quintet: piano, two violins, viola, and cello. The string quintet includes two violins, viola, and two cellos. There are various other combinations, such as clarinet and string quartet, five brass instruments, and so on. Schubert's *Die Forelle Quintet* is for the unusual combination of violin, viola, cello, piano and double-bass.

For the development of the quintet, see fourth section in this Part.

## RHAPSODY

As a form of piano music, the rhapsody was created by a Bohemian composer named Tomaschek, who produced six rhapsodies. Franz Liszt made the form famous with his fifteen *Hungarian Rhapsodies* which are the prototypes for all later rhapsodies. Liszt drew his languorous and sentimental melodies out of the storehouse of Hungarian-gypsy folk music. There is one distinguishing trait to all Liszt rhapsodies: they contrast dramatically gay and passionate moods (called *friska*) with sentimental ones (*lassan*). The second Hungarian rhapsody is outstandingly popular with its spirited rhythms, sentimental moods, breath-taking contrasts and climaxes. Also familiar are the fifth, ninth, twelfth, and fourteenth rhapsodies. The ninth is entitled *The Carnival of Pesth,* and portions of the fourteenth were used by the composer for his *Hungarian Fantasy,* for piano and orchestra.

In writing three rhapsodies for the piano, Brahms carried out the Greek concept of the term: a poetic utterance of epical character. Brahms' rhapsodies are powerful and passionate, dramatic and heroic; they reveal the composer in his more tempestuous moods.

The rhapsody has often been used in orchestral music, and is further commented upon in the orchestral section.

## RIGAUDON

*See below:* Suite.

## RONDO

A form which first achieved considerable popularity in the late eighteenth and early nineteenth century with the classical composers for the piano. The form can best be designated by the letters: A-B-A-C-A. "A" denotes the principal theme which returns consistently; "B" and "C" represent second and third themes. Sometimes this form can be further extended into A-B-A-C-A-D-A, or can be altered into A-B-A-C-A-B-A.

The form was derived from the early round dance, which alternated song and dance, from the thirteenth century choral rondeaux, and the fifteenth century rondeaux for solo voice and accompaniment. The salient traits of the rondo are first found in early harpsichord literature. In Rameau's rondeau we find a repetition of the principal first section after the interpolation of new material. A fine example of the classical rondo is found in Joseph Haydn's *Gypsy Rondo,* which is best known in a transcription for the piano, but which originated as the last movement of the *Trio No. 1 in G Major* ("Rondo all' ongarese" movement). Mozart wrote rondos for piano solo, for piano and orchestra, for violin and orchestra, and for horn and orchestra. Beethoven also wrote several rondos for piano solo, one of which (G major, op. 129) has the droll title of *Fury over the Lost Penny,* and another of which (G major) is for violin and piano. These and other composers incorporated the rondo within the sonata and string quartet, where it often appears as the finale. The rondo is also found in the concerto and the symphony, and in this connection is discussed in the orchestral section.

## SARABANDE

*See below:* Suite.

## SCHERZO

The scherzo form is most familiar within the framework of the symphony where it appears as the third movement (see orchestral section). It is also one of the movements of the sonata (see below). In these instances, the scherzo is meant to be of light character, sometimes even droll, and with a brisk pace. It carries out the actual meaning of the word as a "joke." But Chopin wrote four scherzi for piano which do not comply with this definition, they are for the most part somber pieces of music with more strength than gaiety.

## SEPTET

A musical composition for seven instruments.

## SEXTET

A musical composition for six instruments.

## SONATA

A large work for piano, or for a solo instrument and a piano. It is most often in three movements, carrying out the pattern of the symphony. The first movement is generally in the so-called sonata form. This form is made up of three distinct sections: the first, exposition, presents the themes; the second, development, enlarges upon and varies them; the concluding part, recapitulation, repeats the themes as they first emerged in the opening exposition. The sonata form employs two themes. The first is in the key of the work; the second, a subject of contrasting feeling and mood, is in a complementary key, sometimes dominant, sometimes in the relative major or minor. The second movement of the classical sonata is in a slow tempo; it is lyrical and emotional. Here a customary practice is to use either the song form or the form of theme and variations. The third movement, or finale, is very lively. Various forms are used, sometimes the sonata form, sometimes the rondo form, sometimes the theme and variations. Some sonatas are in four movements. In that event, there is usually a minuet or a scherzo between the slow movement and the finale.

The word "sonata" is believed to have originated with a composer named Graziani in the seventeenth century. Graziani and his immediate successors regarded the sonata as the instrumental equivalent of the "cantata." If the cantata was a piece of music to be *sung* (*see* Choral Music), then the sonata was a piece to be *sounded* or *played*. Whereas the cantata was for a voice, or group of voices, and accompanying instruments, Graziani conceived the sonata for a solo instrument, or group of instruments, and accompaniment.

The sonata was evolved from the canzona, the earliest of instrumental forms. The canzona was music for instruments written in a polyphonic style. Giovanni Gabrieli wrote canzone for quartet and double quartet as early as 1600, having the instruments emulate the a cappella singing of polyphonic music. Before long, the word "canzona" and "sonata" became interchangeable for instrumental music; and eventually the word "sonata" completely replaced "canzona."

The earliest sonatas—the sonatas da chiesa—usually began with a majestic introduction and continued with a fugato passage; then came a short largo which also culminated in a fugato. In the earliest sonatas, these four movements were integrated into a single piece of music. Later composers separated the movements. The sonata da chiesa is, then, the forerunner of the present-day sonata. There was, however, another kind of sonata: sonata da camera. This composition collated a group of dances, and is the ancestor of the suite.

The first master of the sonata was Arcangelo Corelli. He wrote twelve sonatas for violin and accompaniment which were published in 1694 as op. 5. These works established a definite style of violin writing and amplified violin technique. Corelli's slow movements are particularly noble—an immense step away from counterpoint and to homophony. Corelli's most famous sonata is the last, entitled *La Folia*.

Corelli's pupils and immediate successors in Italy were inspired by him to write violin sonatas. Some of these works are still in the repertory. One of them is *The Devil's Trill Sonata* of Tartini, so called because it was said to have been inspired in a dream during which the composer received the main melody from the Devil. *The Devil's Trill* is in four movements, a slow section followed by a fast one; in the fast part trills decorate the melodies. Vivaldi's sonatas for violin and figured bass—particularly the one in A major (op. 2, no. 2)—are also occasionally heard today. Sonatas by Tartini and Vivaldi—and those by Viotti, Purcell, and Handel—increased the technique of violin writing and brought a new expressiveness to lyricism.

Johann Sebastian Bach wrote six sonatas for violin and piano and three sonatas for unaccompanied violin. He achieved a stateliness of form, in the violin and piano sonatas, an independence for the two instruments not realized before his time. The violin and piano sonatas are of historic significance for another reason, too. Before Bach's time, the accompaniment was a figured bass—that is, numerals were placed before the melody to indicate the formal harmonies; Bach's sonatas were the first in which the harmonies were completely written out.

The Bach sonata is generally in four sections with alternating slow and fast movements. Thus the C major and D minor unaccompanied sonatas open with an adagio and continue with a fugue, a largo and an allegro. The *Sonata in G Minor,* for violin and piano, is an exception in that it has five movements instead of four: Allegro, Largo, Allegro, Adagio, and Allegro.

It was to be expected that composers write sonatas for solo instruments other than the violin. We find sonatas for flute and accompaniment, for cello and accompaniment, among such early Italian instrumental composers as Locatelli and Marcello. Handel wrote sonatas for flute and accompaniment. Bach wrote six sonatas for unaccompanied cello and various sonatas for flute and accompaniment, and cello and accompaniment.

Meanwhile, the first sonata was written for the piano. In 1695 (one year after the appearance of Corelli's sonatas for violin and accompaniment) there appeared a volume of piano pieces by Johann Kuhnau called *Frische Klavier Früchte.* Seven pieces in this collection were designated as "sonatas." As Kuhnau himself inquired in the preface— aware as he was of the revolutionary nature of this nomenclature: "Why should not one try to write for the piano in a form that has been utilized for other instruments?" Kuhnau subsequently wrote six other sonatas in a publication entitled *Musical Representation of Some Stories of the Bible.* In this latter volume we find a work still heard occasionally: *The Combat Between David and Goliath,* an early example of program music.

Kuhnau's sonatas bear little resemblance to the classical sonata of Haydn and Mozart. Kuhnau's works are usually in three, four, or five movements, each episodic, with little concern for thematic development. Naturally, too, there is still little understanding of the sonata form; but there is here an awareness of piano style. And it is the technique of writing for the piano, much more than the development of the sonata form, that we also find in the remarkable pieces for piano which Domenico Scarlatti called *Esercizi,* but which today we refer to as sonatas.

It was Bach's son, Karl Philipp Emanuel, who was among the first to clarify the sonata form. Bach wrote the first set of his piano sonatas in 1742. Two years later he issued his *Wurttemberg Sonatas,* and in 1781 still another set of sonatas called *For Connoisseurs and Amateurs.* His finest sonatas are in three movements in which many of the identifying traits of later sonata writing are clearly evident. In the *F Minor Sonata,* in *For Connoisseurs and Amateurs,* two contrasting themes are used, and an exposition, development and recapitulation section definitely presented. Bach, therefore, must be singled out as the first master of the classic sonata. We know how indebted both Haydn and Mozart were to him, how they profited from his piano works. Haydn said: "For what I know I have to thank Philipp Emanuel Bach." And Mozart remarked: "He is the father and we his children; those of us who know what is right have learned it from him."

The classic sonata acquired its present-day identity with Haydn and Mozart. Haydn wrote fifty-two sonatas for piano, the best of these including those in C major, D major, and F major, familiar to piano students everywhere. Haydn also wrote several sonatas for violin and piano, but these are rarely heard. Mozart wrote seventeen sonatas for piano. A few are genuine masterworks, among them those in A major (K. 331), F major (K. 332), C minor (K. 457), C major (K. 545), B flat major (K. 570) and D major (K. 576). The *Sonata in A Major* is known as the *Turkish March Sonata* because the finale (*Rondo alla turca*) is in the style of Turkish music in vogue in Vienna in Mozart's time; its first movement, a theme and variations, is also celebrated. Mozart also wrote several interesting sonatas for four hands, and a delightful sonata for two pianos in D major (K. 448).

Mozart's literature for sonata includes nineteen works for violin and piano. Mozart's violin sonatas differ from later works in this genre in that it is the piano that assumes the commanding role, while the violin is subsidiary; frequently, the violin is no more than an obbligato, while the piano presents the principal thoughts. Mozart's violin sonatas are filled with melodic treasures, one beautiful thought following another in rapid succession. If Mozart is rarely profound and never dramatic in these sonatas, he is always graceful, and charming—a delightful companion. His finest violin sonatas are: C major (K. 296); E minor (K. 304); F major (K. 377); B flat major (K. 454).

The sonata, a province with Haydn and Mozart, became a veritable continent with Beethoven. The thirty-two sonatas for piano, ten for violin and piano, and five for cello and piano, represent a brave new world for music.

In his first three piano sonatas, Beethoven is still writing in the style, and within the crystal-clear and precise form, of Haydn and Mozart. But the great emancipator, impatient with tradition, is not slow in bringing new dimensions to the form and an incomparably rich gamut of expression to the style. Even an early work like the celebrated *Sonata pathétique* (published as op. 13, in 1799) dwarfs every sonata written before it. Never before had the poetic idea been given such prominent attention; never before had virtuosity and technique been made to serve the idea so humbly. The torment of Beethoven's soul is translated in the first movement into music of immense grief; and the slow movement is a noble and philosophic resignation to that grief. There is human feeling in many of the slow movements of the Mozart sonatas, but never such personal, deeply felt, powerfully projected emotions—and expressed in harmonic and melodic language and a rhythmic force new to piano music.

With each succeeding Beethoven sonata, the idea grows richer and more penetrating, the emotion fuller and deeper, the atmosphere more dramatic, the temper more fiery. By the same token, with each succeeding sonata, the structure grows and expands until it seems ready to burst at the seams; the concepts of harmony, tonality, modulation, rhythm become more independent and daring; the technique of thematic development becomes more subtle and involved. Finally, in the last sonatas—in the *Hammerklavier* (op. 101) and the *Sonata in C Minor* (op. 111) particularly—piano music acquires symphonic breadth and depth; the content achieves a spiritual-like mysticism and profundity, which open new avenues for musical writing.

The most popular of the Beethoven piano sonatas are the so-called *Moonlight Sonata* in C sharp minor (op. 27, no. 2); the *Waldstein Sonata* in C minor (op. 53) and the *Appassionata Sonata* in F minor (op. 57).

There are many stories to explain why the *Sonata in C Sharp Minor* acquired the name of "Moonlight." (The name, incidentally, was given to the work not by the composer but after the composer's death by the German critic, Rellstab.) These stories make dramatic reading, but none of them are founded on fact. Beethoven himself called this composition the *Sonata quasi una fantasia* (a sonata somewhat in the nature of a fantasia), and for two reasons: the work violated the then established concept of the sonata by opening with a slow movement instead of a movement in the sonata form; and in the same movement the material is treated freely, in fantasia style. It is the poetic and gentle first movement that won the work the sobriquet "Moonlight"; even if Beethoven himself had no such picture in mind when writing the music, it does suggest the peace and serenity of a moonlit night. But the nocturnal picture ends with the first movement. The second movement is light and fanciful, in the character of a scherzo; while the closing movement has recognizable Beethoven turbulence.

The *Waldstein Sonata* acquired its name by virtue of its dedication to Beethoven's patron, Count Waldstein. More and more spacious does Beethoven's design become as he pours into it the feverish and tempestuous moods found in the first movement, the profound emotional depths of the slow movement, and the exuberant spirits of the concluding rondo. In the *Appassionata* the feeling is even more intense, the conflicts of the soul even more heroic, and the spiritual peace that comes after the struggle even more complete. This is Beethoven at his creative greatest—and this is one of the noblest and most stirring sonatas ever written.

In his ten sonatas for violin and piano, and five sonatas for cello and piano, Beethoven emphasized the individuality of the solo instrument. At the same time, the piano is not merely an accompaniment but an equal partner in an artistic venture. The most popular of the violin sonatas is the *Kreutzer,* in A major, dedicated to the violinist Rodolph Kreutzer. Because, in later years, Count Tolstoy wrote a romantic story about a jealous husband who kills his wife, and called that story *The Kreutzer Sonata,* many programmatic ideas have been ascribed to the music. The music has that kind of dramatic and turbulent character that lends itself to extra-musical interpretation, but Beethoven conceived it as pure music. The most frequently heard of the cello sonatas is that in A major (op. 69) which has a dignity and a nobility not often encountered in the other cello sonatas.

The Romantic composers of piano music preferred the smaller forms to the sonata, or larger forms made up of many small pieces. However the sonata was not altogether neglected. Schubert wrote many piano sonatas which he filled with many happy lyrical ideas. Generally speaking, few of these works are integrated compositions; they are more appealing in parts than in the whole. Only in his last three sonatas, written in the last year of his life and published posthumously, was Schubert able to rise above the constrictions of his form and the limitations imposed by his inability to think in large concepts, to produce music of immense emotional power and soaring romantic spirit.

As was the case with Schubert, so it was with Chopin: he was not at his best in the large form of the sonata. Chopin wrote three such works, none of them possessing that organic unity and that singleness of artistic purpose we find in his smaller masterpieces. Actually, each of his sonatas is really made up of four independent pieces of music. Yet there is wonderful music in each work. The most famous is the *Sonata No. 2,* in B flat minor, three of whose movements have an irresistible surge and dramatic thrust only intermittently interrupted by a felicitous lyric idea. The slow movement (the third) is the popular Funeral March—surely the best known funeral march in all music.

Liszt's *Piano Sonata in B Minor,* one of his most ambitious piano works, has such sprawling form and freedom of melodic treatment that it resembles a fantasia much more than a sonata. It has demoniac power, found in the bold leap of the opening bars and in the strong drive of the first theme. But strength is combined with deep religious feeling as a chorale enters in the first movement as a second theme. After a lyrical slow section, a fugato passage leads to a whirlwind finale.

Romantic music did not neglect the sonata for solo instrument and piano. Schubert wrote sonatinas, rather than sonatas, for violin and piano; one of these, in D major, is occasionally heard and enjoyed for its lovable melodies. A sonata for "arpeggione" and piano—the "arpeggione" being a now obsolete instrument that looked something like a guitar—is today heard exclusively for cello and piano. Schumann wrote two poetic sonatas for violin and piano; and Chopin made one of his rare excursions out of the field of solo piano music with a melodious sonata for cello and piano. Much more significant than any of these works is the literature produced by Brahms in the sonata form. Brahms wrote three piano sonatas that are the works of his youth, and rarely heard. But his sonatas for violin, for cello, and for clarinet are among his finest creations. The first of his violin sonatas, in G major, is sometimes known as the *Rain Sonata* because of a repetitious sixteenth-note figure in the third movement suggesting (to some) the sound of falling rain. The second sonata, in A major, is called the *Thun Sonata* because Brahms wrote it during a summer vacation at Lake Thun. This work begins with a theme that bears a striking resemblance to the melody of the "Prize Song" in Wagner's *Die Meistersinger*. The third sonata, in D minor, is said to be a tonal portrait of Brahms' friend, the famous conductor-pianist Hans von Bülow; it is as volatile in mood and as high-tensioned as Hans von Bülow was reported to have been.

The cello *Sonata in E Minor* (op. 38) was Brahms' first work for a solo instrument and piano. The finer of his two cello sonatas is that in F major, a work of tremendous force and passionate utterances. The two clarinet sonatas are Brahms' last compositions in chamber music; they have the quiet introspection, philosophic resignation, the gentle glow of twilight that move us so deeply in Brahms' greatest last works. It is sometimes customary to hear these sonatas played by the viola instead of the clarinet.

French Romantic music produced few piano sonatas of any permanent value, but many remarkable sonatas for violin and piano. Gabriel Fauré's *Sonata No. 1 in A Major* is one of the most beautiful works in the violin repertory, filled with tender moods and ardent feelings within an exquisite structure. It foreshadowed the objectivity and serenity of one of the masterworks in sonata literature: César Franck's *Sonata in A Major,* for violin and piano. Even greater refinement and sensitivity is found in Debussy's *Sonata for Violin and Piano,* which he wrote one year before his death. These sonatas of Franck and Debussy are cyclic in their form: material from earlier movements is later repeated to integrate the entire composition. Ravel's *Sonata for Violin and Piano* (whose last movement is in an unorthodox "blues" style) and his delightful *Sonatine,* for piano, carry on the traditions of Franck and Debussy.

The Russian composer, Scriabin, wrote ten sonatas for the piano. The first three betray their indebtedness to Chopin and Liszt. With the fourth, Scriabin assumes the one-movement form which he was henceforth to employ; he also begins to append a program to his music as he tries to endow musical tones with metaphysical concepts. With the

*Sixth Sonata,* Scriabin dispenses with key signatures, while the Seventh probes deeply into mysticism. The form henceforth becomes tenuous, the thought elusive, and the technique complex. His harmonic language acquires individuality through the extensive use of the so-called "Mystery Chord" of his own invention, built out of the interval of the fourth, rather than the third.

Contemporary Soviet composers have created significant piano sonatas, the most important coming from Shostakovich, Prokofiev, and Kabalevsky. In America, Charles Ives wrote a piano sonata called *Concord* which was many years ahead of its time (1915) with its audacious experiments with harmonies and tonalities. More conservative, and much more appealing aurally, are sonatas by Edward Mac-Dowell, Samuel Barber, and Aaron Copland.

Significant sonatas for violin and piano have been written, in recent decades, by Ildebrando Pizzetti, Georges Enesco and Ernest Bloch. Fauré's *Sonata No. 2* and Shostakovich's *Sonata No. 2* are notable contributions to contemporary cello literature.

## SONATINE (or SONATINA)

A small sonata, generally easy in technical demands. In this category belong the piano sonatinas of Beethoven, Clementi, Kuhlau and Dussek familiar to piano students. There are sonatinas which are not necessarily easy to play but whose structure is less ambitious than that of the sonata: in these works the first movement is brief, and the development section is either greatly curtailed or dispensed with completely. Schubert's sonatinas for violin and piano and Ravel's *Sonatine,* for piano, are significant examples.

## SONG WITHOUT WORDS

A one-movement piece for the piano in which the melody has the character of a song, and in which the left hand provides a song accompaniment. This form was created by Mendelssohn who wrote forty-eight pieces, each with an identifying title. It is important to remark that most of the titles in Mendelssohn's *Songs Without Words* were added by imaginative editors and publishers rather than by the composer. Only the following titles originated with Mendelssohn himself: "Venetian Boat Song" (three pieces with that name), "Duetto," and "Folk Song." The most popular of all these Mendelssohn pieces is the perennial favorite of the salon, "Spring Song." Other familiar Songs Without Words are the three "Venetian Boat Songs," the "Spinning Song," "Hunting Song," "Duetto," and "Folk Song." Tchaikovsky also wrote a celebrated piano piece in this form, though he preferred to use the French term, *"Chanson sans paroles."*

## SUITE

In the music of the sixteenth and seventeenth centuries, a suite consisted of a group of old dances. Subsequently, the term was used for a series of pieces unified by a single title, subject, or program.

The old suite was evolved from the sonata da camera (which included dances) and certain English virginal music in which two or more dances were combined into a single piece of music. It was the seventeenth-century German composer, Froberger, who set the first pattern of the old suite. The Froberger suite was usually in four movements, including the following old dances: allemande, courante, sarabande, and gigue. Soon there were deviations from this pattern. Chambonnières, Purcell, and Corelli wrote suites in which, at times, one of these dances was substituted by another, or other dances were interpolated to provide additional movements. Purcell's suites contain the rigaudon, chaconne, march, minuet together with the dances already mentioned; in Couperin's suites we find such additional dances as the gavotte, and the rondeau. The suites (or partitas) of Johann Sebastian Bach have more than four movements. The *Partita No. 4 in D Major,* for piano, includes: Overture, Allemande, Courante, Aria, Sarabande, Minuet, and Gigue. The *Partita No. 2 in D Minor,* for unaccompanied violin, contains: Allemande, Courante, Sarabande, Gigue, and Chaconne.

A brief description of each of these old dances follows:

ALLEMANDE. A dance in duple time, and in two parts, with a highly decorated melody. The allemande was generally the first movement of the suite, unless it was preceded by a prelude.

BOURRÉE. A dance of either Spanish or French origin, generally in ²⁄₄ or ⁴⁄₄ time and in two sections. In the old suite it was the custom to use two bourrées in succession, repeating the first after the second.

COURANTE. A dance of French origin, formerly in duple time, but within the suite changed to ³⁄₂, ³⁄₄ or ⁶⁄₄ time. It is in two sections.

FORLANE. A happy Italian dance like the gigue in ⁶⁄₄ or ⁶⁄₈ time.

GAVOTTE. A dance of French origin, in two sections, and in ¼ time. It begins on the third beat. In the old suite it was sometimes customary to use two gavottes in succession, repeating the first after the second. Unlike most of the other old dances, the gavotte did not pass out of existence after the seventeenth century. One of the most popular of all gavottes was written by François Joseph Gossec in the eighteenth century. In the nineteenth century, Thomas introduced a gavotte in his opera, *Mignon;* while in the twentieth century, Prokofiev revived the dance in his *Classical Symphony*.

GIGUE. A lively dance of rustic English origin. It is usually in two sections and in ⅝ time. In the old suite, the gigue was generally the concluding movement.

LOURE. A slow and strongly accented country dance similar to the gigue, in ⁶⁄₄ time.

MINUET. This dance is discussed earlier in this section.

PASSEPIED. A dance similar to the minuet, but quicker, said to have originated in Brittany. It is lively in character, is either in ¾ or ⅝ time.

PAVANE. This dance is discussed earlier in this section.

POLONAISE. This dance is discussed earlier in this section.

RIGAUDON. An old French dance in either ²⁄₄ or ¼ time, in three or four parts. In the twentieth century, Maurice Ravel revived this dance for one of the movements of *Le Tombeau de Couperin*.

SARABANDE. A slow, dignified dance said to have originated in Spain. It is in triple time, and its phrase usually begins on the first beat.

After the age of Bach and Handel, the suite abandoned old dances. (Occasionally, however, some later composers revived the old suite. When Grieg wrote the *Holberg Suite* to commemorate the two hundredth anniversary of the birth of the great Danish writer, he decided to concentrate on the forms and dances in vogue in Holberg's time; his suite, then, is in the old style, includes a sarabande, gavotte, and rigaudon. Maurice Ravel's *Le Tombeau de Couperin,* for piano, is also in the old tradition—it pays tribute to the seventeenth-century French harpsichord composer—and includes a minuet and a rigaudon.)

In the Romantic Era, and afterwards, the suite combined several pieces under a single unifying title. Robert Schumann collected various items about children and child's life in his piano suites, *Albums for the*

*Young* and *Scenes from Childhood;* Debussy did the same thing in his piano suite, *Children's Corner.*

The twelve pieces (gathered in four books) in Albéniz' piano suite, *Iberia,* are collectively a panorama of Spain: its sights and sounds; songs and dances; harbors and haunts. But each piece has interest apart from the other compositions, and is often played independently, as, for example, the highly popular "El Corpus Christi en Sevilla," or "Triana." The three movements of Ernest Bloch's *Baal Shem Suite,* for violin and piano, provide three different facets of a Hebraic sect known as *Hasidism;* each of the movements is a separate and complete entity, and one of them—"Nigun"—is often heard by itself.

Debussy gathered various subtle impressions in several piano suites, including *Images* and *Suite bergamasque;* the latter contains one of Debussy's most sensitive pictures, "Clair de lune." Ravel combined five different tone pictures in a piano suite, *Miroirs;* and three descriptive pieces in another suite, *Gaspard de la Nuit.*

Bartók's *Mikrokosmos,* Debussy's *Children's Corner,* Prokofiev's *Music for Children,* Schumann's *Album for the Young* and *Scenes from Childhood* are piano suites discussed in Part Six.

The suite, as orchestral music, is discussed in the section on orchestral music.

## TARANTELLA

A very fast dance, popular in Naples, generally in ⅜ or ⁶⁄₈ time. The form became popular in instrumental music, assuming the style of a perpetual motion. Chopin's *Tarantelle in A Flat Major* is familiar; so are Liszt's tarantelle from *Années de pélérinage* ("Venezia e Napoli"); Mendelssohn's in *Songs Without Words;* and Rossini's in *Péchés de vieillesse.* Henri Wieniawski's *Scherzo tarantelle* is a staple in the violin repertory.

## THEME AND VARIATIONS

*See below:* Variations.

## TOCCATA

A piece for the organ, or the piano, improvisational in style, emphasizing the virtuosity of the performer. It has elaborate runs, figurations, fugal passages, and so forth.

The earliest use of the word "toccata" is found in a publication dated 1508. The prelude to Monteverdi's opera *Orfeo* (a fanfare for trumpets) is a toccata. But it was the early contrapuntists, such as the Gabrielis and Sweelinck, who first evolved the form, and the early organ composers (Frescobaldi, Froberger, Scheidt, Buxtehude) who developed it. As with the other organ forms, the toccata became a spacious and vital form of art with Johann Sebastian Bach. Bach's toccatas—of which the one in D minor is the most famous—is music of powerful dramatic impact and stunning effects. Another celebrated Bach toccata (C major) is in three sections, the first being the toccata itself, the second a short and poignant adagio, and the third a majestic fugue.

There are not many examples of the toccata in the period following Bach. But a few isolated examples are worthy of mention. Schumann wrote a dazzling virtuoso piece for the piano, called a toccata; and the concluding movement of Ravel's *Le Tombeau de Couperin,* for piano, is also a toccata.

## TRIO

A musical composition for three instruments.

Specifically, a trio is a large work in four movements which follows the general pattern of a quartet, sonata, and symphony.

The most familiar combination of three instruments is piano, violin, and cello. But there are other trio combinations for which the great composers produced notable works. Haydn wrote his *London Trios* for two flutes and a cello; Brahms wrote trios for clarinet, cello and piano, and for violin, horn, and piano; Mozart wrote a trio for clarinet, viola, and piano.

## VARIATIONS

The technique of giving a theme and then subjecting it to a series of harmonic, rhythmic, and melodic alterations is believed to have originated in sixteenth-century Spain. But it acquired popularity in the seventeenth century with the English composers for the virginal. The early instrumental composers made extensive use of the variation form, beginning with such elementary methods as the ground bass: a simple melody stated in the bass and given embellishments in the treble. Development of the ground bass resulted in the evolution of such forms as the chaconne and the passacaglia whose main characteristic is a series of variations on a theme in the bass.

Most of the famous seventeenth-century composers produced instrumental works in the variation form. Corelli's sonata for violin, *La Folia,* is a significant example. Locatelli, Frescobaldi, Kuhnau, Lully all wrote variations. Handel's frequently played *The Harmonious Blacksmith*—a movement from his fifth suite for harpsichord—is also in this form. The monumental *Goldberg Variations* for piano of Johann Sebastian Bach represents a landmark.

The classical composers who followed Bach frequently interpolated the variation form in their sonatas and quartets. Notable examples include the first movement of Mozart's *Sonata in A Major,* for piano, and the slow movement of Haydn's *Emperor Quartet.* Haydn and Mozart also wrote independent pieces in this technique: Haydn's *Variations in F Minor,* Mozart's *Variations on Ah, vous dirai-je maman,* and *Variations on a Theme of Gluck,* all for piano.

Beethoven was one of the supreme masters in the writing of variations; his masterworks in virtually every instrumental and orchestral form reveal his tremendous skill in this department. Among Beethoven's works for solo instrument in this form is the *Thirty-Two Variations,* for piano.

While variations did not greatly interest the Romantic composer, we find significant examples of the use of this form in chamber music by Schubert (as in the *Death and the Maiden Quartet,* and *Die Forelle Quintet*), and in piano music by Mendelssohn (*Variations sérieuses*), Schumann (*Études symphoniques*), and Brahms (*Variations and Fugue on a Theme of Handel, Variations on a Theme of Paganini*).

Since the variation technique has been used extensively in orchestral music, it is further discussed in the orchestral section.

## VOLUNTARY

A brief introductory piece for the organ that is usually extemporaneous.

## WALTZ

A dance in ¾ time, evolved from the Austrian *Ländler* and *Teutsche,* and which became extraordinarily popular first in Austria and Bohemia in the late eighteenth century, and then throughout all of Europe in the nineteenth.

Originally slow and sedate, the waltz soon grew more and more abandoned until it was considered indecent: as late as 1825, the waltz was defined in a European handbook of terms as "the name of a riotous and obscene German dance." But in Vienna it thrived, beloved by both the nobility and the masses. It was the favorite of all dances, and toward the close of the eighteenth century, it was computed that every fourth person in Vienna could be found at one time or another dancing the waltz in a ballroom.

But the music of the waltz was not used exclusively for dancing. Many important composers produced instrumental works in the waltz form, intended for listening. We find examples of instrumental waltz music in the works of Haydn, Mozart, Beethoven, and Schubert. The technique of gathering several different waltzes into a single work, with an introduction and a coda, was first suggested by Schubert, and realized by Karl Maria von Weber in his famous *Invitation to the Dance* (originally for piano, but best known in transcriptions for orchestra by Berlioz and Weingartner).

Chopin wrote fourteen waltzes for piano; Brahms, sixteen waltzes, originally for four hands, but later transcribed by the composer for two hands. Chopin's most popular waltzes include the *Grande Valse brillante* in E flat major, the so-called *Minute Waltz* in D flat major, and the *Waltz in C Sharp Minor*. Brahms' best-loved waltz is his fifteenth, in A flat major (also famous in a transcription for violin and piano). The essential difference between a waltz of Chopin and one by Brahms is essentially that of place of origin. Brahms' waltz is from Vienna—the Vienna of the café house—it is charming and filled with the joy of good living. The Chopin waltz came from Paris—the Paris of the salon; it is suave, sophisticated, and elegant.

Ravel wrote a set of waltzes for the piano entitled *Valses nobles et sentimentales,* in which he paid homage to the Viennese waltz of Schubert and Brahms. This is a set of seven waltzes which are touched with those infectious and sentimental moods for which the Viennese waltz is celebrated.

The waltz was used extensively in music for the orchestra. Further discussion is found in the orchestral section.

# 6

# One Hundred Basic Works of Instrumental Music

Albéniz: *Iberia,* for piano.
Bach, J. S.: *Fantasia and Fugue in G Minor,* for organ.
Bach, J. S.: *Italian Concerto,* for piano.
Bach, J. S.: *Partita in C Minor,* for piano.
Bach, J. S.: *Partita No. 2 in D Minor,* for unaccompanied violin (including the chaconne).
Bach, J. S.: *Passacaglia in C Minor,* for organ.
Bach, J. S.: *Sonata No. 2 in D Major,* for cello and piano.
Bach, J. S.: *Toccata and Fugue in D Minor,* for organ.
Bach, J. S.: *The Well-Tempered Clavier,* for piano.
Bartók: *Quartet No. 2 in A Minor.*
Beethoven: *Quartet in G Major,* op. 18, no. 2.
Beethoven: *Quartet in E Minor,* op. 59, no. 2.
Beethoven: *Quartet in C Sharp Minor,* op. 131.
Beethoven: *Sonata in C Minor, (Pathétique),* for piano.
Beethoven: *Sonata in C Sharp Minor, (Moonlight),* for piano.
Beethoven: *Sonata in C Minor, (Waldstein),* for piano.
Beethoven: *Sonata in F Minor, (Appassionata),* for piano.

Beethoven: *Sonata in A Major, (Kreutzer)*, for violin and piano.

Beethoven: *Sonata in A Major,* for cello and piano.

Beethoven: *Trio in B Flat Major, (Archduke)*.

Bloch: *Baal Shem,* suite for violin and piano.

Bloch: *Quintet,* for piano and strings.

Brahms: *Ballade No. 5 in G Minor,* for piano.

Brahms: *Capriccio No. 2 in B Minor,* for piano.

Brahms: *Intermezzo in B Flat Minor,* for piano.

Brahms: *Quartet in A Minor.*

Brahms: *Quintet in B Minor,* for clarinet and strings.

Brahms: *Quintet in F Minor,* for piano and strings.

Brahms: *Rhapsody No. 2 in G Minor,* for piano.

Brahms: *Sonata No. 3 in D Minor,* for violin and piano.

Brahms: *Sonata No. 2 in F Major,* for cello and piano.

Brahms: *Waltz in A Flat Major,* for piano.

Chopin: Three études for piano: No. 5 in G flat major, (*Black Key*); No. 12 in C minor, (*Revolutionary*); No. 21 in G flat major, (*Butterfly*).

Chopin: *Mazurka No. 5 in B Flat Major,* for piano.

Chopin: Two nocturnes for piano: No. 2 in E flat major; No. 10 in A flat major.

Chopin: *Polonaise No. 3 in A Major, (Military)*, for piano.

Chopin: Two preludes for piano: No. 4 in E minor; No. 6 in B minor, (*Raindrop*).

Chopin: *Sonata No. 2 in B Flat Minor,* for piano.

Chopin: Two waltzes for piano: No. 1 in E flat major, (*Grande valse brillante*); No. 6 in D flat major, (*Minute*).

Corelli: *La Folia Sonata,* for violin and piano.

Debussy: "Clair de lune," from *Suite bergamasque,* for piano.

Debussy: Two preludes for piano: *The Girl with the Flaxen Hair; The Engulfed Cathedral.*

Debussy: *Quartet in G Minor.*

Dvořák: *Quartet in F Major, (American)*.

Falla: *Concerto for Harpsichord, Flute, Oboe, Clarinet, Violin, and Piano.*

Franck: *Quintet in F Minor,* for piano and strings.

Franck: *Sonata in A Major,* for violin and piano.

Handel: *Suite No. 7 in G Minor,* for piano (including "The Harmonious Blacksmith").

Haydn: *Quartet in D Minor,* op. 76, no. 2.

Haydn: *Quartet in D Major,* op. 76, no. 5.

Haydn: *Quartet in E Flat Major,* op. 50, no. 2.

Haydn: *Sonata No. 52 in E Flat Major,* for piano.

Haydn: *Variations in F Minor,* for piano.

Kreisler: *Caprice Viennois,* for violin and piano.

Kreisler: *Schön Rosmarin,* for violin and piano.

Liszt: *Hungarian Rhapsody No. 2,* for piano.

Liszt: *Liebestraum No. 3 in A Flat Major,* for piano.

Liszt: *Sonata in B Minor,* for piano.

Mendelssohn: Two songs without words, for piano: No. 30, (*Spring Song*); No. 34, (*Tarantelle*).

Mozart: *Fantasia in C Minor* (K. 475), for piano.

Mozart: *Quartet in C Major* (K. 465), (*Dissonant*).

Mozart: *Quartet in B Flat Major* (K. 458), (*Hunt*).

Mozart: *Quartet in G Minor* (K. 478), for piano and strings.

Mozart: *Quintet in A Major* (K. 581), for clarinet and piano.

Mozart: *Sonata in A Major* (K. 331), (*Turkish March*), for piano.

Mozart: *Sonata in B Flat Major* (K. 378), for violin and piano.

Paganini: *Caprice No. 24,* in A minor, for violin.

Paganini: *Perpetual Motion,* for violin.

Prokofiev: *Sonata No. 7,* for piano.

Rachmaninoff: Two preludes for piano: G minor; C sharp minor.

Ravel: *Pavane pour une Infante défunte,* for piano.

Ravel: *Quartet in F.*

Ravel: *Sonatine,* for piano.

Saint-Saëns: *Introduction and Rondo Capriccioso,* for violin and piano (also orchestra).

Sarasate: *Habanera,* op. 21, no. 2, for violin and piano.

Scarlatti, Domenico: Two sonatas for piano: D minor, (*Pastorale*), (L. 413); D major (L. 460).

Schubert: *Impromptu in B Flat Major,* for piano.

Schubert: *Moment musical in F Minor,* for piano.

Schubert: *Quartet in A Minor.*

Schubert: *Quartet in D Minor,* (*Death and the Maiden*).

Schubert: *Quintet in A Major* (*Die Forelle*), for piano and strings.

Schubert: *Trio in E Flat Major.*

Schumann: *Carnival,* for piano.

Schumann: *Fantasia,* in C major, for piano.

Schumann: *Quintet in E Flat Major,* for piano and strings.

Scriabin: *Étude No. 11 in B Flat Minor,* for piano.

Scriabin: *Nocturne, op. 9, no. 2,* for piano.

Scriabin: *Sonata No. 4 in F Sharp Major,* for piano.

Tartini: *Devil's Trill Sonata,* for violin and piano.

Wieniawski: *Polonaise brillante,* for violin and piano.

Wieniawski: *Scherzo tarantelle,* for violin and piano.

# PART FIVE

# *Orchestral Music*

# How the Orchestra Developed

Historical documents reveal that orchestral concerts existed at the court of Edward IV, in the fourteenth century, and, one century after that, at the court of Francis I. These early orchestras included lutes, viols, flutes, drums, and a virginal. In the sixteenth century, the opera *Euridice* by Peri—in 1600—required an orchestra of lutes and a harpsichord. All these ensembles were, to be sure, primitive. But less than two decades after the première of Peri's opera, the orchestra experienced a revolutionary transformation. Claudio Monteverdi, that towering operatic figure of the seventeenth century, used an orchestra of thirty-nine performers for his opera *Orfeo* (1607), including many instruments never previously found in an orchestra. Monteverdi's ensemble embraced an entire family of viols, flute, cornets, sackbuts (predecessor of the trombone), lutes, organ, harpsichord, harp. For this enlarged and varied orchestra, Monteverdi devised completely new effects to increase the expressive capabilities of the ensemble: pizzicato, for example, and tremolo.

Monteverdi assigned an importance to the orchestra that no opera composer before him had done. He used it to intensify the drama on the stage. With introductions and ritornelli he set the mood for the action to follow. He wrote with such a sound instinct for orchestral style that he is sometimes looked upon as history's first composer for the orchestra: a composer who (as Adam Carse wrote) made "possible only on string instruments, music in which the interest is that of harmony, texture, and tone color, and is completely independent of imitative movement of parts." Monteverdi so greatly amplified the vocabulary of harmony that it is also possible to look upon him as the father of this modern science. With Monteverdi, the voice is no longer supported by formal and elementary chords. In *Orfeo* we have a rich orchestral fabric of sounds, with many inner strands. Monteverdi even utilized dissonance to achieve contrasts of color.

Composers of the seventeenth century continually experimented with the organization of the orchestra. Lully was one of the first to assign to the strings the prominence they were henceforth to know, and Alessandro Scarlatti was among the first to indicate that the string quartet was the nucleus of the string section. Increasing richness in string writing, striking contrasts, a growing awareness of the important role of the string quartet are found in the concerto grosso compositions of Handel and Bach.

The physiognomy of the orchestra assumes recognizable features for us in the eighteenth century. The orchestra used by Haydn and Mozart in their symphonies was developed, in their day, in the German city of Mannheim. In 1745, Johann Wenzel Anton Stamitz became the conductor of the Mannheim Orchestra. He was one of the earliest musicians to lay stress upon and to pay fastidious attention to the details of performance. He demanded the most rigid discipline from his men. His performances created the first symphony orchestra, an organization unique in that age. Stamitz explored for the first time such dynamic resources of orchestral performance as crescendo and diminuendo. He amazed his contemporaries (who included the young Mozart on a visit to Mannheim) with the decisiveness and unanimity with which his men played under his lead. The venerable historian, Burney, remarked that the Mannheim orchestra was unsurpassed in its execution: "Its forte is thunder, its crescendo is cataract, its diminuendo is a crystal stream babbling along in the distance, its piano is a breath of spring."

The Mannheim orchestra was made up of between forty and fifty men. For the first time we find a coordination in and a balance between the various instrumental sections. There were twenty violins— ten firsts, ten seconds; four violas and four cellos; two basses; and two each of flutes, oboes, horns, and bassoons; also, one trumpet; and a kettledrum. Except for minor amplifications in the woodwind (two clarinets, particularly) this is basically the orchestra for which Haydn and Mozart wrote their finest works. Mozart, even more than Haydn, increased the significance of the woodwind within the orchestral texture.

With Beethoven, many orchestral instruments achieved a new position of importance in the orchestral family: notably the brass, the double-bass, and the kettledrums. Beethoven also introduced some new instruments of his own: piccolo, double-bassoon, trombone, and such percussion instruments as the triangle, cymbals, and bass drum. Most important of all, Beethoven—much more than Haydn and Mozart—developed the artistic resources of orchestral music by opening up new spheres for sonority, dynamics, and tone color.

After Beethoven, many composers interpolated new instruments into the orchestra to arrive at new timbres, colors, and effects. Mendelssohn was the first to use the tuba in symphonic music; with Wagner, the tubas achieved unprecedented significance. Meyerbeer introduced the bass-clarinet; Rossini, the English horn; Berlioz, several varieties of clarinet.

The virtuosity of many orchestral instruments was greatly extended after Beethoven's time. Berlioz' introduction of keyed woodwind instruments (invented by Boehm) virtually revolutionized the science of woodwind performance. As H. C. Colles explained in the *Oxford History of Music,* before this invention "certain scales were very difficult to play in, rapid chromatic passages were uncertain, and many chromatic shakes impossible. Moreover, the holes had to be placed where the players' fingers could cover them and not in the exact positions which acoustical laws dictated. And the result of this was uncertain intonation which the player had to correct as far as possible by his manner of blowing." No less revolutionary was the introduction of valves and piston in horns and trumpets, which simplified the production of any scale.

The orchestra, after Beethoven, developed a more brilliant coat of colors. With the use of divided strings (first found in Weber, Schubert, and Mendelssohn)—the traditional quartet being split into more groupings—the texture of string music became richer and deeper. Berlioz, Wagner, and Mahler brought a greater gamut of tone color to the brass and woodwind than composers had done before them, and they used the percussion with increased dramatic effect.

The search for new colors, new tonal qualities, new nuances has not ceased. We continually find introduced unorthodox instruments into the orchestra. Many contemporary composers have written large orchestral works requiring a piano, or an organ, or both. Gustav Mahler and Richard Strauss brought to the orchestra such unorthodox instruments as a mandolin, or a guitar, or a saxophone. Strauss even invented instruments of his own to bring greater realism to his programmatic writing, as, for example, the "wind instrument" in *Don Quixote* and the "thunder instrument" in *An Alpine Symphony*. Respighi used an actual phonograph in *The Pines of Rome* to inject the voice of a nightingale into his music through a recording. Twentieth-century extremists were even more daring. George Antheil wrote a work called *Ballet mécanique* for an orchestra that included anvils, airplane propellers, electric bells and automobile horns; Gershwin used real French taxi-horns for *An American in Paris;* there is a banging typewriter in Ferde Grofe's *Tabloid;* in Vaughan Williams' *Seventh Symphony,* the score requires the use of a whistling wind machine and a clanging vibraphone.

# The Modern Symphony Orchestra

The modern symphony orchestra has about one hundred men. More than half of them belong in the strings. The nucleus of this string section is the string quartet—first and second violins, viola and cello; but the strings also include double-basses and harps. The usual number of strings in our greatest orchestras is seventy, distributed more or less in the following manner: seventeen first violins and seventeen second violins; twelve violas; twelve cellos; ten double-basses; two harps.

The violin is the basic instrument in the string section; no other instrument comes closer in achieving the expressiveness of the human voice. With a range of four octaves, the violin is capable of a wide gamut of colors and nuances, but is at its best in tender and lyrical moods.

The leader of the first violin is known as the concertmaster. It is his duty to unravel for the other violins any unusual or knotty technical problem that may arise in the music. When the score calls for a violin solo—as in Rimsky-Korsakov's *Scheherezade* or Richard Strauss' *A Hero's Life*—the concertmaster performs the passages.

The viola is larger in size than the violin and is tuned one-fifth below. It is also an expressive instrument, but its emotional range is more limited than that of the violin, and its voice is richer and more melancholy.

The cello is tuned one octave below the viola. Its deep, rich timbre makes it particularly effective in elegiac or soulful passages. Where the violin and viola are played with the instrument under the chin, the cello is placed between the knees.

The double-bass, which is considerably larger than the cello, is also played in a vertical position. It has the lowest register in the string section—an octave lower than the cello. Its very deep voice makes it more useful in emphasizing rhythm than in projecting a lyric line.

The harp is the only instrument among the strings that differs radically in shape, and in the number of its strings. Where all other string instruments have four strings, the harp has forty-six, the C notes being red-colored, and the F, blue. Seven pedals help to raise the tone of the scale by one or two semitones. Its arpeggio sweeps and plucked notes contribute delicate effects.

The second important section of the orchestra is the woodwind. As the name implies these instruments are "wind," which means that their sound is produced by blowing air into them. Most of them are made out of wood.

The highest register is found in the flute. The flute differs from the other woodwinds in two important respects. It is made not out of wood but generally out of silver or gold; the air is blown into a flue or mouthpiece, whereas in other woodwinds the air is blown through a delicate reed, or double reed, which fits into the mouthpiece. The gentle, poetic, and silvery tone of the flute is familiar. So are the shrill pipings of the piccolo, which belong to the flute family. The piccolo is half the size of the flute, and an octave higher.

The oboe, a double-reed instrument, produces a poignant, bittersweet tone. The English horn is actually an oboe. It is somewhat larger in size, and its tone is a melancholy wail compared to the bittersweet voice of the oboe.

The masculine member of the woodwind family is the clarinet. The clarinet has a wide range, and nobility and beauty of sound. The most functional clarinet in the modern orchestra is that in B flat; but in scores where there are sharps in the key signature, the clarinet in A is used. This family also includes a bass clarinet.

The bass voice of the woodwind is the bassoon. It has a double reed, and its voice is heavy and ponderous, thus making it particularly apt for comical or whimsical passages. There is also a double-bassoon among the woodwinds, whose voice is the lowest in the whole orchestra.

The modern fully equipped symphony orchestra has sixteen wood-wind instruments: three flutes and a piccolo; three oboes and an English horn; three clarinets and a bass clarinet; three bassoons and a double bassoon.

The third orchestral group—the most brilliant in resonance—is the brass. In this family, the trumpet has the highest pitch. Its tone is piercing, making the trumpet particularly useful for brilliant colors. There are two kinds of trumpets, that in C being the most useful; the other is in B flat.

The French horn, an octave lower than the trumpet, is made up of circular tubes. One end of these is a large open mouth from which the musical sounds emanate; the other end is a small funnel-shaped cup, the mouthpiece. The tone of the French horn is majestic, and ro-mantic.

The trombone is manipulated by a slide, the tone becoming lower each time the slide is drawn out. The trombone sounds almost like a trumpet, except that it is somewhat more subdued, more solemn and dignified. The brass includes tenor and bass trombones.

The lowest brass voice is the tuba—the bass of the trombones. Its tone has great depth and mellowness.

The modern symphony orchestra has seventeen brass instruments: four trumpets, eight French horns, four trombones, and one tuba.

The loudest section in the orchestra is the percussion. This is the group that gives stress to the rhythm and plays an important role in building up powerful sonorous effects and climaxes.

The most important percussion instrument is the kettledrum, usually consisting of two large round drums beaten upon with two felt-covered drumsticks. There are snare or side drums used to produce rolls, and a bass drum. Brilliant sonorities are contributed by the cymbals (made up of two metal plates, the edges of which touch each other in a sliding motion; another way to use the cymbal is to beat a kettledrum stick on one of the plates to produce a roll).

Other percussion instruments include the following: the glocken-spiel, or bells, a series of horizontal metal bars; the celesta, which has a keyboard like a harmonium but yields a tinkling tone; the triangle, which is a steel rod shaped into a triangle, producing soft bell-like tones when it is tapped with a piece of metal; the xylophone; chimes; and when the score calls for it, a piano.

The symphony orchestra requires the services of two timpanists (or kettledrum performers), and two additional percussion players who between them can double on all the other percussion instruments. Most of the large orchestras also include a staff pianist.

The position of the various groups of instruments on the concert stage varies slightly with different conductors. The most usual pattern is to have the first violins at the right hand of the conductor, and the second violins and harps at his left. The cellos and violas are directly in front of him. At the back of the cellos and violas are the woodwinds, and after that come the rows of brass and percussions. The double-basses are lined up in the rear.

One variation of this formation is found in the Boston Symphony Orchestra where the first and second violins are grouped together at the right of the conductor, with the violas at his left.

Still another variation is found in the Philadelphia Orchestra. There, the first violins are at the right hand of the conductor, while at his left are the cellos and harps. The second row includes flutes, oboes and viols; and directly behind them, the clarinets and bassoons. French horns are seated behind the clarinets and bassoons, and are followed by a row of trumpets and trombones and a row of timpani. In the right-hand corner of the stage come the tuba, celesta and double-basses; in the left-hand corner, the piano and various other percussion instruments.

# 3

## *The Conductor*

The famous composer and conductor, Gustav Mahler, once said that there are no great orchestras, only great conductors. There is a great deal of truth to this aphorism, if it is not interpreted too literally. Of course, not even Toscanini can make a high-school orchestra sound like the Boston Symphony; and by the same token even a fourth-rate conductor cannot make the Boston Symphony sound like a high-school orchestra. But where a great orchestra is involved, its artistic significance varies directly with the ability of its conductor. The same orchestra, on alternate weeks, can sound inspired and perfunctory depending on the capabilities of the man at its head.

The art of conducting is the most complex in the entire realm of musical interpretation, because the instrument used by the conductor —the symphony orchestra—is the most complicated. The conductor must know his orchestra and the score he is conducting; he must have the ability to transmit his concept of the music to the men under him; he must have the personal magnetism to electrify and inspire them.

It is only comparatively recently that the conductor has become the musical interpreter *in excelsis*. Until the middle of the nineteenth century, his only function was to beat out the time for his musicians. The

Germans called him a *"Taktschlager"*—a time beater—and that is precisely what he was.

The function of time-beating is as old as music itself. The methods of beating time varied with different men and in different periods in music history. As Johann Bähr wrote, in 1719, "One man conducts with the foot, another with the head, a third with the hand, some with both hands, some again take a roll of paper, others a stick." Some even used a handkerchief tied to a stick; others hammered a key on the organ bench. In the Sistine Chapel of Rome, in the sixteenth century, it was customary to beat time with a roll of paper called the "sol-fa." One century later, Jean-Baptiste Lully conducted by pounding his walking stick on the floor. One more century and we find the conductor at the Paris Opéra striking time with a stick on one of the desks; he disturbed performances with this regular beating so frequently that he came to be known as a "woodchopper."

In the eighteenth century, time beating was combined with the playing of the organ or harpsichord, and less frequently, with the playing of the violin or flute. This practice is said to have originated early in the seventeenth century with Adolphe Hasse in Dresden, and was subsequently practiced by Handel and Johann Sebastian Bach. In the nineteenth century, this method became more complicated. The musician at the harpsichord would signal the beat with his head to the concertmaster who faced him; the concertmaster, in turn, designated the beat to the rest of the men with movements of his violin when he was playing or with his bow when he was at rest.

Slowly and almost unrecognizably the conductor emerged out of the shadow of the time beater. Time beaters like Lully and Handel yielded to fits of temperament. Lully used to break violins in demoniac fits of rage when errors were committed; Handel once threw a kettledrum at an offending player; Gluck was a veritable tyrant. Time beaters, in short, were making their whims and tempers and personalities strongly felt in the closing decades of the eighteenth century—so much so that a code of personal conduct was drawn up for them by the men of the orchestra.

The time beater was asserting his personality. He was also beginning to bring to his perfunctory task both musicianship and taste, both discrimination and personal style. Time beaters like Bach, Haydn or Beethoven—directing performances of their own masterworks—or like Johann Wenzel Stamitz in Mannheim whipping his orchestra into shape, were conductors in the contemporary sense of that term. They imposed both their will and their conception of a musical work upon their musicians.

Conducting as a science and an art did not develop fully until the baton came into general use. The baton freed the conductor from the necessity of playing an instrument; it compelled him to focus his entire attention on the job of directing his men and shaping a performance.

Though the baton had been in sporadic use for many centuries, and had been employed by various time beaters, it did not come into its own until 1820. In that year Ludwig Spohr, eminent German violinist, conductor and composer, visited England to direct a few concerts of the Royal Philharmonic Society. He bewildered the musicians of the orchestra by refusing to direct them from a place at the concert-master's desk, but rather by standing in front of them and waving a stick at them. Spohr has written about this event, a red-letter day in the history of conducting, in his autobiography: "Incited thereby to more than attention, and conducted with certainty by the *visible* manner of giving the time, they played with a spirit and correctness such as, until then, they had never before been heard to play. Surprised and inspired by the result, the orchestra immediately after the first part of the symphony expressed aloud its united assent to the new mode of conducting, and thereby overruled all further opposition on the part of the directors. . . . The triumph of the baton as a time-giver was decisive."

Henceforth the baton was to be an all-important instrument in the hand of the conductor—an instrument that changed him from a time beater to an interpretative artist.

One of the first to recognize the artistic mission of the conductor was Felix Mendelssohn during his eight-year period as director of the Leipzig Gewandhaus Orchestra. With Mendelssohn, the conductor began to personalize his performances, to make them a reflection of his temperament and genius; and with Mendelssohn, the conductor began to assume the responsibility of giving design to each of his performances. Others also understood the true function of the conductor: Berlioz in France; Franz Liszt in Weimar; Hans von Bülow in Germany. Hans von Bülow was particularly fastidious about rehearsals, particularly attentive to details. "Only when one has mastered an opera . . . in which each nuance, each instrument, has its special determination, is it possible to rehearse and conduct it," he wrote. He also said: "A score should be in a conductor's head, not the conductor's head in the score." With words such as these the conductor ceased once and for all to be a time beater. He has become a sensitive artist, an interpreter, a recreator. He is to play on his instrument—the symphony orchestra—the way Heifetz plays on a violin, Casals on a cello, and Horowitz on a piano.

It is possible to dissect the conductor, as a biologist dissects a frog, and uncover those anatomical qualities that go into the making of greatness. This writer has done so in his book, *Dictators of the Baton:* *

"The ear, first of all: a conductor obviously must have unusual aural sensitivity to musical sound, to tone colors, to different shades and tints of orchestral texture. . . .

"Then comes the brain. The conductor must have a comprehensive musical training which embraces a working knowledge of most instruments of the orchestra. To this he must add a good memory. A conductor must know the music he is directing thoroughly—every note of it—for only then can he give specific and exact directions.

"Finally, the conductor must have that innermost sensitivity that comes from the heart. He must feel the emotional qualities of the music he is directing keenly and spontaneously, if he is to impress these emotional qualities on his men.

"But ear, brain, and heart . . . are not everything. . . . We must search beyond anatomy in our dissection of the great conductor. In our search we come to an element difficult to describe, but whose presence is felt electrically; an element which for want of a better word we speak of as 'personality.' . . . Without a magnetic personality no conductor can achieve greatness. Toscanini, Stokowski, Mitropoulos have the capacity to galvanize the men who play under them, and the audience as well. No sooner do these conductors come on the stage than one feels the contact of some inexplicable electric currents. The very atmosphere suddenly becomes highly charged. In such an atmosphere, a performance becomes cogent and dynamic, bursting with vitality.

"Genius has not only the capacity of creating great art; it is often capable of producing great art in others. It has not only the power of being inspired, but also that of inspiring. A minor orchestra under a great conductor will sound like a major one; and a major orchestra will outdo itself in the presence of genius. More than one important soloist has confessed that playing under Toscanini's direction has made him achieve heights which he formerly thought unattainable."

* *Dictators of the Baton,* by David Ewen. Revised Edition. Prentice-Hall, Inc., 1948.

# *Basic Forms of Orchestral Music*

## BOLERO

A Spanish dance in triple rhythm, usually accompanied by castanets. It was created in 1780 by Sebastian Cerezo. Chopin wrote a bolero for the piano (op. 19), but the form is essentially orchestral. The most celebrated work in this form is the *Bolero* of Maurice Ravel, written for the dancer Ida Rubinstein in 1928, and subsequently a tremendous favorite at orchestral concerts everywhere; it has also been heard in numerous arrangements for different instrumental combinations.

## CONCERTANTE

The most familiar meaning of this form is: a concerto for two or more instruments and orchestra. Mozart's *Sinfonia Concertante in E Flat Major,* for violin, viola, and orchestra (K. 364) is a notable example.

## CONCERTINO

A little concerto. This term bears the same relation to concerto that sonatina does to the sonata. The structure of the concertino is slighter than that of the concerto; the movements are brief; and development sections are invariably either curtailed or eliminated. Several contemporary French composers have produced delightful concertinos for piano and orchestra, among them Jean Françaix, Arthur Honegger, and Francis Poulenc.

## CONCERTO

### (also *Concerto Grosso*)

The concerto is a major work for one, two, three, or more solo instruments and orchestra (though most usually for a single instrument), intended primarily to emphasize the individuality of the solo instrument and to exhibit the virtuosity of the performer. The concerto is most often in three movements. The first is in sonata form, traditionally ending in a cadenza in which the performer further demonstrates his powers but without orchestral accompaniment. (In Mozart's time it was customary for the performer to improvise his own cadenzas during the performance. Later on, the composer—or a performer, or some other musician—wrote out special cadenzas which were interpolated into the concerto. Thus the cadenzas used today in the violin concertos of Beethoven, Mendelssohn, or Brahms, are either by Joachim or Kreisler; much less frequently by some other violinist.) The second movement of the concerto is slow and lyrical, sometimes in the song form, sometimes a theme and variations. A lively closing movement follows, most often in the rondo form. Cadenzas are at times interpolated to close the second and third movements.

The word "concerto" was used for the first time in 1602 by Ludovico Viadana for a series of motets, for voice and organ. But as an instrumental form, the concerto appears first in a work for two violins and figured bass by Giuseppe Torelli, in 1686. Torelli's concerto was actually a sonata da camera, since it was for three instruments only.

An orchestral concerto was created by Arcangelo Corelli, who was also responsible for the early development of the sonata and of chamber music. Corelli's sixth volume of works (op. 6) consists of a set of concerti grossi for two violins, cello and a "concertino obbligato," or accompaniment. This is the source of all later concerto-grosso writing; Corelli succeeded in formulating a concert-grosso style which remained a model for his contemporaries and successors.

He developed the essential form of the concerto grosso. It became a work in which a small group of solo instruments (called the concertino, or small concerto) was combined with the rest of the orchestra (called the ripieno, meaning "full"), in unison or in contrast, antiphonally or contrapuntally. Corelli wrote with such richness of musical ideas, such effective contrasts of light and shade, and such skill in the interplay of solo groups and orchestra, that the concerto grosso became a valid and significant form.

The best known concerto grosso by Corelli is the eighth, called the *Christmas Concerto*. It is made up of several short movements contrasting one another in tempo and mood. The last movement is called "Pastorale," and it is because of this section that the entire work is known as the *Christmas Concerto*. The "Pastorale" is a religious melody describing the birth of Christ, with angels hovering over Bethlehem; in its simple, pastoral beauty it is the godfather for later similar pastorales in such masterworks as Handel's *Messiah* and Bach's *Christmas Oratorio*.

Corelli's concerto grosso, widely heard and distributed through publication, had an enormous influence. Italian composers were inspired by him to write works in the same form—among them Geminiani, Locatelli, Sammartini, and most important of all, Vivaldi. Vivaldi wrote more than four hundred concertos, works which led music out of the maze of polyphony into the clearer and purer atmosphere of homophony. We know how profound was Vivaldi's influence on Bach; how Bach used to copy out Vivaldi's concertos and transcribe them for different instruments. Vivaldi's influence on the evolution of musical style was no less powerful. He helped to establish the concerto-grosso form more firmly, to give it both clarity of design and solidity of structure. He taught his contemporaries to write a singing melody. He pointed the way to contrast of thematic ideas and to thematic development, basic tools of the later orchestral composer. He was one of the first outstanding exponents of program music.

Vivaldi produced two sets of concerti grossi. The first, gathered in op. 3, was entitled by the composer *Harmonic Inspiration* (*L'Estro armonico*), and includes twelve works. The eleventh in D minor is particularly famous, but usually in the modern transcription by Alexander Siloti. It is in three movements, the first being a spacious slow section leading into a fugue; the second, a song of wondrous beauty; the third, a vigorous and dramatic finale. The second set of concerti grossi, op. 8, was published under the title of *The Trial of Harmony and Invention* (*Il Cimento dell' armonia e dell' invenzioni*). In this group we find a remarkable quartet of concertos collectively entitled

*The Four Seasons.* Each is concerned with one of the seasons of the year, beginning with spring; an unidentified sonnet at the head of each work provides a clue to its emotional and programmatic content. For *The Four Seasons* is program music—one of the earliest notable examples of such writing; each work can be justifiably looked upon as a tone poem. Realistic effects produce the sounds of birds, the merry-making of farmers, the chattering of teeth with the "shiver, and tingle of the chilling snow," the murmur of running fountains, the fall of the spring rain.

Handel heard Corelli's concerti grossi in Italy. It is no coincidence that he, too, published a set of twelve concerti grossi—eighteen years after Corelli published his; though the fact that the works of both Handel and Corelli are opus 6 is more curious than significant. (Six years earlier, in 1734, Handel had published his first set of concerti grossi, opus 3.) The Handel concerto grosso, like that of Corelli, consists of a group of solo instruments (often two violins and a cello) with the rest of the orchestra. It follows a more or less regular pattern, beginning with a slow and sedate movement, continuing with an allegro and an adagio in both of which principal themes are given embellishments by the solo instruments; a fugal allegro follows, and the work concludes with a vivacious finale. For variety of lyricism, for spaciousness of design, and for nobility of concept, the twelve Handel concerti grossi, in op. 6, represent a marked advance beyond both Corelli and Vivaldi.

Johann Sebastian Bach was also familiar with the Corelli concerto grosso and profited by this intimacy when he produced his own six *Brandenburg Concertos* for orchestra. The name "Brandenburg" was derived from the fact that this set of works was commissioned by Christian Ludwig, Margrave of Brandenburg. It cannot be said that the Margrave was perceptive enough to recognize the value of the Bach compositions. The concertos do not appear listed in a catalogue of the Margrave's musical collection, and there is good reason to believe that each of the manuscripts was sold for about ten cents a piece!

The Bach Brandenburg concerto is usually in three movements: the first is fast; the second, lyrical; the third, vivacious. (The first concerto, however, has a fourth movement—a minuet; and the third concerto has only two fast movements separated by two slow chords.) There is no set solo group in the first concerto, the only work in the entire set which conforms less to the concerto grosso style than to the suite form. The solo group in the second concerto is a trumpet, flute, oboe, and violin; in this work there are particularly effective arabesque passages for the solo trumpet. In the third concerto, Bach uses three string choirs, each consisting of three instruments (three violins; three violas; three cellos). The fourth is written for a solo violin and two solo flutes. The fifth also has three solo instruments—a flute, a violin, and a harpsichord; a remarkable feature of this composition is an extended unaccompanied cadenza for harpsichord in the first movement, the first time a keyboard instrument was given such importance in the concerto grosso. The last of the concertos has unique orchestration, in that it is entirely for strings (except for a cembalo), but with the violins and violas omitted. Instead of the viols and violas we have a pair of obsolete instruments—the viola da braccia and the viola da gamba—to make up the solo group.

Throughout the six *Brandenburg Concertos* lyrical pages are combined with polyphonic writing in Bach's most ingenious and effective manner.

It is a small step from the use of a *group* of solo instruments with orchestral background to that of a single *solo* instrument and orchestra. And it was a step which early composers of the concerto grosso were not hesitant to take. Tartini, Valentini, Vivaldi, Handel, and Johann Sebastian Bach all wrote numerous concertos for some solo instrument and orchestra. But these concertos are not yet in the pattern of later works in the same form. They still carry out the prevailing tradition of the concerto grosso: pitting the single instrument against, and combining it with, the rest of the orchestra. But these composers were responsible for certain salient developments in the concerto. In the Handel concertos for solo instrument and orchestra, we find the first prevalent use of the cadenza—subsequently a distinguishing characteristic of all concertos; we have already noted the remarkable use of the cadenza in Bach's *Sixth Brandenburg Concerto*. And Bach was the first composer to apply the concerto form to a keyboard instrument. Bach wrote seven concertos for piano and orchestra, and it is with these works that the piano concerto is born. Actually, all these seven works were transcriptions of other works, some of them originating as violin concertos; indeed, two of these works in their original violin version—the *Concertos in A Minor* and *E Major*—remain staples in the violin concerto repertory. Even more greatly favored by present-day concert audiences is Bach's *Concerto in D Minor*, for two violins and orchestra.

After the age of Bach, composers lost interest in the concerto-grosso form, preferring to concentrate on its legitimate successor, the concerto. But before speaking the last word on the concerto grosso it is necessary to add that some composers, of a later day, revived the form. Brahms' so-called *Double Concerto*—the concerto for violin, cello and orchestra —is a reversion to the concerto-grosso technique an adaptation of it to modern concerto. In the twentieth century, Ernest Bloch wrote a *Concerto Grosso,* for chamber orchestra, to prove that it is possible to incorporate modern thinking and idioms within older forms. The contemporary Czech composer, Bohuslav Martinu, has made extensive use of the concerto-grosso form in works like the *Concerto Grosso, Double Concerto,* and various concertos for solo instrument and orchestra. The twentieth-century Hungarian, Béla Bartók, also returned to the concerto-grosso style in his finest orchestral work, *Concerto for Orchestra.*

It is first with Mozart that we arrive at the contemporary concept of the concerto. Mozart wrote numerous concertos for single piano and orchestra, two and three pianos and orchestra, violin and orchestra, flute and orchestra, etc. The concerto structure is now fully clarified: the first movement in sonata form is followed by a song-like slow movement, and concluded with a finale generally in rondo form. Mozart was also the first to understand the role of the solo instrument, and its relationship to the accompanying orchestra. He allowed the solo instrument a freedom of movement and an independence not known before him; and yet the significance of the orchestra is by no means slighted. Instrument and orchestra become equal partners in the artistic scheme.

The noblest of Mozart's more than twenty concertos for the piano include the following: D minor (K. 466); A major (K. 488); C minor (K. 491); C major (K. 503). The most often heard Mozart concertos for violin include the fourth in D major (K. 218); and the fifth in A major (K. 219), the latter known as the *Turkish Concerto* because the last movement includes a theme in the pseudo-Turkish style in vogue in Vienna in Mozart's day. Of the other Mozart concertos, the most famous is the *Concerto in E Flat Major* (K. 365) for two pianos and orchestra. Mozart also wrote two splendid concertos for flute and orchestra; and a *Concerto for Flute, Harp and Orchestra,* together with a *Sinfonia Concertante for Violin, Viola and Orchestra* which is really a concerto.

The concerto before Mozart emphasized virtuosity; the Mozart concerto combined virtuosity with a profound depth of feeling and an enchantment of lyricism. There is suaveness and sophistication in his two finest violin concertos; there is the immensity of tragedy and dramatic restlessness in the C minor and D minor piano concertos; there is bright-faced gaiety and light heart in the A major and B flat major concertos for pianos; and there is a seraphic beauty, almost otherworldly, in the two concertos for flute and the *Concerto for Flute, Harp and Orchestra*.

Beethoven completely banishes virtuosity for its own sake to concentrate on the poetic idea. Beethoven's first three piano concertos—he wrote five—are in the Mozart vein: lucid in structure, formal in approach, correct in idiom. But in the *Fourth Concerto in G Major,* in the *Fifth Piano Concerto in E Flat Major* (best known as the *Emperor Concerto*) and in the *Violin Concerto,* the concerto form assumes epic proportions and is filled with epic poetry. So dramatic is the *Fourth Piano Concerto* that it is not difficult to interpret it as the composer's own Herculean struggle with Fate (the Fate that condemned him to deafness)—particularly in the slow movement, a dialogue between piano and orchestra, in which the orchestra is defiant Fate and the piano the resigned victim. The *Fifth Concerto* has acquired the sobriquet of "Emperor" because of the majesty of its form and content. Here, as in the *Fourth Concerto,* the concerto form assumes the expanse of a symphony as nobility and grandeur of thought unfolds. The same immensity of design and majesty of content is found in Beethoven's *Violin Concerto in D Major,* deservedly one of the most celebrated of all violin concertos.

The Romantics who followed Beethoven brought to the concerto greater ardor, deeper emotion, greater flexibility of expression. The peaks in the Romantic literature for the concerto include the Schumann *Piano Concerto in A Minor,* the Mendelssohn *Violin Concerto in E Minor,* the two piano concertos of Chopin (E minor and F minor), the two piano concertos of Brahms (D minor and B flat major), the *Violin Concerto* of Brahms (D major), the *Violin Concerto* (D major) and the *First Piano Concerto* (B flat minor) of Tchaikovsky, and the *Piano Concerto in A Minor* of Grieg. Liszt wrote two piano concertos which are comparatively minor efforts, but they are of interest because they experiment with the one-movement form. His *Concerto No. 1 in E Flat Major*—the more popular of the two—was in Liszt's day derisively referred to as the "Triangle Concerto," because the instrumentation included the triangle.

In the twentieth century, concertos in a Romantic vein have been written for the violin by Sibelius, Glazunov and Elgar, and for the piano by Rachmaninoff. Rachmaninoff's *Concerto No. 2 in C Minor* has become one of the most popular of all concertos, filled as it is with the most beguiling sentiments and melodies. It has been used successfully in several motion pictures, such as Noel Coward's *Brief Encounter* and in *Rhapsody;* and one of its principal melodies was confiscated for the song hit, "Full Moon and Empty Arms."

Concertos in a more advanced and experimental technique, now permanent in the repertory, include the following for piano: Prokofiev's *Concerto No. 3 in C Minor;* Khatchaturian's *Piano Concerto;* Gershwin's *Concerto in F;* Ravel's *Concerto for the Left Hand,* and *Concerto for Piano and Orchestra;* Bartók's *Second Piano Concerto.* Violin concertos include: Prokofiev's *Concerto No. 1;* Alban Berg's *Concerto for Violin and Orchestra;* William Walton's *Concerto for Violin and Orchestra.* Both Bartók and Walton have also produced fine concertos for viola and orchestra, and so has Hindemith; Hindemith's viola concerto entitled *Der Schwanendreher* (*The Organgrinder*), is based upon old folk melodies one of which is called "Seid ihr nicht der Schwanendreher."

## DIVERTIMENTO

A term used extensively in the eighteenth century interchangeably with serenade, cassation, and nocturne; it would be difficult to draw a fine line separating these terms. They were all works for various combinations of instruments, including the orchestra. These compositions were often used for outdoor performance or for court entertainments, and were light in character. They were made up of several short movements, varied in style—usually more than four in number.

Haydn and Mozart wrote many divertimenti. Haydn's first string quartets were really divertimenti. Mozart's *Divertimento in B Flat Major* (K. 287)—scored for two horns and strings, and in six movements—is popular. A contemporary use of this form was made by Béla Bartók in his *Divertimento,* for strings.

## FANTASIA

This form, popular in solo instrumental music, is discussed in an earlier section. Several sporadic attempts have been made to adapt the form for orchestral music. Beethoven wrote a *Fantasia for Piano, Chorus and Orchestra in C Minor* (op. 80) that is rarely heard. One of the most celebrated orchestral fantasias is by the contemporary English composer, Ralph Vaughan Williams—the *Fantasia on a Theme by Thomas Tallis,* in which a theme by the sixteenth-century English church composer, Thomas Tallis, is freely developed.

The term "fantasia" is also sometimes used in orchestral music to designate a potpourri of melodies. Vaughan Williams wrote a *Fantasia on Christmas Carols;* fantasias on a famous opera are often represented at concerts of salon and band music.

## INTERMEZZO

An orchestral interlude in an opera played to denote a passage of time as the curtain remains raised. Popular examples of such pieces of music include the extremely popular intermezzo from Mascagni's *Cavalleria Rusticana* and that from Granados' *Goyescas.*

The term "intermezzo" is often used interchangeably with "entr'-acte"—music for orchestra between scenes or acts. When used in a symphony—as in Schumann's *Symphony No. 4 in D Minor*—the intermezzo is a short movement of poetic content intended as a transition between two larger movements.

The intermezzo is also a form of piano music and is further analyzed in that section.

## MARCH

Music intended to accompany marching, usually in three sections, the middle one being a lyrical trio, and the third part repeating the first. It is most often in $\frac{6}{8}$ time, but sometimes in $\frac{2}{4}$ and $\frac{4}{4}$ time. One of the earliest examples of a march is found in a collection of dances by Arbeau in 1489. Marches are found in operas by Lully and Mozart; and in oratorios by Handel. Beethoven wrote a very popular "Turkish March" in his incidental music to the *Ruins of Athens.* Marches are also found in keyboard music, and the form is further commented upon in the section on solo instrumental music.

As a form of orchestral music, the march is varied in character and personality.

The most popular kind of march is the military march, of which Johann Strauss' *Radetzky March* and the famous marches of John Philip Sousa (*Stars and Stripes Forever, Semper Fidelis,* and so forth) are notable examples. Then there is the wedding march—the two most famous being that of Mendelssohn (in his *A Midsummer Night's Dream Suite*) and Wagner (from the opera, *Lohengrin*). Finally there is the funeral march. While the most celebrated of these is for the piano (the slow movement of Chopin's *Sonata No. 2*), it is familiar in band and orchestral arrangement. The funeral march in Beethoven's *Eroica Symphony* is also famous.

Other popular marches for the orchestra include the stirring "Rakóczy March" (or "Hungarian March") from Berlioz' *Damnation of Faust;* the "Coronation March" from Meyerbeer's opera, *Le Prophète;* and the march from Wagner's *Tannhäuser.*

Sir Edward Elgar wrote a set of five marches for orchestra, entitled *Pomp and Circumstance.* The first of these, in D major, has become as intimately identified with the British Empire as the British national anthem; its middle section has become popular in a song for which Laurence Housman wrote the lyric, "Land of Hope and Glory."

## MINUET

The minuet is analyzed in the section on instrumental music.

As a form of orchestral music, the minuet first appears in the old classical suite. It was also interpolated as a movement in some of the so-called *French overtures* of Lully, Purcell, and Handel, and is even found in some overtures to Handel's oratorios. Mozart wrote many delightful minuets, the most celebrated being that found in his opera *Don Giovanni.* There is also a very charming minuet in Verdi's opera, *Rigoletto.*

The greatest musical significance of the minuet in orchestral music is as a movement—the third—of the classical sonata, quartet, and symphony. Minuets are found in such works of Haydn and Mozart, and in the earliest sonatas and quartets and in the *First Symphony* of Beethoven. Beginning with the *Second Symphony,* Beethoven changed the mood and tempo of the minuet movement and rechristened the form "scherzo," thereby beginning a new tradition in symphonic writing. (Beethoven, however, returned to the minuet in the *Eighth Symphony*.)

## NOCTURNE

While the nocturne is basically a form of piano music (see section on Solo Instrumental Music), it makes an occasional appearance in orchestral music. In the early classical period composers like Haydn, and many of his immediate predecessors, wrote nocturnes (or notturnos) for various instrumental ensembles—the nocturne being the same as the divertimento and the serenade.

The connotation of nocturne—as a piece of "night music"—is carried out by Mendelssohn in the nocturne in his *Midsummer Night's Dream Suite*. This beautiful song for the horn gently lulls to sleep the characters of the play at the close of Act 3.

Claude Debussy wrote three nocturnes for orchestra, but as Debussy explained, "We are not concerned with the form of the nocturne, but everything that this word includes in the way of diversified impression and special lights." The three nocturnes are subtitled: "Clouds" (Nuages), "Festival" (Fêtes), and "Sirens" (Sirènes).

## OVERTURE

An orchestral prelude to an opera and play; in the Classical Era, the first movement of a suite.

The earliest operas did not have an overture, but a vocal prologue. But in the seventeenth century, opera composers started prefacing the first act with an instrumental piece sometimes called "sinfonia," and other times a "toccata." The overture becomes prominent in opera with two composers. One was Alessandro Scarlatti, who prefaced his operas with a three-part overture: an allegro, culminating in a fugue; a grave section; a vivacious finale. (This type of overture came to be known as the *Italian overture*.) A second type was perfected in France by Lully—and consequently became known as the *French overture*. This was also in three sections: the first, slow and sedate; the second, lively and frequently in fugal form; the third, a dance—usually a minuet. French overtures became extremely popular in England, as well as in France, and were written by Purcell and Handel.

Thus far there was only a most tenuous relation—if there was any relation at all—between the overture and the work it prefaced; in fact, it was not unusual for a composer to use for one opera an overture written for another. Two composers worked toward creating a closer tie between overture and the opera that follows it. One of them was Gluck. In his search for dramatic truth, Gluck dispensed with the formal overture of his predecessors and contemporaries. For *Alceste* and *Iphigénie en Aulide* he produced an *"intrada"* (an introduction) —a one-movement piece which sets the mood for the play to come and is integrally bound up with the character and style of the opera. In his attempt to make his intrada an inextricable part of the opera, Gluck joined the final bars of the overture to the opening scene without interruption.

Mozart carried on this new concept of the overture, and went one step further. In *Don Giovanni* and *The Magic Flute* he incorporated in his overture melodies from the opera itself. Henceforth most opera composers had a double purpose in writing overtures: to include some of the basic material of the opera; and to capture the spirit and atmosphere of the work. Beethoven, in the overtures to his opera *Fidelio*—he wrote four of them, the most celebrated and the greatest being the *Leonore Overture No. 3*—not only quotes thematic ideas from the opera but has them so intimately related to the opera in feeling and mood and emotional impact that they are regarded as miniature dramas.

Generally, Rossini did not place too much artistic importance on the overtures to his operas. Many times he did not hesitate to take the overture of one opera and use it for another; and he could do this because his overtures generally bore no relation to the operas that followed. But in writing his most ambitious opera, *William Tell,* Rossini took special pains with every facet, including the overture. The *William Tell Overture* is probably one of the most familiar overtures ever written. It is really a set of four tone poems, integrated into a single work. The first is a beautiful nature picture of a morning in the Swiss Alps; the second is a vivid description of a storm; the third is a pastoral scene in which is heard the shepherd's song of thanksgiving for the passing of the storm; the concluding part is military music descriptive of the triumph of Swiss soldiers over their Austrian rulers.

Weber's overtures to his greatest Romantic operas—*Oberon, Der Freischütz,* and *Euryanthe*—are miniature dramas in the vein of Beethoven's overtures to *Fidelio*. Even more than Mozart, Weber made a conscious effort to incorporate into these overtures the chief materials from the operas: motives connected with principal characters and incidents; parts of the most significant arias. These three overtures epitomize the subject of the operas themselves, but they are self-sufficient masterworks apart from their operas and have survived in the orchestral repertory.

The overtures written by Wagner for some of his earlier operas—notably, *Rienzi, The Flying Dutchman,* and *Tannhäuser*—follow the direction pointed out by Weber in assembling ideas from the operas themselves. Beginning with *Lohengrin,* Wagner replaced the overture with a prelude—a short orchestral preface whose sole function is to reflect the spiritual or emotional climate of the music drama. Thus we find an otherworldly radiance in the prelude to *Lohengrin;* sensual yearnings and fevers in that to *Tristan und Isolde;* religious ecstasy in the *Parsifal Prelude.* Each of the *Ring* dramas also has a short prelude. (While the introduction to *Die Meistersinger* was called a prelude by the composer, it is really an overture in the style of that found in *Tannhäuser. Die Meistersinger Overture* is an elaborate canvas on which the composer brings some of the main themes and melodies from the music drama.) Claude Debussy also utilizes brief preludes—one before each act, to foreshadow the atmosphere or mood—in *Pelléas et Mélisande.*

There is another kind of overture which has nothing to do with the opera. This is a genre created by Beethoven—the concert overture. As the term suggests, these overtures are intended exclusively for concert use. Beethoven's overtures to *Egmont* and *Coriolanus* preface the incidental music he wrote for these plays; but they are completely independent of the other pieces, and continually provide pleasure to the music lover at symphony concerts.

After Beethoven many composers wrote overtures exclusively for concert performance. These works were inspired by some specific program and are usually in the sonata form. We can point to a few of the most familiar such works. Brahms' *Academic Festival Overture* is made up of several German student songs—including the universally known "Gaudeamus igitur," which arrives as a climax; Brahms wrote it to express his gratitude for an honorary doctorate given him by the University of Breslau in 1879. Tchaikovsky's *Overture 1812,* about Napoleon's defeat in Russia, quotes the Russian national hymn and the French "Marseillaise." In the body of the overture the music describes the battle of Borodino, and the overture is climaxed by the triumphant strains of the Russian anthem. Tchaikovsky's *Romeo and Juliet* is no less popular. Inspired by the Shakespeare tragedy it translates literally the principal episodes, including the feud of the Montague and Capulet houses, the passionate love of Romeo and Juliet, and their death. The main love melody achieved "Hit Parade" status in the popular song, "Our Love."

## RHAPSODY

As a form of piano music, the rhapsody is discussed in the section on solo instrumental music.

Orchestral composers expropriated the form from piano literature and adapted it for symphonic music. Sometimes the Greek meaning of "rhapsody" is carried—a poetic utterance of epic character—as, for example, Brahms' *Alto Rhapsody*.

Most often, the term has come to apply to an orchestral fantasia of folk or popular melodies, usually gay, with sharp contrasts of feeling. The prototype of this kind of work is the Liszt *Hungarian Rhapsody* which, since it originated as a work for the piano (though also frequently heard in orchestral versions), is analyzed in the solo instrumental section. In this vein is Chabrier's *España,* one of several famous orchestral works recreating Spain through the use of authentic folk melodies and rhythms; this work is built around two native Spanish dances, the jota and the malagueña.

Antonín Dvořák wrote three *Slavonic Rhapsodies* with the character of Czech sagas. They are filled with Bohemian folk melodies. The *Rhapsody in D Major* seems to describe knightly trysts and tournaments. The *G Minor Rhapsody* speaks of a knightly love idyll. The *Rhapsody in A Flat Major* recreates a knighty hunt.

Georges Enesco wrote two *Rumanian Rhapsodies,* the first of which (A major) is the more frequently played. This work is vitalized by the robust rhythms of such Rumanian dances as the hora and the sirba. The music has rapidly changing moods.

Rachmaninoff took Paganini's melody from the *Twenty-Fourth Caprice* and used it as the basis for his *Rhapsody on a Theme of Paganini;* but, while rhapsodic in treatment, the work is more accurately a theme and variations.

The Bible was the source for Ernest Bloch's rhapsody for orchestra with cello obbligato—*Schelomo*. "Schelomo" is the Hebraic name for King Solomon, and Bloch's rhapsody is a portrait of the King, who is represented by the solo cello.

The most familiar rhapsody in American music is unquestionably Gershwin's *Rhapsody in Blue,* which utilizes the popular idioms of American music with symphonic breadth and freshness. This is a work that is American to the core, from the opening wail of the clarinet, through the jaunty jazz ideas for the piano, up to the climactic, wonderful and deservedly famous melody for the strings.

## RONDO

A form found in early solo instrumental music, particularly in music for the piano; it is analyzed in an earlier section. The rondo was transferred to symphonic music. It is most often found as the last movement of concertos, as in Mozart's *D Minor Piano Concerto* (K. 466) and *D Major Violin Concerto* (K. 218), in Beethoven's *Fourth* and *Fifth Piano Concertos* and *Violin Concerto,* Chopin's *First Piano Concerto,* Brahms' *First Piano Concerto,* and so on.

## SCHERZO

Literally, "a joke,"—consequently a light piece of music deft in pace and light in mood. In symphonic music, the scherzo is most often found as the third movement of the symphony, evolved from the minuet. It was Beethoven who, in his *Second Symphony,* replaced the minuet with a scherzo. While retaining the minuet form (though sometimes extended and amplified) and its ¾ time, the scherzo has a quickening of pace and a lightness of heart, even whimsy, the minuet never possessed.

Mendelssohn was particularly masterful in writing music in the scherzo form, giving it a fairy nimbleness and grace, as in his early *Octet* and in the famous Scherzo of his *A Midsummer Night's Dream Suite.* In the symphonies of Bruckner and Mahler, the scherzo often acquires the personality of Austrian folk dances.

There are times when composers write scherzi as self-sufficient pieces of music. The most famous of these works is Dukas' *The Sorcerer's Apprentice* (see Part Six).

The scherzo, as a form of piano music, is treated in the section on solo instrumental music.

## SERENADE

Essentially a form of vocal music (see section on choral and vocal music). But, in the eighteenth century, serenades were written for small chamber groups and orchestras. This was essentially music for the outdoors, and in several brief movements, usually more than four. The material is light and unpretentious, since most of the works were written to order for some festivity. In the eighteenth century, the serenade was used interchangeably with divertimento, nocturne, cassation to designate a little suite. The most celebrated example of such early serenades is Mozart's lovable *Eine kleine Nachtmusik*. This is only in four movements, but it is believed that an additional minuet movement has been lost.

After Beethoven, the serenade—as a form of orchestral music—passed out of general usage. Brahms resurrected the form in his first attempts at orchestral writing, creating two serenades; the first was for full orchestra, and the second for orchestra without violins. Brahms chose the term "serenade" for these works advisedly, wishing to produce music that was light in character; but, of course, his form is much more ambitious and spacious than that found in eighteenth-century orchestral music. Tchaikovsky also used the form for his delightful *Serenade for Strings,* which includes the ever-popular "Waltz."

## SINFONIETTA

A little symphony. It is smaller in structure and in length than the symphony and slighter in orchestration. Several twentieth-century composers have used the form successfully, including Janáček, Prokofiev, and Miaskovsky.

## SUITE

The early structure and evolution of the suite, and its application to instrumental music, is found in the section on Solo Instrumental Music.

Instrumental composers soon began utilizing the suite form—a collation of old dances—for orchestral music. Besides writing various suites for solo instruments, both Handel and Bach created orchestral suites. Handel wrote a familiar work called *Water Music,* a suite in the old style for orchestra, for a royal water-party on the Thames River in London, in 1717, attended by King George I. Fifty musicians were in a boat by the side of the royal barge playing this music written for that occasion. "It was so strongly approved by His Majesty"—we learn from a contemporary document—"that he commanded it to be repeated once before and once after supper, although it took an hour for each performance." In its original version, the *Water Music* comprised twenty pieces—fanfares as well as dances. But as heard today—and frequently in the modern adaptation of Sir Hamilton Harty—the suite includes only six parts: Overture (in the French style), Air, Bourrée, Hornpipe, Andante, and Allegro deciso.

Johann Sebastian Bach wrote four orchestral suites (sometimes designated as overtures). Two are particularly famous. The second, in B minor, is made up of an overture, rondo, sarabande, bourrée, polonaise, minuet, and badinerie. (The classical suite usually ended in a gigue; Bach substituted a frivolous piece, called badinerie.) The third suite, in D major, contains the celebrated Air, so famous in Wilhelmj's transcription for violin and piano (*Air on the G String*). This air appears after an overture, and is followed by two gavottes, a bourrée, and a gigue.

The classical suite—a grouping of old dances—passed into obsolescence between the middle of the eighteenth century and the beginning of the twentieth. In the twentieth century, several neo-classicists revived the form successfully. Georges Enesco wrote an orchestral suite, in 1915, whose movements include an overture, sarabande, gigue, minuet, air and bourrée. Albert Roussel's excellent *Suite in F Major* for orchestra, written in 1926, has only three movements: Prelude, Sarabande, and Gigue. The orchestral suite that Stravinsky adapted from his ballet, *Pulcinella*—that ballet score, in turn, was derived from the music of Pergolesi—is also in the classical tradition; its movements include an overture, toccata, gavotte, and minuet.

After the death of Bach, a different connotation was given to the orchestral suite. It became a large work, in several movements, united by some integrating idea, or program. Such a suite is Rimsky-Korsakov's *Scheherezade*. The unifying element in this work is the story-telling of Scheherezade. We know from *The Arabian Nights* that the Sultan, bent on killing the beautiful Scheherezade, delays this fatal act because she keeps on telling him wonderful tales for a thousand and one nights; finally, he spares her life. Four such tales are retold musically in the four movements of Rimsky-Korsakov's suite: "The Sea and Sinbad's Ship"; "The Tale of the Kalendar Prince"; "The

Young Prince and the Young Princess"; and "The Festival at Bag-dad." The music of the suite is further integrated through the repeti-tion of two melodic ideas throughout the work: the theme of Scheherezade herself, in the solo violin; and the stern theme of the Sultan, first heard in the very opening.

Many other orchestral suites of this kind have acquired permanence in the symphonic repertory. We need concern ourselves only with a few of the most popular.

Modest Mussorgsky's suite, *Pictures at an Exhibition,* originated as a work for the piano but became famous in the orchestral transcription by Maurice Ravel. Ten pictures by the artist Victor Hartmann, which Mussorgsky saw at an exhibition, become ten realistic tone poems. The suite opens with a brief section called the "Promenade," describing the composer walking through the gallery (this theme is repeated throughout the work). The following pictures are then interpreted tonally: "The Gnome"; "The Old Castle"; "Tuileries"; "Bydlo" (a Polish oxcart); "Ballet of the Unhatched Chickens"; "Samuel Gold-enberg and Schmuyle"; "The Market Place at Limoges"; "The Cata-combs"; "The Hut on Fowl's Legs"; "The Great Gave at Kiev."

Debussy's *La Mer* is a suite of three impressionistic tone poems about the sea. The first pictures "From Dawn Till Noon on the Sea"; the second describes "The Play of the Waves"; and the third retells the "Dialogue of the Wind and the Sea." Ravel's *Rapsodie espagnole* is a suite of four Spanish portraits, two of them native Spanish dances: *"Prélude à la nuit"; "Malagueña"; "Habanera"; and "Feria."*

A very popular orchestral suite by an American composer is made up of five graphic tonal descriptions of America's Grand Canyon. It is, to be sure, Ferde Grofe's *Grand Canyon Suite.* The five parts are: "Sunrise"; "The Painted Desert"; "On the Trail"; "Sunset"; and "Cloudburst."

There is still another kind of orchestral suite besides those already described above. This includes excerpts from an opera or ballet score, or from incidental music to a play, integrated into a unified symphonic composition, for concert performance.

Mendelssohn's most celebrated orchestral composition is just such a work, the *Midsummer Night's Dream Suite.* Mendelssohn wrote the *Overture to A Midsummer Night's Dream* long before he contem-plated producing other numbers for the Shakespeare play—when he was only seventeen years old. It was his first masterwork, a composition which realizes amazingly his later mature style at its very best. Seventeen years after writing this overture, Mendelssohn was asked by King Frederick William of Prussia to write music for a projected performance of the Shakespeare play that was to be given in Potsdam on October 14, 1843. Mendelssohn now produced thirteen numbers. But when Mendelssohn's suite is now performed, we do not hear all these excerpts; only the best are given. Besides the overture, the suite—in present-day performances—includes the Nocturne, Scherzo, and Wedding March.

Bizet's familiar *L'Arlésienne Suite No. 1* comes from the incidental music he wrote for a performance of Daudet's play, *L'Arlésienne*. Bizet's entire score includes twenty-seven pieces, but the first suite has only four of these: Prelude, Minuet, Adagietto, and Carillon. Bizet's friends took four other selections from the incidental music to arrange a *Second L'Arlésienne Suite:* Pastorale, Intermezzo, Minuet, and Farandole.

There are also two orchestral suites derived from the incidental music Edvard Grieg wrote for Ibsen's play, *Peer Gynt;* and, once again, it is the first of the two suites that is the more popular. The *Peer Gynt Suite No. 1* has four movements: "Morning"; "Åse's Death"; "Anitra's Dance"; and "In the Hall of the Mountain King." Only one part of the second suite is as celebrated as any movement of the first: "Solveig's Song." This is the concluding movement of the second suite, the three preceding parts being: "Ingrid's Lament"; "Arabian Dance"; "The Return of Peer Gynt."

It has become a practice with many contemporary composers to write new scores for the ballet, and then to adapt this music into orchestral suites for performance at symphony concerts. Stravinsky's three most familiar scores are *The Fire-Bird, Petrushka,* and *The Rite of Spring;* but they are even better known in their adaptations as suites than in their original ballet version. The same thing is true of Manuel de Falla's *El Amor Brujo,* Ravel's *Daphnis and Chloë,* Khatchaturian's *Gayne,* or Copland's *Appalachian Spring:* the ballets are rarely seen, and consequently the original ballet scores rarely heard; but the suites from these scores are permanent fixtures in the contemporary symphonic repertory.

John Alden Carpenter's *Adventures in a Perambulator,* Copland's *The Red Pony,* Kabalevsky's *The Comedians,* Khatchaturian's *Mas-*

*querade,* Ravel's *Mother Goose Suite,* and Tchaikovsky's *Nutcracker Suite*—all of them suites for orchestra—are described in Part Six.

## SYMPHONIC POEM (or TONE POEM)

A one-movement work for orchestra, extremely flexible in form, in which a specific program, or a poem, or a story is realistically told through musical means.

This form was created by Franz Liszt. Influenced by the Wagnerian music drama, he wanted to introduce Wagnerian principles into symphonic music. Consequently, he produced a dramatic kind of orchestral work, but without any accompanying text, which told a story; and to give this work greater unity he applied to symphonic music Wagner's technique of the *leading motive.*

Liszt wrote twelve symphonic poems, his programs derived from literary works by Goethe, Victor Hugo, Shakespeare, Lamartine, and Schiller. The most frequently heard of these is *Les Préludes* inspired by Lamartine's *Méditations poétiques.* Liszt himself has summarized that part of Lamartine's poem which served him as a program for his music: "What is life but a series of preludes to that unknown song whose initial solemn note is tolled by death? The enchanted dawn of every life is love; but where is the destiny on whose first delicious joys some storm does not break—a storm whose deadly blast disperses youth's illusions, whose fatal bolt consumes its altar? And what soul, thus cruelly bruised, when the tempest rolls away, seeks not to rest its memories in the calm and rural life? Yet man allows himself not long to taste the kindly quiet which first attracted him to Nature's lap; but when the trumpet gives the signal he hastens to join his comrades, no matter what the cause that calls him to arms. He rushes into the thick of the fight, and amid the uproar of the battle regains confidence in himself and his powers."

Liszt's other symphonic poems include *Tasso* and *Mazeppa. Tasso* (after Goethe) is the portrait of a hero. "I first called up his august spirit as he still haunts the waters of Venice," explained Liszt. "Then I beheld his proud and melancholy figure as he passed through the festivals of Ferrara where he had produced his masterpieces. Finally, I followed him to Rome, the eternal city, and offered him the crown and glorified in him the martyr and the poet." *Mazeppa* (after Victor Hugo) is a literal musical delineation of the sufferings of the Asiatic chieftain during a historic three-day ride, as he gallops on a fiery steed over the plains and hills, finally to have his horse succumb to fatigue.

The first important composer to emulate Liszt in writing symphonic poems was the Bohemian Bedrich Smetana. Between 1874 and 1879 he wrote a cycle of six symphonic poems collectively entitled *My Country (Ma Vlast)*. In line with the composer's nationalist tendencies, this huge work pays tribute to Bohemia, its traditions and people and culture.

One composition in this group is particularly favored by concert audiences: the second, *The Moldau (Vltava)*. The composer provided his own program for this music: "Two springs pour forth their streams in the shade of the Bohemian forest . . . their waves joyfully following over the rocky beds. The forest brook, rushing on, becomes the River Moldau which . . . grows into a mighty stream. It flows through the dense woods from which come the joyous sounds of the chase, and the notes of the hunter's horn are heard ever nearer and nearer. It flows through emerald meadows and lowlands where a wedding feast is being celebrated with song and dance. At night in its shining waves, wood and water nymphs hold their revels, and in these waves are reflected many a fortress and castle—witnesses to the bygone splendor of chivalry. . . . At the rapids of St. John, the stream speeds on . . . into the broad river bed in which it flows on in majestic calm towards Prague."

Only two years after Liszt's death, Richard Strauss wrote the first of his symphonic poems: *Macbeth*. This is descriptive, realistic, dramatic music—using the most advanced techniques of orchestration, harmony, and rhythm—and far different from the post-Romantic music Strauss had been writing before this. Having found a medium uniquely sympathetic to his temperament and ideas—and the medium was the Liszt symphonic poem—Strauss began writing works that made him world famous. His greatest symphonic poems were written between 1889 and 1897, each inspired by some program which the music frequently interpreted with amazing literalness. *Don Juan* (inspired by a poem of Nicolas Lenau) is the passionate quest of Don Juan for a woman who is to him woman incarnate. "Because he does not find her," explains Lenau, "although he reels from one to another, at last disgust seizes him and this disgust is the devil that fetches him." *Death and Transfiguration (Tod und Verklaerung)*—after a poem by Alexander Ritter —brings up a death scene, the frightful wrestling of the dying man with Death, and his final deliverance from the world. *Till Eulenspiegel's Merry Pranks* (based on an old German legend) relates the various pranks perpetrated by the practical jokester, Till, which finally bring him to his doom at a gibbet. *Thus Spake Zarathustra* conveys musically—as Strauss himself said—"the development of the human race from its origin, through the various phases of its development, religious, and scientific, up to Nietzsche's idea of the Superman." *Don Quixote,* subtitled by the composer "fantastic variations on a theme of knightly character," describes the fabulous exploits of Cervantes' famous and lovable Don and the Don's squire in a series of ten variations. *A Hero's Life* (*Ein Heldenleben*) portrays a hero in peace and war, in love and in achievements to the time he resignedly takes his leave of the world; the hero, apparently, is Strauss himself, for in the fifth section (entitled "The Hero's Mission of Peace," summarizing the achievements of the hero) Strauss quotes snatches from some of his earlier works.

These Strauss symphonic poems electrified the world of music with their passion and strength, their technical virtuosity and instrumental wizardry, above all with their gift in translating extra-musical experiences into tones. Composers everywhere were inspired by Strauss to write symphonic poems, a form that now became favored among writers of orchestral music.

Some symphonic poems were in a highly pictorial vein, as in Ottorino Respighi's set of three works picturing life in Rome: *Fountains of Rome, Pines of Rome,* and *Roman Festivals*. The first two are particularly liked by audiences everywhere. The *Fountains of Rome* is a group of four picturesque landscapes, while the *Pines of Rome* reveals the memories and thoughts aroused in the composer by four pine-flanked Roman scenes. There is a distinct novelty in the latter work: in the third section we hear a recording of a nightingale's song skilfully interpolated into the orchestral texture.

Sometimes composers wrote sensitive and impressionistic symphonic poems. Delius produced exquisite mood-etchings in tone in *On Hearing the First Cuckoo in Spring* and *Summer Night on the River*. Rachmaninoff translated a famous painting by Arnold Böcklin in *The Isle of the Dead*. In this Rachmaninoff music we recognize the massive cliffs, surrounded by grim cypresses, overlooking the water, as a Stygian boatman draws near with a flag-draped coffin and a lonely mourner in his ship. Arnold Schoenberg, on the other hand, interprets a poem by Richard Dehmel in *Transfigured Night* (*Verklaerte Nacht*). The Schoenberg music, and the poem of Dehmel, tells of a woman who asks forgiveness from her lover for having been unfaithful to him. As they walk through a lonely moonlit grove, she receives that forgiveness, and the world becomes transfigured by this display of compassion.

Some composers endowed the symphonic poem with their nationalistic feelings as Sibelius did in *Finlandia* and *En Saga*. The familiar melodies in *Finlandia* have such a folk character that some believe they are actual quotations of Finnish folk songs; but all the thematic material is of Sibelius' creation. *Finlandia* was written just before the turn of the twentieth century when Finland was still under the domination of Russia. So passionate a national document is this music—and so greatly did it inflame the patriotic ardor of the Finnish people—that it is sometimes said that this music did more than all the propaganda speeches and pamphlets in bringing about the emancipation of that little country.

Popular idioms have also found their way into the symphonic poem. One of the most frequently heard of Aaron Copland's works is his symphonic poem, *El Salón México*, in which many popular Mexican melodies are gathered. George Gershwin's symphonic poem, *An American in Paris*—in the jazz idiom of the 1920's—is a great favorite in American music. It describes an American walking in the streets of Paris, enjoying the exhilarating spirit in the air, but feeling a powerful nostalgia for home.

## SYMPHONY

The symphony is the most significant form in orchestral music. It is a sonata for orchestra, generally in four movements. The first is in sonata form; the second, slow in lyrical, in song form, theme and variations, or some other form; the third, a minuet in the classical symphony of Haydn and Mozart, and a scherzo with and after Beethoven; the finale in sonata, rondo, or theme and variations form.

The word "symphony" was derived from "sinfonia." In the seventeenth century, sinfonia applied to any piece of music for a group of instruments. Overtures and orchestral interludes in many of the earliest operas were often designated as sinfonias. With Monteverdi, these sinfonias became extended pieces of music rather than fragmentary items. There are also sinfonias in many of Bach's cantatas.

As interest in instrumental music grew late in the seventeenth century, the sinfonia became a medium apart from incidental passages in operas or cantatas. Composers began writing sinfonias exclusively for various instrumental groups. The three-movement sinfonia was gradually evolved through the application of such forms as the sonata da chiesa and the Italian overture, both of which had two fast movements flanking a slow one.

We find the word "symphony" used in the eighteenth century among such early Italian instrumental composers as Sammartini, who wrote more than twenty works under that name. But these works are really sinfonias: the instrumentation is haphazard, depending upon the kind of instruments at hand; the writing is episodic, with thematic ideas rarely developed or transformed.

To the contemporary music lover the symphony becomes more recognizable with the kind of music Johann Stamitz wrote in Mannheim in the middle of the eighteenth century. We have already commented on how, as concertmaster and leader of the Mannheim Orchestra, Stamitz developed the first "modern" symphony orchestra. The emergence of the first "modern" symphony orchestra went hand in hand with that of the first "modern" symphony. Stamitz wrote about fifty symphonies whose form, style, and instrumentation are not far removed from the symphonies of Haydn and Mozart. Stamitz produced a three- or four-movement work in which unity, balance, and contrast were finally achieved. The architectonic structure was clear. Sometimes he suggested the two-theme form of the later first-movement sonata form; in the lyricism of his slow movements he achieved complete emancipation from the restrictions of polyphony. The instrumentation is effective in its dynamics and color.

In Vienna, too—just at about the time that the eight-year-old Haydn came to live in the city—there were many respectable composers writing symphonies. These men are all forgotten now, and their music is never played. (For the record, these composers included Georg Matthias Monn, Giuseppe Bonno, and Christoph Wagenseil.) But they prepared the ground that Haydn was soon to fertilize. These men also succeeded in realizing a new concept of symphonic writing which was to have a profound influence on the young Haydn.

Haydn wrote his first symphony in 1759. Actually it was not a symphony such as Stamitz and the Viennese were writing at the time, but a three-part overture. Haydn kept on writing such overtures—and serenades, divertimenti, and nocturnes—and for a while he persisted in calling them symphonies without realizing that the symphony had an individual physiognomy and personality of its own. But the influence of Stamitz, the Viennese composers, and Karl Philipp Emanuel Bach (who was also producing symphonies in the new manner) was inescapable. By 1770, Haydn was writing symphonies that permanently and completely parted company with the older instrumental forms.

The first of these early Haydn symphonies which is still performed is the *Symphony in F Sharp Minor,* written in 1772. It is better known as the *Farewell Symphony.* The story is told that Haydn wrote this work to give his employer a hint that his musicians needed a vacation: in the last movement, the musicians leave the platform one by one, while the music is still in progress, until only the conductor is left. The story is more interesting than significant. What is significant is that in structure, instrumentation, variety of feeling, and melodic charm the *Farewell Symphony* is in that symphonic form which was henceforth to serve the composer of the symphony.

Haydn kept on developing and growing as a symphonic composer. His forms and designs kept on acquiring greater breadth; the orchestration became fuller and richer all the time; the ideas grew more original and more personal. The new era of the symphony was now unfolding. In 1784, Haydn wrote two sets of symphonies on a commission from Paris, and one of these is a masterwork: the *Symphony in G Major* (No. 88).

Haydn's greatest symphonies, however, are the two sets of six works each which he wrote toward the end of his life in conjunction with his two visits to London. Each of these is a work of major importance, and each is still alive in our symphonic repertory. These twelve symphonies represent Haydn at the apex of his career as a composer; they are the summit of his symphonic writing. Within a precise yet pliable form, he brought wit and grace, or grandeur and majesty, or rustic humor, or poignant emotion, more spontaneously and more freshly than anyone had done up to this time. In many pages of these symphonies he is the poet who transforms the world around him into enchantment.

These are the most frequently performed of the "London" symphonies: the *Symphony No. 92 in G Major,* known as the *Oxford* because it was performed when Haydn received an honorary degree from Oxford University in 1791; the *Symphony No. 94 in G Major,* named *Surprise,* because a loud chord comes suddenly after a quiet and sensitive melody in the second movement; the *Symphony No. 100 in G Major,* the *Military,* a name derived from the fact that the instrumentation calls for a bass drum, cymbals, and a triangle then associated with military music; the *Symphony No. 101 in D Major,* known as the *Clock,* after the regular rhythmic clock-like pulse in the slow movement; and the *Symphony No. 103 in E Flat Major,* the *Drum Roll*—the first bar being a roll of the timpani.

Mozart—who transformed everything in music with which he came into contact—enlarged the structure of the symphony, enriched the instrumentation, intensified the emotion, and extended thematic development. Mozart wrote more than forty symphonies, the first when he was only eight. The greatest (like those by Haydn) came at the end of his life. But many of the earlier Mozart symphonies are well able to enchant present-day music lovers with their beauty and vernal freshness and spontaneity. Among these are: *Symphony No. 31 in D Major (Paris)* (K. 297); *Symphony No. 35 in D Major (Haffner)* (K. 385); *Symphony No. 36 in C Major (Linz)* (K. 425); and *Symphony No. 38 in D Major (Prague)* (K. 504).

The crown of Mozart's symphonic output is the trio of masterworks which he wrote within a period of six weeks in 1788: the *Symphony No. 39 in E Flat Major* (K. 543); the *Symphony No. 40 in G Minor* (K. 550); and the *Symphony No. 41 in C Major* (Jupiter) (K. 551). Not only does Mozart open up here new vistas of eloquence and drama, but he parts company with eighteenth-century formalism through his daring harmonic writing, enlarged proportions of his development, increasing grandeur of design, and increased intensity of emotion. It was because of its divine perfection that the last of these symphonies was given the name of *Jupiter* by J. B. Cramer, when that work was performed by the London Philharmonic in 1821.

The *Jupiter Symphony* is a monument in classical literature. But even a work of such dimensions becomes dwarfed when placed at the side of one of Beethoven's greatest symphonies. With Beethoven, the symphonic form assumes truly epic outlines. Beethoven's search for ever deeper, ever profounder poetic concepts brings with it innovation after innovation until the classical traditions of Haydn and Mozart are completely shattered. For spaciousness of form, for nobility and sublimity of thinking, for dramatic power and Titanic emotions, there is nothing in all music to surpass the greatest pages in the nine symphonies.

In the first two Beethoven symphonies we are still in the eighteenth century, for they are characterized by the grace and refinement and the respect for classic structure found in Haydn's symphonies. But occasionally, Beethoven even here is impatient with the accepted rules. The opening bar of the *First Symphony,* in C major, is not in the key of the work as practice up to then dictated; and in the *Second Symphony,* in D major, Beethoven creates a tradition of his own by replacing the third-movement minuet of the Haydn and Mozart symphony with a scherzo. But, despite such indiscretions, both symphonies belong to the Classical Age.

Then Beethoven made a Herculean leap into a new era, with a symphony that was unquestionably a child of the nineteenth century. In no other branch of music did he make so prodigious an advance with a single work as he now did in the symphony. The *Symphony No. 3,* in E flat major—called the *Eroica Symphony*—is of imposing structural dimensions and filled with demoniac passions and Titanic struggles on the one hand, and on the other with a pathos that combines anguish with resignation. The iconoclast spoke in the piercing dissonances of the first movement, and in the second where a funeral march makes its first appearance in a symphony. The poet and philosopher spoke in the now turbulent and now gently contemplative pages of the first movement, in the eloquent threnody of the second, and in the violent surges that proclaim victory for the hero in the finale.

It is now a familiar story that Beethoven had intended dedicating his *Third Symphony* to Napoleon, whom he regarded as mankind's benefactor, and a true democrat. When Napoleon became Emperor, Beethoven angrily tore up his title page and rededicated his symphony to a nameless hero. But to understand the music of the *Eroica* it is necessary to bear in mind that Beethoven's hero is no soldier or politician, but the hero of the spirit who fights for a noble cause.

The *Symphony No. 4,* in B flat major, is in the gentle and idyllic vein of the *Second Symphony.* But the ever-popular *Symphony No. 5,* in C minor, is once again an epic. It has been interpreted as man's struggle against Fate—or, more specifically, as Beethoven's struggle against the terrible Fate that doomed him to deafness. This is a program superimposed on the music by others, and not by the composer—but it fits. The first theme of the first movement—the three short notes followed by a long one—surely sounds like the knock of fate; and the poignant second theme resembles the answering plea of the victim. The melancholy second movement can be interpreted as a resignation to Fate; but the ominous rising theme that opens the scherzo movement suggests the resumption of a struggle. That struggle erupts in the finale, where it culminates in a resounding victory over Fate.

The *Symphony No. 6,* in F major—appropriately named the *Pastoral*—is a nature picture. It is the only one of the nine symphonies which the composer intended to be programmatic. The subtitles to the five movements provide all the clue the listener requires: "Awakening of Joyful Feelings Upon Arrival in the Country"; "The Brook"; "Village Festival"; "The Storm"; "The Shepherd's Song." The *Symphony No. 8,* in F major, is also in a comparatively light vein— consistently gay and infectious in mood, and at one point even mildly satirical: in the second movement the composer is believed to have made fun of the metronome, invented by his friend, Mälzel.

The emotional force and the passion found in the *Third* and *Fifth Symphonies* are also present in the *Seventh* and *Ninth.* The *Symphony No. 7,* in A major, is so frenetic in its rhythms (particularly in the last two movements) that Wagner called the entire work an "apotheosis of the dance."

In the *Symphony No. 9,* in D minor, Beethoven introduces the human voice for the first time in a symphony—in the last movement, in which Schiller's "Ode to Joy" receives a setting for a quartet of solo voices and chorus. There is something symbolic about the fact that in the last movement of his last symphony Beethoven should have resorted to the human voice. It is almost as if the symphony had structurally and contextually developed so far that it could not possibly progress further without enlisting the human voice to supplement the musical instrument.

Beethoven's *Ninth Symphony* ushers in the Romantic Era in symphonic music. After Beethoven, the symphony acquired a more varied instrumentation, a greater subjectivity of emotion, and at times new techniques. The first important Romantic symphony after Beethoven was Berlioz' *Symphonie fantastique,* written only five years after Beethoven's *Ninth Symphony.* This work was a radical departure for symphonic music for two reasons. First, it relied completely on a program provided by the composer—a program which the music fulfilled realistically. Second, it introduced a new technique in structural unity which Berlioz himself described as the *idée fixe*—a recurrent motive that appears and reappears through the work as a connecting link. Subtitled "An Episode in the Life of an Artist," this symphony graphically relates the struggle of a hero to win the ideal woman. In the first movement, "Visions and Passions," the love of the hero and the ideal is aroused. The hero plunges into meditation about his beloved in the second movement, "The Ball." In the third part, "Scenes in the Country," the beauty of nature brings back to his mind the vision of his beloved's loveliness. The hero attempts suicide through an overdose of opium, but succeeds only in inducing nightmares in one of which he kills his loved one. The fourth movement, "March to the Gallows," describes his execution for his crime. In the finale, "Witches' Sabbath," the hero sees witches dancing demoniacally around the bier of his beloved.

The *idée fixe* of Berlioz was supplanted by still another structural technique by a later French composer. In his only symphony (D minor) César Franck utilizes a method he had invented and used in earlier works, namely the cyclic form. This calls for a repetition of themes from earlier movements in the finale, and constructing thematic subjects out of germinal ideas, for the purpose of achieving integration. The César Franck *Symphony* is unusual in still another respect—it was the first symphony to make serious use of the English horn (the opening beautiful melody of the second movement), an innovation that shocked his contemporaries. The symphony is more dramatic and impassioned than other Franck works; but in the second movement it has the spiritual radiance we associate with Franck. It is in three, instead of the more customary four, movements.

Other distinguished Romantic symphonies created in France include two by Vincent d'Indy. The first is entitled *Symphony on a French Mountain Air*, and is built out of a mountain folk song the composer learned in the French Alps; it is first heard at the beginning of the symphony in the English horn. A later, and no less notable, symphony by d'Indy is the *Symphony in B Flat Major*. Camille Saint-Saëns wrote several symphonies, the finest being the third in C minor, for organ, piano, and orchestra. Ernest Chausson's *Symphony in B Flat Major*—profoundly influenced by the Wagnerian style—is also famous.

In Germany, the symphony flourished with Schubert, Schumann,

Mendelssohn, and Brahms. Schubert, like Beethoven before him, wrote nine symphonies. The earlier ones are soundly classical in form and Mozartean in style. But the two masterworks by which Schubert is represented at symphony concerts—the *Symphony No. 8,* in B minor, known as the *Unfinished,* and the *Symphony No. 9,* in C major—have the unmistakable fingerprints of Schubert: his wonderful lyricism, his engaging personal charm, his Viennese *Gemütlichkeit.* The *Unfinished Symphony* has only two movements instead of the traditional four; Schubert made sketches for a third, but never completed them, and he never attempted a fourth. Why Schubert did not finish his symphony— he who never lacked for inspiration—is something of a mystery. He wrote it in 1822, consequently living for another six years and writing another symphony. Yet he allowed this symphony to remain truncated. The explanation may lie in the fact that, in its two movements, the symphony has such inevitability and perfection that even Schubert was incapable of sustaining so high a level of inspiration for another two movements.

The *Unfinished Symphony* is outstanding for its melodic purity and beauty. But Schubert's last symphony, in C major, has much more to recommend it than lyricism. It also has persuasive strength of sonority and rhythm. The sublimity of some of its melodic ideas and the expressiveness of its emotion is something we do not find in other Schubert symphonies. Schubert, who knew the Beethoven symphonies and admired them profoundly, was influenced by them to extend his own musical horizons. The *C Major Symphony* proves how far Schubert would have traveled within the symphony had he been granted a full life's span.

Lyricism is also the strong point of Schumann's four symphonies. He was not a master of thematic development and he was notably deficient in his instrumentation. But he could endow melodic subjects with such a sensitive beauty, such a tender melancholy, and such a poetic content, that his symphonies never fail to provide pleasure. Schumann's *First Symphony,* in B flat major, is called the *Spring Symphony.* But it is not a realistic portrait of nature in the way Beethoven's *Pastoral Symphony* is. Schumann's music, rather, represents his emotional responses to the vernal season; it is filled with ebullience and inner joy. This symphony was written in the year of Schumann's marriage to Clara and voices the springtime in Schumann's heart as a result of this happy event.

The most familiar of the Schumann symphonies is the third, in E flat major, the *Rhenish*. It was intended by its composer as a picture of Rhenish life. The principal melody of the second movement is an old German drinking song. In the fourth movement, the music portrays the installation of the Archbishop of Geissel as Cardinal in the Cologne Cathedral, while the fifth and concluding movement provides a picture of a rustic festival in a small Rhenish town.

In his youth, Mendelssohn wrote more than a dozen symphonies in the spirit of Mozart and Schubert. But the three Mendelssohn symphonies heard most often are the products of his full maturity. The *Symphony No. 3*, in A minor, is called the *Scotch* because it was inspired by the composer's visit to Scotland. However, there is nothing particularly Scotch about this music, which is in the composer's purest Romantic style. The fourth, in A major—the consequence of a trip to Italy—has acquired the sobriquet of *Italian Symphony*. Throughout the work we feel the warmth of the Italian sun in the ebullient melodies and radiant harmonies; the first movement can easily be interpreted as the composer's exhilaration on paying his first visit to the land of the South. In the finale, Mendelssohn introduces the exciting rhythms of a leaping Italian carnival dance known as the saltarello. Mendelssohn's *Fifth Symphony,* in D major, pays tribute to the Reformation Movement. In the first part, Mendelssohn quotes the strains of the familiar sixteenth or seventeenth century "Dresden Amen," which Wagner uses in *Parsifal*. The concluding movement makes stirring use of Luther's chorale, *Ein' feste Burg*.

It took Brahms many years to write his first symphony. He began making outlines for a symphony as early as 1855, but did not complete a work in that form until two decades after that. Meanwhile, he had produced masterworks in chamber, choral, and vocal music. He was forty-three years old when his *First Symphony,* in C minor, was written. It was, consequently, a work of his fullest maturity and genius. In few other works did he bring such sensuous beauty, such impassioned speech and dramatic force—and with a majestic structure—as he did in this masterwork. Brahms' *First Symphony* has been called "Beethoven's Tenth Symphony." It is the first symphony since Beethoven to approximate Beethoven's giant strength and grandeur.

Brahms wrote four symphonies in all. Each differs markedly from the other. Walter Niemann, a German writer, has identified each one in the following way. He called the first, "Brahms' *Pathetic Sym-*

*phony,"* because it is a veritable drama of struggle and resignation, tragedy and nobility. The second, in D minor, was "Brahms' *Pastoral Symphony.*" While it has no program, this symphony throughout has such an idyllic character as to bring up pictures of beautiful landscapes and countrysides. To Niemann the third, in F major, was "Brahms' *Eroica Symphony,*" for Niemann read into this music heroic conflicts and victories. The fourth, in E minor, was "Brahms' *Elegiac Symphony"*: the struggles of the *Third Symphony* are over; what we get in the fourth is philosophic peace and resignation. In the finale of the *Fourth Symphony,* Brahms resurrects the seventeenth-century form of the passacaglia which, in his hands, becomes a mighty dramatic exposition.

The German Romantic symphony reached a culmination with Bruckner and Mahler, each of whom completed nine symphonies. The symphonic structure now assumes truly Gargantuan proportions, and calls for huge orchestral forces. Here we have a multiplication of details, and a complication of ornaments. Here, too, we find an attempt to make music express metaphysical or philosophical concepts: the meaning of life; the mystery of Nature; and so forth. In truth, Mahler, even more than Bruckner, tried to make music express things which up to now had not been within its province. In the *Second Symphony,* in D minor—known as the *Resurrection Symphony*—Mahler speaks of the idealistic struggle of a hero trying to attain the goal of learning the meaning of life and death. After inquiring the "why" of human existence and human suffering in the first four movements, Mahler poses an answer in the finale by setting Klopstock's poem, "The Resurrection," for soprano, contralto, chorus and orchestra. In the *Third Symphony,* in D minor, Mahler tries to unravel the mystery of Nature, and in the *Fifth,* also in D minor, the riddle of Death. The *Eighth Symphony,* in E flat major, describes a Faustian pursuit for a happiness that cannot be realized, while the *Ninth Symphony,* in D major, is man's resignation to Fate.

Bruckner's symphonies are less pretentious in their content, but no less ambitious in structure and style. His finest symphonies include the *Fourth* in E flat major, known as the *Romantic Symphony* and the *Seventh* in E major, whose sublime slow movement is said to have been inspired by a premonition of the imminent death of the one whom Bruckner admired above all others—Wagner.

The weaknesses of the symphonies of Bruckner and Mahler are

many. Expanse is sometimes mistaken for grandeur; dull declamation for drama and eloquence; emotional extravagance for genuine feelings. Sometimes they are too long, too garrulous, too fussy with details. But at their best these symphonies have many pages of nobility and profundity. Repeated hearings of the greatest symphonies of Mahler and Bruckner convincingly prove that the strength of these works more than make up for the weaknesses.

Borodin's two symphonies, which carry out the national ideals of the "Russian Five," are among the earliest Russian symphonies to gain any degree of importance. We still hear performed Borodin's *Second Symphony*, in B minor, written in 1876, which has all the vivid Oriental colors and barbaric rhythmic force we associate with Borodin's best music.

The greatest Russian symphonist undoubtedly was Tchaikovsky. In his symphonies, Tchaikovsky combined some of the national traits of the "Russian Five" (several Tchaikovsky melodies have the unmistakable identity of the Russian folk song) with European sophistication and culture. Tchaikovsky wrote six symphonies; the last three are among the best-loved works ever written for orchestra. In these three masterpieces, Tchaikovsky poured out a flood of emotion without inhibitions; their appeal is tremendous. As James Gibbons Huneker said of Tchaikovsky: "He is first and last a dramatic poet. He delineates the human soul in convulsions of love, hate, joy, and fear; he is an unique master of rhythms and of the torrential dynamics that express primal emotions in the full flood." Huneker might have added that the human soul Tchaikovsky was expressing was his own tortured self.

The concept of Fate dominates both the *Fourth* and *Fifth Symphonies*. In the *Symphony No. 4*, in F minor, we sense the presence of Fate in the introduction of the first movement which, as the composer himself explained, is the "kernel, the quintessence, the chief thought of the whole symphony." Tchaikovsky adds: "This is Fate, the fatal power, which hinders one in the pursuit of happiness from gaining the goal, which jealously provides that peace and comfort do not prevail, that the sky is not free from clouds." The feeling of despondency generated in this introduction deepens in the rest of the first movement, and in the lyrical second movement. But there is optimism in the next two parts. In the finale, Tchaikovsky incorporates a famous Russian folk song, "In the Fields There Stands a Birch Tree."

Fate is even more prominent in the *Symphony No. 5,* in E minor. It is evoked by the mysterious and gloomy opening theme of the first movement which recurs in all succeeding movements. The symphony has lighter moods, too, particularly in the delightful waltz which appears as the third movement. But there always returns the grim melody representing Fate to remind us that the pleasures of life are evanescent. In the finale, the Fate theme comes back in a major key, proud and triumphant, as if to establish the fact that, in the end, it is Fate that is always triumphant.

Tchaikovsky's last symphony, in B minor, known as the *Pathétique,* is probably the most lugubrious symphony ever written. It was the composer's last will and testament to the world, the quintessence of his deep-rooted torment and frustrations. Appropriately enough, Tchaikovsky placed his slow movement as the finale—a plangent wail, one of the most pessimistic utterances in all music. Tchaikovsky died soon after writing this work, but he had written his own requiem before dying.

The most popular Slavic symphony, other than those by Tchaikovsky, was written by Antonín Dvořák: the *Symphony in E Minor, From the New World.* Like his finest chamber-music works, this symphony was inspired by an American folk idiom. During his stay in the United States, Dvořák came into contact with the music of the Negro and was profoundly moved by it. In writing a symphony in the new world, he modeled his thematic and rhythmic material after the Negro song—and so successfully that his melodies sound genuinely American. One of the themes in the first movement gives a suggestion of the well-known Spiritual, "Swing Low, Sweet Chariot." The beautiful and poignant melody in the second movement—which is entirely of Dvořák's invention—might have been a Spiritual; Williams Arms Fisher fashioned this melody into the now familiar song, "Goin' Home."

The music of the most distinguished symphonic composer of the twentieth century is deeply rooted in nationalism. Jean Sibelius, Finland's greatest composer, has produced seven symphonies which are his finest works. The first two—they are still his most popular one—are in the style of the German Romantic composers of the late nineteenth century. The first, in E minor, was written in 1899; the second, in D major, in 1901. Both were influenced by the sensuous and passionate speech of Brahms and by the hyperemotional content of Tchaikovsky. But though apparently imitative, both works have such youthful impetuousness, buoyancy, and freshness—and they generate such excitement among audiences—that they have never lost favor. The *Second Symphony* is particularly famous. The Finnish conductor, Georg Schneevoigt, interpreted its first movement as a picture of Finnish pastoral life; the second movement as an expression of the composer's patriotic ardor; the third, as a patriotic manifesto on the part of all Finns; and the finale, as the hope for freedom and deliverance that stirred in the heart of every true Finn in 1901.

As Sibelius kept on writing symphonies he became less subjective, and less faithful to traditional form. He began striving for greater conciseness, economy, and directness. This tendency is first apparent in the *Symphony No. 4,* in A minor. There is greater sobriety here than in the preceding three symphonies—a quiet restraint that is most effective. With his next three symphonies, Sibelius reduced his orchestral forces, utilized short, epigrammatic themes, and arrived at a simplification of contrapuntal and harmonic writing. These works have the power of understatement. The finest of these last three symphonies is the concluding one, the *Seventh,* in C major, written in 1924. It is in a single movement with a logic all its own. The work is built out of episodic thematic subjects into an organic unity with tremendous power, and with many changing moods.

The seven symphonies of Sibelius do not have a program; but their national identity is unmistakable. This is always music by a Finnish composer, speaking of Finland—the country, the people, the history, the folklore.

Two outstanding symphonic composers of the twentieth century emerged in the Soviet Union—Shostakovich and Prokofiev. Both have used music as an instrument to express the culture and ideals of their native land. Shostakovich's best and most famous symphony is still the *First,* completed when the composer was only nineteen years old. Though its indebtedness to Tchaikovsky and Prokofiev is obvious, this symphony is, for the most part, a highly original work with a dynamic power and an electrifying momentum that are magnetizing. It is in the traditional four movements, and is at its best when the composer allows his wind-swept ideas and youthful energy unrepressed expression.

Curious to note, Shostakovich has been at his best in the odd-numbered symphonies. The *Fifth Symphony* has majesty of design and is filled with passionate and agitated ideas alternating with more tranquil feelings. Great emotional depths are reached. The *Seventh Symphony* was the most publicized symphony of our time because it was written during historic times and helped to interpret them. Shostakovich completed the work in 1941, a year in which the hammer blows of the invading Nazi armies were devastating the Soviet Union. Most of the symphony was written in Leningrad, during the siege by the Nazis. But it was completed in the Volga city of Kuibishev, to which the Soviet government had moved in October 1941. Shostakovich intended his music as "an embodiment of the supreme ideal of patriotic war." The first movement tells of the disruption of civilian life by the war and its tragic impact and concludes with a requiem for the victims of the war. The next two movements are, by contrast, an optimistic affirmation of life: art and beauty and science being more durable than the achievements of war. The finale is a prophecy of and a paean to ultimate Soviet victory over the enemy. The *Seventh Symphony* was a triumph wherever and whenever it was played in the free world, for it acquired dramatic and emotional significance owing to the stirring times which it reflected and interpreted.

The *Symphony No. 9* is one of the most joyous of Shostakovich's works. Some critics like to consider this work as a single unit with the two symphonies that preceded it. They explain that if the *Seventh* speaks of the war spirit of the people, the *Eighth* reflects the grim aftermath of the war; and the lighthearted *Ninth* is the voice of victory and happy readjustment to peacetime life. The melodies and dance themes are delightful and frequently good humored, bringing up the picture of a bright and pleasant world.

Like Shostakovich, Prokofiev produced his most celebrated symphony first. Named the *Classical Symphony,* Prokofiev's first symphony tried to employ modern techniques of melody, harmony, and tonality within the classical symphonic form of Haydn and Mozart. The structure, the instrumentation, and the brevity of thematic material belong to the eighteenth century; but the tart harmonies, the surprising melodic leaps, the brisk rhythms are of our own day. But there is nothing anachronistic about this music. The synchronization of the old and new is achieved with such subtlety and mastery that the symphony— far from being a curiosity—is vibrant and vital. In the third movement, Prokofiev replaced the traditional minuet of the classical symphony with another old dance form, the gavotte.

The *Symphony No. 5*, written twenty-seven years later, is a work of far different character. It has huge dimensions, as opposed to the slight proportions of the early symphony; harmonically, melodically, and rhythmically it is along huge and impressive lines as compared to the simplicity and terseness of the *Classical Symphony*. Prokofiev planned his *Fifth Symphony* as a tribute to the spirit of man—a spirit that neither war nor disaster can completely conquer. There is heroic stride to this music; and in the slow movement, there is a compelling and a profound sense of tragedy. For the *Fifth Symphony*, written in 1944, is (like Shostakovich's *Seventh*) a child of World War II.

Igor Stravinsky, the most famous composer to emerge from Russia, also produced several symphonies. His first was an apprentice effort, and is never given. Thirty-five years later he wrote a second symphony, in C major. This work is in a hybrid classical form, with the first movement in strict sonata form, and the other movements suggesting the old suite and concerto-grosso forms. The *Symphony in Three Movements*, written five years later, is much more complex in form and style. This is music not easy to comprehend because of its complete independence of formal symphonic construction and its highly unorthodox thematic procedures.

The foremost symphonic composer in England today is Ralph Vaughan Williams. His early symphonies are Romantic in character; two of them are programmatic. He called the first symphony *A London Symphony;* it is a portrait of a great city. The first movement describes London asleep. In the second, we get a picture of the section known as Bloomsbury. The third depicts Saturday evening at the Embankment; and the finale portrays the crueler aspects of the city, the unemployed and the unfortunate.

Vaughan Williams' second symphony was derived from Walt Whitman: the *Sea Symphony*, for chorus and orchestra. The third, called *Pastoral Symphony*, is not a picture of nature, but a quiet and contemplative work with a pastoral character throughout; all four movements are comparatively slow and serene.

With the *Symphony No. 4*, in F minor, Vaughan Williams' style changed suddenly. This is music modern in technique and idiom. But this modernistic tendency is abandoned in the *Symphony No. 5*, in D major, and reverts to the introspective and gentle moods of the *Third*. The *Symphony No. 6*, in E minor, was completed in 1947, and reflects the effect of the recent war and the postwar period on the composer.

The first movement is a kind of lamentation, expressive of the tragedy of the times. There is a more philosophic outlook in the second movement, but the scherzo once again recalls the misery of the times. The finale has been described as the serenest piece of music ever written—a whisper from beginning to end. The four movements are played without interruption, one movement tying in with the next.

Vaughan Williams' seventh symphony, entitled *Antarctica,* was developed out of the score which the composer had written for a motion picture, *Scott of the Antarctic.*

Two leaders in contemporary French music have been productive in the symphonic field. Arthur Honegger's symphonies include the highly successful second—the *Symphony for Strings*—which reflects the mood of Paris during the terrible war year of 1941. The symphony that followed, the *Liturgique,* was interpreted by the conductor, Charles Munch, as posing "the problem of humanity vis-à-vis God"—man's revolt against a Higher Will and his subjugation to that Will. The three movements have liturgical nomenclatures: Dies Irae; De Profundis; Dona Nobis Pacem.

Milhaud's first symphony came comparatively late in his career, in 1939. But his finest is the *Third Symphony,* for chorus and orchestra, written to celebrate the liberation of France after World War II. We find the indomitable spirit of France in the fiery first movement. The second is quietly reflective, and the third was intended to portray the return to grass roots. In the closing movement, the symphony is filled with religious ardor and exaltation.

The number "3" has proved lucky for American symphonic composers. Three splendid symphonies bear that number, and they represent the finest orchestral works of each composer: Roy Harris, Aaron Copland, and Walter Piston. Harris' *Third Symphony,* while in five sections, is in a single uninterrupted movement, and is in a sixteenth-century contrapuntal style combined with modern approaches to melody and tonality. Copland's *Third Symphony,* without ever resorting to actual quotation from folk sources, is in the spirit of American folk music; but Copland does incorporate into his score quoted material—material from his own earlier works, *Appalachian Spring* and *Fanfare for the Common Man.* The four movements of Walter Piston's *Third Symphony* have great emotional range; but the symphony is at its best in the calm and introspective music of the Adagio movement.

## VARIATIONS

The form of variations (or theme and variations) is discussed in the solo instrumental section since it is found in the early history of music for the harpsichord, for the violin, and for the organ.

In orchestral music, the variation form is first used extensively within the larger format of the symphony and concerto. Many of the Haydn and Mozart symphonies have movements in the theme and variations form; the form is also found in the slow movements of Beethoven's *Third, Fifth, Seventh* and *Ninth Symphonies.*

One of the earliest examples of the variation form being used for a self-sufficient and independent orchestral work is Brahms' *Variations on a Theme by Haydn,* written in 1873. (Another version of this work is for two unaccompanied pianos.) Taking for his theme a melody in Haydn's *Divertimento in B Flat Major,* Brahms altered and varied it in the most subtle disguises—so much so that there are times when it is difficult to recognize the basic subject. A rhythmic phrase, a melodic turn of the original melody, is capable of inspiring Brahms into sensuous lyric flights, or into delicate and graceful expression. All the resources of Brahms' skill is found in these eight variations. The composition ends with a dramatic restatement of the main melody by the entire orchestra.

One of the finest applications of the variation technique to orchestral music is found in Elgar's *Variations on an Original Theme,* or the *Enigma Variations* as it is better known. Elgar intended this work as a series of fourteen personal portraits of his friend, each variation being a portrait. To each section he appended a set of initials or a nickname revealing the identity of the person under discussion. After the poetic melody is heard, the first variation presents a self-portrait. Another variation is a picture of Elgar's wife, while still other variations represent frequently informal glimpses of personal friends.

An unorthodox use of the variation form was made by Vincent d'Indy in his *Istar Variations.* Most theme and variations present the theme before the variations. But in the d'Indy work, we get the variations first. The theme grows and develops and evolves throughout the series of variations and only at the end of the work does it appear—in unison and octaves. The reason for this method is to be found in the program which d'Indy was expounding in his music. For the work tells about Istar approaching the doorway to Death, in search of her love. She must pass through seven gates, at each of which she must disrobe a part of her garments. Finally, she stands in her nudity at the seventh gate, and is permitted to drink the waters of life and to save her lover. Each variation, then, represents a different stage of disrobing; and the theme at the end, in unison and octaves, portrays Istar in her nudity.

## WALTZ

The waltz is analyzed in the solo instrumental section, since it makes its earliest appearance in serious music in compositions for the piano.

In orchestral music, the waltz was first glorified by the great waltz kings of Vienna, notably Johann Strauss, father and son. The son is the greater and the more famous of the two. Though Johann Strauss II wrote his waltzes for popular consumption, he brought to them such a refreshing charm, such melodic inventiveness, and such rhythmic vitality and such tasteful instrumentation that they have become immortal, and are often heard at symphony concerts performed by the greatest conductors. His most popular waltz is *The Beautiful Blue Danube*. But other waltzes are equally favored throughout the world: *Tales from the Vienna Woods; Emperor Waltz; Artist's Life; Wine, Women and Song; Voices of Spring;* and so on.

Waltzes have been used in symphonies and operas. In symphonies, we find the waltz as one of the movements of Berlioz' *Symphonie fantastique* and Tchaikovsky's *Symphony No. 5.* Now-familiar waltzes stem from various operas including Gounod's *Romeo and Juliet,* Tchaikovsky's *Eugene Onegin,* Puccini's *La Bohème,* and Richard Strauss' *Der Rosenkavalier.*

Maurice Ravel wrote a major orchestral work entitled *La Valse* which describes a ballroom scene in Vienna in 1855. The couples are whirling in a dance as there rises from the orchestra first a suggestion, then a phrase, then the fully developed melody of a waltz. All is gay and lighthearted as the waltz grows and develops. But dissonant chords suggest impending tragedy. The gay waltz becomes music of despair— as Ravel remembers that the Vienna of post-World War I is no longer the gay Vienna of the past.

## 5

# One Hundred Basic Orchestral Works

Bach, J. S.: *Brandenburg Concerto No. 4.*
Bach, J. S.: *Concerto No. 1 in D Minor,* for piano and orchestra.
Bach, J. S.: *Concerto in D Minor,* for two violins and orchestra.
Bach, J. S.: *Suite No. 3.*
Bartók: *Concerto for Orchestra.*
Beethoven: *Concerto No. 5,* for piano and orchestra, (*Emperor*).
Beethoven: *Concerto in D Major,* for violin and orchestra.
Beethoven: *Coriolon Overture.*
Beethoven: *Leonore Overture No. 3.*
Beethoven: *Symphony No. 3,* (*Eroica*).
Beethoven: *Symphony No. 5,* in C minor.
Beethoven: *Symphony No. 7,* in A major.
Beethoven: *Symphony No. 9,* in D minor, (*Choral*).
Berlioz: "Dance of the Sylphs" and "Rakóczy March" from *The Damnation of Faust.*
Berlioz: *Symphonie fantastique.*
Bizet: *L'Arlésienne Suite No. 1.*
Bloch: *Schelomo,* for cello obbligato and orchestra.
Brahms: *Academic Festival Overture.*
Brahms: *Concerto No. 2,* in B flat major, for piano and orchestra.

Brahms: *Concerto in D Major,* for violin and orchestra.

Brahms: *Symphony No. 1,* in C minor.

Brahms: *Symphony No. 4,* in E minor.

Brahms: *Variations on a Theme by Haydn.*

Chabrier: *España.*

Chopin: *Concerto No. 1,* in E minor, for piano and orchestra.

Copland: *El salón México,* for orchestra.

Corelli: *Christmas Concerto.*

Debussy: *La mer.*

Debussy: *Nocturnes.*

Elgar: *Enigma Variations.*

Elgar: *Pomp and Circumstance March No. 1.*

Enesco: *Rumanian Rhapsody No. 1.*

Franck: *Symphony in D Minor.*

Gershwin: *Rhapsody in Blue.*

Gluck: *Overture to Iphigénie en Aulide.*

Grieg: *Concerto in A Minor,* for piano and orchestra.

Grieg: *Peer Gynt Suite No. 1.*

Handel: *Concerto Grosso No. 6,* in G minor.

Handel: *Water Music.*

Haydn: *Symphony No. 88,* in G major.

Haydn: *Symphony in G Major,* (*Surprise*).

Haydn: *Symphony in D Major,* (*Clock*).

Lalo: *Symphonie espagnole,* for violin and orchestra.

Liszt: *Concerto No. 1,* in E flat major, for piano and orchestra

Liszt: *Les Préludes,* for orchestra.

Mahler: *Symphony No. 2,* (*Resurrection*).

Mendelssohn: *Concerto in E Minor,* for violin and orchestra.

Mendelssohn: *A Midsummer Night's Dream Suite.*

Mendelssohn: *Symphony No. 4,* (*Italian*).

Mozart: *Concerto No. 20,* in D minor, for piano and orchestra.

Mozart: *Concerto No. 4,* in D major, for violin and orchestra.

Mozart: *Eine kleine Nachtmusik.*

Mozart: *Symphony No. 40,* in G minor.

Mozart: *Symphony No. 41,* in C major, (*Jupiter*).

Mussorgsky: *Pictures at an Exhibition* (transcribed for orchestra by Ravel).

Prokofiev: *Concerto No. 1,* for violin and orchestra.

Prokofiev: *Concerto No. 3,* for piano and orchestra.

Prokofiev: *Symphony No. 1, (Classical).*

Prokofiev: *Symphony No. 5.*

Purcell: *Fantasia on One Note.*

Rachmaninoff: *Concerto No. 2,* in C minor, for piano and orchestra.

Rachmaninoff: *Isle of the Dead,* for orchestra.

Ravel: *Bolero.*

Ravel: *La Valse.*

Rimsky-Korsakov: *Scheherezade.*

Rossini: *William Tell Overture.*

Schoenberg: *Verklaerte Nacht.*

Schubert: *Symphony No. 8, (Unfinished).*

Schubert: *Symphony No. 9.*

Schumann: *Concerto in A Minor,* for piano and orchestra.

Schumann: *Symphony No. 3, (Rhenish).*

Shostakovich: *Symphony No. 1.*

Shostakovich: *Symphony No. 5.*

Sibelius: *Finlandia.*

Sibelius: *The Swan of Tuonela.*

Sibelius: *Symphony No. 2.*

Sidelius: *Symphony No. 7.*

Smetana: *The Moldau.*

Strauss, J.: *The Beautiful Blue Danube.*

Strauss, J.: *Tales from the Vienna Woods.*

Strauss, R.: *Don Juan.*

Strauss, R.: *Till Eulenspiegel.*

Strauss, R.: Waltzes from *Der Rosenkavalier.*

Tchaikovsky: *Concerto No. 1,* in B flat minor, for piano and orchestra.

Tchaikovsky: *Concerto in D Major,* for violin and orchestra.

Tchaikovsky: *Overture 1812.*

Tchaikovsky: *Romeo and Juliet.*

Tchaikovsky: *Symphony No. 4,* in F minor.

Tchaikovsky: *Symphony No. 5,* in E minor.

Tchaikovsky: *Symphony No. 6,* in B minor, *(Pathétique).*

Vaughan Williams: *Fantasia on a Theme of Thomas Tallis.*

Vaughan Williams: *A London Symphony.*

Vaughan Williams: *Symphony No. 6.*
Vivaldi: *Concerto Grosso No. 11,* in D minor.
Wagner: *Overture* and *Venusberg Music* from *Tannhäuser.*
Wagner: *Prelude* and *Good Friday Spell* from *Parsifal.*
Wagner: *Prelude* and *Love-Death* from *Tristan und Isolde.*
Weber: *Overture to Euryanthe.*
Weber: *Overture to Der Freischütz.*
Weber: *Overture to Oberon.*

# PART SIX

*Music for Children*

# Music for Children

The repertory of great music by the foremost composers of the past and the present embraces many works that are excellent for child consumption. Some of these works were written expressly for children. They are consequently simple and direct in technique and style and with limited esthetic demands on the listener. Other works, while not written for children, are *about* children—their make-believe world and the world of their everyday experiences; it is not difficult, in works such as these, for the child to identify himself with the music he hears and to respond to it favorably. Still another category includes musical works which, though intended for adults, have a story appeal to make them easily assimilable by children.

There is probably no better way for a child to get to know and love great music than through an acquaintance with works such as these. A representative selection is discussed below, all works in it being outstanding music, and some of it very great music. This selection includes different fields from song and piano pieces to ballet and opera. A child who gets to know these compositions, who has learned to understand and love them (and he can do so through phonograph records, since most of them are recorded), has gone a long way toward learning to understand and love *all* great music—even that on an adult level.

## BALLET

DEBUSSY: *La Boîte à joujoux (The Toy Box)*.

In 1913, Debussy completed a ballet for his eight-year-old daughter, Chouchou—simple music for a simple text. The scenario (by André Helle) describes a toy soldier in a toy box falling in love with a dancing doll; she, in turn, is interested in a quarrelsome polichinelle. A battle is fought between the forces of the toy soldier and those of the polichinelle. The toy soldier is wounded, and is nursed back to health by the doll who falls in love with him. The little play ends with the soldier's marriage with the dancing doll, and the polichinelle to his new sweetheart.

Utilizing parodies of familiar tunes, music-box effects, martial strains, and bugle calls, the score is delicately unpretentious, without sacrificing the composer's interest in advanced harmonies.

PROKOFIEV: *Cinderella*.

One of Prokofiev's most delightful works for the stage is this children's ballet based, of course, on the famous fairy tale. One of the most charming features of this work is Prokofiev's witty use of old classic dances—such as the gavotte, passepied, bourrée, and minuet—without abandoning his twentieth-century harmonic and melodic mannerisms. There are also modern dances (the waltz and the mazurka) and there is an oriental dance. Musical realism intrudes in Prokofiev's character portrayals: from the delicate pictures of fairies (the fairies of Spring, Summer, Autumn, and Winter), dwarfs and dragon-flies, to the hard lines of his caricatures of Cinderella's cruel sister and the pompous cavaliers and guests at the Prince's reception. The score is filled with satiric and ironic overtones, as in the scene where Cinderella offers the Prince some oranges and the music quotes a passage from the composer's opera, *The Love for Three Oranges*.

## OPERAS

BRITTEN: *Let's Make an Opera*.

In this child's opera, Britten and his librettist (Eric Crozier) show children how an opera is created. The work is divided into two acts. In the first, six children and five adults discuss the idea of writing and producing an opera. This discussion enables both librettist and composer to transmit their individual problems to young audiences. The second act is the opera itself, entitled "The Little Sweep." Its story is centered around a pathetic little English chimney-sweep who bungles his first attempt at sweeping so badly that he fears punishment from his father. Five other children hide the victim and send him safely in a trunk to the country.

One of the interesting novelties of this opera is the audience participation. Between the two acts, the audience is taught its music. In the second act, the audience is called upon four times to participate in the choral numbers. All are simple and lively little songs, easy to learn and remember.

### COPLAND: *The Second Hurricane.*

This opera was written for performance by high-school children, the text prepared by Edward Denby. The authors describe the work as a "play opera," because parts consist of spoken scenes, and parts of songs. No curtain rises to announce that the opera has begun. A chorus files upon the empty stage as if for a rehearsal (the main characters of the opera are in the chorus). The Principal of the school arrives and briefly explains to the audience what it is about to see and hear. A simple story then unfolds: Four boys and two girls, realizing the shortage of hand laborers, enlist their efforts to bring food and help to victims of a flood. The sets, the music, the orchestration are as simple as the story. The children require no elaborate musical training to perform the principal leads, to sing in the chorus, or play in the orchestra; children are also expected to design the sets.

### HUMPERDINCK: *Hänsel und Gretel.*

It is a magic child's world that unfolds in the opera. This is its great strength, and the reason why it has become a classic in the opera house—loved by old as well as young. Though frequently Wagnerian in technique, the score never loses contact with the fairy tale and its characters. The melodies are frequently wistful, or ingenuous, and always fresh as folk songs; the entire score is touched with fantasy and enchantment. Humperdinck can truly be said to have originated the operatic fairy tale.

The Grimm fairy tale which inspired the opera is well known.

(Those who have forgotten the details of the plot will find them in Part Three, in Stories of Famous Operas.)

The score is filled with numerous delights. First of all there is the overture—a potpourri of some of the most famous melodies of the opera. In the first act we hear the delightful song in which Gretel teaches Hänsel to sing and dance. In the second act there is the "Sandman's Song" with which the terrified children, alone in the woods, are put to sleep. They first say their prayers in the "Evening Prayer" and when slumber comes, fairies descend to protect them to the gossamer music of the "Dream Pantomime." In the third act, the witch sings her weird incantation as she prepares to victimize the children. But they thwart her by shoving her into the hot oven and jubilantly sing the lovable "Gingerbread Waltz."

RAVEL: *L'Enfant et les sortilèges (The Child and the Sorcerers)*.

Colette, the famous French writer, prepared the text for this "comedy of magic" to which Ravel wrote the music. It is called a "fantasy," but it is actually a child's opera. Colette's story—or fairy tale—concerns a boy who, punished by his mother for failing to do his homework, avenges himself by breaking up the furniture in the room and torturing his pet animals. Suddenly the furniture comes to life and upbraids the boy for his temper. Out of one of the destroyed books emerges a Princess who says she will have nothing more to do with him. Outside the house, trees, frogs, and a squirrel also come to scold him. But when the squirrel gets hurt, and the boy looks after him solicitously, the animals are appeased. They take the boy back into the house where his mother is waiting for him anxiously.

Ravel's score is full of the kind of unexpected humor in which children find delight. There is a duet in cat language; a funny dance of the cup and the teapot; a burlesque on American fox-trot music. But children are also able to find joy in Ravel's incomparable gift for evoking the world of a child's imagination with a wonderful feeling for fantasy.

## ORCHESTRAL MUSIC

BRITTEN: *A Young Person's Guide to the Orchestra*.

This work was intended by the composer to teach listeners the instruments of the orchestra. It consists of a theme and variations. In

each variation, a different instrument, or group of instruments, is fea-
tured. The theme itself is taken from Purcell's incidental music to
*Abdelazar*. After the theme is given, thirteen variations follow in which
the following instruments appear in the given order: flutes and piccolo; oboes; clarinets, bassoons; violins; violas; cellos; basses; harp;
French horn; trumpets; trombones; percussion. In the concluding
section, which is a fugue, the instruments return in the same order they
had appeared in the variations. (Another work for children illustrating
the instruments of the orchestra is discussed below—Prokofiev's *Peter
and the Wolf*.)

## CARPENTER: *Adventures in a Perambulator*.

This witty suite, by the twentieth-century American composer
John Alden Carpenter, portrays the impressions of a child as he is
being wheeled around by his nurse in his perambulator. The expedition
begins in the first section ("En voiture"). The next part ("The Policeman") relates the child's reaction to the formidable man in uniform
flirting with the nurse. We next hear the pleasant sound of hand-organ
music (the observant ear will recognize a quotation from Irving Berlin's "Alexander's Ragtime Band") in a section appropriately called
"The Hurdy-Gurdy." In "The Lake," the child's response to the
expanse of water in front of him is described. The child's next experience is the frightening and in a way fascinating sight of growling
dogs ("Dogs"); once again the observant ear will recognize quotations
from "Where, Oh Where Has My Little Dog Gone" and "Ach du
lieber Augustin." The concluding part is "Dreams"; the child succumbs to fatigue and sleep after his day's adventures.

## COPLAND: *Outdoor Overture*.

Like *The Second Hurricane*, this work is intended for high-
school performance. It has simple melodies, concise developments,
together with a tartness of harmony and orchestra that make for enjoy-
able playing and listening. The melodic highlight is a piece for trumpet
solo.

## COPLAND: *The Red Pony*.

This is an orchestral suite adapted by Copland from the score
for a Hollywood film—John Steinbeck's *The Red Pony*. One of its

central characters is a boy named Jody who lives on a California ranch. Jody is also the central character of Copland's children's suite, which tries to reproduce the world as Jody sees it. The suite is in six parts. In the first, "Morning on the Ranch," the daily chores are described. The next part, "The Gift," reproduces Jody's delight in getting from his father the gift of a real live red pony. "Dream March and Circus Music" is concerned with Jody's daydreams. In "Walk to the Bunkhouse," Jody's admiration for Billy Buck, the horsehand, is re-created in music. "Grandfather Story" is one of those adventure tales that Jody loved to hear his grandfather relate. The suite concludes with "Happy Ending," in which the music of the first section is repeated; the farmhands, and Jody, must return to the daily chores.

### DUKAS: *L'Apprenti sorcier (The Sorcerer's Apprentice).*

This delightful scherzo for orchestra is the composer's best known work—an established classic in symphonic music as well as a favorite of children everywhere. The story is familiar, and it is retold in the music with charming realism as well as with disarming wit.

A magician has the secret of transforming a broom handle into a human being capable of performing any required menial task. The magician's apprentice, one day, overhears the incantation and, eager to emulate his master, decides to put it to test. When the broom acquires life, the apprentice orders it to bring water. Pail after pail is brought into the den, to the immense delight of the apprentice. When the apprentice wishes to arrest the efforts of the conscientious broom, he realizes with horror that he does not know the necessary formula with which to restore it to its inanimate state. Frantically, the apprentice seizes a hatchet and splits the broom in two. But there are now two, instead of one, to bring the water into a rapidly flooded den. The apprentice screams out to his master for help. The master, returning, utters the necessary magic words and peace and normalcy are restored.

### HAYDN: *Toy Symphony.*

Contemporary musical research leads us to suspect that Joseph Haydn is not the author of this novelty; it is now believed to have been written by Mozart's father. In any case, for years we have known this work as "Haydn's" *Toy Symphony,* and it will probably be called that for a long time to come.

Within an abbreviated symphonic form, Haydn—or whoever wrote it—produced music primarily for toy instruments. Only three of the regular orchestral instruments are utilized: two violins and a bass. Among the toy instruments are: a penny trumpet, a quail call, a cuckoo, a screech-owl, a whistle, a drum. The tunes are as ingenuous as the instruments to play them. The story goes—though it is now subject to question—that the idea for this symphony came to Haydn during a visit to Berchtesgaden, Bavaria, where he came upon some toy musical instruments that amused him greatly.

### KABALEVSKY: *The Comedians.*

In 1938, the Soviet composer, Dmitri Kabalevsky, wrote incidental music for a children's play produced in Moscow. This play centered around a band of wandering comedians and told of their amusing escapades as they went from town to town, appearing in public squares, fairs, and so forth.

In writing music for this play, Kabalevsky assumed a witty, pictorial, nostalgic, and simple style. From this incidental-music score he prepared a suite of ten numbers which has become extremely popular at children's concerts everywhere (as well as at regular symphony concerts). The movements are: Prologue, Galop, March, Waltz, Pantomime, Intermezzo, Little Lyrical Scene, Gavotte, Scherzo, and Epilogue.

### KHATCHATURIAN: *Masquerade.*

This is also an orchestral suite adapted from incidental music to a play for children; it is light and breezy in musical content. It is in five parts: Waltz, Nocturne, Romance, Mazurka, and Galop.

### McDONALD: *Children's Symphony.*

The contemporary American composer, Harl McDonald, has taken nursery melodies known to children everywhere and used them within a conventional symphony form. McDonald's idea is—and it is a good one—that since children know these tunes they can easily see how they are developed within the symphonic form. Each movement has a main and secondary theme; both themes are stated briefly and developed. In the first movement, McDonald used "London Bridge" and "Baa Baa Black Sheep." In the second, "Little Bo Peep" and "Oh,

Dear What Can the Matter Be" are presented. The third movement has "Farmer in the Dell" and "Jingle Bells," while the finale employs "Honey Bee" and "Snow Is Falling on My Garden."

### PROKOFIEV: *Peter and the Wolf.*

This musical setting of a modern Soviet fairy tale is already a classic. Prokofiev wrote it to teach children the instruments of the orchestra. Each character in the tale is depicted by a different instrument: the bird by a flute; the duck by an oboe; the cat by a clarinet in the low register; Grandpapa, by the bassoon; the wolf, by three French horns; Peter, by a string quartet; the hunter's shots by kettle-drums and bass drums. Each character and incident is also portrayed by a musical motive which returns whenever that character or incident appears or is talked about. With an ingenious use of recurring motives and instrumentation—and a graceful blend of the spoken word and musical sounds—a delightful story unfolds about young Peter's success-ful attempt to capture a wolf and bring it to a zoo.

### RAVEL: *Ma Mère l'oye (Mother Goose Suite).*

Ravel, who loved children and wrote enchantingly for them, was here inspired by the stories in Mother Goose. He originally wrote a suite for four-hand piano duet to be played by two children. Later on, he orchestrated it. It is in five sections. The first, "Pavane of the Sleeping Beauty," is a short dance of stately character. The second was inspired by the story of Hop o' My Thumb. The third retells the story of Laidernnette, Empress of the Pagodas, who is cursed with ugliness but whose beauty is restored through the love of a Prince. The fourth section, "Conversations of Beauty and the Beast" is a little waltz melody. The suite ends with an enchanting melody in a movement entitled "The Fairy Garden."

### SAINT-SAËNS: *Le Carnaval des animaux (The Carnival of the Animals).*

This suite, for two pianos and orchestra, is one of the happiest attempts to portray animals through music. With vivid programmatic writing, Saint-Saëns describes the lumbering elephants with a ponder-ous melody in the double-bass; the cuckoo, with a sprightly tune in the clarinet; the graceful swan with a wonderful song for the cello; kangaroos, by swirling phrases in two pianos; and so forth. Throughout, the composer has tongue-in-cheek, as when he includes "Pianists" in his zoo of animals. He also indulges in sly quotations from the works of other composers. The graceless elephant is made to prance to a strain from Berlioz' delicate *Dance of the Sylphs*. In other parts there are quotations from Rossini's *The Barber of Seville*, Offenbach's *Orpheus in the Underworld*, Mendelssohn's Scherzo from *A Midsummer Night's Dream*, and Saint-Saëns' *Danse macabre*.

The suite is in fourteen parts: Introduction and Royal March of the Lion; Hen and Cocks; Mules; Tortoises; The Elephant; Kangaroos; Aquarium; Personages with Long Ears; Cuckoo in the Woods; Birds; Pianists; Fossils; The Swan; Finale. In the finale, all the characters of the "zoo" return for a last bow.

Recently, brilliant verses were written by Ogden Nash to preface each of these sections. While they are sophisticated, they are sufficiently amusing and absurd to please children. The entire suite, with the Ogden Nash verses, is available in recording.

TCHAIKOVSKY: *Nutcracker Suite.*

This lovable work is a far cry from the frequently lugubrious and pessimistic symphonies of the same composer. Here his inspiration was a story by E. T. A. Hoffmann, in a French adaptation by Dumas. The story tells about a girl who, receiving a nutcracker for Christmas, dreams that it is a handsome prince who leads the toys in a victorious battle against the mice, and who conducts the girl to Jam Mountain where there are song, dance, and festivities. Tchaikovsky originally wrote this music as a ballet; but it is the orchestral suite that is most famous. The suite is in eight parts: Miniature Overture; Russian Dance; March; Dance of the Sugarplum Fairy; Arabian Dance; Chinese Dance; Reed-Pipe Dance; and Waltz of the Flowers. It is interesting to remark that in the fourth section Tchaikovsky introduced a new percussion instrument into the orchestra—the celesta—with which to describe the gossamer delicacy of the sugarplum fairy.

## PIANO MUSIC

BACH, J. S.: *Inventions.*

Bach wrote two sets of little educational pieces for the piano which he termed "inventions"; there are fifteen in each set. One book is made up of two-part inventions (or two themes developed in imitation); another book, of three-part pieces.

Bach wrote this music as teaching material for his sons. As he himself put it, it was intended to be "a guide for clean performance in two, later in three, independent parts and to the conception of development of good ideas ('inventions'), with special emphasis on the cultivation of a cantabile style of playing and the acquisition of a strong foretaste of composition."

These inventions are important steps in mastering the more complex fugal style of Bach's adult piano works. They are charming contrapuntal pieces, fresh in thematic ideas, and skilful in the interplay of the voices—and are of esthetic as well as pedagogical value.

### BACH, J. S.: *The Little Notebook of Anna Magdalena Bach.*

Bach's second wife, Anna Magdalena, had a notebook into which she copied out pieces of music as exercises (for her own, and her children's, use) together with other pieces written for such special occasions as wedding, christening, or birthday. Most of these compositions were by her husband—written either for pedagogical or functional purpose; some were by other composers. The notebook is a veritable cornucopia of little jewels of children's piano pieces. It contains a variety of marches, minuets, polonaises, musettes—all of them the last word in simplicity yet of unfailing musical charm. The little Bach minuets and other delightful little Bach dances studied by beginners at the piano come from this collection. It also includes several songs for voice and piano.

### BACH, K. P. E.: *Solfegietto.*

This graceful little piece effectively imitates on the piano the fluid runs of a vocal exercise—"solfegietto" meaning a "little solfeggio," or a "little vocal exercise."

### BARTÓK: *Mikrokosmos.*

This is a suite of one hundred and fifty-three pieces (gathered in six volumes) introducing children to the contemporary idiom. In the first four volumes the composer concentrates on exercises for beginners in which the particular lesson is designated by the title: "Syncopation," "Dotted Notes," "Parallel Motion," "Alternating Hands," and so forth. The next two volumes are written in the distinctive styles of the folk music of various Balkan countries. Some pieces are descriptive ("Pastorale" or "Boating") ; some are imitative of sounds of the extra-musical world ("Buzzing") ; some explore new acoustic sounds for the piano. The student is frequently made to play in the language of poly-tonality, polyrhythm, dissonance—but reduced to the simplest terms—until the seemingly complex world of modern music acquires logic. But beyond the instructional value of this suite, each piece is a delightful and provocative composition capable of pleasing and stimulating.

## BEETHOVEN: *Bagatelles.*

"Bagatelle" is a French word for "trifle." These pieces, then, are trifles for the piano. Beethoven wrote three sets of these works all of them pleasing melodically, even if slight in form and content. The most celebrated of these is "Fuer Elise," familiar to every piano student.

## BEETHOVEN: *Sonatas, op. 49, nos. 1 and 2.*

Though the opus number would indicate that these sonatas are works of Beethoven's maturity, they are actually early productions. Technically and structurally they are the easiest piano sonatas by Beethoven; they are invaluable for the young listener in getting to learn something about the sonata form.

## DEBUSSY: *Children's Corner.*

Debussy wrote this infectious suite of children's piano pieces for his daughter, Chouchou, trying to recreate a child's world. It is interesting to note that Debussy himself gave the work English, instead of French, title and subtitles—his idea being that an English governess is playing games with a French child.

The suite opens with "Doctor Gradus ad Parnassum," a satire on a child's painful experiences with piano exercises. "Jimbo's Lullaby" follows—Jimbo being a toy elephant which the child is crooning to sleep. After a poignant "Serenade for the Doll," we hear a delightful description of snowfall as seen by a child from a window—"The Snow Is Falling." The fifth section is called "The Little Shepherd"; it is a delicate pastoral piece. The famous "Golliwogg's Cakewalk" closes the work. (The cakewalk was a dance famous in American popular music in the 1890's and early 1900's, which intrigued the composer because of its jaunty rhythms.)

### HAYDN: *Sonatas.*

Haydn, of course, wrote his piano sonatas for the mature music lover. But they are so clear and explicit in their classical design, so elementary in technical and esthetic demands, that they are ideal fare for the young. Haydn sonatas particularly suited for the performing and listening pleasure of children include the C major, D major, and A flat major.

### IBERT: *The Little White Donkey.*

This witty and highly descriptive little piece by the contemporary French composer, Jacques Ibert, is one of ten numbers in a set entitled *The Wind in the Ruins.*

### LIADOV: *The Music Box.*

In this piece, the late nineteenth-century Russian composer, Anatol Liadov, imitates the tinkling musical sounds of a music box when the cover is lifted. It is the only piece by Liadov to survive.

### MENDELSSOHN: *Songs Without Words.*

Once again, the composer intended here music for adult consumption. But the programmatic interest of some of these pieces, and the simple appeal of the melodies, makes them ideal for youthful consumption. Children will particularly like the "Spinning Song" and the three "Venetian Boat Songs." (For further comment, see Part Four.)

### MOZART: *Minuets; Variations on Ah, vous dirai-je maman.*

As a child of five and six, Mozart wrote several delightful morsels for the piano, including several minuets (K. 1, 2, 4, 5, 9a), and an Allegro in B flat major (K. 3). They have the disarming ingenuousness of childhood, but childhood charm as well. A later piano work by Mozart is just as easily assimilated by children: *Variations on Ah, vous dirai-je maman* (K. 265), which Mozart wrote in his maturity. The melody will be familiar to every child, since it is the same tune to which he is taught the alphabet. There are twelve pleasing little variations on this tune.

## PROKOFIEV: *Music for Children*.

The famous Soviet composer wrote a set of twelve easy pieces for children in 1935. They are descriptive of a child's world and a child's activities, including a game of tag (trippingly reproduced in the melody), a children's march, a child's morning and evening, a stroll, a child's impressions of a rainbow, a grasshopper parade, and so forth. The last piece in the set, "The Moon Goes Over the Meadows" has the poignancy of a Russian folk song.

## SCHUMANN: *Scenes from Childhood (Kinderscenen)*.

This is the first of two sets for the piano which Schumann wrote with children in mind. Here Schumann contemplates the world of the child. In thirteen numbers he gives a man's reaction to the thoughts, games, and moods of little people. The impressions are frequently subtle and sophisticated, but they recreate a child's environment so magically that children will feel completely at home with this music. The most celebrated piece in this set is "Dreaming" (Träumerei), probably one of Schumann's best known instrumental pieces. Other charming items include "Pleading Child," "Perfect Happiness," and "Rocking Horse."

## SCHUMANN: *Album for the Young (Album für die Jugend)*.

This set was written one decade later. There is a marked difference between the two works. Whereas the *Scenes from Childhood* is an adult's concept of the child's world, the *Album for the Young* is music written directly for children. It is, consequently, elementary in technique and unsophisticated in programmatic interest. There are forty-three pieces, including games, stories, moods, thoughts, and so on. We find here such delightful miniatures as "Soldier's March," "Little Hunting Song," "The Wild Horseman," "Santa Claus," and "War Song."

## VOCAL MUSIC

## MUSSORGSKY: *The Nursery*.

Mussorgsky, probably the greatest song composer to emerge in Russia, wrote a song cycle for children and about children that is a classic. In the first song, "Tell Me a Story," the child pleads for a tale about a boogey-man who haunts the forest. In the second, "The Beetle," he tells his nurse about the horrible beetle he has seen. This is followed by a "Dolly's Lullaby," in which a child is tenderly putting his doll to sleep. "Prayer at Bedtime" is a child's prayer to God for forgiveness for his "wickedness." "The Hobby Horseman" describes the child's ride astride his hobby horse, though in his imagination he is sweeping gallantly through great and mysterious spaces. The last song, "No, You Don't, Pussy," is a child's story to his mother about a cat whom he punishes when it tries to invade a bird's cage.

# PART SEVEN

## A Glossary of Basic Terms in Music

# A Glossary of Basic Terms in Music

## A

| | |
|---|---|
| ABSOLUTE MUSIC: | Pure music; music requiring no programmatic interpretation or extra-musical associations to be appreciated. |
| A CAPPELLA (MUSIC): | Unaccompanied choral music. |
| ACCIDENTAL: | A sharp or flat not designated by the signature. |
| ADAGIO: | Very slow. |
| ALLEGRETTO: | A bit quickly, but slower than Allegro. |
| ALLEGRO: | Quick. |
| ANDANTE: | Slow. |
| ANDANTINO: | Quicker than Andante, but still slow. |
| ANTIPHONY: | In choral music, the method of singing with alternate choral groups. |
| APPOGIATURA: | Grace note or embellishment. |
| ARCO: | After a pizzicato passage in string music the term "arco" denotes that the bow is to be used again. |

ARPEGGIO:    Playing the ascending or descending notes of a chord consecutively.

ATONALITY:    Absence of a tonality, or key center.

AUGMENTATION:    Repeating a melodic theme by lengthening the value of each note.

## B

BAR:    Measure.

BASSO OSTINATO:    A repetitious theme in the bass.

BEL CANTO:    Literally "beautiful song." The art of beautiful song, or lyrical aria, in Italian opera.

BINARY FORM:    The procedure of using two contrasting themes in a movement of symphony, sonata, etc.

BRAVURA:    A brilliant, virtuoso style.

## C

CADENCE:    End of phrase, section, or movement.

CANTABILE:    A singing style.

CASTRATO:    A male eunuch with an artificial female voice, popular in the eighteenth century in opera performances.

CHORD:    The combination of three or more tones.

CHROMATIC:    A tone, interval, chord, or scale varying from the major or minor usually by a semitone. A chromatic scale is one made up of half-steps.

CLEF:    The sign at the beginning of each stave indicating exact pitch. In piano music, two clefs are employed: The "G clef" in the treble and the "F clef" in the bass. In viola music, the C clef is used.

CODA:

A concluding section in an instrumental work.

COUNTERPOINT:

Procedure of using two or more independent melodies simultaneously.

CRESCENDO:

Getting louder gradually.

## D

DA CAPO:

Literally "from the beginning"; a term signifying that the first part of a composition is to be repeated.

DEVELOPMENT:

The working out of thematic material.

DIATONIC:

A step, interval, progression, melody made up exclusively of those notes in the scale out of which it is constructed. A diatonic scale is one made up of consecutive tone degrees.

DIMINUENDO:

Getting softer gradually.

DISCORD:

Dissonant combination of tones.

DISSONANT:

Combination of tones giving the feeling of unrest and requiring other tones for resolution.

DIVISI:

Divided; the division into two or more parts of a group of performers playing in unison.

DOMINANT:

Fifth step in the scale.

DOUBLE STOP:

In string music, the simultaneous playing of two strings.

DYNAMICS:

Gradations of sound from loud to soft, and soft to loud.

## E

ENHARMONIC:

A difference in notation but not in pitch, as in F sharp and G flat.

| | |
|---|---|
| EQUAL TEMPERAMENT: | Method of tuning now in use dividing octave into twelve equal semitones. |
| EXPOSITION: | The first section in sonata form in which themes are presented. |

**F**

| | |
|---|---|
| FERMATA: | A symbol designating long pause. |
| FIGURED BASS: | A stenographic system employed in the sixteenth and seventeenth centuries whereby a numeral in the bass indicates the harmony. |
| FINALE: | Concluding movement of symphony, sonata, etc. or concluding scene in opera. |
| FLAT: | Symbol lowering note a semitone. |
| FORTE: | Loud. |
| FORTISSIMO: | Very loud. |
| FUGATO: | In fugal style. |
| FUNDAMENTAL: | Root tone of a chord. |

**G**

| | |
|---|---|
| GIOCOSO: | Joyful. |
| GIUSTO: | Precise, exact (used in connection with speed). |
| GLISSANDO: | A sliding tone produced by sliding finger across keys of a piano, or strings of a string instrument. |
| GRACE NOTE: | An ornament. |
| GROUND BASS: | A thematic subject repeated throughout a composition in the bass with variations. |

**H**

| | |
|---|---|
| HARMONICS: | A whistle-like sound produced on string instruments by touching the |

finger lightly on the string, instead of pressing it.

HARMONY: The science of chord construction and progression.

HOMOPHONY: The style calling for a single melody and its harmonic accompaniment.

## I

IMITATION: A contrapuntal method whereby a theme or a phrase is repeated by another voice, usually in a lower or higher pitch.

INTERVAL: Distance in pitch between two tones.

INTONATION: Playing or singing in tune.

INVERSION: Turning upside down two notes of an interval; or, changing tones of a chord so that the bass note assumes a position other than root; or, reversing intervals of a melodic line; or, in counterpoint, changing position of two melodic lines.

## K

KEY: Scale.

## L

LARGHETTO: Slow and dignified, but faster than Largo.

LARGO: Very slow and with great dignity; slower than Adagio.

LEGATO: Connected; smooth transition from one note to the next.

LEITMOTIV: Leading motive; a device developed by Wagner whereby a recurrent theme identifies a character, emotion, incident, etc.

| | |
|---|---|
| LENTO: | Slow, but faster than Largo. |
| L'ISTESSO TEMPO: | The same speed. |

## M

| | |
|---|---|
| MAESTOSO: | Majestic. |
| MARCATO: | Accented. |
| MEDIANT: | Third note in scale. |
| MENO: | Less. |
| MODE: | A type of scale (major, minor). |
| MODERATO: | Of moderate speed. |
| MODULATION: | Change of key or tonality. |
| MORDENT: | Grace note. |
| MOSSO: | Animated. |

## N

| | |
|---|---|
| NATURAL: | A sign restoring the natural pitch of a tone that has had a sharp or flat. |

## O

| | |
|---|---|
| OBBLIGATO: | A voice or instrumental accompaniment. |
| OCTAVE: | Eight consecutive diatonic notes. |
| ORGAN POINT: | Same as pedal point; a bass tone that is sustained for some time against moving voices. |
| ORNAMENT: | An embellishment; grace note. |
| OSTINATO: | Ground bass. |

## P

| | |
|---|---|
| PART-SONG: | A song for two or more voices. |
| PEDAL POINT: | See organ point. |
| PIACERE (A): | At pleasure; an indication that style, tempo, etc. are at discretion of performer. |

| | |
|---|---|
| PIACEVOLE: | Graceful, free of excessive expression. |
| PIANISSIMO: | Very soft. |
| PIANO: | Soft. |
| PITCH: | Relation in sound of one tone to another. |
| PIU: | More. |
| PIZZICATO: | Plucked string. |
| POCO: | A little. |
| POLYPHONY: | Same as counterpoint; the employment of several different melodies at the same time. |
| POLYTONALITY: | Use of several different keys at the same time. |
| PORTAMENTO: | Gliding from one note to the next. |
| POTPOURRI: | A medley. |
| PRESTO: | Very fast, faster than Allegro. |
| PRESTISSIMO: | Faster than Presto. |
| PROGRAM MUSIC: | Music that tells a story, describes a mood, or depends upon some literary program. |
| PROGRESSION: | The advance from one chord to another. |

## Q

| | |
|---|---|
| QUASI: | Almost; as if. |
| QUAVER: | Eighth note. |

## R

| | |
|---|---|
| RALLENTANDO: | Getting slower. |
| RECAPITULATION: | Final section in sonata form in which exposition is repeated. |

RECITATIVE:                  Declamation for voice.

RECITATIVO SECCO:            Literally "dry recitative"; in opera,
                             recitative that is accompanied by
                             random chords.

REGISTER:                    Apart of the compass of the voice.

REPRISE:                     Repeat.

RESOLUTION:                  Movement from dissonance to con-
                             sonance.

RHYTHM:                      Arrangement of short and long
                             notes, accented and unaccented
                             notes.

RITARDANDO                   Gradual retarding of tempo.

RITENUTO:                    Immediate retarding of tempo.

ROOT:                        Tone upon which chord is con-
                             structed.

RUBATO:                      Literally "stolen"; changing the
                             tempo by giving some of the time
                             values of longer notes to shorter
                             ones without changing the basic
                             rhythm.

## S

SCALE:                       A formal succession of notes within
                             an octave, such as diatonic or chro-
                             matic scales.

SCORDATURA:                  Mistuning of string instrument for
                             special effect.

SECULAR (MUSIC):             Any music not religious or litur-
                             gical.

SEMITONE:                    Half-tone.

SEQUENCE:                    A melodic or rhythmic phrase fre-
                             quently repeated.

SEVENTH CHORD:               Chords of four notes made up of
                             thirds.

| | |
|---|---|
| SFORZANDO: | Sudden force. |
| SHARP: | Symbol raising note half a tone. |
| SIGNATURE: | Symbol used at beginning of composition to indicate key and tempo. |
| SLUR: | Curved symbol indicating two or more notes are to be played legato, or held. |
| SOLFEGE: | Exercise for the voice. |
| SOPRANO: | Highest register of female or boy voice. |
| SORDINO: | Mute. |
| SOSTENUTO: | Sustained. |
| SOTTO: | Below. |
| SOTTO VOCE: | Toneless voice. |
| SPICCATO: | Staccato bowing in rapid string passage. |
| STACCATO: | Brief, sharp, detached notes. |
| STAFF: | The five parallel horizontal lines on which music is written. |
| STRETTO: | Concluding passage in instrumental music, or finale of opera, in which the tempo is quickened; in a fugue, a stretto passage is one in which the subject and answer tend to overlap. |
| SUBDOMINANT: | Fourth degree in scale. |
| SUBMEDIANT: | Sixth degree in scale. |
| SUL PONTICELLO: | On the bridge; indication to string players that bow is to be played as close to bridge as possible. |
| SUSPENSION: | A discord created by holding one or more notes of a chord while the rest of the notes move on to the succeeding chord. |

| | |
|---|---|
| SYNCOPATION: | Alteration of natural accent by shifting accent to normally weak beat. |

## T

| | |
|---|---|
| TEMPO: | Time. |
| TEMPO GIUSTO: | Exact time. |
| TENOR: | Highest range of male voice. |
| TENUTO: | Held. |
| TESSITURA: | Average range of song or voice. |
| THOROUGH BASS: | *See* Figured Bass. |
| TONALITY: | Key or mode. |
| TONIC: | First note of scale. |
| TONIC CHORD: | Chord built on the tonic. |
| TRANSCRIPTION: | Arrangement of a musical piece. |
| TRANSPOSE: | Change pitch of composition to different key. |
| TREBLE: | Highest register. |
| TREMOLO: | On string instrument, rapid reiteration of single note. |
| TRIAD: | Chord in three tones: root, third, and fifth. |
| TRILL: | Quivering sound produced by rapidly alternating note with its major or minor second. |
| TRIPLET: | Three notes grouped together as a single unit and given same time value as two normal notes. |
| TROPPO: | Too much. |
| TUTTI: | Entrance of entire orchestra. |

## U

| | |
|---|---|
| UNISON: | Sameness of pitch in two or more notes. |

## V

| | |
|---|---|
| VIBRATO: | A vibrating, tremulous note on a string instrument. |
| VIVACE: | Lively. |
| VOCALISE: | Exercise for the voice. |

# Index